The Mind and the machine
Should we fear artificial intelligence?

The Mind and The Machine

The Mind
and
the Machine

Should we fear Artificial Intelligence?

Serge Boisse

The Mind and The Machine

To Françoise,

*For her love, her generosity,
and her continued support throughout my
writing of this book.*

*For Corine,
her warm friendliness and
Invaluable support.*

From the same author:
All title Available at Amazon.com

Soul Shifter,
Novel, (in French)

Alice et la boîte de Pandore
Novel, (in French)

Vendre son livre sur Internet,
Essay (in French)

One day when I was about four years old, I had a revelation. Suddenly, for a mysterious reason, a new thought appeared in my mind: "I exist!" This thought was so original! It made me somebody, a small person different from the others, and now I *knew* it.

Since that day, I have never ceased questioning myself: but if I do exist because I think (thank you Descartes!), how can I also think *because I exist*? How is it possible that the human being thinks, that it has a mind, and that apparently this mind has a quality that distinguishes it from the animal intelligence?

When I became a little taller, I learned how to read and write. One of my favorite book was titled "How does it work?" It explained, with lot of details and diagrams, the operation of a thousand of electrical or mechanical appliances of the daily life. However, even though I discovered then with ecstasy how a power plant or a vacuum cleaner could function, the book did not answer the question of my four years: in the end, how does the mind work?

The question of finding out how we think is not new. There exist many textbooks on that matter, some highly technical and specialized, some others more general. As a Teenager, then a young person, an adult, and eventually a not-so-young adult (sob…), I ate up many erudite booklets about psychology, biology, neurology, data processing, philosophy, logic, game theory, artificial intelligence, robotics, and others whose even titles still are completely incomprehensible for the layman, not to mention their abstract, unintelligible, meaningless and sometime even stupid contents!. Because a lot of nonsense was also uttered on the subject!

However, the more I read, the more I deepened into the subject, and the more I had the feeling to move away from the question. It is a fact that this issue is definitely not a simple one, and to answer it, you have to take a multidisciplinary and generalist approach, something which is unfortunately rare in our times of scientific specialization.

Over the past ten years, however, our understanding of the human mind has progressed in leaps and bounds. It is now possible to answer the question. We now know how the mind does really work. However, this answer can be found only through the synthesis of a few high level scientific papers.

I have never found a simple book that would provide a simple and accessible answer to a question, which is so simple in its form and so complicated in its contents. I hope that this book will meet this desire. I try here something impossible, that is to say to explain in a simple way this deeply unsettling phenomenon: how could spirit come to matter, and how does our mind work.

It will appear to some that this issue is totally heretical. According to some people, the existence of the mind can only be explained because our brains, the seat of thought, are driven by an "influx" of possibly divine origin, and that we call soul. Without soul, our minds are only able to perform basic "animal" tasks, but would be devoid of this "creative spark" that makes us human. I think it is an extremely interesting idea that deserves to be scientifically examined, in light of what we now know about brain function. How come that humans seem to have "something more" than animals, and what is this "something"? Today, it seems possible to answer without the assumption of the soul. It is now possible to fully describe the mechanism of our mind.

This is brand new. I will try to explain why in this book.

On the contrary, stating that the mind can be fully explained by its hardware organization - Let us call it "the brain" and its software "the brainware" - is a pure mechanical assumption, and would end in believing we would undoubtedly be able to create a true artificial intelligence (AI). This idea has very important consequences, and you can bet that the general audience and even political leaders greatly underestimate theses consequences. It is high time to scan some ideas about AI and to get ready for its coming.

Indeed the arrival of true AI is close, very close. This is no longer science fiction. As early as 2005, DARPA, the U.S. agency for Armaments, launched a first tender for the realization of conscious combat robots. Other organizations, which are hopefully more peaceful, but are all American, which is very significant, are engaged in the practical realization of artificial entities capable of creative thinking, emotions, and sense of "self" is identical to what we call consciousness.

It is urgent for the layperson, especially for the European layperson, to awake!

The advent of AI will have greater consequences than anything we can imagine. Far greater. Our civilization is on the verge of a huge global impact. It will likely happen within twenty years from now, maybe even ten years. This may sound hypothetical, or even impossible, but it will happen.

Terms such as "future Shock" or "global shock" are now part of our culture, and we use them far too frequently. Saying that there is a planetary shock because the price of the barrel of oil is now ten dollars more is ridiculous and laughable. The impact of AI will be a *real* shock.

Today, we are on the eve of singularity, an event that will be as important as the invention of language or writing for our civilization. Maybe even more important than that. Maybe as important as the emergence of humankind on Earth. *Superintelligence* is this very singular event.

What is this all about? Quite simply this: the mind of AI will not be a mere copy of the human mind. If we create one day an AI, it will not be "as intelligent as a human being". It will be a million times more! This is not a speculation but a demonstrable fact, which is (we will prove it) as valid as a mathematical theorem. Its consequences will be huge and will transform our civilization. There will be a world "before" and "after" singularity, and the two worlds will be as dissimilar as can be our civilization from that of the hunters-gatherers twenty thousand years ago. Perhaps even more.

By reading this book, you will understand what intelligence is, what superintelligence will be, and why we must prepare ourselves, quickly and NOW!

In fact, a huge danger that is very new and ignored by the general audience is threatening our civilization and even our planet, and nothing but the superintelligence can help us out.

This danger is the *Grey Goo*. What is it? Read more…

I

A small tour of the mind

The Mind, this unknown

TheCubeBehindOurArtificialMind, painting of Sabin Corneliu Buraga

A Little story of mind

As of high antiquity, as soon as the human being was able to have some free time to think about something other than its own survival, the issues of mind, consciousness and intelligence have haunted philosophers. At first, these three questions were a little confused. Thereafter they were separated and then become more complex to the point where almost every philosopher has a separate definition of these three words, which are often confused in the collective consciousness or popular wisdom.

For example: "intelligence is what separates humans from animals," or "intelligence is what gives the ability to solve problems," or "That's property of a mind to invent strategies in response to a new situation. ". In the same way, one can hear that "the mind is what gives the ability to think", or "consciousness is what makes that that I know that I am me". Definitely not clear!

Talking about absence of clarity, here is my preferred definition: "Intelligence is all that we cannot explain in our mind". Not bad, is it? Still this definition implies that intelligence is a bit like the Terra incognita of old maps, shrinking as time flies. When we can explain everything in mind, because we will be super smart, intelligence will be reduced to zero. Well... there seems to be a little contradiction here?

In ancient times, having a mind was attributed to some human beings (all male, very convenient for them) and others humans did not have a mind and could therefore be used as slaves (even more practical!) The distinction between mind and soul intervened with the advent of Christian religion, and the question of knowing whether females had a soul then was of the utmost importance! Thus, Soul and mind became two separate concepts: During the Middle Ages only human beings had a soul, but all living creatures had at least an embryo of mind. Many people still think this way today. Others just have replaced the word "soul" with "consciousness". Which is even more confusing.

Anyway, having a mind seems to be a property that the humans share with at least some higher animals, while consciousness is still a property of human beings alone (until further notice). Nowadays intelligence is more seen as set of measurable qualities rather than a single property: We might say that Albert is more intelligent than Bob, but we also know that there are different forms of intelligence. There are many intelligence tests, but no mind tests!

Any definition has its practical utility. In this book, because I want to explain how our mind works, I will say quite simply that "the mind, it is the whole set of the brain functions". Over-simplifying, the brain is the hardware and the "Brainware", or mind, is the software.

We will not need definition for the intelligence. In this book I will explain you how the mind functions; it is up to you to see whether my explanations help you understand what you identify with intelligence.

All right, OK, OK, you really want a single and functional definition of intelligence? Then here is mine:

Intelligence is the ability to reduce entropy during the compression of information.

Does this help you? To really understand this definition you will need advanced mathematical concepts that I do not want to dwell here. Basically this means that intelligence is "the ability to make summaries". This seems rather simplistic at first, but it is in fact a very general and complete definition (and even in a sense, the most complete one). Anyway, as I said, we do not need a definition.

As for consciousness, we can keep the naive definition above: "The fact that I know I am me"

The very fact that the mind can be analyzed is not obvious at first sight. The mind has this strange quality to resist its own introspection. The vast majority of its functions work silently, unconsciously, and thereby pass unnoticed.

For millennia, the only identified functions of the mind were:

- The function of speech,

- And the ability to choose what we do, the famous "free will".

Two functions in all and for all!

Finding the good angle of attack had been be a centuries-long job!

For example we have known only for barely a century that the visual system is not only "what makes us see things", but is a system that manages to include the light pulses received by the retina into a coherent and three-dimensional but abstract representation of the objects around us, and then modify that representation according to what is perceived or imagined, and consequently the visual system is a full part of the mind!

Indeed, it can be shown that the visual system in the human brain is an extremely complex system that performs hundreds of billions of calculations per second (including additions and multiplications), simply to allow us to "see"... This explains for example that no current computer program can analyze a photograph and undoubtedly answer by yes or no to the question "is there a human being in this picture?", even after months of calculations, when a human comes almost instantly with the answer with no error, and can even further say the gender of that human being, but also his/her hair color, attitude, expression, and style of clothing, all things that our current computers are quite unable to do.

In the same way, we have only known for a few decades that "speaking" and "understanding someone who speaks" are two very different functions, although localized in close places in the brain. Truly, it is relatively easy to have a computer speak, but it is much more difficult for a computer to understand what is being said...

Thus, historically, philosophers have begun to analyze the mind starting with the higher level functions; then gradually lower level functions were identified, and very often found far more complex than the higher ones! However, mistakes were numerous. For example two centuries ago it was thought that the function "to calculate" was broken down into "to make an addition", "to make a multiplication", etc., that "to make an addition" required "to seek in a table", which required the function "to remember"…

The Mind and The Machine

It was a good idea, but it was totally wrong! There is not such a module as "to make an addition" in the brain, just as there is no function like "to remember the table of addition"! We know now that our arithmetic competences are actually based on a "substrate" of countless hidden functions that are necessary for a mind to simply grasp the concept of "five", or of "to add", and to plan the operations needed to achieve a given goal. We will come back to this point later.

Only recently have scientists begun to understand the brain and our mind. This understanding is the synthesis of many very different approaches, including neurology, psychology and computer science.

Nuclear magnetic resonance imaging (NMRI) offers a way to "see" live brain activity: it allows to measure in real time the consumption of sugar in different areas of our "brainware" or cerebral hardware, which reflects the neurons activity. It happens not only to map precisely this remarkable organ, but can show how different areas are activated in turn, for example when we talk about a memory. Note that we are still unable to prove that the language center devoted to cars in men brains is roughly as big as the center dedicated to purse in women brains (Well, almost!)

On a smaller scale, the electron microscopic study of the nervous system of primitive animals, such as worms or insects, has allowed us to understand the operation of simple sensory systems, like the locomotion system of insects (neurons that control the legs and synchronize them). Neurobiologists thus have managed to draw up the complete neuronal map of certain species! (Obviously, for humans, were are still far from that)

To some extent, we are now able to partially understand the operation of the first few layers of processing in our visual system, starting with the retina, which not only collects the light information but also carries out a lot of very complex calculations!

Psychologists then enter the scene: they have designed very ingenious experiments in which they can precisely measure the reaction time of a human subject to various stimuli. They have managed for example to understand the reason of "optical illusions", such situations in which the eye does not manage to see whether a detail is "concave" or "convex", or perceives parallel straight lines as curved because they are surrounded by other convergent lines, etc.

All this helps us understand how some parts of our mind work, related to our senses or our reflex actions. But how on earth is our intelligence working?

Then the computer scientists have tackled the problem with an ax. Since the 60's, having a wonderful tool named computer, often called an "electronic brain", they have tried to, if not replicate, at least simulate some mental processes such as "problem solving" or mind games (like chess). That gave rise to a new discipline, the artificial intelligence (AI).

After the excitement of the beginnings, where "the thinking machine" was predicted for 1980 (!) and the bitter disillusionment that followed, the AI science entered a phase of maturity. It sticks to limited objectives, sometimes with success, sometimes with failures (but those are full of lessons), and manages gradually to give more and more power and competences to the computer and to restrict the scope of what was considered impossible. Importantly, AI specialists now cooperate with other disciplines, including psychologists and neurobiologists, and these collaborations between different disciplines are very hopeful.

Computer and brain are very different. Some tasks that are impossible with our brain, like calculating the logarithm of numbers with dozens of figures, are easily done by a computer, and vice versa. No computer program can recognize the musical instruments which appear in a CD- recorded song, nor even extract the melody from it (if there are several voices). Whereas a child would effortlessly succeed!

17

The Mind and The Machine

It seems that all the tasks that are ultimately the most difficult for a computer are those that are the easiest for us: pattern recognition, analogies, perceptions of the regularities of the world around us: the mere task of finding its way in a cluttered room is for a robot a task of almost insurmountable complexity.

Finally, the main contribution of AI is this one:

The human mind carries out a fantastic number of calculations: its power is thousands of times higher than the most powerful computer of planet. However, this colossal power is not enough. The organization of the mind, its decompositions in numerous sub-functions, either complex or simple, is the key.

Reasoning and logic

Let us attack first a generally accepted idea: thinking is reasoning, and reasoning is deducting. In other terms, "to think, we use our knowledge and logical reasoning, so as to construct new knowledge from what we know and of what we observe".

In other words, our mind would work because it has a memory: it would get the information provided by "sensors" which are our senses, and would contain an "inference engine" that is certainly subtle and complicated but whose primary role would be to confront and mix our perceptions and our knowledge in order to infer new knowledge and actions to be undertaken. This "engine" would function according to rules that are still largely undiscovered, but can be approximated by the rules of mathematical logic.

As a consequence, cognitive psychology researchers as well as teachers believed in the 1960ies and 1970ies that the ideal knowledge would be an abstract and perfectly decontextualized knowledge that may apply for everything, whatever the considered topic. Mathematics and logic are regarded as major disciplines precisely because they involve a maximum level of abstraction: they seek towards universality.

This is completely wrong!

Yet this belief is only the reformulation of an intuition which is deeply rooted in everyone, even if you are not a psychologist nor a teacher; and which could be summed up as follows: "being logical means being intelligent", or: "logical reasoning means reasoning". The fact that one gives a disproportionate importance to logic and abstraction when one seeks to understand intelligent reasoning is indeed an echo of the work of former logicians and philosophers (Boole, Leibniz...) who supposed, wrongly it seems, that human cognition is governed by abstract rules of a logical type.

But actually this belief, we even say this faith, in the essential importance of logical and deductive thought, stems from another even more fundamental belief: The belief that most of the cognitive activity consists in thinking and solving problems. Consequently, the main objective of research was to describe, formalize and to model rules, heuristic and algorithms that govern our ability to think and reason.

Nevertheless, the results of this common research in artificial intelligence, logic, and psychology did not live up to expectations.

The Mind and The Machine

On the one hand, such models hardly handle the human cognitive capacities and on the other hand, many cognitive functions remain out of the reach of such models (induction, pattern recognition, decision making in situation of uncertainty, …) Eventually many empirical data have proved the wrongness of this first design of "reason".

Thus, it has become increasingly clear that abstract and logic thinking is uncommon. Even the most "sophisticated" human experts show a surprising resilience to handle abstraction and proceed logically. Logicians themselves, when out of their area of expertise, i.e. taken out of context, appear unable to use the most basic rule of logic, the modus ponens (which I will explain a little further).

There is a well-known test (the "Wason task") that remarkably illustrates this point. In this test, a subject is presented four cards, printed on both sides, so that he could only see one side:

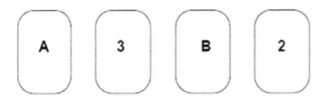

The subject is told that to create these cards the following rule was followed:

"If there is a vowel on a side, there must be an even figure on the other side".

The question is:

Which card(s) must be turned over to know if the rule has been respected? You must turn over a minimal number of cards.

Now try to solve the problem! Do not pass this line before you have found!

This one either! (Cheater!) Try it, come on!

Did you find? I will give you the right answer below. But be careful, it's not that easy! It is noted that only 10% of the subjects are answering correctly, although the knowledge of the elementary logical rule of the modus ponens should be enough to find the solution.

This rule, which is the most fundamental rule and simplest of formal logic, is:

> If we have: "if P then Q",
>
> AND if P is true,
>
> THEN Q is true.

In our example, P is the proposal "there is a vowel on one side" and Q is the proposal "there an even number on one side". It is easy to see that the rule "if P then Q" is not respected if and only if there is P and non-Q together. This is why we must turn over the first card labeled "A" (to check that there is an even figure on the other side) and the second card labeled "3" (to check that there is not a vowel of the other side). In fact, it is necessary to turn over the P cards and the non-Q cards.

The good answer is thus: first and the second card. Have You found it? No? You are not alone! Although the "logical" solution of this test requires only one ultra-simple logical rule that is so much "obvious", the modus ponens rule, it seems to be so difficult to reason with. We simply do *not* think that way!

Come on, here is another test for you to catch up:

You are presented four stamped envelopes, as follows:

With the rule:

"If an envelope is closed, then it must wear a 2.80 stamp".

The question is the same one: "**which envelope(s) should you turn over to know if the rule has been respected**?"

Come on, try it! This test is passed by 90% of people, you should be able to do it!

No, but oh, really try, right? It's not that complicated ... It is far less hard than the other... All right, OK, I do it! I seek!

Did you find? How? By using the modus ponens rule? Wow! I would be surprised. I rather believe that you wondered something like:

Hmm. If an envelope is closed, it must be stamped to 2.80. Good! Then I must turn over the first envelope, which is closed, to see whether this is well the case. And then? Turning over the open envelope (the third) will not tell us anything new. Then the fourth one can be open or closed, the rule will nevertheless be complied with since I have the right to put a 2.80 stamp even onto an open envelope. Now the second one... it can be opened and the rule does not apply, or else closed and... in this case it should be stamped to 2.80, but it has a 2.10 stamp, therefore I must turn it over it to check that it is quite open... OK, therefore I will turn over the first and the second envelope.

Ah Ah! This the same problem as with the cards, under a different disguise, the very same logic applies, the answer is the same!

And yet, 10% of people pass the 1st test, and 90% the second...

In fact people do not use same logic as the logicians: they do not use abstract proposals such as "this rule has type: if P then Q", but rather they use their knowledge of the field, they make analogies, and deduce what is "plausible" and what is not. Envelopes, stamps, are much more speaking than letters and figures. You can imagine yourself turning over the envelope, or sticking the stamp. Moreover, you did it while you were thinking, did you?

Okay, but then, if logic does actually not "run" our mind, what does?

Little Introspection

The thinker by Rodin

The human mind is the result of an evolution whose goal was to get humans to survive and reproduce, not to understand themselves. The mind was not designed for that. We have no "mind probe" that would tell us how we think. It is a pity! However, nothing prevents us to investigate how we might think, and to compare these ideas to reality. This is called introspection.

Let us try to see what happens...

When I think about a problem, sentences are formed in my mind. That is what we might call the "narrative thread" of consciousness. However, where are these thoughts coming from? It is difficult to know. I have the feeling that the next sentence is formed in a flash, then the words become clearer, and I recite them to me to memorize, but the sentence was already there before I start verbalization. It seems to me that ideas come from a deeper layer, where they "live" without being verbalized, and that I become aware of them only when they reach the "language service" in my brain.

I often say that there are hidden processes in my mind that I call "little elves" and that are launched when we need to dig a specific fact from our long-term memory. They are working in the background, invisible until they found. Possibly many little elves are working together simultaneously, not only for retrieving "forgotten" facts, but also to find new ideas. In this book, we will stumble upon little elves everywhere. Do not forget the little elves! Even when you rest, they are still at work!

The mind has curious gaps. For example we have all made the experience one day to have a name "on the tip of your tongue", but not being able to remember it. We know that we know, but we do not know what we know. It is very strange. When this happens, I just say "Wait, it will come back to me" In general, we try a little, then as it does not come, we move on to something else, and suddenly, a few minutes later (or days!) the forgotten name pops up in our mind, with obvious clarity: "How could I forget that!" Thank you, little elf!

In the same way the mathematician Poincaré tells he has for months sought a demonstration to a difficult theorem, then he was discouraged and thought no more to it, until the solution appeared to him suddenly, limpid and complete, and weeks later, while he was preparing to board a bus! It seems that Poincaré had in his mind a particularly stubborn little elf!

I also feel that I know how to think in a non-verbal way. When I was a child, I imagined that I was assembling blocks to build a tower or an arch. I piled them in my head, considering their stability before building my tower "for real". Contrary to popular belief, the human visual system not only can see and decode what is seen, but can also produce images or sensations that are perceived as images. Just close your eyes and imagine... You can even imagine things while keeping your eyes open, "forgetting" temporarily to see the real world... In addition, the same is true for the auditory system (you can sing in your head or even listen to an inner symphony), etc... In other words, all our senses can act as *decoders* (their primary function) but also as *encoders*.

Put yourself in the dark and close your eyes. What do you see? First, you still sense for a few seconds the contours of the bright objects that were in front of you, gradually fading. This phenomenon called retinal afterimage comes as its name suggests, from the retina, which is the first layer of the visual nervous system.

The retina calculates and stores for some time the trace of the average light intensity in the different areas of the visual field, and what is actually transmitted to the next layer of treatment is the *differences* in intensity compared to this time average. Note that if our eyes did not move continuously, this difference would become zero in a few seconds, and we would not see anything! That is why our eyes are constantly animated by unconscious micro-saccades, which make the eyes live.

Then, darkness. No! Not just darkness! You begin to see color stains, or parallel lines, or textures, fairly regular, rapidly scrolling without any apparent order. Your visual system believes it sees things. You might think it is a "noise", that is to say, what remains when we remove the visual signal. Actually, although noise is present, it is not enough to fully explain these kinds of visual hallucinations.

Our visual system certainly contains thousands of highly specialized small decoders, all running in parallel. One of them is responsible for detecting horizontal lines; another for finding inclined lines, a third one identifies sudden changes in intensity or color, etc.

Moreover it also contains encoders, which receive their orders from "above", (we will see later what that means), and whose job is to produce visual signals. One creates horizontal lines, another builds leaning lines, a third one deals with "texturing" surfaces, much like the graphics card is a video game! There are also thousands of them. Most collect their input signals from the output of other coders and transform or mix them.

When we are in the dark, our eyes closed, these basic shapes encoders and generators contained in our visual system give heart to joy, they function in a "freewheeling mode".

Then finally your mind eventually recognized some vaguely familiar image in this whole random mess, it "locks on", requires coders generator to provide details on this image, and you then start to "see" a full scene which may be part of a memory, or may be entirely new.

It is quite possible that this faculty of creating simulated visual impressions for ourselves is necessary for the "decoding" of complex scenes or objects: when the eye does not know what he sees, he creates virtual images and textures, and compares them to what he sees in order to detect coincidences.

However, in fact, that mental imagery is also used for another purpose: it allows the formation and manipulation of concepts.

The mind has a wonderful ability to combine completely different concepts into a whole that seems consistent. Try to think of a "red lemon": Your mind immediately produces an image of this new concept, doesn't it? But what you "see" is a lemon whose surface is red, not a red uniform lemon-shaped spot, which is just another possible definition of a "red lemon".

Nevertheless, when I said "a red lemon-shaped spot", this time you see in 2D because the word "spot" implies a flat surface.

It is also fascinating to note that when I mentally visualize a red lemon-shaped spot, I see it on a white background. Do you see it as well? Strangely enough, as "lemon" should "activate" the concept of yellow and "red" the color red, a third color, white, is actually selected by our internal visualization system to serve as a background for the red spot! The words "shaped spot" may make us think of a drawing and a drawing is usually done on a blank sheet.

The mind prefers to create three-dimensional representations rather than flat ones. We are designed to live in a three-dimensional world. When we "see" a scene or an object such as a table and chairs, we not only analyze the image received by our two eyes, but we also design a simultaneous representation of 3D objects that we can even mentally move. We can imagine putting the chairs on the table and we "see" the result immediately.

When we move inside a room, or when we just turn our head, our eyes see very different things: but indeed we do not think that the room is changing, but rather that our point of view has changed with respect to the position of 3D objects that our mind "sees" as fixed!

(i) A triangular bulb

The Mind and The Machine

Let us continue a little this exploration of our hidden faculties:

Imagine a standard light bulb. We "see" immediately a roughly round form, made of clear glass with a metal cap. I see it above the bulb, as if it were set in a chandelier: and you? Do you "see" the cap up, or down as in the icon of "I have an idea"? And why not right or left? Or front? This is apparently never the first image that comes to mind. Again, the visual system must make choices for us to visualize concepts, and these choices involve memory.

Now consider a "triangular light bulb".

What do you imagine? What do you see? The first time I thought about this concept, I "saw" a kind of glass pyramid, with rounded edges and a light blue color. Perhaps you saw a tetrahedron instead of a pyramid. But what you did *not* see is a glass triangle (Or maybe it was a neon tube bent to make a triangle?) But no, you saw a 3D shape, didn't you?) This is an extremely fast process: the image pops up before you have time to say it is popping up.

Yet it is a complicated one, more complicated, for example, than a "red light" or "triangular parking".

It seems that the concepts of "triangle" and "light bulb" mix to achieve a credible result, despite the conflict. It seems that bulb refers to "round", "ball", "3D", "glass", and "triangle" refers to "acute corners," "three", "edges", "2D". The process mixing the two sets of description selected "3D", "straight edges", "rounded corners", "glass", leading to "glass pyramid with rounded edges".

The white blueish color that I visualize might come from "glass" since that makes me think of "transparent" and "water" but also from "bulb" which suggests white or yellow. The mixture of these colors makes me therefore think of a white blueish color and a more opaque than transparent material, fairly thick (like glass with air bubbles trapped inside) Where does this concept come from? I cannot remember having even thought about it.

In fact, I did not think of anything! This whole process took place instantaneously, without the intervention of my conscience, and as it seems, directly inside my visual system. Isn't it extraordinary?

Let us sum up the properties of the mental imagery that we have just discovered:

The visual system (but it is true for any sensory system) can both recognize and produce images. This production is possible because the concepts that we think about require special features in the image to produce (or part of the image, or in an object to integrate in an image). It is as if the concepts had relations with one another (to detect associations and conflicts) but also with images generators, and actually by using these generators of mental images, they connect with one another.

The production of mental images is also used by the motor system: Before you perform a movement, you visualize mentally (and usually unconsciously) this movement. This system allows the motor system to decide which muscles must be activated and in what order.

We will return with more details on this mechanism when we try to explain the global operations of the mind.

We humans, have eight senses (and not five!):

-   Sight
-   Hearing
-   Touch
-   Smell

- Taste
- The sense of balance, provided by the inner ear
- Proprioception: the sense of the position of our members, allowing us to know where they are even when our eyes are closed and without the help of touch. It also allows us to move our arms without bumping our body (a well-known and very hard problem in robotics!)
- Female intuition.

Uh, sorry about this... there are only seven senses in fact! Where is the error?

It reminds me a little riddle of Pierre Desproges: What is wrong in the following list:

Leukemia, metastasis, polyp, melanoma, joy.

Okay, it is not the best taste, but I love Desproges. Moreover, I think these small tests, such as "seek error" do reveal a lot about deep mechanisms of our mind. We shall see it later when we discuss how we can make analogies and find similarities and differences between concepts. But back to the subject.

As with vision, our seven senses all have sensory imagery and are thus bi-directional: they provide sensations, but our mind can "simulate" or "impose" sensations perceived by the senses and create concepts from these simulations.

For example, imaging of the seventh sense (proprioception) is activated when a golfer mentally repeats the swing he will do to send the ball. Even a sense as "limited" as the sixth (the sense of balance) has a mental imagery: it comes into play for example if I ask you to imagine that you are driving over a speed bump, or when a diver or acrobat mentally repeat the somersault he will perform.

Multi-sensory perceptions

From our young childhood, and even from birth, our senses are used to draw up a mental picture of the world around us: The primary purpose of nature seems to have been to make the new-born understand he is surrounded by 3D objects (and other living things), that these objects have a location, and that he himself is one of those "objects".

One of the first skills that young children gain is to learn the relationship among the parts of their body, and between their body and the world. Watch a baby waving his arms and legs: he grabs his foot with his hand, very well! He is not just playing but learning. His seventh sense tells him that his foot is "there", that his hand "is there" too, and his sense of touch tells him": ah, it's touching, I feel the contact! The baby will then understand the link between his sense of the position of its members and his sense of touch. He will then attempt to use his sense of touch to "make a map of his body." It is remarkable that this is coincidence detection between the information provided by two different senses! This ability to detect coincidences seems to be innate, pre-wired in our brains.

The areas of the cerebral cortex that process the tactile information which are close to each other in the skin are also close to each other in the brain. It is no coincidence. These areas are interconnected, and by sliding a finger on the skin, you active successive yet close areas, and that gives you a feeling of continuity; This allows the young child to understand which areas of his/her body are close to one another, and eventually "where they are." All this, even before he/she can understand that he/she can consciously move his/her members!

When a young child touches the wall of his cradle with his hand, his seventh sense told him that the hand "is there", and if he has already internalized the map of his body, he knows that the object his hand touch is not on his body. Moreover, he does only sense a single contact, not two. Therefore, he is touching "something else". In exploring by touching the limits of this "something else", he will draw a mental map of it. And, miracle, he will understand the relationship between what he touches and what he sees. He will understands that what he sees, he can touch. Assuming he has long enough arms.

Isn't it an extraordinary mechanism? No mechanical robot is able to do such things even if running the most sophisticated programs, but yet a newborn child does it in the simplest way!

Psychology

- *After 12 years of therapy, my psychiatrist said to me something that brought me to tears.*
- Oh yeah? What did he say?
- He said: "No hablo Inglés"

So finally, what can we say about the mind, based on introspection and the observations we can make of other minds? This question is the central question of psychology. Here are some basic observations on the mechanism of our minds, asserted by psychologists:

- The mind receives its information through sensory channels: the well-known five senses, plus the vestibular system of the inner ear (orientation), and the sense the position of our members (proprioception).

- A "sensory overload" can create *pleasure* or *pain*

- From information received, the mind is capable of building an *internal representation* of its environment

- Conversely, it is able to "see" a desired or imagined situation.

- The mind has *conscious* and *unconscious* functions.

- It is capable of acting through conscious actions or unconscious reflexes. These reflexes can be conditioned.

- The human mind seems to have a narrative thread and be able to "talk" to himself silently.

- Among the functions of the mind, there is a motivational system that drives us to act towards the goals that we set consciously or not, (the impulses and drives).

- Among the mind features there are unconscious *censorship* functions that prevents us from thinking unpleasant things.

- The mind dreams during REM sleep, and during dreams the censors are "released" and censor less things. They learn their trade.

- The mind is not built at once, but requires a *learning process* with step by step skill acquisition. The newborn has some skills, at least those that will enable it to learn more. The most powerful drive for the learning process for the newborn is the *attachment* to his mother. Then they will learn by imitation and then by "symbolic representation"

- The mind has a linguistic or language competence and it can be shown that the newborn already has a grammar parsing ability.

- The mind seems to have a short-term memory, whose maximum capacity is five or six simultaneous ideas or concepts, which fade after a couple of minutes.

- It also has a long-term memory, which stores up our memories but also our beliefs and our skills, and whose capacity seems to be of the order of tens of Tera bytes (1TB = 1000 gigabytes or GB). It is interesting to note that many computers already have this memory to disk. (It does not make them smarter insofar...)

- The transfer of short-term memory to long-term memory is a process that takes time, sometimes several minutes to several hours. That is the reason why people who have had a car accident and lost consciousness as a result of the shock often cannot remember what was immediately preceding the accident: their short-term memory has not had time to transfer data in the long-term memory.

- Conversely, the recall of a memory buried in the long-term memory may take several hours or even days!

- The overall state of mind seems to suddenly change under the influence of chemical discharges triggered by *emotions*. These emotions are very diverse, but it seems there is a group of "basic" emotions which can be combined with one another and give other emotions. Opinions differ, however, about the list of basic emotions, and even on their number.

- Each individual is unique, not only because his/her personal experience, memories and skills are different from those of other people, but also because each individual "has his/her own personality." What does this mean, doc?

Emotions and character traits

We all know that we are prone to emotions; we all know that our characters are quite different. What does this mean? What is the difference between emotions, feelings, character traits? Can we be more specific? How many separate emotions are there, exactly?

Answering these questions is equivalent to substituting uncertainty with error: there is no single answer. But why? Let us try to see it up closer.

What do you think of the following list? Do you think this is an exhaustive list?

- Hunger, thirst, satiety
- Pleasure, Pain
- Calm, agitation, impatience, excitement, anger,
- Imperturbability, stability, passivity, emotionality, compulsivity, instability, hysteria
- Habit, familiarity, Surprise, Astonishment
- Curiosity, enthusiasm, indifference, laziness, passivity, Boredom
- Serenity, disquietness, anxiety, fear
- Happiness, joy, sorrow, sadness, depression
- Fullness, satisfaction, dissatisfaction, frustration, greed
- Enthusiasm, weariness, laziness

- Love, desire, affection, friendship, attachment, indifference, disdain, contempt, hatred
- Attraction, repulsion, revulsion
- Reverence, awe, lust, ambition, jealousy
- Trust, distrust, paranoia
- Pride, shame
- Recklessness, Courage, Cowardice
- Extroversion, friendliness, scowling, Introversion
- Sincerity, rectitude, hypocrisy, lying
- Kindness, indifference, malice, sadism
- Hypochondria, Narcissism, Paying attention to himself, being indifferent to himself, masochism
- Being a revolutionary, a reformer, cautious, conservative
- Being direct, fleeing, beating about the bush, calculating, a Machiavellian
- Being simple, complicated, twisted
- Altruism, caring for others, indifference, selfishness

In every line of this list, are terms that seem to be related to the intensity (positive or negative) of one single variable on a single scale. However I do not pretend that inside our minds there really exists a single scale that goes (for example) from hatred to love through indifference. These words are helpful; they can quickly characterize our "mental states". However, beware, do not believe that these "variables" have a real existence!

Is it possible however that the apparently so wide variety of our emotions and character traits may be in fact only quantitative differences of a few variables?

The top items of my list included "basic" physiological emotions. The bottom part of the list includes terms that are much more character traits. In-between are listed what might be called mental and social attitudes. It seems that the transitions among these categories are somewhat fuzzy. I believe that the origin of the higher items on my list (probably chemical messengers in the brain) is completely different for the classes in the lower end, which appear to stem from our education and to be fairly stable.

Basic emotions are probably *summaries of mental states*. Our brains may contain lots of "probes" for measuring the activity of particular areas, all connected to a synthesis process that develops a felt emotion. (We will see later, addressing the theme of consciousness, how we can consciously "feel" something). However, as with any sensory system, this process is bidirectional: some thoughts create emotions too. Again, we will focus on this fascinating subject later on.

Some chemical messengers have clearly a direct influence on the state of our mind (think of adrenaline, or hunger and thirst). Nevertheless, this does not mean that all categories of my list are linked to the chemistry of the brain!

The central question that should concern us is this one: Are these emotions, attitudes and character traits really intrinsic properties of a mind, or only emergent characteristics, resulting from the complex organization of our mental systems?

For example the concept of "liking something" is, at first, very simple: it boils down to a single summon:

- Like what your senses feel good! (Mom's tits...)

In particular, the sense of taste is probably the most capable (for the very young child) to feed up higher levels with "pleasant" or "unpleasant" sensations.

Then, it becomes more complicated... Other "commandments" appear to be added:

- Like what/who you know well! (Your mother, your blanket, your toys...)
- Dislike what/who you do not know!

Then others:

- Like what comes from whom you like (gifts, awards...)
- Like what looks like what you like!
- Dislike what looks like something you dislike (or that has the same smell or touch, etc.).
- Like doing things you well know how to do (the beginning of the feeling of pride)

However, where do these "commandments" come from? What are the rules that make us change our emotions?

Worden modeled in 1996 the emotional behavior of primates. When a young monkey sees a potential threat, like a big bird on top of him, then it looks at the behavior of an experienced adult monkey and models its own behavior after it. Indeed, evolution did not give the young monkeys innate knowledge to distinguish between dangerous large bird like eagles and not dangerous ones like vultures. This leads to the following two rules:

If something can be dangerous

If someone more experienced than I am feels fear

Then I feel fear too

If something can be dangerous

If someone more experienced than I am doesn't feel
   any fear

Then I will not feel fear either

Note that these last two rules imply that the young monkey is able to recognize the emotions of another individual. Something we now know is built-in in our brain. More about this later.

With a thousand similar rules, we come to model correctly many emotional behaviors of primates (Warning: this is only to model emotions: intellectual behavior, even for primates, cannot be reduced to a set of rules).

What about if human beings were having similar rules? After all, it is an interesting idea. In 1985, Pfeifer tried to use rules to predict the behavior of an individual. For example:

> If the condition is negative for myself
>
> If the condition was caused by another person
>
> If the other person was in control
>
> Then generate anger towards the other.

Suppose we wanted to create an artificial intelligence (AI) by means of computer programs: should we then encode directly the variables "love" and "fear" into the program and give them a scale of numerical values, and then implement complex procedures for varying the value of these variables according to the "commandments" above, to rules, and probably to many other things?

On the other hand, should we... do nothing and hope that love or altruism will result of the education we give to our AI and of its digital hard-coded mental structure?

I think we should choose the second option! I believe that the hardest challenge for an AI programmer will be to guess what should *not* be hand-coded. I shall go back to that later on.

What is certain is that *attachment* and *love* are the very young child's most powerful engine of learning. It seems that here too, other "commandments" are at work:

- Mimic the actions of the people you love!
- Like imitating!

- Do over and over what you like doing!

Very quickly, the child experiences the other as "something that can do the same thing" as he/she does. By imitating and being imitated, the children learn that among the objects around only human beings can live the same experiences as he/she would.

How exactly does this process of imitation work?

Imitation

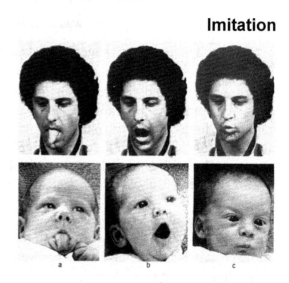

The famous Swiss psychologist Piaget has created a remarkable model of the succession of competences that the child must acquire, and therefore the steps that he must pass before moving to a higher skill. For him, "imitating" is a skill that requires an ability to "symbolic representation" and therefore only appears around the age of one year. Piaget made four assumptions:

- Human beings gradually learn to mimic during their early childhood.

- A basic form of symbolic representation is needed to mimic
- Newborns are unable to link what they see in others and what they feel in themselves.
- Once the child is able to mimic, mimicry remains a minor and childish skill.

In 1983, two American researchers, Andrew Meltzoff and Keith Moore, proved that Piaget was wrong: A newborn *is* able to mimic, and within 32 hours of his/her birth! These two researchers proved that the four above assumptions were wrong! In fact, imitation is probably the most important human basic skill!

In 2003, Meltzoff mounted a series of experiments to understand how children come to imitate adults, and reached a really surprising conclusion:

In a first experiment, a researcher showed to little ones of approximately 18 months how he tried to remove the tip of a 'mini-dumbbell' for children. But instead of completing the work, he was pretending he could not remove the tip of the toy. The children thus never saw the precise representation of the true purpose of the action. Using different control groups the researchers noted that the babies had seized the focus of the process (remove the end of the dumbbell), and they imitated the intention of the researcher and not what they had actually seen, and that they were happy when they managed to do so.

Children therefore understand the *intentions* of adults, even if these adults are unable to perform the task. They imitate what the researchers wanted to do rather than what they were doing in practice. However, there is more to it:

The second experiment was designed to see whether children attribute reasons for things. For this experiment, the researchers had made a small machine (with arms and grabs) that performed exactly the same aborted action as in the first experiment. Soon it was found that toddlers who had taken advantage of this demonstration were not more willing to attribute intent to the machine than others who were faced with the small dumbbell without demonstration. It seems that children do not grant any intentions to inanimate objects.

A third experiment made it even clearer that a child pays attention to the will of his/her fellows, and how these motives and intents are important to him/her. In this test, the ends of the small dumbbell were firmly glued to the bar. They could not be removed. The researcher repeated the same demonstration as in the previous experiments: he tried to remove the outer part of the toy, but his hand slipped from the tip without grasping it. The same thing necessarily happened when the children tried (since the tips were glued), but the kids were not at all satisfied with the mere reproduction of what they had seen adults do. They tried over and over again to remove the tip, biting it and imploringly glancing at their Mum and at the researchers.

Meltzoff's work reinforces the idea that toddlers are beginning to focus on the goals of adults and not just on their actions. Several scholars go further and suggest that imitation in humans is always - at a fundamental level - the imitation of intentions and goals rather than of actions and representations.

Animists, who believe that even inanimate objects can have a spirit, are not so far from the truth: our sensory modalities are "wired" to assign roles to the objects, be they animated or not, they have detected. Better than that, they come to assign goals to animated objects (humans) only!

This indicates that the ability to distinguish between animate and inanimate objects exists from the very young age. In fact, it is likely that there are already in our brain and from birth visual circuits that are pre-wired to recognize a human face.

We will address the goals and intentions later on, and how they appear in our mind. Let us continue to explore the fascinating field of mimicry, because we may be even more surprised:

How on earth can therefore the very young children discern at first attempt the intentions of adults, while they are still incapable of the "symbolic representation" treasured by Piaget?

This is where another very recent and little known discovery interferes. This discovery was not done by a psychologist, but by an Italian neurologist, Giacomo Rizzolati (1996). This is the discovery of *mirror neurons*. Although not reported by the media, it is probably the most important psychological discovery of the decade, probably as important to psychology as the discovery of DNA was for biology.

What is it about?

The researchers found - by chance - that some neurons (in the F5 area of the premotor cortex) that were activated when a monkey made a movement with a specific purpose (e.g., to take an object) were also activated when the monkey simply observed this movement done by another monkey or by the researcher, who gave an example.

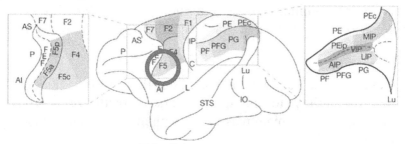

Area F5 of the premotor cortex

Therefore, a direct link between *action* and *observation* exists in the brains of primates. This discovery was first made with monkeys, but the existence and importance of mirror neurons in humans has been confirmed.

Shirley Fecteau showed that this mechanism of mirror neurons is active in the brain of immature little children and that those networks of mirror neurons continue to develop in the later stages of childhood. We must add here that the scientists agree that these networks are not only more developed in adults (compared to children), but they are considerably more advanced in humans in general compared to other primates

The mirror neurons are part of a complex brain machinery that identifies animated objects in what is seen, and seeks to assign *goals* to animated objects and *roles* to inanimate objects.

Human, Animal, Imitation and violence

Man is a social animal, which differs from other animals in that it is better at imitation; Aristotle said it already (Poetics 4). Today we can understand and trace the brain sources of this human specificity.

Nevertheless, we are not at the end of the surprises: this discovery that the ability to imitate is rooted directly in neurons, and probably in all mammals, can explain the innate tendency of humans to rivalry and violence:

Man has the highest capacity for mimicry in the whole animal kingdom. It is also the most violent. Are these two facts related?

This seems paradoxical, because it is likely that imitation plays a key role in the herd instinct and social harmony. Therefore, the man should be the least violent animal!

Yet it is dangerous to imitate! Too much imitation leads inevitably to violence.

Where does this danger of mimicry come from? Remember that in the premotor cortex of the monkeys studied by Rizzolati, mirror neurons were activated when the animal made a movement with a purpose, most often "to pick up an object." Now imagine a monkey who tries to seize an object and another one who blindly imitates its fellow monkey, but without being aware of it. Those two eager hands that converge towards a single object cannot help generating a conflict...

Hence, imitation can be the cause of conflicts and violence, knowing that any behavior of acquisition and ownership (as grasping an object for itself) is also likely to be imitated.

Yet another example: Imagine there are two toddlers in a room full of identical toys. The first takes a toy, but he does not seem very interested by the trinket. The second observes and tries to pull the toy to his little friend. He was not very enthralled by the knick-knack, but suddenly, because the other shows interest in it, this is changing, and he does not want to release it. Tears, frustration and violence ensue. In a very short time an object for which neither had a particular interest become the stake of a stubborn rivalry between them.

Everything in this too much desired but unshareable object is notably imitation, even the intensity of one's desire depends from the others' desire. This is what Girard *calls mimetic rivalry*, a strange process of "positive feedback" that secretes large quantities of jealousy, envy and hatred.

If imitation happens to be often dangerous for monkeys, this is also true for humans. But the big difference is that monkeys are unlikely to fight to death for food, partners, territory, etc. because relationships made of domination and submission are curbs to instinctive violence No such brakes exist anymore among men.

As said already Jacques Monod:

> Now dominating its environment, the man had in front of him no serious opponent but himself. The direct intra-specific fight, fight to death, thereby became a major factor of selection in the human species. This is an extremely rare phenomenon in the evolution of animals [...] In what direction should have this pressure of selection pushed the evolution of humankind? (Monod, 1970).

Here I will risk a personal theory: emotions are needed to create a system of goals and intentions, which in turn is a prerequisite for the design of thoughts. The human capacity to think is the result of the richness of our emotions and this richness would have not been able to emerge but in an environment of rivalry and violence. The presence of many biological mirror neurons in the human brain, leading to an immense ability to mimic, has therefore been the cause of the creation of our consciousness.

Violence was necessary for the emergence of humankind. Of course, humanity could have disappeared because of the mutual extermination of its members! That did not happen, because humans have, through their new ability to think creatively, set up barriers and social taboos, which were beyond the instincts of submission / domination of the monkeys. Let us quote, for example, the creation of 'leaders' and 'wizards' social classes, the invention of religion, etc.

Thinking

Let us continue our "guided tour" of the mind: up to now, we have talked a little bit about our senses and our mental imagery, and then we have made a detour to higher-level concepts such as our emotions, our mental and social attitudes, and how we learn by mimicry. Between these two lines lies the terra incognita of "how on earth do we think?"

It seems that "thinking is to recite ideas to oneself." Big mistake! We know that we are able to think in a non-verbal way, using our mental imagery. Still worse, the fact that we "recite ideas to ourselves", i.e. the "internal narrative thread" is something that does not just happen like this! I said above that when I begin to think, I feel that the next sentence I am going to think of is «already coming complete from deeper layers of my mind," and I do verbalize it to myself only to become aware of it and remember... and to know if I can use it or reject it. Actually, the narrative thread is a process of *deliberation*, which is a layer of mind above the layer where thoughts are formed. The layers of thought and deliberation are distinct. In addition, thoughts have nothing to do with words. *Thoughts are arrangements of concepts*, just as concepts are arrangements of percepts from our mental imagery.

The main idea of all this is that our mind seems to be made up of countless "little elves" or *agents*, and that these agents are organized into five layers that seem to be almost disjoint (at least conceptually), each using the skills of the layers below it:

- The layer of consciousness and the "narrative thread"
- The layer of deliberation and goals
- The layer of thoughts and ideas
- The layer of concepts
- The layer of senses, specifically that of the sensory modalities,

This organization reflects the development of the brain: the services that manage the sensory modalities are the oldest ones; the genes that encode them are dozens, even hundreds, or millions of years old. The "deliberation" layer is present in human beings, but also at least partly in higher mammals, some of which are capable of developing plans according to their goals (A famous example is that of the monkey that must push a box and climb onto

47

it to get bananas that are suspended too high to catch them another way).

The layer of *concepts* is probably shared by all mammals, and perhaps by other classes of animals. It receives the sometime very complex information developed by our sensory modalities, and derives new concepts. Conversely, it can display a concept by requiring the generators in our sensory modalities.

When a dog carrying a large bone in its mouth "thinks" to tilt its head to pass through the bars of a grid, and well before reaching the grid, we can say this is probably because it has the concepts of "width" and "length" and "It goes through or not" and also "tilting the head", and probably others. The dog also has a higher-level layer, the level of "thought" (possibly different from that of humans), and this layer is capable of creating the idea of "when the bone is wider than the bars, I should tilt the head so that it goes through", an idea that is mixing different concepts.

Concepts

However, what is a concept?

To find out, nothing is worth but an example. Think of the concept of "butterfly". When I think of a butterfly, many things are happening:

1) I immediately visualize a butterfly (for me it is yellow and black, and for you?).

2) But that's not all: I am able to recognize a butterfly if I see one. Yet I know that my visual system knows nothing of butterflies. My visual system "knows" something about color, orientation, contours and edge detection, motion detection, and volume, but nothing about butterflies...

3) I am able to learn on my own what a butterfly is, even if I have never seen one. In my childhood, I saw butterflies. I realized that they were things that fly by fluttering wings, a bit like birds (but I recognized straight away that butterfly are not birds). Moreover, all this took place long before an adult told me "it's a butterfly, my child."

4) I know to associate some characteristics with a butterfly. I know that butterfly have wings and a body, that these wings are bright and multicolored, and have this so characteristic shape, that their bodies have long legs and so on.

5) I can imagine a butterfly that would have other characteristics: for example, a white butterfly, a translucent butterfly, a butterfly without wings, a sailor butterfly, a dragonfly with butterfly wings, etc…

6) Finally, I can give a name to this concept: butterfly.

It seems that my mind can do four things with concepts:

- It can detect that a concept is present in my current mental imagery.

49

- It can create new concepts automatically from my sensory imaging (especially visual, but not only).
- It also knows when it should *not* create unnecessary new concepts. If I were to create a new concept for every new thing I see, my memory would become quickly saturated.
- He knows how to "reify" a concept, that is to give it a "special place", to save it in memory, but also to link it to other concepts, manipulate it, change it in response to a goal, "moving it to the next level," the thought layer.

Look at our AI programmer who wants to create the concept of "butterfly" for the AI. His first idea would be to create a structure in memory, with attached fields such as the name of the concept, close other concepts, the original properties of the new concept or the differences with close concepts, and methods to assign a value to these fields. In AI-oriented computer science, this is called a *frame*. What you must understand is that this is a false good idea. A concept is much more than a frame with properties and methods.

The concepts of *left* and *right* for example, even though they seem superficially very simple, are certainly very complicated internally. The *lateralization* of a young child, the way he learns to distinguish his left from his right and the left and right sides of objects and people around him, takes years. A concept not only describes things, it *does* things. The evocation of a concept triggers extraordinarily subtle mechanisms in our mind.

The main feature of the concept of concept (ah ah!) is that concepts are emerging from our sensory imagery, and can in turn be imposed on our mental imagery. A frame cannot be imposed on our mental imagery, and cannot arise spontaneously from our imagery. To create a computer model of a concept, we should perhaps need frames, but certainly something else. It is not enough to know what concepts are made of; we must understand how they are created, and what they do, i.e. how they act.

But what? How does it work exactly? How do we create new concepts, *useful* concepts?

To find out, let us start with a very simple concept: The concept of *red*.

Red

Our visual system has been designed to recognize objects in a 3D world, and to provide information on these objects. One of this information is color. We perceive that an object has an intrinsic color, regardless of lighting conditions. A pink object under a white light could emit the same light (the same spectrum) than a white object under a reddish light, but the human visual system is able to maintain the *consistency of color* and see the object as white even it appears pink because of lighting. It was utterly important for our ancestors (and even our primitive mammal's ancestors) to perceive the regularities of their environment.

It has actually been shown that the variations of natural light have only three degrees of freedom, and that the eye and the human visual system are configured to measure these three degrees of freedom. They are:

- The *light-dark* variation, which depends on the total light received by an object
- The *yellow-blue* variation, which determines if a portion of an object is directly exposed to sunlight or is in the shade (in which case it is illuminated by the sky)

- The *red-green* variation, which depends on the height of the sun in the sky and the presence of water vapor in the air.

The three-color channels provided by the human visual system are precisely what is needed to maintain the consistency of color. This allows recognizing the same object when viewed later under a (natural) different light.

Our senses allow us to recognize not only patterns, but also and above all some invariants in the world around us. One of these invariants is the (intrinsic) color of objects.

Now, how has the concept of 'red' been able to form in my mind? Very simply by a mechanism detecting repetitions of a unique feature provided by the visual system. When the number of objects for which the color features is identical or very similar over a certain threshold, my mind (the part of me responsible for creating concepts) automatically creates a concept to characterize these "very close" in the color space.

When I was a young child, I was presented objects and asked which ones were "red". I suppose that I initially responded randomly, but fortunately, my mind contained a "little elf" whose job was detect duplication of a feature provided by my visual system. The "color" characteristic of objects that I was presented as "red" was identical (or very close), so the little elf was quick to understand that (it was his job, he did nothing else). And voilà! The concept of *red* was born, with as a bonus some examples in memory (red objects), and the unconscious knowledge that the characteristic "color" was the one which was most important for this concept, allowing me to impose a red color to a mental image, for example, to imagine a red lemon.

Then I was able to mentally change color from red and get ready to recognize and conceptualize other colors! Obviously other similar concepts ("purple", "magenta", etc.) Can be created by this process, and these categories overlap in the color space. Then the frequency of future use of these concepts will determine whether to keep them or not.

Of course, this mechanism of focusing on one characteristic and of detection of repetitions is too primitive to give birth to all concepts. However, there are other little elves in my mind: some are responsible for detecting the correlation between the variation of two characteristics, or the coincidence of events in time, for example.

Obviously, the creation of concept as I just described is too dependent on the sense of sight, whereas I am able to reason about an object without any visual image, sometimes without even knowing what sensory modality I should assign: for example, I can think about an object that is worth 50 euros. I can imagine, in the absence of an appearance, how big could that object be (not too big), and possibly even its smell if this is a perfume (which I do not know, but I know this is a likely possibility)

Lesson learned: concepts do arise from the sensory imagery and are created by "little elves", which are continuously fired to detect patterns or linkages in invariants provided by the sensory system.

Even for complex concepts, which seems to result purely from our thoughts, these thoughts create mental images (not only visual) in which the concepts are then detected.

Five

Now a concept a little more complicated concept: the number *five*:

Let us be clear: I try to imagine how, as I was three or four (maybe less), I understood the concept of "five" while I did know nothing yet about the concepts of addition or numbers, and did even not know how to count. Here I will to suppose that my visual system was not automatically counting identical objects, which is wrong because it is now assumed that we perceive immediately the number of objects in a set, as far as this number remains small, less than five or six in general. I will also assume that when I learned the concept of "five" I cannot count, I did even not know the existence of the word "five" and maybe even that of "four"! (A little later, when I started to count, I have persisted for months to recite "one, two, three, six, four," to the disappointment of my parents...)

To identify the "five" in what I saw or heard (clap your hands five times), the problem was not to identify the numerical characteristic in what I saw, but to know there was a numerical characteristic to search at first, a "five-ness".

Understanding a concept is about knowing how to recognize it, how to impose it to our mental images, and how to identify and manipulate its features.

Let us begin by the end: suppose that I have the concept of "five", but I am still not counting. How can I manage (assuming that my visual system does not count either) to identify that there are five apples in a basket?

I look at the basket. I recall from my memory an instance of "five" I have already seen, for example five oranges. (Much more likely, for "five", a typical example would be our five fingers. But for six, the example of oranges would be better suited! So I still go on my explanation with oranges, but remember I could have used anything that I have previously associated with "five", for example, the five arms of a sea star.) *So I visualize these five oranges. I make a one to one correspondence between oranges and apples. If there is no apple nor orange left on one side then there are indeed five apples.*

Let us go into a little more details about the key phase: to make a 1-1 correspondence between oranges and apples, I must connect an orange with an apple, and then do it again being careful not to link with an object already used. I should continue as long as there are unused couples of orange-apple.

Whew! It is a bit complicated for the sake of verifying a concept! Right, but it just happens to be the most general test of the concept of "five-ness". Moreover, it suffices to modify slightly the procedure to find other concepts: if some oranges remain at the end, there is *less-than-five* apples. If an apple is remaining we had *more-than-five* apples. Two new concepts for the same price!

Furthermore, this procedure only uses the ability (or concept) of 1-1 Correspondence, which appears to be a prerequisite for the competence of recognizing a number of items. This concept of 1-1 correspondence in turn uses "link two objects", which is a skill that children learn very quickly, "to repeat" (even faster learned, probably innate) and "recognize that we have already used this object", a more complex skill that is acquired later, actually just before learning "five"!

Proof: you have probably noticed with amusement how young children draw a stick person, with a circle and two lines: they draw one single oval for the body and head, then four lines that are attached to the oval, and then they add a mouth and two eyes in the oval.

This is because they follow the following *algorithm*:

- Draw a round circle (the body).
- Add arms
- Add legs
- Draw a round circle (head) *Hey! But there is already a circle, it's magic! Well, well too bad, I do not trace it.*
- Draw the mouth and eyes

They know they have already drawn a circle and do not understand why they should draw another one, since there is already one! This proves that "recognize that we have already used this object" has not been yet acquired the children who knows he needs a round circle for the head, but don't see that actually an *other* circle is needed.

We can now explain how to create the concept of "five" or more precisely "five-ness." This requires a number of skills:

1. Understanding that objects do not appear or disappear spontaneously, that they are still there even when we do not look. This is what we call the *physical continuity*, and the understanding of it is greatly eased by the invariants searches performed by the visual system

2. Understanding the concept of correspondence between two objects, or binary relation. This is facilitated by the fact that our visual system "tells" us that an object has one position, not two, no objects have two positions at once, and if there are two things at to two different positions,

these are two separate objects and we can link them or mentally move one in the position of another.

3. Understanding the concept of "looking over all objects in a set" and "apply a relationship to all objects in a set." Realizing that as long as unused objects remain "this not good", but when we managed to use all the objects, "it's good".

4. Understanding the concept of a 1-1 correspondence between two sets of objects, which uses the previous two concepts: look over all objects in a set and link them to objects from another set. Realizing that as long as unused objects remain "this not good", but when we managed to *pair* all objects, "it's good".

5. It becomes possible to build the concept of "five" when there is a "typical exemplar" in mind. To understand that there is a "five" in what is seen, we must assume that many "little elves" are continuously testing our previously acquired concepts; one of these "little elves" is in particular responsible to test the concept of 1-1 relationship: it continuously seeks connections between objects that are seen and examples in our memory, for which the concept of "1-1 relationship" has already been used: our five fingers, or a basket of five oranges, or the arms of sea star. Ah Ah, there are five!

Now that we know all that is hidden behind "five", perhaps we can generalize to all numbers? Ah Ah! This is not that simple! The concept of *number* is much more than the juxtaposition of the concepts of "one" "two" three", etc.

To create the concept of *numbers*, our mind will need to understand that the concept of "1 to 1 relationship" is *transitive*, i.e. if two groups of different objects can each be 1-1 connected with an example of "five", then these two groups can also be 1-1 linked together. The 1-1 relationship defines equivalence classes and these classes *are* precisely the numbers.

It looks like math's, but on second thoughts we do not see why an intelligent mind should not perceive in the long run that when we use the concept of "1 to 1 relationship" between two groups of objects, and then between one of these groups and a third one, there is still a 1-1 relationship between all groups related this way... After all coincidence detection is one of the basic mechanisms of our mind.

Specifically, to associate two concepts is the job of the "thoughts" layer. Our thoughts are "one level above" concepts. They mix and combine concepts, they realize the similarities between concepts. They also lead to the creation of new concepts (such as the concept of number) exactly the same way as concepts creates new mental images, "one level below".

Another thing about concepts: they are permanent, which means they can be and are stored in our long-term memory. We will see that this is generally not the case for thoughts.

Thoughts

As we said, *thoughts are arrangements of concepts*. Obviously, concepts inside a though are not arranged randomly. This arrangement has a "syntax" and a "grammar".

The first thoughts of a young child seems to be simple juxtapositions of concepts. In, fact, they are already much more than that, otherwise they would just remain little more developed concepts.

I am going to tell you two short stories:

When my son Rémi, two years old, had for the first time a night walk with his parents, he saw suddenly a star in the sky. He had never seen one and did not even know the word "star":

- "Oh, little light!" He exclaimed
- "Yes, this is a star," I replied.

This thought is more than the discovery of a new concept. It reflects the combination of two concepts, "small" and "light", and an emotion "oh, this is something new", plus a wish: "I wish Dad would tell me what it is." The thought has occurred because the "concepts" layer of his mind had given to the "thoughts" layer the information that "there was something new, a small light in the sky", but also because the level above, the goals level, generated an emotion and a desire. Unless it was some sort of reflex or injunction: "When you see something new, tell it".

At about the same age, but I believe that it was even before two years, my son had fun watching a fountain, when a drop of water fell on his hand. As he did not like it, he spoke in an offended tone to the water jet, saying:

- Not hand, Water!

What could be translated as "Hey you, Water, do not come on my hand!"

Again there is a mix between those two concepts "No, don't do that", and "falling on the hand", and an emotion: "I do not like it", which together have generated a new thought and its verbalization, which was incomplete because the child did not say "come (or fall) on my hand", but simply said "hand". There was probably also a "goal" that was active somewhere with a heuristic such as "when someone does something you do not like, tell him/her and protest", which led to the verbalization of the idea, a real new thought. In addition, my son spoke to the stream of water because he had the idea that this water, moving and agitated, was to be alive and would understand what he said! I find this an absolutely formidable mental mechanism, especially knowing that the interjection "Not hand, water!" was in fact the *first sentence ever pronounced* by my son, who until this day had only spoken a few isolated words.

To understand thoughts, we must understand what they *are*, what they *do* and how they *appear*.

Thoughts are arrangements of concepts that are following a syntax, and that meet a *goal*.

The typical example is the phrases that we recite to ourselves in our minds, but there are other kinds of thoughts. For example, when we think of a scene involving several objects, the "syntax" is the geometric arrangement of this objects, their positions, the fact they cannot intersect, but can move, turn , etc.. When we think of an event, there is a succession of images within our mind, and the "syntax" there is given by the causal relationships: the facts that are causing other facts and consequences.

Just as concepts, thoughts can activate our sensory imagery. However, unlike a concept, a single thought can activate multiple images simultaneously, probably as many as there are "places" in our short-term memory, five or six.

Thoughts are closer our mind's level of "deliberation" that concepts, and are best suited to introspection. Intuitively, we "realize" that there might be several types of thoughts:

- Comments, observations, findings, related to the sensory imagery, but also to our emotions and feelings
- Questions

- Goals, objectives and desires
- Problems to solve
- Ideas and intuitions
- Etc…

Note that decisions are not thoughts: decisions belong to the "deliberation" level in our mind, not to thoughts level. Only comments or justifications of decisions are thoughts.

Thoughts are *immediate*: unlike concepts, that have some permanence, thoughts are created "on the fly" and allow our minds to take into account changes in the state of the world around us as well as inside ourselves, inside our goal system.

To create a thought, mixing concepts is not enough. Otherwise, it would be sufficient to mix arbitrarily concepts to create thoughts and our minds would be overwhelmed by an unlimited number of irrelevant thoughts. The example of "triangular light bulb" cited above also shows that when two concepts are mixed, they create a new concept, not a thought.

Thoughts do not have a single origin. Our mind contains several "thoughts generators". Together, they continuously create an ocean of potential thoughts or *proto-thoughts*. Only the "interesting" proto-thoughts acquire the right to become real, the right to activate sensory imagery. So in addition to generators there are also *thought filters* that remove uninteresting proto-thoughts.

As it is a bit abstract, let us give examples of generators of (proto) thoughts:

- The emergence of a new concept creates a thought: "hey, it's new!"

- The recognition of an *analogy* between two concepts creates a thought: "but it is almost the same!", and three goals: "find the differences", "find the common ground" and "seek whether this analogy may help to solve a current problem or achieve a goal".

- The aggregation of sensory images (linked with different concepts) in a small space creates a thought: "why have these concepts something in common?" When I say the aggregation of sensory images, I not only refer to the position of objects, but also to their color, shape, size, texture, in fact any characteristic returned by the visual system. For the auditory system, the mind also searches for common ground between sound events: pitch, timbre, interval, rhythm, volume, etc. Actually, any observed regularity (or irregularity) may be the starting point for new thought.

- The observation of a series of events creates a series of concepts of cause and effect, and questions like "How can this event be the cause of the next one?", "What other effect could it cause?", "What else can cause this?" and so on. Questions are a special kind of thought.

- When a goal G is active, similar concepts (via sensory imagery) are sought, and if they are already known as the effect of a concept X, a thought "a neighbor of concept X could help achieve G "is generated.

This list is non-exhaustive; we have without doubt dozens of such specialized small generators of proto-thoughts. Together, they create probably tens or hundreds of them per second, which is far less than what would produce a random mixer of concepts, but is still too much because the vast majority of these proto-thoughts are of no interest and are not worth being saved.

When we want to design a bicycle, we imagine its wheels made of metal, maybe plastic, but not tapioca pudding. When the phone rings, we believe that someone calls us, but *not* that the phone is hungry and calls to eat. (However when a Tamagoshi rings it does cry out for eating!)

This is where *thoughts filters* come in the scene. Again, there are several kinds of them, but probably less than generators:

- If a thought relates to the object of an emotion, it is interesting.
- If a thought was created by an active goal it is interesting
- If no concept in a proto-thought is active in sensory imagery (either current or generated by previous thoughts) it is better to reject it (this helps to preserve a minimal continuity in the train of our thoughts)
- If a thought is dangerous, it must be rejected

The last sentence refers to the existence in our minds of *censors*, who tell us what *not to think*. This is the icing on the cake of Freud. We will talk about it later.

How do thoughts filters work? This is a much more complex question than it seems. When Kasparov had the black in a chess opening that starts with the king's pawn, playing the tower's pawn in response seemed to him as absurd as a bicycle wheel made of tapioca soup. That is because he reasons by analogy with chess games he already knows. The same applies to a bicycle wheel for which we imagine that we need a single material, hard, solid, that will stand the weight of the rider, and by analogy we can see immediately that it takes metal. We understand immediately why the head of Louis Philippe looks like a pear, not an orange, and why Italy looks like a boot, not a sock. What a fascinating mechanism!

Analogies

« I hate, detest, abhor, abominate and curse synonyms! »

We have seen that analogies are one of the most powerful engine to create new thoughts. When we want to design a flying machine, we instantly think of birds, and this analogy will help us a lot...

The human mind constantly creates new analogies. It has disconcerting ease for this. Consider the following question:

What is to France what London is to Great Britain?

Paris, of course, too easy!

Okay, but then *what is to the French Midi-Pyrénées region what London is to Great Britain?*

Here we hesitate a little more: "Paris" is a plausible answer for the same reason as in the previous question, because it is the capital of France, and London is the capital of Great Britain. Nevertheless, the answer "Toulouse" is certainly better, because actually Great Britain can be seen as a region of the UK, and London played a dual role as the capital of a country and the capital of a region.

Come on, another one: *what is to America what Monte Carlo is to Monaco?* I wonder why I think to "Las Vegas" as an obvious answer! Visibly "Monte Carlo" reminded me of "casino" and seeking "a town in America which has famous casinos, I thought of Las Vegas. This is quite remarkable a mental work!

Let us try something simpler: *What is to seventeen what eleven is to thirteen?* The answer "fifteen" is obvious, because 15 = 17 - 2 just as 11 = 13 - 2.

But some rather "twisted" people (including me) could answer "thirteen" because they have noticed that 17, 11 and 13 are three prime numbers, that 11 is the first prime number below 13, and therefore the correct answer would be "The first prime number below 17", or thirteen!

This reminds me of the question "find the next term of the series" frequently found in QI tests: In these problems, there are sometimes several plausible answers. In fact, there are always dozens! But only one of them seems "easier" or "best".

The "recipe" to be applied to find the next term in a sequence is not always simple. Sometimes it is enough to "translate" or multiply a known suite such as the sequence of natural numbers. Sometimes it is enough to compute the differences between terms and consider these differences. Sometimes each term of the sequence derives only from the previous one, sometimes from two, sometimes from all preceding terms...

One example:

1, 2, 6, 24, 120, ...?

The next term is 720 (120 x 6), because 120 = 24 x 5 and 24 = 6 x 4, etc.

Was it too simple? What do you think of this one, then (caution: it is a *very* hard one):

4, 10^{12}, 5, 2 ,2, 9, ...?

The answer is 20: do you see why? No? And if I tell you that the next number is 8, does it helps you? Not much? Come on, think! I will give you the solution to the end of the chapter.

To find the solution to these problems, we try to "boil it down a known result", i.e. to find a regularity in the suite that will allow us to find an analogy with a known result. However, how do we to find these patterns? In fact, we use the *shape* of the series: for example in the following:

1, 1, 2, 2, 3, 3, 2, 2, 1, ...??

We "see" that the suite is composed of "double numbers" which start from 1, "climbs" up to 3, and then down, so that the solution 1, seems "obvious" and necessary. We made an analogy with a mountain:

```
                    3 3
         2 2                 2 2
      1 1                          1 1
```

It is clear that 3,3 plays the role of the summit, and the two pairs 1,1 are the slopes of the mountain.

Analogies do not take place only on the concept level but they also use sensory imagery. Our sensory imagery (here: visual), does not just give us a visual image "of the series: it "shows" us that the series is made of pairs of identical numbers, that 3 3 is the "central pair" that its *role* is "to stop rising and begin the descent" (remember of the mirror neurons that can assign roles to objects).

In the series: 1, 2, 3, 2, 3, 4, 3, 4, ...?

The most likely answer is 5, because you *see* the following shape:

```
                    ?
            4       4
         3  3       3
         2  2
      1
```

or maybe this one:

```
        3   4   ?
    2   3   4
1   2   3
```

or still:

```
1   2   3
    2   3   4
        3   4   ?
```

And in all cases, the answer can only be 5.

The famous computer scientist Douglas Hofstadter wrote a program, seek-whence (sounds as "sequence"), that manages to infer the roles of numbers in a sequence, and to answer questions like "What is the role of 4 in the following: 1,2,3,4,5,5,4,3,2,1?" Here the answer is "the figure that frames the central pair 5.5". In many ways, seek-whence is truly great: it happens very often to find the same response as human beings, on matters which are in fact far from intuitive. Hofstadter was able to show how these seemingly simple questions are complex: they are in fact at the heart of intelligence. Hofstadter then wrote another program which is even more brilliant, Copycat, who can make analogies and answer questions like: "what is to *iijjkk* what *abd* is to *abc*? (i.e.: if *abc* becomes *abd*, what happens to *iijjkk*?)

I think however that he has underestimated the role of sensory imagery: It allows us not only to see shapes, but also to understand the role of each element that contributes to the shape. In addition, it is precisely this understanding of roles that enables us to guess the role of the missing digit and therefore its … value.

This mechanism of inferring roles through our senses (at least that of the vision) is certainly anything but trivial. Unfortunately, we can make only assumptions about what is really happening in the depths of our mind. We will try to understand how it works a little further when we talk about *goals*.

The lesson to learn is this: Our sensory imaging provides not only images of what surrounds us, but also has functions that detect the *roles* of objects and *goals* of the perceived agents. To do this, it carries out comparisons guided by the purposes and roles, i.e. analogies, rather than simple raw comparisons between perceptions (real or simulated).

So, for our series 4, 10^{12}, 5, 2 ,2, 9, 20, 8, ...?

Ah, yes, here is the solution: the number 4 is the first number whose writing in French, *quatre*, includes the letter 'a'. The number 10^{12}, *un billion* (yes, in french billion means 10^{12}, not 10^9), is the first number which when written in french contains the letter 'b'. The number 5 is the first number whose French writing, *cinq*, includes the letter 'c'. Etc... Hey, that was not easy, was it?!

Language and reading

An example: In writing a word, the *role* of the first letter is to start the word; the role of the last one is to complete it. The role of other letters is to 'fill' the gap, linking the first and last letters. When we skillfully read, we do not spell out words letter after letter: we see the word as a "block" and we decipher by making analogies between the significant features of the word and those words that we already know. These features are significant: the first letter, last letter, and the filling ones (even when not in order). Don't you believe me? Try to read this:

Aoccdrnig to rscheearch at Cmabrigde uinervtisy, it deosn't mttaer waht oredr the ltteers in a wrod are, the olny iprmoetnt tihng is taht the frist and lsat ltteres are at the rghit pclae. The rset can be a tatol mses and you can sitll raed it wouthit a porbelm. Tihs is bcuseae we do not raed ervey lteter by it slef but the wrod as a wlohe.

The same in French:

Sleon une édtue de l'Uvinertisé de Cmabrigde, l'odrre des ltteers dnas un mtos n'a pas d'ipmrotncae, la suele coshe ipmrotnate est que la pmeirère et la drenèire soit à la bnnoe pclae. Le rsete peut êrte dnas un dsérorde ttoal et vuos puoevz tujoruos lrie snas porlblème.

C'est prace que le creaveu hmauin ne lit pas chuaqe ltetre elle-mmêe, mias le mot cmome un tuot.

Be careful: what the text suggests is only partially true, (and definitely *not* proved by Cambridge University!): you can scramble inner letters and still read, but you must preserve some regularities when doing that shuffle e.g. separate vowels, maintain ascenders and descenders in the correct spots and preserve the "sonority" of the world. Not every mix would fit!)

It is still striking, isn't it? To read, we visualize every word as a whole, and we ask our memory to "recall" the words that have about the same length and use roughly the same letters, (almost) regardless of order, but still start and finish with the good letters. Then we make a gross comparison between the read word and the small set of recalled words, and we reduce this list by retaining only those words that have a correct grammatical role for a word in that place in the sentence. In general, there remains only one!

The Mind and The Machine

This mechanism works besides on all levels:

In terms of letters, subjects who are asked to remember letters that are briefly presented to them make more errors on letters with close sounds (F and S, B and V, Q and U, etc.). It is well known that when we read we pronounce silently. To memorize a letter, we carry out an aural analogy, based on "key" sounds.

Another example, the experiment of the "swarming text". When you look at some object, your eyes are driven by jerks and thus skim through the field of your vision. This is especially and continuously the case when you are reading. During an eye saccade, the eye movement is *ballistic*. Once launched towards a certain point of the text, its movement is not adjusted any more along the way; it is entirely determined by the initial impulse. What is then swept by the eye between two fixings is not integrated in the reading. The following experiment is carried out: You are sitting head maintained motionless in front of a computer monitor; a device detects the beginning of each of your jerks, calculates your next point of fixing long before you have reached it, and quietly changes the word you were reading without any notice from your side. Result: you think you read something as stable as it was engraved in stone, but for someone who reads over your shoulder - and whose ocular jerks are not synchronized with yours - this text swarms and changes unceasingly.

Here is a little test to see if you are observant: What read below?

Are you sure? Read again.

Come on, another test:

The challenge is only to count how many times the letter 'F' appears in this text:

> FINISHED FILES ARE THE RE-
> SULT OF YEARS OF SCIENTIF-
> IC STUDY COMBINED WITH
> THE EXPERIENCE OF YEARS.

Go ahead, count... See a little further the solution.

Here another example, at the sentences level: Try to read the following sentences:

For .... the meaning ... .. sentence , we .... keywords, and other......... ... unimportant.

And this sentence no verb!

Have you smurfed the preceding smurfs, in spite of the absence of smurfs?

Cheers! You smurfed a good smurf, even if you did not smurf smurfly. Anyway the smurf of this smurf is smurfly smurf and I smurf that your smurf is not always smurfing, especially if the smurf of smurfs is too large.

Hmm... The last smurf is less easy to smurf, right? The reason is that I put a lot of "smurf" on purpose, whereas when we read a "normal" text the keywords we focus on are selected by our visual system, not by the author of the text.

The Mind and The Machine

However, in a normal text (with no smurf) the visual system selects the keywords that allow our linguistic system to achieve the semantic analysis, the analysis of meaning.

How does the visual system do? It checks the role of all words before choosing the keywords. By role, I mean here their position in the sentence, distance to 'other already selected keywords, importance (here, the memory intervenes and tells the little elf in charge of choosing keywords which words have already proved good in the analysis of sentences).

Finally, the comprehension of written sentences proceeds as follows:

- The visual system decodes words (recognizing beginning, end and filling letters)
- The visual system determines the roles of words and chooses keywords
- The linguistic system searches for the meaning of the phrase: it activates the concepts corresponding to keywords, which in turn activates the sensory imagery, seeking at once analogies and "resonances" with the current goals...
- During this time the decoding of the other words continues in parallel and the meaning of the sentence is consolidated, enriched or canceled, in which case the process performs a "back return" and another choice (of key word, concept, imagery...) is tried.

The training in speed reading that you may have heard of makes it possible to cancel the last step: reading goes faster, but there are risks of semantic ambiguity because the checking steps are skipped altogether.

Just one last thing: when the visual system analyses inanimate objects, it assigns *roles* to them. When analyzing animated objects, it assign their *goals*. Our sense of vision distinguishes very early what is animated and what is not, probably because it is vital for an animal to know if "something which is seen" represents a danger, a predator, or on the contrary, a prey. Finally, the goals analysis is very similar to the analysis of roles. A role can be decomposed into sub-roles in the same way that a goal can be decomposed into subgoals. The system of production and management of goals of the human being is however of immense sophistication, as we shall see.

Oh, yes, and our "F"?

 The letter "F" appears six times. Yes!

> FINISHED FILES ARE THE RE-
> SULT OF YEARS OF SCIENTIF-
> IC STUDY COMBINED WITH
> THE EXPERIENCE OF YEARS.

A person with a sense of observation gets 3.
If you saw 4, then you are above average.
If you've seen 5, then you can sicken a lot of people.
If you've seen 6, then you are a genius.
Personally I saw 4. I could see that I was not a genius...

Roles, analogies and unification

« All generalizations are excessive »

The Mind and The Machine

All right, but what is a role? Consider the very simple analogy problem below:

If A becomes B, what is C becoming?

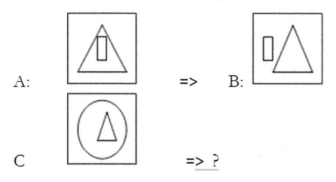

A: => B:

C => ?

Possible solutions:

a: b: c:

You have to find among a, b or c "what is to C what B is to A" Or, if A => B, then C =>?

Got it? You do not even try? How lazy you are! Come on, try it, it is not very difficult... Watch: if A becomes B, then C becomes... then, a, b or c?

In "classical" artificial intelligence, there is a solution for allowing a computer to break this kind of problem: the algorithm of *unification*.

To do this, we carry out a "symbolic" description of the problem, as follows:

A = rectangle inside triangle

74

B = rectangle left-to triangle
C = triangle inside circle

Then we introduce goals, which are descriptions of the three possible solutions:

a = circle inside circle
b = triangle left-to circle
c = circle left-to triangle

Then we attempt to "unify" the problem A => B in turn with C => a, C => b and C => c, until we find a successful "unification" (here with C => b):

> A=>B:
> rectangle inside triangle => rectangle left-to triangle

> Generalization:
> > X inside Y => X left-to Y
> > (in the example, X = rectangle, Y = triangle)

> Try with C => b:
> > Triangle inside circle => triangle left-to circle
> > Success with X = triangle, Y = circle

This unification algorithm (which I will not detail here because it is well known to computer scientists) is the most general one. For this reason many scientists believe that our mind effectively contains a unification algorithm.

However, the major problem lies in the choice of the symbolic description: Should we say that the triangle is a right-of the rectangle or that the rectangle is left-of the triangle? Even harder, should we say "triangle" or "set of three lines whose ends are attached two by two"? (After all, the symbolic system of a child may not know yet the concept of "triangle", but he can still make analogies)

The Mind and The Machine

And then how can you describe figures like this one:

unambiguously, with elementary logical expressions such as "circle", "triangle", "left-of", "below", "overlapping", etc..? This is clearly impossible to do it in a general way, there are too many special cases.

The use of mental imagery solves this problem: we can make deductions (specialists say inferences) directly from our mental images without having to translate them into "symbols"!

To summarize, our mind is able to make inferences and unifications to find similarities, roles and goals, but these analogies are not based on logical expressions, but directly on the images that are produced and analyzed by our sensory imaging.

To find the role of a visual element is to make an analogy with an already known (inanimate) visual element whose role is known.

To find the *purpose* or *goal* of a visual element is to make an analogy with a known visual (animated) element whose goal is known.

Finally not that different!

Goals

A father to his son: "disobey me! »

We have conscious and unconscious goals. Our conscious goals, our objectives, are thoughts like "I have to do this today," or "I must lose three pounds before the holidays". Finally, these "goal-thoughts" do not differ qualitatively from other thoughts, and their processing is done in the level of deliberation to generate the "narrative thread" of our thought.

Our mind also continuously and unconsciously constructs hundreds of *internal goals*. These internal goals are managed by a complex hidden system, which I will simply name our goal management system. I would like to discuss this system here. In a way, it is at the heart of intelligence: the creation of new thoughts could not happen if such a system did not exist.

Let us be clear: all "little elves" that make up our minds have a local goal: searching for memories, analogies, etc. But some of those little elves aim at searching thoughts that might be "global" goals, or solutions to satisfy a goal-thought.

You are in the street, the weather is hot and you are in the mood of a glass of cold and lively drought beer. You ask a person who pass by where the nearest bar is.

To understand this very understandable behavior (!), we must understand that:

- You have a goal: to drink a beer
- You have a plan: go to a pub (because you know beer don't grow on trees, but pubs and bars have beer, and in town there are usually many bars and pubs, and therefore finding a bar would probably be the easiest way for you to drink a beer)
- This generates a new goal: to find a bar
- Which generates a new plan: ask someone (because you need somebody who knows the neighborhood well, and you know that the pedestrians of a district often know it well)
- This in turn focalizes your perception on people close to you, intending to ask them a question

We see that even for a seemingly simple and natural action, several sub-goals are generated, and that a lot of knowledge is needed.

In the same way in visual recognition, let us suppose that we already recognized the contours of a brick:

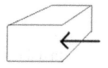

This triggers the creation of a new goal: "find a vertical edge in the indicated zone"

Our mind contains a *goals management system* that is responsible for creating thoughts about our goals:

- Cutting high-level goals into sub goals
- Reasoning from our knowledge to predict future perceptions
- Reasoning from unexplained observations to invent assumptions that may be their cause,

- Understanding the cause and effect relationships between observed phenomena,
- Organize thoughts sequences to solve problems that arise in the pursuit of our goals in the real world.

To manage goals is in principle a very different activity from that of managing concepts or thoughts. Concepts can be learned, thoughts can be manufactured, but the goals must be *invented*.

A goal is an abstract image that "wants to be true". A goal has a *desirability*. Goals are "magnets" that will "attract" certain concepts and thoughts. For example, when our mind produces thoughts about an event E (which may be an action that we intend to do), our thoughts generators (see above) create the question "can you predict the result of E?" However, if a goal B is active, it will "steer" the question manufacturer to the more specific question "can the result of E be B or a known sub goal of B?"

To answer these questions it is most likely that the mind seeks answers in our causal beliefs, our beliefs about the causes and effects of certain events. These causal beliefs are thoughts of a certain type, stored in long-term memory. As with all thoughts, our causal beliefs are first manufactured in the form of proto-thoughts, before taking the thoughts filter test (see above).

The same with goals. Before becoming a real goal, a goal must pass through a filter, Otherwise too many useless goals would be created unnecessary and we simply could not think and reason.

The mechanism is the same as for "ordinary" thoughts: A goal activates a mental image of the desired result, and therefore automatically activates the search for similarities between this goal and other images of known concepts, here images of the causality chain among events. If an active concept is of the form "C is the cause of E", and if E is same as the sought top goal G, then G will survive and C will become a new goal (but a subgoal of G).

However, when a new goal G is created, it is highly unlikely that our causal thinking memory already contains a ready-made thought in the form "X is the cause of G": that would be too simple! What our minds might contain is a thought of the kind "C is the cause of E" where E has a certain analogy with G, but is not identical to it. Knowing that C is the cause of E can help us find a cause for G, this way: C is probably not a direct cause of G, but may well be a modified version of C. We must therefore create a new sub-goal: "how should we change C to become the cause of G, knowing that C is the cause of E that has this analogy with G ". It is complicated!

Another filter is the one that prevents us from thinking the same thing twice: it detects and prevents us from looping round in circles in the chain of goals. The mechanism for detecting loops is very complex and is fact is a true system, that must be trained, and that also uses heuristics, concepts, thoughts and goals.

All these complications account for the level of our mind which manages goals, the level of deliberation, to be a level just as complicated as the layer of concepts, or thoughts. This level includes necessarily a whole system of plans management, which keeps track of goals and their sub-goals.

But this is only part of the story: the reasoning that we just unraveled, which consists of breaking goals into sub goals until we find basic goals for which there is a direct and simple action that lead the way, is not the only way we have to find how to reach a goal:

We also practice "forward thinking", which consists of starting with a list of possible actions and see which ones move us closer our goal.

Our brain was not done once for all, and the evolution of our mind has in fact encouraged the search for cognitive processes that make useful suggestions, and not the optimization of a single searching algorithm exploring all our beliefs. This means that in our catalog there are different forms of research on causal beliefs, e.g. " find a belief whose consequences are similar to a mental image of a goal" or" find an event that leads to the goal", and of course "find if we have not already solved a similar case before"

A goal has a *desirability*, which can be seen as a measure of its potential usefulness, unless this comes from a sort of fundamental and innate, impulse, to which we are subjected permanently

This concept of desirability of goals creates also desirability for actions: an action that leads to a desirable goal is also desirable. However, beware: there are cases where this does not work. For example when we want to seduce a creature of the opposite sex (Goal A, very desirable) we could consider that one way to achieve this goal would be to display our sincerity (a sub-goal B which is then also highly desirable) and a perfect means to achieve this sub-goal B is to say that we are in love with someone else... Yes, but crash! We then get a shingling slap. In doing so, we still achieve the goal B, showing our sincerity, but the same time we have destroyed all ways to achieve goal A!

In the same vein, imagine we pursue a goal G and devise an action A, which leads to G but will have be "side effect" of reducing the desirability of G. This "goals calculus" in our mind is something quite complex!

Another complication comes from the need to distinguish between causal implication and prediction: implication is useful to look for chains of actions that will lead to a goal, while prediction is useful to... predict the currently unknown result of actions and see whether they may lead or not to a given goal. However, prediction is not enough to plan actions: if one predicts that the observation of A leads to the observation of B, this does not mean, we must reach state A to reach state B: the two states may have a common hidden cause C! In this case, A is a good predictor of B, but to reach B we do not need to move through A, but C!

An example: we can observe a strong correlation between the fuel oil consumption and the death rate of the elderly. Should we then suppress fuel heating to reduce mortality? No of course, there is correlation only because both figures increase in winter...

OK. We have described how goals can be broken into sub goals, and ultimately create plans to achieve them, but we did not say anything about the main question: where do proto-goals come from?

A first class of proto-goals generators consists in "filling in the blanks". Our knowledge is imperfect, our predictions are imperfect, and our understanding of the causes and effects is flawed. Subsequently our mind has "goal making little elves" to fill in these blanks:

The *explain* goal generator fills in blanks in our knowledge of the past.
The *predict* goal generator fills in blanks in our knowledge of the future.
The *discover* goal generator fills in blanks in our knowledge of the present.
The *curiosity* goal generator fills in blanks everywhere!

This last generator fills in blanks we do not even know they exist! The activity of the "curiosity" little elf could be summarized as "find anything (a concept, a thought, a goal, an image) which could be useful to remember later". Curiosity maintains very abstract links with the "usefulness calculator" service, but there is one that is intangible: curiosity *is* useful!

A second class of goals generators arises from agents (little elves, again) that are probably innate and active from birth (curiosity might belong to this class):

- Satisfy a body need (to urinate, breath, sleep)
- Imitate (another person)
- Reproduce what has been done by others (an action, a construct)
- Repeat again what we just made
- Get attached to a person

- Play
- Breed
- Explore
- Get in touch with others
- *Etc.*

We have already discussed *imitate* and *get attached* agents, which are the starting point of our learning.

Reproduce and *play* are agents who are very active in children. Evolution introduced these agents because they are useful to improve our skills, but also to train our "loop detectors" that prevent our mind from always misleading in the same mental ruts.

Reproduction becomes really active at the time of puberty (Sure you would not have guessed!) as if evolution had planned this goal to be generated in our minds, to make sure we can be here today to have this conversation!

Explore is an agent which obeys *discover* and *curiosity*. Explore is active as early as the time when we were born, explore can be achieved through tactile, visual means, and even by taste, and later on, thanks to other agents such as *move*, *walk*, etc.

Get in touch with others is a generator that appeared later in evolution but nevertheless this "primary" goal is the foundation upon which our social intelligence, i.e. the possibility that we have to understand and control our interactions with our fellow human being, builds up. Together with the emergence of mirror neurons, which are designed, to calculate the goals of other people, these two super-goals have led to the emergence of social relations and language.

These agents shall together constitute a "mini morality" which is the starting point of our moral sense, and tells us what we *want* to do and not do.

The Mind and The Machine

The moral system will become of utmost importance when we build an artificial intelligence: an AI is potentially dangerous for humans, hence we must either make sure it acquires a moral sense that is being human friendly, or impose it injunctions that would force it to remain friendly (The famous "three laws of robotics" by Isaac Asimov are a good illustration of this.)

We shall extensively discuss these concepts later, but we can already understand that the task is not going to be that easy. In the description of the mind that I have just painted in broad strokes, where should we put Asimov's laws? First of all, are these laws desirable? In fact, it seems they are not. The three laws are incompatible with the freedom of action and reasoning Asimov gave to his dear robots. The "three laws safe" robots belong to science fiction, not to our future.

Anyway, we have to find a way out, though... Okay, here is the solution: *meta-morality*. Go straight to the end of this book if you want to know what this means. However, I would recommend that you should go on reading in order: hyperlinks are good, but you quickly lose tracks of what you want! Long live to paper books!

The puzzle is set up

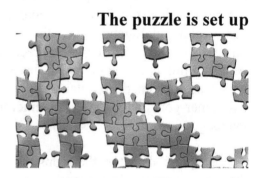

Good! Now we can relax and have a little rest. We now have all we need to understand how goals can create concepts that will help us solve our current problems.

Consider the two lists (next page) of diagrams, each showing four rectangles that contains geometric figures, and separated by a line.

The problem is to find a concept that is common to the diagrams of the "good list" (on the left) but is not shared by any diagram of the "bad list" (on the right)

In other words, what is the concept that underpins all drawings inside the four boxes in our "good list", but which does not apply to any box in the "bad list"?

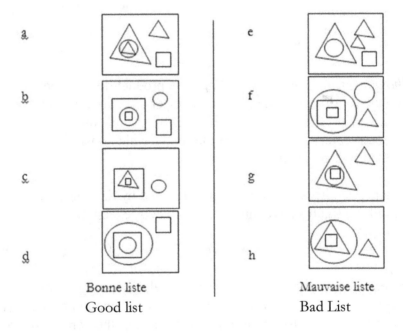

Bonne liste
Good list

Mauvaise liste
Bad List

Come on, get a closer look... We call this kind of problem *Bongard problems*, named after the Russian scientist who has designed them in the sixties (and we will address the computer program *Phaeaco*, which effectively solves such puzzles, later on)

So, try it! *Which concept is common to the four diagrams of the "good list" (a to d) but is not shared by any diagram of the "bad list" (e to h)?* Please think, for once!

Listen to the little elves:

Hmm! Not that easy! Okay, then *explain* will create a new goal: "find a common concept within the four left drawings", and *predict* will seek to whether this concept applies to the figures on the right (it should not)

At the same time our sensory imaging generates descriptions of the eight figures, creates concepts for them and sees that there are many instances of the concepts of "round", "circle", "square", "nested objects", "left / right", "one", "two", "three", and some instances of "four".

Thoughts takes over these findings and product descriptions of the figures: for example, the first in the upper left corner (a) may be described as "there are two groups of objects, one on the left made up of three nested figures, the other to the right consisting of two isolated figures, a square and a triangle".

Imaging endorses the descriptions provided by thoughts, and notes that all the figures have three nested objects, except (e).

Both goals, which were inactive due to lack of food for thought, then wake up and *find a common concept* triumphs: There are "three nested figures" almost everywhere! "All wrong!" says *test if it applies to the figures on the right*: It is not enough because (f), (g) and (h) have also three nested figures, and they are on the bad list...

Explain takes control then and activates *find a common concept in the left figures* again, praying him to find another concept, and creates two new goals: "*find a common concept to (f) (g) and (h)*" and "*find a common concept for the nested figures on the left hand side*". Only the latter succeed so I will therefore not dwell on the path followed by the other goal.

"*Finding a common concept for the nested figures to the left*" launches the *concepts* level by asking it to find another description that merely "three nested figures". *Concepts* runs, increasing the level of details. For the figure (a), this gives "a triangle inside-of a circle inside-of a triangle", for (b) "a square inside-of a circle inside-of a square ", etc. At this stage *concepts* remarks that the intermediate figure is in both cases a circle, and a thought is generated: "interesting, this is the same shape"! , Which resonates with the goal "find a common concept", but unfortunately in figure (c) the intermediate figure is a triangle and this thought is nipped in the bud.

But the goal "*find a common concept*" is looking at the same time in our memory to find a common concept and realizes that we can achieve this by generalizing descriptions, which is then a new goal. This leads to the new thought-question: what feature is common to a square inside-of a circle inside-of a square, a triangle inside-of a circle inside-of a triangle, a square inside-of a square inside a square", etc..

Concepts launches an unification, getting back "X inside-of Y inside-of X" as the most general possible concept explaining the four left figures. (Warning: I do not claim that our mind is doing algebra and uses unknown variables such as X and Y, the expression "X inside-of Y inside-of X" is just a way to express in human language a concept that has nothing to do with language and only uses our faculties of visual imagery).

'Uh-huh!' says *find a common concept*: 'I got another one! The smallest nested figure must be identical to the greatest figure!'

Test whether it applies to the figure on the right, gets hold of the thought and requests *concept* for a unification between "X inside-of Y inside-of X" and the four figures on the left: the unification fails in every case and *unification* is disappointed, but the top level goal, as for itself, knows that this precisely negative result should be obtained: brilliant!

Explain is triumphing: I have got the concept! There must be three nested figures, and the smallest must be identical to the largest one. The other isolated figures are only here for diversion and are of no importance. *Predict* is also happy because this concept applies to the left figures but not to the right one, which is what we wanted.

And voilà! Whew! Naturally, the above description is a very crude view of what really occurs. To describe it fully would take hundreds of pages, and it is likely that billions of calculations have been made to achieve the result.

Let us note two things:

1) The little elves (goals, concepts...) are all working in parallel, and even though it happens that some are sometime waiting for the result of another, very often they are doing alone.

2) The final concept is very general and does not say that the figure that must be both inside and outside should be a square, a rectangle or a circle. If we created a figure with an octagon inside a diamond inside an octagon, we would have no trouble recognizing that it complies with the concept that we have just learned. This is the true power of unification, which we discussed above.

Good! This starts to be set up! We are beginning to understand what is happening in our little head! It is time to step back.

Interlude

So far, I have tried to have you experience first-hand a few facts about the mind, facts that took years of arduous study to update. We peeled a little the operation of our sensory modalities and the way we produce concepts, thoughts, analogies, and goals.

Yet all this seems so general, abstract. This does not provide us in any case with the way how we should construct a mind, or even with an understanding of the way our mind works.

We will stop here this early exploration of our mind through introspection, and focus more on the main subject of this book, the mind: how does it works, and what is its structure?

First, before speaking of *how* we must say a word about *why*.

2

Mind and Brain

The evolution of intelligence

The *cause* of human intelligence is evolution. Intelligence is an evolutionary advantage because it allows us to model the reality, including our internal reality, which in turn allows us to predict, decide, and finally manipulate this reality.

It all started with an ability to model the environment, and then came the ability to feel emotions and imitate behaviors, then model the social environment (other minds), and eventually the ability to model our own behavior.

Indeed, we know that there were three main steps in the evolution of the brain:

Fish were provided with the **reptilian** brain about 500 million years ago. It then developed in amphibians and reached its most advanced step in reptiles, roughly 250 million years ago. It provided the vital functions of the body by controlling heart rate, breathing and body temperature, balance, etc. The reptilian brain includes the brain stem and cerebellum, which essentially forms the brain of a reptile. It is reliable but tends to be rather rigid and compulsive...

The **limbic system**, for its part, appeared in small mammals about 150 million years ago. It is able to remember pleasant or unpleasant behavior, and therefore responsible in humans for what we call our emotions. It mainly includes the hippocampus, the amygdala and the hypothalamus. It is the seat of our often-unconscious value judgments, which exert a great influence on our behavior.

Finally, the **neo-cortex** began its meteoric expansion in primates only 3 million years ago with the emergence of the gender Homo. This is the engine that will develop language, abstract thought, imagination, and consciousness.

I think that evolution has done a good, yet imperfect job. I think the inflated reptilian brain and limbic system cause our great ability for anger and violence. I am convinced that if we should one day create an artificial intelligence, we would be well advised not to slavishly copy nature, and "implement" only some functions of these two primitive systems.

That said, do not throw the baby out with the bath water. During this evolution, we have acquired useful skills for certain problems of adaptation, but also powers that can be used in multiple contexts, what we call general intelligence. The adaptation problems of our ancestors were not limited to picking berries and hunting reindeer. Intelligence has been an evolutionary advantage because it has allowed modeling and predicting our environment, including other humans.

In a sense this ability is weak, it is not as fast and accurate as our ability to see in 3D, for example, but in general we come to explanations of reality that are real enough to enable us to manage our life.

This is what has allowed us to surmount the first "crisis" in human history, the explosion of violence due to the sudden increase of our capacity for imitation, as we have already spoken about. It is likely that the few tens of thousands of people who inhabited the earth then (three million years ago) have narrowly escaped annihilation. They survived only because their intelligence enabled them to predict the behavior of their peers.

To understand the evolution of the human mind, we need more than the classical Darwinism: we need a theory that goes back to 1992 and is the *integrated causal model of population genetics*.

This theory with a complicated name tells us that evolution is a selective pressure exerted on the genes. The contribution of a gene to the success of his own spread is determined by the regularities of its *total* environment, the environment outside the body and the genetic environment - genes that surround it.

Thus, it is not enough if a mutation gives an advantage to a group of individuals for this genetic mutation to persist: Genes also want to get their share and the mutation should give an evolutionary advantage to the individual, *given the other genes it possesses.*

It was found, for example, that the genes that make an animal having a front and a rear, e.g. a human has a head, trunk and members or as an insect has a head, thorax and abdomen, are the same in all animals, vertebrates and invertebrates. They have undoubtedly existed since the time the first worm having a forward and a backward side was manufactured on Earth. The genes responsible for us having vertebrae is a sequence of DNA which is exactly the same as the sequence that makes a fly, for example, have its body divided into rings. The same genetic mechanism is at work to design the body of animals as different as worms, insects, mice or men, which is the best proof ever of the rightness of Lamarck's hypothesis stating that all species must have a common origin from the simplest forms of animal life. This could only be proved a couple of years back whereas Lamarck assumed this more than two centuries ago...

A new adaptation cannot spread unless it constitutes an immediate advantage: genes do nothing but adapting themselves. For the cerebral cortex to develop, it was needed that neurons were there, that the cerebellum was there to coordinate movements, etc. In a sense, the brain has been built by successive layers, but all are needed for intelligence to ultimately exist.

An example: all the higher animals sleep, all mammals dream. Sleeping is a basic need, something we cannot help doing. Our brain secretes sleep hormones, which, when accumulated in sufficient quantity, are *forcing* us to sleep. Yet we do not know exactly why we *need* to sleep. Explanations such as "the body needs to rest" do nothing: the evolution might well have made for us a body that would not need to sleep. Why did it chose not to do? What enormous evolutionary advantage have our genes found in our sleeping?

First, there is the fact that an animal that sleeps in a safe place is during this time less likely to be preyed upon by predators, especially by nocturnal predators, which are better adapted to night. An animal that is not a nocturnal predator, which does not have the "genes of nocturnal predator", has an advantage to sleep during the night. Conversely, an animal that is adapted to the night has no interest to show in the day.

Nevertheless, this may not be the only reason. Our brains also need to rest, to dream. We do not know *why*, but we know that if a cat, for instance, is deprived from the possibility to dream, then it suffers from serious psychological disorders. Why? Maybe, simply because the genes that define the organization of the brain are not perfect. Sleeping first appeared in the brain of the first fish and reptiles, whose organization has determined the subsequent format and organization of all brains of all animals. Maybe it was difficult for the genes to manufacture at first try a 24/24 effective brain, and a "small" defect such as the need to sleep regularly was not, after all, a serious handicap (according to what we have just said about predators).

This explanation may not be the good one. Perhaps the mind, even in a primitive animal, will need to periodically cut the flow of external sensations that are coming in to "take stock", consolidate memories and experiences, and finely adjust the network censors and suppressors that prevent us from thinking absurd things. It is possible that a brain that does not sleep is simply not functional for some reason we do not know yet. In my opinion, it is much more likely that these adjustments that take place in our minds when we sleep and dream have been invented by evolution after the construction of the primitive brain-that-sleep-but-that-does-not-dream, and that our genes have benefited from what was at first a slight disadvantage but was turned to some useful functions.

It is likely that the censor/suppressor system beloved by Freud, which is inside our minds and "regulates" our thoughts in preventing us from believing dangerous or absurd things, stems from the simple fact that genes have first produced a brain-that-sleeps because it was easier to do than a brain-who-does-not-sleep, and then they have improved it by inventing a brain-that-dreams, then a brain-that-dreams-for-regulating-itself, which allowed the mind to achieve a higher grade that would have been impossible otherwise.

Why does our intelligence use our visual cortex? Because it is there! Evolution invented vision long before the emergence of mammals. Then the following developments have used this cortex to their advantage. The repeated failures of AI projects show that designing an intelligent mind without the equivalent of the visual cortex (or any other sensory modality) does not lead to an intelligent system.

The human heart is not an organ that helps to run after a prey. The human heart is an organ that carries blood and oxygen to other organs. Removing the heart does not give birth to a less effective human, but to a human being who has ceased to function. The same happens for an intelligent mind. Deleting one or more important sensory modalities does not lead to a less environment-sensitive intelligence, but no intelligence at all (Blind persons see nothing, but they have a visual cortex and a sensory modality of vision, which allow them to understand the topology of the universe around them and to carry out spatial and temporal reasoning)

However, because evolution has followed a blind path leading to intellect, the brain is probably not the best possible architecture. If we had the possibility of high performance genetic engineering, or if we had more knowledge in artificial intelligence, it is likely that we could create more intelligent beings than us, because, unlike evolution, we will not have to move laboriously from small adaptation to small adaptation, we could design its structure all at once and then manufacture it.

Some of our minds features are absolutely *not* optimized:

- Computation: we are unable to multiply two ten-digit numbers without taking a real headache, let alone to extract a cubic root. Yet our neurons *do* perform internal calculations, and they do well, but "having a sense of numbers" is not an evolutionary advantage, and that is the reason why we are so crappy at calculation, just as we do not know for example how to sort instantly thousands of numbers, or decode a binary file, all things that just any computer can do easily.

- Logical reasoning: try without a real drag to tell whether this argument is valid:

  "If free will does not exist, then the concept of responsibility is nonsense. If responsibility is nonsense, then the judiciary system as well. So if free will is possible then the judiciary system is not nonsense"

  Uh... someone has an aspirin? (Answer below)

- The capacity of introspection: we have no way of knowing and directly monitor what is going on inside our minds. If we were able to better understand our unconscious, we could "control" our impulses and improve ourselves. In fact, we could do much better: we could *reprogram* ourselves.

- The ability to self-improvement. We have no way to change our way of thinking, the algorithms used by our brain. That said it is likely that this capacity would be more dangerous than useful: unless we fully understand what happens inside us, the slightest alteration of the delicate mechanics of the mind might break everything and turn us into vegetables... However, *if* we *really* understood how we operate, we would want to change ourselves because in this case, we would *know* how to become more intelligent and we would want to do so.

- The ability to choose what we want to forget: we have no conscious control over what our memory saves or forgets. There are times that we would love to remember, and others we would like to forget... but hey... forget about it!

Have you ever wished to have one of these capacities? Our genes have created us, but now they limit us. Nevertheless, one day these limits will be exceeded. If we can create a "real" AI, this would radically change the situation. An AI is a program, and it would be easy to provide it with any capability we need, and many more. An AI would not be a copy of a human mind. An AI would be an AI, and (at least) some of its capabilities would be well above that of a human mind, like it or not. It is an inescapable fact, the consequences of which are extraordinary. I will deal with this issue at the end of this book.

Genetic engineering is another way that would allow humanity to improve; we could "program" our genes so that our children have the best brains... provided we understand how they work, but also how they are formed from stem cell, how genes control this formation, and how we could control genes... Hum! That frankly looks like science fiction. In my opinion, the AI will come *well*

The Mind and The Machine

before we can act on our own genes, knowing what we do. I will tell you later the reason why.

By the way, about the sentence on the free will and the judiciary system of the previous page, the argument is *invalid*:

Let us consider the sentences:

F: "free will is possible,"
R: "Responsibility is nonsense," and
J: "The judiciary system is a nonsense."

The assumptions are: "not F => R", and "R => J ",
and the proposed conclusion is:

"F => not J, which is equivalent to "not F or not J", or to "not (F and J)"

But we cannot deduce this conclusion from the assumptions: all we can say is that "not F => J ", i.e. "F or J". It could be that free will is possible and that the judicial system is still nonsense! You have found? Bravo! You could be a good lawyer!

The brain

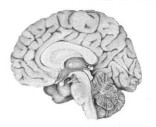

So, how does the brain work?

Have you ever noticed that the brain looks like a cauliflower? Both seem to share almost the same lumpy structure. Specifically, a cauliflower seems to be made of lumps, which are themselves made of lumps, which are themselves made of smaller lumps, like a wild carrot flower seems to be made of flowers that are made of smaller flowers with about four or five levels of organization. These kinds of structures that are abundant in nature are called *fractal structures*. So is our brain fractal?

No! Well, the major structures of the brain (there are 52 per hemisphere) are effectively divided into smaller structures, separated by *grooves*, but these sub-structures do not resemble themselves, nor do they resemble to the main structure at a reduced scale. The "cauliflower" aspect of the brain stems solely from the fact that the brain is actually like a large sheet of paper that is crumpled, folded many times on itself. This folding allows packing a large area in a small volume and can also optimize the length of "phone cables" that provide communications between remote areas. However, the various areas of the brain are not identical and are highly specialized instead.

(Not so sure: although the function of each module is different, their internal architecture may be quite the same: each module could be similar to the whole brain, but at a reduced scale. In addition, a team of researchers has to prove that there are systems for information processing in plants: I wonder if I will continue to like eating cauliflower!)

The Mind and The Machine

This is how we usually cut the brain in functional areas:

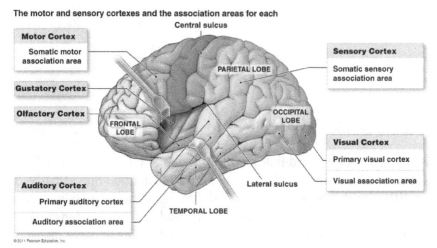

The motor and sensory cortexes and the association areas for each

(Please take another piece of saveloy?)

What is remarkable is that although we are all unique, our brains all have the same shape and the same number of grooves and folds and each fold has the same function for all humans. For example, the prefrontal area is involved in short-term memory.

The physical organization of the cerebral cortex is that of a very thin sheet folded on itself. In the thickness of the sheet, there are six layers of neurons that appear to fill different roles (we will see them later). However, it appears that the different areas of this sheet are highly specialized: we find an area that is dedicated to language processing, and another dedicated to the sensory-motor system (touch and muscles) and we can draw a real map of it. For example, we see that the area of the brain that deals with our hands and fingers has a comparable size with the one that process everything else in our body!

The visual cortex area, which understands what you see, is at the back of your head. This disturbs me because I have always thought that my mind was just behind my eyes, but this was not right! It is at the base of my skull. Similarly, the *left* brain actually processes information from *the* right visual field and vice-versa. Strange, isn't it? It gives me a headache when I think about it.

A very important feature is that the brain has two hemispheres, which play different roles in our thought system. I will not dwell here on the roles of the two hemispheres (logical vs. artistic-emotional), which are well known.

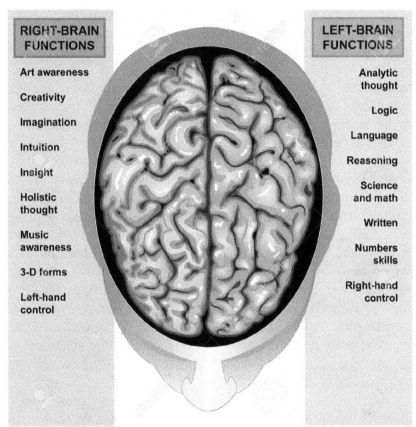

RIGHT-BRAIN FUNCTIONS

Art awareness

Creativity

Imagination

Intuition

Insight

Holistic thought

Music awareness

3-D forms

Left-hand control

LEFT-BRAIN FUNCTIONS

Analytic thought

Logic

Language

Reasoning

Science and math

Written

Numbers skills

Right-hand control

But an important question arises here: *Why* do we have this organization in two hemispheres? What significant evolutionary advantage is there for all animals with a brain to have a brain organized this way? Moreover, if we want to create an artificial intelligence, would it be necessary to provide her with sort of "two artificial brains"?

The Mind and The Machine

This is a fascinating question and I do not know the answer. The philosopher and computer science theorist Marvin Minsky wrote in his wonderful book *the society of mind* that it might be interesting to have a "B-brain", connected to a main "A-brain": The A-Brain would be connected to the outside world through sensory connections, and the B-brain would have a "regulating role" in relation to the A-Brain: Being as smart as the first one, its "senses" would be probes that monitor the activity of the A-Brain: So it would prevent it from constantly rehashing the same thoughts, from succumbing under a roller coaster of emotions, or from spending too much time in fruitless searches. It is a devilishly exciting idea: a second brain that regulates the first one, and why not a third (smaller) one that regulates the second? Alternatively, maybe the first regulates the second, while being controlled by it at the same time?

Nature did not choose to do so, probably because of the inextricable wiring that would be needed. It has found a different solution, which is not spatial but temporal: Our brain regulates itself during sleep; it stores useful knowledge in long-term memory, and destroys knowledge or ideas that are harmful to its own operation. This "delayed" system is coupled with a "real time" one which use chemical messengers that can influence the entire brain overall. (It is also possible that glial cells play a role in regulating the brain. These cells, which are present in the brain, and even more numerous than neurons, acts on the synapses and regulate the sending of neurotransmitters and moreover they communicate with each other).

Minsky's idea of a B-brain is an alternative that would achieve the same result in an artificial brain, without having to sleep or dream. Is this a good idea, or should we follow the pattern of evolution? The debate is open.

We shall see later when we address consciousness that it is not a B-brain in the sense of Minsky but that it still plays an important role in regulating the rest of the brain. Maybe consciousness emerged just because it was a simple process to regulate mental activity!

Nevertheless, the left and right hemispheres of our brains are *not* the A and B brains of Minsky: They are both connected to the same sensory channels and there is not one that controls the other. Their role is well known, but the reason for these roles remain enigmatic.

The functional magnetic resonance imaging (fMRI) allows seeing what happens inside the brain. It measures the instantaneous oxygen consumption in different areas. It has now reached a resolution of about 100x100x100 "voxels" or cubic pixels, meaning that we can measure in real time the individual activity of each of these millions of areas, in the course of our thoughts. And we find that areas that are active simultaneously are linked by "relay areas" whose number is very low.

In other words, the functional architecture of the brain resembles that of the Internet: there are "processing centers" linked to "communications nodes", themselves connected by "motorways". In fact, if we remember that the reaction time of a typical neuron is about one hundredth of a second, each neuron involved in a large brain function is less than two clock ticks, that is to say two hundredths of seconds, away from those of other "processing centers" involved in the same function! This is a devilishly effective architecture!

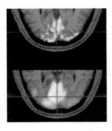

Here are the areas of your brain that are activated when you see a very bright picture (the front of the brain is at right).

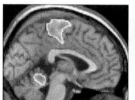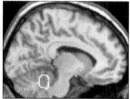

The brain during real (left) and simulated (right) orgasm

The basic component of the brain is the neuron, or nerve cell. There are a hundred billion in your brain. A neuron can be compared to a small unit of information processing. However, in fact information is distributed in the neuron itself, but also in its connections with its neighbors. These connections are numerous, allowing the neuron to communicate with its neighbors by chemical and electrochemical signals. A neuron has "input" connections, or *dendrites*, which are fairly short filaments close to the main body of the cell, and "output" connections, often much longer, arranged along a "common trunk», called the *axon*.

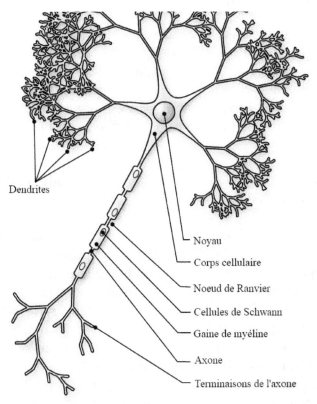

Dendrites

Noyau

Corps cellulaire

Noeud de Ranvier

Cellules de Schwann

Gaine de myéline

Axone

Terminaisons de l'axone

The connection between a termination of the axon of a transmitter neuron and a dendrite of a neighbor receiving neuron is called a *synapse*. Each neuron is connected to thousands of neighbors.

It is noted that, although we know a lot about neurons, it is unclear how they really work, especially how they process information.

A neuron is capable of performing simple mathematical operations such as sum, multiplication by a constant, and comparison to a threshold. However, a neuron does not seem to have memory by itself: on the other hand, the connections between neurons, synapses, appear to be a component of this memory: the synapse is able to "learn" which signals must pass, and which must be blocked.

You may have heard of "networks of artificial neurons", which are mathematical and computer models that replicate the operation of a set of neurons. Please note that this is an excessive simplification of the operation of a real neuron, which seems to perform more calculations than simple additions, multiplications and comparison to a threshold. However, this simplistic model is enough to demonstrate the phenomenon of *emergence*, which certainly plays an important role in real brains. I will discuss this in further detail later.

There are two ways (in fact not contradictory at all) to study what happens in the brain:

- The bottom-up approach: starting with neurons, trying to understand how they organize themselves into groups, units, zones, areas, etc. And how these physical functions create mental functions. For example, we can study simple animals such as worms or insects and try to reconstitute their entire nervous system, and see what happens then (exciting experiments were conducted on the locomotion of insects). Or else analyze with an electron microscope the connections between neurons, say in the visual system, and try to understand which processing takes place.

- The "top down" approach: starting with the whole brain, trying to understand what role each part and subpart plays, etc. We can therefore rely on the fMRI, or study people who have suffered from brain damage. That is the way we have found out about the famous difference between the left and right hemispheres, which I will not dwell here.

A fascinating question is: to achieve artificial intelligence, should we reproduce the brain at the level of neurons? In other words, for our thoughts to exist, do we need the "substrate" of the hundred billion neurons connections that we all possess, or else can mental function be equally well fulfilled by another "substrate" such as a super computer?

To answer this, I propose to choose first the "top-down" approach, and to explore the major sensory systems of the human being, starting with the visual system. We will return to the "bottom-up" approach later when we discuss the networks of artificial neurons and exciting findings that can be learned from them.

The human visual system

The human eye focuses light rays onto the retina at the back of the eye, where our light-sensitive cells are located: *cones* (sensitive to color, and close to the focal point or *fovea*, where vision is clearer), and *rods* laying around the circle occupied by the cones: they are much more sensitive but do not distinguish colors and that's the reason why you see in black and white and fuzzy when in the dark.

Too bright a light destroys the rods, which take a long time to rebuild and that is why it takes time to get used to darkness.

There are about ten million light-sensitive cells in the retina: one could compare it to a ten million pixels digital camera. However the pixels of the retina are not square, and are not linearly laid out: there are more of them close to the fovea than in the periphery: it is as if the brain could see through a 'fish eye' of short focal length: but the further processing of visual signal occults that characteristic, and we have not the impression of seeing things distorted at all!

A small region of the retina located at the beginning of the optic nerve has no light-sensitive cells: the eye can see nothing in the region of the visual field corresponding to this *blind spot*, and actually the visual cortex reconstructs the "probable" image that you "should" see in this area, so that you don't have the impression of a "hole" in your field of vision at all... and yet this hole exists! Isn't it fascinating? The process reconstituting the images seen by the blind spot seem to use *encoders*, neurons that produce false images and are an essential component of visual reasoning, as essential as *shapes decoders*.

Cones are of three types and sensitive to three wavelength bands of light, respectively in red, green and blue. We reconstitute the colors from this information. But very quickly, even before the optical signal enters the visual cortex, the color information is processed and the visual signals are no longer intensities of red, green and blue, but *differences* between the perceptions red-green , yellow-blue and black-white (contrast). Our visual system handles six basics colors, operating in three antagonistic pairs. As I explained in the first part of this book, this is exactly what is necessary to discriminate the real colors of seen objects, despite the differences in natural light (sun/shadow => yellow/blue, noon/evening => green/red).

Color blinds have a congenital atrophy of the "red-green" channel: they discriminate very well between yellow and blue, but very little between red and green. Bulls have also no red-green channel. Shaking a red cape or a green cloak in front of them is the same for them. On the other hand a very large number of animals can discriminate between yellow and blue, simply because it is vital for an animal trying to escape a predator and running to a partially shadowed rock to realize that the sun-exposed part of the rock (yellowish) and the shadowed part (rather blue) are on the same rock indeed.

These three "differential" channels: red-green, blue and yellow-black-white, have different evolutionary significance and the most important channel is the black-white or contrast one, because it allows recognizing objects. Then comes the yellow-blue channel, then the red-green channel. However, they are similarly processed by the visual system. This processing consists in detecting sudden changes which generally represent the limits of objects (or of shades on an object), and then in deducing the most likely spatial arrangement of the facets or surfaces, that make up these objects in a universe supposed to be in 3D. Simultaneously, the comparison between the images seen by the left eye and the right eye provides us with an estimate of how far theses surfaces are. By comparing these estimated distances to assumptions about the 3D world, the visual cortex refines and validates the 3D model of the objects that surrounds us.

This raises a fascinating philosophical question: As our visual system is based on the fact that the world around us is in three dimensions, and that this system exploits the many constraints that arise from this assumption, we are then persuaded to live in a three-dimensional world. However, what if our senses were not based on that assumption? By the way: is the world really in 3D, or is it an illusion of our senses?

Let us stop this philosophical digression, and get back to the subject:

The retina does already perform some early complex processing of the visual signal, as we have already seen: among others things it calculates, and for each area of the visual field, the differences between the mean and instantaneous intensity, which is the cause of the phenomenon of "retinal impression". You can find retina cells that already detect the direction of large variations in contrast (such as objects edges), and others that are sensitive only to vertical, diagonal or horizontal lines.

From the retina, the visual signal travels in the optic nerve to an X-shaped area at the front of the brain, the optic chiasm, where the signals from the left and right eye mix:

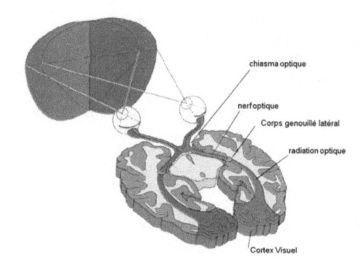

Here an interesting phenomenon takes place: the signals corresponding to the right visual field of each eye are sent towards the left visual cortex while signals from the left visual field of each eye are sent to the right visual cortex.

What is it good for? It is probably "securing" the processing design: if each hemisphere would care of one eye only, it should make more calculations, since there would be twice as many pixels. In addition, suppose you had lost an eye, then that would result in a useless whole visual cortex, which would be a real waste of neurons. In addition, relief detection processing, which requires a comparison between what is seen by the right and left eyes, would be much more difficult: then it is better to mix the signals and carry out this detection as soon as possible.

A word on depth perception: it is based on the fact that when the lines of sight of our two eyes are parallel, distant objects will appear with roughly the same position in the perceived image, while closer objects will be at different positions.

What looks simple in appearance is *not* in reality: researchers have shown that depth perception required millions of calculations. Therefore, there are millions of neurons involved in there! However, we know how to connect a computer to two cameras and have it mapping the relief of the terrain it sees with good accuracy but we are still far from the performance of the human visual system, which happens in particular to precisely discern depth even when one of the two images is blurred.

Depth Information is solely used in our brains as a *confirmation* of the assumptions about those conformations of 3D surfaces viewed through the eyes. The calculation (since this is a real calculation) of these assumptions is based on the many regularities of a world of 3D objects perceived by an organ of vision. For example the corners of an angular object are generally at the convergence point of three edges if this corner is turned to us, or of two edges if one of them is hidden; in the same way the shadows of an object are all on the same side if there is a single source of illumination (which is the general case in nature) and so on.

Here again, computer scientists came to write programs that can "recognize" the different objects in a scene; even though they are still very far from the wonderful accuracy of our visual system.

The Mind and The Machine

But this can be at fault because, remember, it is designed to discern in a natural environment the contours and surfaces of 3D objects that surround us, despite the contrasts of shadows and objects that are partially hidden. The "white-black" channel is usually the most useful for this work. Nevertheless, the two other channels have a role to play: they can build the abstract concept of "intrinsic color" of an object: In a room with white-painted walls, we see the walls as white... Yet, if one takes a picture of the room and analyzes the colors, then one would realize that what is perceived as "white" might cover many different colors, some of which may appear yellow, gray, blue... in a different context!

Here is an extraordinary example of this:

Edward H. Adelson

Look at the above checkerboard, made up of light and dark gray cases, with a cylinder placed above, and tell me if the boxes marked A and B have the same color.

No, definitely not! Box B is much clearer than A, even if it is in the shadow of the cylinder.

Well...

You are wrong: A and B have the same color, exactly!

What?

112

They have! Look at the image below:

Using a drawing software, I took a sample of the color of each box. The two colors are identical! Yes, the lower circle has the color of the box B!

Proof:

The gradient of gray you seem to see only exists in your imagination! Awesome, isn't it?

Remember the path of visual information: having passed through the optic chiasm, information reaches the visual cortex. The latter represents 15% of the brain surface, just to say how important this is. More specifically, the area of visual cortex, located at the back of the brain, can be divided into five sub-specialized areas:

The first one, or area V1, is the primary visual cortex. This is the most important one. Without it, we would be blind. Information directly coming from the retina arrives straight on it. The primary visual cortex V1 carries out a first analysis of the collected information (shape, color, movement) and then distributes it to other areas.

The area V2 refines this information sorting. It processes and parses contours, orientation (horizontal, vertical), textures and colors.

V3 analyses forms in motion and calculates the distances

V4 handles the processing of still shapes and colors.

V5 is responsible for the perception of movement (direction and speed).

Here is an illusion that brings the V5 area into play:

Move your eyes closer and away from the figure while looking at the central point: the circles appear to revolve! This is because the simplest basic movement is translation, not rotation: when you approach your eyes the area V5 provides for each diamond a translation traveling information... but in a direction that is not exactly that of the radius (central point to diamond), but rather that of the diagonal of the diamond (which is, on purpose, not directed towards the central point), giving therefore an impression of overall rotation.

And actually there is a very early layer of processing in the visual system, which performs a conversion from rectangular coordinates (i.e. x, y) to polar coordinates (i.e. distance from the center, angle). Thus, a circle seems a "perfect shape" to us only because it is the simplest form in polar coordinates. This illusion shows a malfunction of this coordinates conversion of in some cases. But the detection of movement is a complex process: from a sequence of raw images, how to determine what changes, what is moving and how, and first is there any move at all, or is it just an apparent motion due to the rotation of our eyes or head?

Consider what happens on a ultra-simplified example: Suppose that our eyes could not see full 2D images, but merely one horizontal line, formed only with bright and dark dots that we can symbolize with "X" and "O" letters, like this:

OOOOXXOOOOOXOOOXXOOOOXXXXOOOOXXOXOXOOOX

Well, OK, this is not easy to understand. But now, Let us assume that our " XO sensory modality " perceives the following sequence of "frames" (just imagine that the X and O represent off and on lights on an advertising sign made of a single line of light bulbs):

```
OOOOXXOOOOOXOOXOXOOOOOXXXXOOOOXXOXOXOOOX,
OOOOXXOOOOOXOOOXOXOOOOXXXXOOOOXXOXOXOOOX,
OOOOXXOOOOOXOOOOXOXOOOXXXXOOOOXXOXOXOOOX,   T
OOOOXXOOOOOXOOOOOXOXOOXXXXOOOOXXOXOXOOOX,   i
OOOOXXOOOOOXOOOOOOXOXOXXXXOOOOXXOXOXOOOX,   m
OOOOXXOOOOOXOOOOOOOXOXXXXXOOOOXXOXOXOOOX,   e
OOOOXXOOOOOXOOOOOOOOXOXXXXOOOOXXOXOXOOOX,
OOOOXXOOOOOXOOOOOOOOOXXXXXOOOOXXOXOXOOOX,
OOOOXXOOOOOXOOOOOOOOOOXXXXOOOOXXOXOXOOOX,
```

It will become "obvious" that the X and O are the "echoes" of fixed or moving objects, and that one of these objects, shaped like "XOX" (or OXOX? Or maybe XOXO?) is moving to the right, passing "behind" another object represented by XXXX (or may be XXXXO we do not know yet we must wait until the moving object appears on the other side)

Yes, it may be obvious for us (in any case it would be if I had shown you their video series, as in an animated film instead of the above single lined "frames", - but it is not possible within a book).

Yes, but how the hell does the visual system infer that?

First, it must "understand" that objects persist over time, and that if a part of the frame remains unchanged it means that objects have not moved. Conversely, if all X and O have moved in the same direction, then it is likely that the observer is actually moving relatively to these objects: When we turn our head, or when we walk, our eyes do see something completely different at every moment, yet we don't have the impression that the objects are circling around us at all: we just "see" that objects are fixed, and that we are actually moving! This process requires very complex mental calculations, and yet it seems so natural and "obvious".

Then it will be necessary for the system to detect the sub-structures that are stable but shift at the same speed (or approximately) compared to others, to "know" that this might be a moving object, that a moving object can pass in front of or behind another object, and that this may mask partially or completely one or the other. It must make assumptions about what might the next frame look like, and compare what he sees with the assumption made previously. Many assumptions are maintained in parallel, some will be reinforced, others abandoned. God! It may involve a lot of calculations!

And it does. Even with our simplistic "XO vision", the visual system needs to make thousands of comparisons to "understand" what is happening. In real 2D, with a ten million pixels image, it's getting even worse! In fact, there are specialized groups of neurons, which seek to detect "movements" in five directions: up, down, left, right or diagonal (and not more: for example when an object is moving "to the right and slightly up, with a slope of 15%" in our visual field, it is detected as such because the right motion sensor outputs a strong signal, and the 45° diagonal sensor gives a slightly less strong signal. Why not, if this is enough?)

What is truly remarkable is that the eye can scan approximately ten frames per second, although the "processors" of the system, the visual neurons, need already five to ten milliseconds to make a simple addition! This shows the degree of parallelism of visual processing.

Finally after all these calculations area V5outputs a synthesized description of the observed scene: This is an intermediate level description, which does not yet call upon our memory. This description does not yet say "What I see is a car" nor "this is the face of Grandma", but tells "there is a self-connected object, composed of different surfaces, with such characteristics (color , texture, shape, edges, movement...) and these surfaces and areas are linked together by relations like "above", "right-of", "within", "moves", "in-front-of", "behind", etc.

In short, the visual system provides a description of the 3D scene it was able to reconstruct, and this description is made of the description of all objects and spatial relationships between them. These descriptions are themselves rather short "sentences" with "words" chosen from a (quite large, but fixed) number of *visual primitives*, which will enable further processing by *unification* of what is perceived with known concepts, as we saw in the first part of this book.

This description is often incomplete or imprecise, allowing many optical illusions like this one:

All horizontal lines are straight and parallel!

The description of the scene provided by the visual cortex to the higher level of identification of concepts, uses words like "white square", "black square", "Above and left," "above and right", but not "horizontal line with above and below it some alternating black and white squares, the series which is below being shifted": such a concept is far too complicated to rank among our visual primitives. And that's why you do not see the parallel lines! There are no primitives of combination of primitives to describe them fully: but well, this kind of pathological surface is not so common in nature!

Here is another one:

All lines are straight!

The vision works a bit like the opposite of the 3D graphics card of a computer running a video game. You know that 3D cards take as input descriptions of 3D surfaces (shape, texture, light and movement) provided by the game, and then they synthesize an image on our screens. Well, our visual cortex does the opposite.

However, vision acts as a 3D graphic card *plus* its inverse. Like all our senses, vision has a way of working both ways and use all means to find what a perceived scene means (Ah Ah! Have you noticed the change in what the word *means* meant? How and by which means do we so easily detect such shifts of meaning?)

As a 3D card that would be "bidirectional", human vision transforms descriptions of 3D objects in pictures and vice versa.

When analyzing, it detects the positions and movements of objects, recognizes their textures, color, etc...

When synthesizing, it produces images from the description of objects and their movements.

However, "analysis" is a little more complicated than "synthesis": oh, say about a million times, maybe?

On top of the fact that this is used in our dreams or in our mental imagery, this synthesis is probably used by the visual system itself, to check if this was not wrong in complicated cases. This often happens when there are several possible interpretations of the same scene:

The mind has a hard time choosing... and wavers between the two.

Here is another example of how the visual system uses encoders: The image below is nothing but a set of black spots:

What is it?

Yet our mind comes to complete the picture with the missing features and to recognize the image of a hand resting against a wall, with his shadow. Quite remarkable, isn't it? The encoders are well and truly handling this task. Some of them add strokes where there is none, to facilitate the task of concepts recognition.

Eventually, at the end of visual processing, the intermediate symbolic description of the viewed scene is compared to concepts stored in our memory, to check if what is seen looks like something that has already been seen before, at least partially. As we saw at the beginning of this book, a new concept is created when a number of patterns are detected. Therefore, at this level a kind of detector of repetitive or curious facts, or regularities, exists, which allows creating new visual concepts (like "red" or "cube").

Functionally, a visual concept is something that can be activated when these patterns are detected again (by unification) in the descriptions provided by the intermediate visual cortex.

On the contrary, a concept can be used as a generator and activates the encoders, which allows us to imagine the concept. Eventually, a visual concept can link visual imagery to other sensory imageries and other concepts.

In the 1960s, neuropsychologists wondered if there was somewhere a "grandmother neuron" that would we activated when and only when grandma appears in our visual field. It seemed absurd, but they did not otherwise understand how we could manage to recognize this dear old lady.

We now can say with certainty: of course not! There is no grandmother neuron. However, there is indeed a visual concept of our grandmother.

The visual cortex outputs a symbolic description (using primitives) of a set of percepts, but at this stage the mind does not know yet it is your grandmother. However, your concept of "grandmother" is always on the lookout for grandma's image (in fact it seeks to unify the descriptions provided by the symbolic visual cortex with those it knows, the ones that created it).

Moreover, when a certain set of percepts are activated simultaneously, they *signal* the recognition of our grandmother by the "grandmother" concept.

Hello Ma!

Real things, of course, does not happen quite like this: if each concept should permanently compare all percepts with its own set of "expected percepts", it would be much dumb computing time, even with millions of neurons working in parallel. What really happens is that there is a simultaneous comparison of each set of percepts from the visual system with a very large number of concepts, through an *associative memory*, also called "content-addressable memory"

You probably know that a computer memory is a set of boxes each having a number, or address: to find the content of a box, we *must* have its address, or no salvation.

In contrast, our brain circuitry is capable of content addressing: if you submit some content to this memory, even partial or garbled, it is able to find and "output" the entire content!

We will talk again about this quasi-magical associative memory function when we tackle the study of memory.

The auditory system

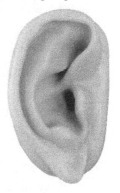

If our visual system is amazing, the human auditory system is equally, if not more!

"Hello, my child," says your beloved grandma. We are so used to understand instantly what is said that we do not realize at all what miracle it is.

No later than thirty years ago, it was thought that it would be just a little bit more complicated for a computer to understand what we have said (the problem of recognition) than to have it talk (the problem of synthesis). We now know that the first problem is infinitely more complicated: there are talking machines everywhere, but none of them can understand us without error.

Our auditory system is able:

- To almost instantly recognize where a sound comes from, and if it comes from front or behind, even with only two ears (where we would need three in theory)
- To recognize the words of our mother tongue and understand them, even if we do not know the voice of the person who speaks and whatever she speaks normally, cries, sings or whispers.
- To follow the melody of a single musical instrument, even when it is part of a whole orchestra, as well as to follow a conversation in a cocktail bar or a very noisy nightclub!
- To recognize, the pitch, intensity, and tone in a sound: to say what source (person, musical instrument, animal, sounding object...) it comes from.
- To estimate the distance between the sound source and the ear, by mitigation of frequencies with distance, i.e. to compare the received signal with what it *should be* if it was closer! A far away gong sound seems stronger than a whisper in our ear...
- To identify speakers only through listening, provided we have already heard their voice; otherwise, at least to guess their gender and often even their emotional state and stress level.

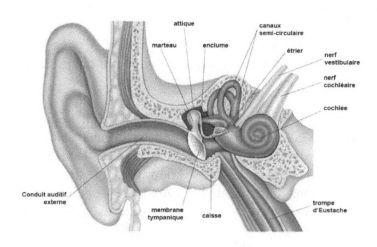

The audio signal is recorded in the *cochlea* by a series of ultra-sensitive hair cells that vibrate gently, and the intensity of this vibration is transmitted to the auditory nerve. The vibration of the eardrum, transmitted by a series of tiny bones, eventually arrives in this strange snail shell, which acts as a filter, so that some of these micro-lashes are mainly sensitive to high frequencies, others to midrange, and others to bass frequencies.

Downstream the auditory nerves, the first stages of the sound signal processing in the nervous system amplify these differences, performing a real frequency analysis of the signal.

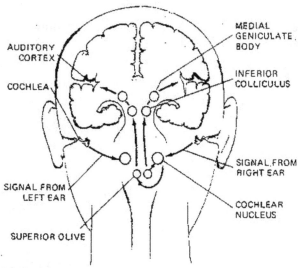

It is possible to plot the intensity of the different perceived frequencies as a function of time. This is called a *sonogram*. Here is how it looks:

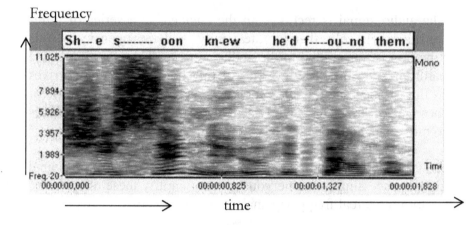

The image above is the sonogram of the pronunciation of an English sentence. "She soon knew he'd found them". Time is shown on the horizontal axis, running from left to right. The frequency (or pitch of the sound) is on the vertical axis, grave at the bottom, treble at the top. Stronger the signal, darker the picture: the beginning of the word *soon* contains many high frequencies (dark spot toward the top of the image).

Let us say we wanted to have this sentence understood by a computer, or even worse, by a Frenchman. All this poor guy would understand is a French-like gobbledygook, something like "cheessoonew-eedfaounzem". *By Jove!*

The first thing would be to recognize phonemes in there and then to try to see what words they could match.

One way to do this with a computer is to draw the image of the sonogram from the acoustic signal recorded by a microphone, using the so-called *Fourier analysis*. That is, from the sound signal, which represents the change in air pressure as a function of time, detecting the different frequencies present in the signal, and calculate the "intensity" of each instantaneous frequency. A sonogram is a graphic representation of these intensities. The mathematical treatment of this problem has been well known for two centuries, and there are electronic circuits that carry out the Fourier transformation in real time.

In a second phase, we analyze the computed frequency array (or the image of the sonogram obtained), comparing some parts with stored templates for each phoneme, trying to reconstitute the succession of phonemes that were pronounced. Unfortunately, the scientists who have tried this method have faced a formidable obstacle:

Many phonemes are very similar, so that their images are almost identical. To reach our goal would require a sonogram with a frequency and temporal resolution much finer than the above "fuzzy" image of a sonogram (the human ear is able to discriminate minute frequency deviations; it is estimated to analyze about three thousands frequency bands, so that's the number of lines that would be needed in the image of the sonogram)

Returning to our French guy and his "cheessoonew-eedfaounzem": What is he wondering about?

It could start with the phoneme "shee" as the English word "she", but also by "sheess" as in "she's." Therefore, the first words of the sentence could be "she soon knew" but also "she's onions", "she owns you," "she saw you", "seasons new", and dozens of other possibilities. And even that is assuming that the consonants and vowels were correctly recognized, but in English there is little difference between the pronunciation of "o" and "a", and between "or" and "a", "e" and "i", "d" and "t", etc. So our Frenchman (or the program) should consider the possibility of his (its) own mistakes. For example, the first phoneme "sh" might be the English "th", so then the phrase could also begin with "this onion", "this harms you", etc. In addition, what if "Sheessoo" were a proper name that the program does not know? If the system were making five attempts for each of the ten phonemes in a ten syllables sentence, there are five to the power ten possibilities to understand, or 1 953 125 possibilities, many of which would be syntactically correct (conforming to the syntax of the language). Which one is correct? This is called "combinatorial explosion".

OK, Let us go! Let us increase the resolution of the Fourier analysis, so that of the image, hoping to reduce the phonemes ambiguity. Then, besides the fact that it takes a lot of computation time even with a very fast computer, we just come to recognize no phoneme at all! In fact, no speaker does pronounce the same word twice in exactly the same way: there are variations in timbre, pitch, etc. that are so much changing the image of the sonogram that in practice this does match to none of the templates. (It is even worse if we try to recognize sentences that are spoken by a different speaker from the one who recorded the templates).

If we adopt a probabilistic approach, by calculating "the chances that it might be a particular phoneme" we are back to the problem of blurred image: the number of candidate phonemes is too large. In practice, even if adjusting all parameters at best, the performance of computers is simply... bad. The performance of speech recognition systems become fair only when used with a limited vocabulary, and only after a laborious learning phase, where the speaker is to record all of the words that the system should be able to recognize. (I must admit that computer scientists have made a lot of progress in this field during the last ten years: both *Google* and *Apple* voice recognition applications are now quite impressive)

Then how does our mind succeed? It seems to use an "all-out" strategy by making several things at once. In fact, the (quite unconscious) work performed by our auditory system to understand and analyze the sounds it perceives is huge:

First, it speculates on what the sequence of sound it hears could mean. For example, to recognize a sentence, the auditory system anticipates the next phonemes that the speaker could eventually pronounce. In other words, it uses a *predictive coding* of what is expected.

It then compares what is heard with what is expected in a smart way: not with all possible or imaginable sounds, phonemes, noise etc., but only with those it has already identified as the most plausible, based on assumptions that might of course be refined or challenged at any time.

The best automatic speech recognition systems also use such a predictive coding based on the syntax and grammar of the language to recognize. Even so, their performance remains far below what we humans can achieve. This gives rise anyway to useful applications such as the recognition of simple instructions we give to a mobile phone or to an elevator (because the expected list of phonemes in a given situation is very limited in these applications)

It seems that going further should require, in addition to Fourier analysis and predictive coding, other strategies, which are indeed at work in our mind.

There is a fairly strong analogy between auditory recognition and visual recognition. Like the latter, auditory recognition carries out an "extraction" of the most relevant percepts, the "basic shapes" that are likely to appear in the sonogram of what we hear. These basic shapes, when repeated, result in the creation of auditory concepts, or of concepts at all (when we hear a drummer giving three fast bangs of bass drum, there is no doubt that our concept of *three* is enabled)

Among the "basic concepts of hearing" are those of the pitch of a sound, the change of tone (or its spectrum) over time, its location, its movement, its probable origin, its perceived and absolute intensity, etc.

As for visual cues, our mind creates (unconscious) thoughts on auditory concepts, and develops a real grammar of the sequence of these concepts over time.

Also as in the visual domain, the auditory system is capable of operating in both directions: recognition and synthesis. We can fully "hear" what a sound we imagine is going to sound like. I am not saying we perform a full sound synthesis, but that we at least recreate the sound percepts and concepts that we would expect when hearing that sound.

The comparison between expected and heard percepts is much easier than the gross comparison between two sonograms. The extraction of auditory concepts then favors predictive coding.

There are still many other "tricks" used in the auditory system. We will not list them here. Scientists have studied this process in detail; in particular, they have found acoustic illusions that just as visual illusions help us to better understand how our mind is to analyze the sound signal. There is a whole bunch of literature on this subject.

Nevertheless, the truth is, we understand what is said because we are human, because we share the same mental resources than the speaker, and therefore we are able to put ourselves in the same mental state than him, and to anticipate what he/she will say. I suspect that a machine would have to do the same to *fully* recognize spoken language. Note that knowing the speaker, and being attached to him, often helps to understand: Mothers are able to recognize words spoken by their baby, even if they are incomprehensible to others! That is because they *want* to understand what baby says, and mobilize more brain resources on hearing. We will see a little further how the mechanism of attention works.

Vision and hearing are very complex and very useful sensory modalities, which have many similarities. Both are also well studied and we know a lot about them. However, I will now speak about a far less known and very different sense, which most people have never heard of: *proprioception*.

Proprioception and coordination of our movements

Proprioception? Wassat? This barbaric word means the sense that allows us to know the position of our members. This seems so natural to us that we may even doubt that there is a "sense", sensory organs and processing systems fully dedicated to this sense. However, proprioception is there, and those who are lacking it are severely disabled. These people, for example, must constantly check with their eyes the position of their members, they have difficulty in performing gestures as simple as eating with a fork without getting hurt, they are unable to throw an object with precision, etc.

The sensors of Proprioception are neuromuscular spindles (sensitive to nerve vibration), the tendon organs of Colgi (which measure the tension on muscles), joint receptors (which detect the extreme angles of joints, and measure the movement of articulation), and cutaneous receptors. All this information converge in the cerebellum, which processes them and calculates the angles of all our joints. Conversely, control of muscle movements from the cortex pass through the cerebellum, which synchronizes all muscles involved, and verify that our members are well moving to the desired position at the needed speed to perform the requested movement.

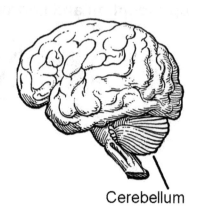

Cerebellum

The size of the cerebellum, which is quite respectable, gives an idea of the complexity of the processing taking place in that organ. The cerebellum is a primitive relic, a very old organ, which was invented by evolution as soon as animals began to have several members that must be synchronized to perform useful actions.

You may say that the insects do not have a cerebellum, and yet they are capable of coordinated movements, but it is an illusion: each leg of an insect is an independent system, operating on a purely reflex basis, and the walk of an insect for instance is just an *emerging* function arising from the simultaneity of many simple uncoordinated reflexes. We have been able to construct robots that move like insects, and yet the motors of these robots are driven by very simple commands laws and only react to a few basic signals.

However, when it comes to implement actions *for a given purpose*, such as running after a moving prey, the required computing power is huge, and for living organisms, a proprioception system and a cerebellum are necessary.

But why is it so difficult to determine the position of our members, from the angles measured on each articulation? Ask a robotics specialist and he will lift his eyes to heaven! Imagine the number of muscles and actions to be coordinated for simply pouring a cup of tea!

More simply, consider a robot equipped with a mobile, adjustable arm, with a joint half-length. The problem is to have the extremity of the arm (the clamp) translate horizontally, at constant speed:

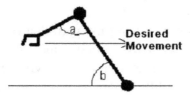

More formally, the problem is to find the *control law* for both motors attached to the joints, i.e. to find what angles they should turn and how fast (depending on the time!) so that the extremity of the arm completes the requested movement. You will agree with me that this is a formidable mathematical problem, involving many trigonometric calculations. What to say then about what we can do unconsciously with members that have *dozens of degrees of freedom* and can perform complex movements without colliding with obstacles being either on our own body or external ones?

Imagine the following situation: you are sitting at your desk, a sheet of white paper in front of you, and a pencil in hand. Now close your eyes and try to draw a circle on paper. Open your eyes and see what you have drawn: it is not a perfect circle (unless you are very gifted), but it is very similar. Consider now all the commands that your mind has given to *each of* the muscles of your fingers, your hand, your arm, and even your shoulders to accomplish that result. But how has he managed to calculate all this?

In the case of an industrial robot, the control laws are mathematically calculated in advance, using trigonometric relations. This is sometimes a challenge, which requires very sophisticated and complicated mathematical calculations, even on large computers. At the end, we get the list of angles to obtain for each joint and at each moment, and there is not any more but to send commands to the motors and actuators.

The Mind and The Machine

Is the brain be able to calculate sines and cosines? Is there an innate knowledge of the Pythagorean theorem and of the properties of triangles and circles? Of course, there is not!

We actually proceed by *seeing* the path that our hand will follow, we break the movement into smaller movements, and we try to accomplish every little movement by visualizing what would happen if we tense a little more such or such muscle, even if it means correcting (possibly with another joint) in case of an error compared to the ideal path. In addition, we are trying to accomplish the overall gesture in the most flexible possible manner, i.e. minimizing discontinuities: any muscle (or joint) that is used at a given time should be monitored throughout the duration of the movement.

Returning to our robotic arm, Let us imagine it being controlled by our mind: How can this work? What is happening in our mind when we try to have one of our tips follow given path? Maybe something like this:

Er...having the clamp to accomplish a horizontal movement to the left, huh?
Let us see: if I close the angle (a), the clamp will go roughly in the desired direction (left). It is less clear for the angle (b), which instead will move the clamp up (if I open it) or down (if I close it).
Okay, well. Let us see what would happen if I started to close down the angle (a), say by (da) = 20 degrees:

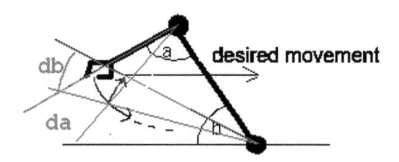

Well it progresses, but it does not go well, the clamp goes down too much... We must compensate... necessarily with articulation b. We must climb the clamp up, so we open the angle (b) with an angle (db) such that the clamp path will be horizontal. On the figure above (my mental image of the move), (db) is a bit smaller than (da).

Okay, well it's perfect, I'll start by closing the angle (a) with a speed v, while opening angle (b) with a speed v x 90% to see what happens: hup, Let us do it!

Moving... it goes well, it looks like I am not mistaken. I am still here... Oh! What happens! I'm no longer on the right path!

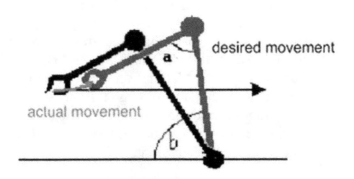

desired movement

actual movement

It's a bit too high... Well, I must either reduce the opening speed of the angle (b), or accelerate the closing speed of the angle (a). I will rather choose the first option, it will go slower and I can better catch future errors...

Let us be clear: when we do such gestures in an automatic way, "without thinking of it", that goes without saying that we do not tell ourselves the same phrases that are above in italics. I do not pretend this. I just tried to formulate or to describe verbally unconscious, nonverbal, processes that take place in our internal systems of coordination of actions and of representation of our body attitudes.

The Mind and The Machine

In my view, such a scenario is much closer to what really happens in our mind than the "robotics" scenario, which consists in calculating all control laws in advance. Our scenario uses a detection of qualitative characteristics, such as "left-of", "above", "further", "faster", "too high", etc. Which involve skills and services that we would more expect in the visual system.

Because not everything is calculated in advance, we must monitor the actual movement, compare to the expected movement, and make decisions based on these comparisons. We will see later how these processes of unconscious micro decisions that occur constantly in our minds might work.

That is how we control our movements. It is a complicated process, but less complicated and above all much more resistant to uncertainties and errors than the "robotics" scenario.

This system does not just happen; it requires an apprenticeship. When small children shake hands and arms in their cradle, they produces hundreds of observations on the correlation between what they see and what they feel through their senses of touch and their sense of proprioception. Moreover, from these hundreds of observations they construct a visual and tactile representation of their body and its immediate environment.

It is certain that a system of spatial representation of the attitudes of our bodies and our members exists in our mind and that this system strongly interacts with the visual system. It is no coincidence that the center of the vision of our cortex is located at the back of our head, near the cerebellum. It is interesting to note that the primary motor cortex is located quite far away from these areas at the rear of the frontal lobe. In this cortex are located deliberation processes leading to decisions to move this or that member, but the coordination of these movements is not there.

Knowing which muscles to move and how to perform a gesture is a problem. Knowing what gestures must be accomplished for a given purpose is yet another matter!

Well, we will not talk here of other senses: touch, taste, smell, sense of balance. It is enough to know that each of our senses has its own escort of neurons responsible for processing received signals, and that the set of all of these neurons accounts for almost half the neurons in our brain.

Sensory (and motor) systems make up a large part of our mind, and probably of any mind. I argue further that no intelligent mind can exist without a sensory system, and that is one explanation for the slow progress of artificial intelligence.

Now Let us leave the field of perception and senses to explore one of the most amazing abilities of our brain: human memory.

Long-term memory

Long-term memory is the place where we store... our long-term memories. There are indeed several kinds of memory in our mind, starting with the internal memory of our sensory systems, short-term memory, and finally medium and long-term memory.

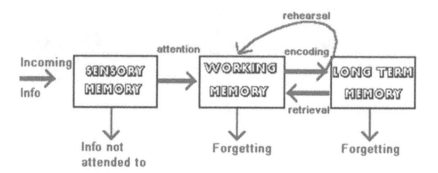

How many memories, how many facts can we remember? It is generally accepted that the capacity of human memory is about 10^15 bits, which is roughly a thousand times the capacity of the hard disk of an average PC (one TB). This estimate is based on the number of neurons that we have, and on an estimate of the number of bits stored by each neuron. But this approach suffers from many flaws, not least because human memory is very redundant, and because it is not at all sure that each synapse in the brain contributes to human memory!

However, there is another estimate, due to Thomas K. Landauer in 1986. In contrast to the above "hardware" estimate, Landauer provides a *functional* estimate, based on what we can learn from our experiences. He analyzed a number of experiments made by himself and others, during which subjects were asked to read texts, view images, listen to short passages of music, phrases and meaningless syllables. After a delay ranging from several minutes to several days, the subjects took tests to determine what they had learned. These tests were very specific, to know precisely what was actually used or not, even vaguely. The same questionnaires were also posed to humans who had not heard or seen the stimuli, to control precisely the part that a human could guess from the sole questions.

Landauer eventually came with an impressive body of tests, which is robust and almost insensitive to random errors. By calculating the sum of what had actually been retained, and then dividing by the time allotted to memorization, he was able to determine how many bits per second actually pass in our long-term memory.

The very interesting result of this test is that in all cases, it was shown that subjects memorized *two* bits of information per second. Two, no more. Whether it is text, music, words, or anything else, always two bits per second!

When accumulated over a lifetime, this learning rate gives us a total of one billion bits, or 125 MB, not even a thousandth of the capacity of your hard disk!

Although this is only approximately true, because Landauer has not measured anything (e.g. how quickly do we acquire information on how to ride a bicycle? And how much information?), It 'remains as much *a million times smaller* than the hardware estimate! This suggests that, perhaps, the computing power needed to build a mind capable of general intelligence, whose memory would be even greater than ours, is already on your desktop!

However, beware. These two bits per second that we record in our long-term memory are a concentrate, the marrow of the bone, the quintessence of the thought, the elixir of our memories! This is the result of a *compression* that can take days!

This compression is necessary for any intelligent mind, because a smart mind is every day collecting billions of information and cannot afford to store them in memory as such, like a stupid computer without intelligence. That would be too much, and furthermore, how then could we get the *useful* information from this morass? It is necessary to *arrange* our memories, but that is not enough: they must be linked to other information, so that we can recall them later, if necessary, in very different contexts. The key word in the preceding sentence is "if necessary": The ways that can lead to the recall of our memories are so twisted! Think of Marcel Proust, crunching a madeleine (a cookie), and recalling, by this familiar taste, in one fell swoop all the memories of his childhood he thought he had lost forever!

However, linking information to each other is already compressing it: if you know how to reconstitute a complex idea from others who were already saved, it is unnecessary to memorize the complicated new idea: just store the (simple) way that allows reconstituting it from the others. And voila!

Maybe you have been taken aback by my personal definition of intelligence I gave at the beginning of the first chapter: *Intelligence is the ability to reduce entropy during the compression of information.* It is our ability to compress, without too much loss, millions of small facts collected at every moment into... two bits per second. With this definition, *WinZip* and *WinRAR*, two widely used file compression programs, are among the most intelligent computer programs ever designed! In fact, it's just a joke: these programs do compress well, but to find a specific piece of the file, you need to decompress the entire file. I dare not think what would happen if we "uncompressed" all of a sudden all of our memories... An "MPEG" or "DivX" Codec is already doing better: it allows to compress on the fly a huge sequence of images (a movie), and to unpack only that part that interests us.

Especially since our memory does not store only memories but also concepts, thoughts, ideas, procedures and methods. It is both *declarative* and *procedural*:

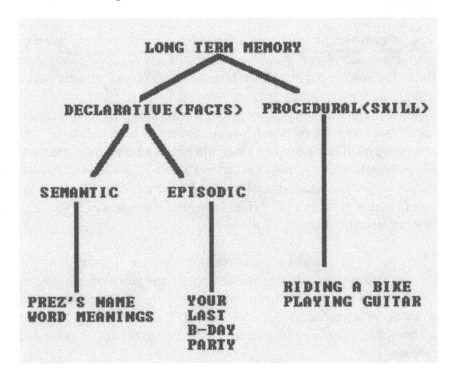

Just a quick word on what is called "Memory priming": the fact that if you are in the correct state of mind, you will remember certain facts or certain words much easier and faster. For example, subjects who are presented a series of unlinked words to be remembered, such as "car, cloud, shark, doctor, tree, swimming" will take more time to read and will remember less well the word "doctor" than if they had been submitted the list "accident, hospital, nurse, doctor, care"

The Mind and The Machine

As we briefly mentioned earlier about the visual system, human memory is *associative*, or "addressed by content." It is sufficient (in principle) to give it up a few bits of memorabilia, a few facts that are relevant to the memory we tried to recall, and poof! It is recalled in full. (More precisely, it is reconstituted for you: the "little elves" of our mind, memory research agents, put you at least partly in the state of mind you were during the recording of memory).

You already know one type of addressing by content: Internet search engines. When you type a series of keywords in Google or Bing, the search engine will return a list of complete web pages containing the keywords or even words that are semantically close. Thus, associative memory works this way: Suppose you want to remember an event, of which you do not recall all the details. You remember well, on the other hand, the place where this event took place, people who were involved, and so on. Do not worry; your mind creates for you, without you being aware of it, some "little elves" that will search your memory, just like a search engine, to "output" the full memory of the event.

These agents do not always succeed: they need some time, because the fact is too deeply buried in memory. Then you say, "ah, damn, I have it on the tip of my tongue"... and the next morning you wake up with you striking your forehead: "Ah there it is!" Yes, but it's too late.... And if you continue, you will eventually have a flat forehead!

By the way, what does "too deeply buried" mean?

This simply means that to reconstruct the memory, we had to rebuild many others, and we had to use too many other agents and services of our mind. Research agents have therefore their own working memory, which is used to store these temporary reconstructions, which is disposable after work. It is likely that memories are scattered throughout the brain, but the temporary memory required for their recovery is in the hippocampus, a small structure that is part of the limbic system (see below).

142

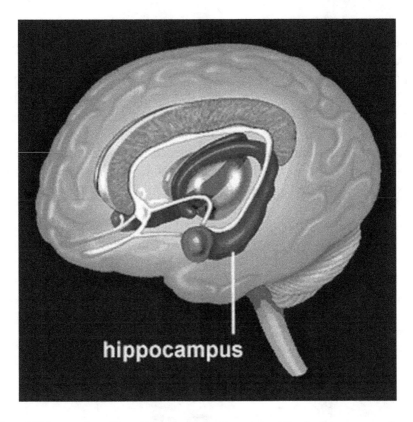

hippocampus

In addition, what does "get back to the state of mind you were in at the time of the recording of the event" mean? How to save a state of mind?

The clearest response to this question is that we have in our mind some "little elves" called K-lines, or knowledge lines, by their inventor, Marvin Minsky, and whose role is precisely to activate partial states of mind. How does it work?

Suppose that you are a particularly handy person, and that you spend with delight all your weekends repairing the lawnmower, adjusting the car engine, redoing the ceilings of your home. However, you never remember what tools you need to do this or that, and you never have the right tool at hand. Damn! How to stop getting upset every day?

Here is a good idea: next time you need to repair the mower, soak your hands in red paint just before you start: in this way, all tools you need for the mower will be colored in red, and the next time, you will just have to remember "red for the mower". Also, soak your hands with green paint just before setting the ignition timing of the car, and in blue paint before doing masonry, etc. After some time, not only can you easily remember what tools you need for a given task (of course, some tools used for several things will be marked with different colors), but you will also see what tools in your possession are useless: they are not marked!

Similarly, when your mind has solved a problem, it may mark the little elves that have been used to solve this problem. But in fact, instead of marking it with a color (which would be difficult!), the mind creates an agent that maintains a list of agents involved, and who can "activate" them altogether: the K-line:

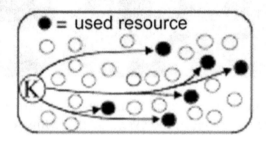

In this way, the next time we have to solve a similar problem, it is sufficient to activate the K-line and not all agents one by one. The same applies for memories. The concept of "apple" for example, involves many other concepts like "red or yellow or green color", "round shape", "the size of a fist", "crunchy texture", "acid taste"... which can be all activated by one K-line, which is also connected to the name "apple".

In a memory such as "cousin Jack was flying his kite," the concepts of "Jack" and "kite" are both activated, but also those of "young cousin, playing, laughing, running, wind, string , lozenge shaped, canvas mounted on sticks", etc. Really, a huge number of tiny details, some related to Jacks, others to kiting, others to both.

When recalling this, you have inside your mind a memory K-line that activates at least two other K lines, one for Jack and one for the kite. A K-line is an agent who puts you into a partial state of mind, the one that is related to the current memory.

To store something in long-term memory, it becomes unnecessary to record every detail, but only what K lines will be needed to reactivate the memory. This is obviously much less data to store! This is how the impressive data compression that we discussed above works.

Naturally, as the mind changes in time, new K-lines are created every day, and others, becoming useless, are removed: thus, in order to "revive" a remembrance of our childhood, which was recorded in a context (in fact in a mind) that was possibly very different from what it is today, it is necessary to reconstruct the K-lines that existed at that time (at least those that were activated at the time of registration). This is the role of our memory researchers little elves, whose humble task, perfectly unconscious and unknown, can last a few seconds to several days or even weeks!

Artificial neural networks and memory

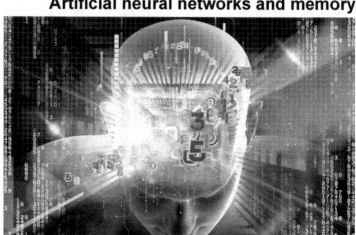

If one wishes to know more detail on how the mind comes to use its "brain hardware", sometimes referred to as "Brainware" or "wetware" to physically perform all these functions of memory, we must study neural networks. Specifically, the simulations of neurons that were performed on computers provided fascinating results, particularly with regard to memory: researchers managed to build associative memories with very simple "logic circuits", which are supposed to represent some functions of a neuron!

An artificial neural network (ANN) is a network consisting of a set (usually a few hundred to several thousands) of very simple and all identical logic devices, interconnected with each other: the artificial neurons, or we might say or "simplified neurons".

Just like a real neuron, an artificial neuron has a series of input synapses, where digital messages (numbers) are put in, referring to the intensity of each input signal. The artificial neuron multiplies each input by a constant known as the "*connection weight*" then computes the sum of these results and compare this sum to a fixed value called the *threshold*, and generates an output based on this comparison:

146

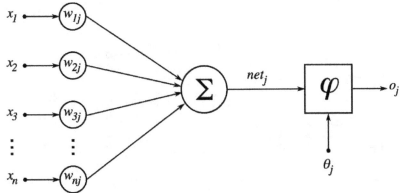

The simplest output function sends "1" if the sum exceeds the threshold, and "-1" if it does not, but you can also use other functions such as "sigmoid" (This does not qualitatively change the results).

Having these artificial neurons (realized concretely in the form of electronic circuits, or simulated on a computer), we can combine them together to form an artificial neural network or ANN:

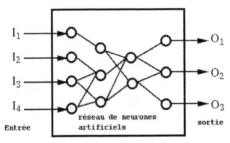

Since the 1990s, ANNs have been extensively studied, and some of them involving tens of thousands of artificial neurons have been made.

What for? The two main applications of ANNs are pattern recognition and associative memory. Let us assume we want to recognize a series of scanned text characters (i.e. the post office uses such systems to automatically recognize the zip codes on the envelopes). The network is fed with bits from the scan, representing a character, and outputs the ASCII code of the letter:

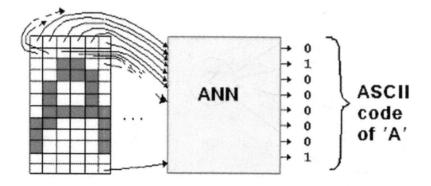

To achieve such an application identifying many characters, we must determine the parameters needed to set up the RNA, i.e. find the weight to be assigned to each connection of each neuron. This may amount to tens of thousands of interrelated parameters to adjust! As this would be extremely difficult to do, even with a computer (and how should we then program it?), theorists have developed a *learning model* of RNA, which gradually adjusts the weights:

We start with randomly drawn weights, then this ANN is presented different inputs, and we slightly adjust the weights so that the output is as close as to what is expected. Then we start all over again. After dozens or even hundreds of thousands of such tiny adjustments, the network is declared "ready for service."

TA curious phenomenon, which is the whole point of the RNA, applies then: It is to be noticed that the network is able to recognize the entries that have been presented as reference patterns, as well as *other entries* that might be slightly different. In character recognition, for example, the network is capable of recognizing the letters 'A', 'B', etc. even if they are *badly written*, provided that they do not look too similar to another "model" letter. In fact, the network is doing just as the human mind would!

(This should not be literally understood: we have seen that the human visual system is much more complex than a simple ANN is. Nevertheless, undoubtedly similar mechanisms to those simulated by ANNs are also used by our mind, not only in our sensory systems, but everywhere, especially in the memory)

To achieve an associative memory with an ANN, we use a network that has as many outputs as inputs. The network outputs the "model" shape that has been learned and that is the closest to the "poorly written" input shape:

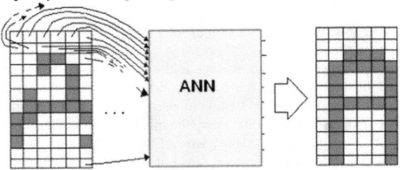

One interpretation of this would consist in saying that the ANN recreates the memories of what has been learned from a possibly incomplete or slightly distorted fragment of these memories! How fascinating!

By the way, what do we mean by "the closest to the input model" and "slightly distorted?" To answer this, we must take a quick look at the theoretical model of an associative memory. Here is a very simple experiment:

Let us assume you have a large sheet of thin metal, horizontally put on trestles. Take a hammer and give random blows to the sheet so as to distort it, forming cups here and there. Turn the sheet over and smash it in the other direction. You are at a point when your sheet has "learned" basic shapes it may recognize later on. Now take a small ball, hold it a few inches above this all bumpy sheet, and release the ball: it will roll towards the bottom of the closest bowl. You have just made your first ANN model!

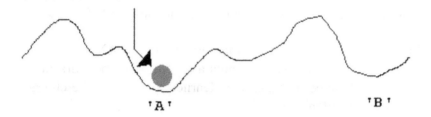

The coordinates of the position of the ball when you have released it, expressed in inches and horizontally and vertically measured from a corner of the sheet, encode the symbol to be recognized. The final position of the ball encodes the recognized symbol. Scientists say that the system composed of the ball and the metal sheet moves from an initial state (the initial position of the ball) to a final state that is a *stable attractor* of the system: a large number of initial states, constituting a *basin of attraction* will lead to the same state.

Of course, to take into account the many incoming and outgoing connections of a real ANN, mathematicians have made a somewhat more complicated model where the piece of metal is replaced by a set of attractors in an abstract space with many dimensions. Forget it.

When we adjust the weights of neural connections, we change the "geography" of these attractors. This will distort some bumps, increase or decrease some others or even delete them and create new ones. Learning *is* changing the geography of the attractors of memory, creating new bumps and cups in a new landscape.

As nothing is hardly perfect in this world, the system may contain a number of attractors that are not provided and do not conform to learned patterns.

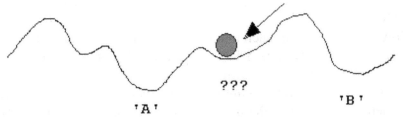

'A'   ???   'B'

The "ball" which symbolizes the calculation by the ANN can be locked in an unexpected "local minimum", a sort of a "parasite" attractor. In the case of an associative memory, this could lead to recall a memory that has not been recorded, or even does not exist. This is what happens when you have a sense of *déjà vu*: in fact, you have *not* already seen what you happen to see: your memory is just playing tricks because of the occurrence of an unforeseen attractor.

Mathematicians have proved that the phenomenon of déjà vu has a probability of occurrence that decreases with the number of neurons in the system: for the human brain, which implements millions or even billions of neurons in each sub-system, and that this phenomenon is very rare.

Forgetting

However if we try to teach too much things to a too small network, it begins to forget certain facts, if not all of them. This is called "catastrophic erasure". We must then have the network re-learning everything again. How do humans avoid that? The gradual burying of memories, which is the process of compression in the long-term memory, is likely to take place during deep sleep, whereas we recall things during REM sleep to avoid catastrophic deletions.

By the way, how do we manage to forget things?

In a passage of 2001: A Space Odyssey from Arthur C Clarke, the hero Dave Bowman speaks to the computer HAL:

> *"Well, Hal, stay in there."*
> *He nearly added, "and forget about it"*
> *But HAL could not do so.*

I think that Clarke did a mistake here: Indeed, today's computers never forget anything except when being asked to delete files, but a true AI should have a true associative memory, which in turn *is* able to forget.

An outstanding result from recent research is that the performance of a learning system increases when it is capable of forgetting knowledge! Learning AI systems reach a maximum after a certain time, then their memory is cluttered with unnecessary or knowledge of little use, so the number of tries needed to solve a given problem is increasing instead of decreasing when the number of knowledge becomes very large. The problem is that accumulating knowledge is not enough, it is also important to store but the *useful* knowledge. Human beings do forget, but it is not at all a handicap!

Conversely, a patient followed for 30 years by the great Soviet neurologist Alexander Luria had the amazing ability not to forget! Looking for a few minutes at pages filled with 30, 50, 70 words or numbers, he was able to repeat them without any lapse of memory, one week, six months or even 15 years later (!)

Without being autistic or crazy, this patient was not normal however. His various senses had no separation (synesthesia), which allowed him to do strange connections. He had among others the strange ability to associate a color, a sound or a texture to a word or a number. This way he had many possible ways to store the souvenirs in his memory.

However, this ability was not without drawbacks: the man found extremely difficult to remember the meaning of a text he learned, for instance. To answer a single question about this text, he had to read the whole text again in his head! By contrast, we can see the strength of our small "ordinary" memory: encode significance first. In other words, we forget the words of the text, but we retain most of the story, which is still much more useful in life...

Forgetting was the subject of various theories, which can be summarized in four processes, which seem to be at work in our mind: *decay*, *motivated forgetting*, *obstruction* and *interference*.

Decay:

Memory deteriorates and becomes fragmented over time as with all biological processes.

Forgetting is meant to occur because of a lack of exercise and absence or scarcity of reminders.

This is confirmed in the way we statistically forget the words of our language. Proper nouns, less often repeated, disappear first, then nouns and adjectives this is common as they can characterize several nouns), then verbs, then exclamations and interjections.

Motivated forgetting

Unconscious mechanisms would make us forget the unpleasant or distressing events.

Psychoanalysts show that forgetfulness is often associated with events causing well-known discomfort or carrying stress.

Freud assumed there was a selective process at work for dismissing or maintaining memories unconscious: these memories would be linked to some past trauma the evocation of which would be unbearable for the person. Psychoanalysis is based on the idea that these driven back memories are not forgotten and can be brought back to consciousness.

Obstruction

This kind of forgetting mechanism is a disturbance of the recovery and not of the storage of information. The temporary inaccessibility of information would occur due to insufficient encoding, lack of relationship with the acquired semantic, or inappropriate clues for recovery.

But information is still stored somewhere in memory, since at any other time, you can suddenly have access to it.

Interference

Forgetting would happen because another data prevents recovery.

In retroactive interference, new memories tend to erase old memories. And vice versa in proactive interference were older memories prevents a good storage of new memories.

The proactive and retroactive interference would allow us to update our knowledge of the world: the new information takes precedence over older information pieces (retroactive interference) without erasing all of them (proactive interference).

Then...

I think that all these four forgetting processes exist in our mind. In fact, forgetting is a *necessary* mechanism. The reason for forgetfulness is that it allows learning a concept from examples alone, even without having seen counterexamples. We will see this later on when we talk about human learning process.

Which associative memory for an AI?

Just one last word before we finish with memory. To create an artificial intelligence, we will probably need to create an associative memory from scratch. However, that does not mean we should slavishly copy what happens in the brain. Admittedly, the latter seems to be working with a mechanism quite similar to ANNs... Nevertheless, the brain is dependent on a hardware consisting of biological neurons, and given this "Brainware" there are few other ways to achieve an effective associative memory. However, with a computer, there are certainly methods that are faster in computing time, and much easier to implement, such as files indexing (the method that is used by search engines like *google*).

Good! It is time to broaden the debate a little. To sum up:

Eventually, what is intelligence?

As for human beings, intelligence is a special quality of a mind supported by a brain composed of one hundred billion neurons and a thousand times more synapses, a complex brain made of complex parts, each one playing a specific role. Intelligence is possible thanks to the combination of a large number of sub-systems; each of them is not designed to give us a particular capacity, but to fill a specific internal function.

To be able to work, an intelligent mind needs *sensory systems*, which allow the acquisition of new *concepts* about the world around it, but also the perception, or more generally the recollection of them. It requires a *thought* generation system that enables to link different concepts to one another. It needs a *short-term memory*, which allows the temporary storage of the thoughts and current concepts. It needs a *long-term associative memory* to store memories and procedures. In addition, it also needs a system for *goal planning*, a system of *deliberation* to decide what to do, and a motor system to coordinate its actions. (Besides, reflex systems also bypass the "deliberation" level by triggering actions directly from certain well-defined percepts). Eventually, a *control system* efficiently allocates available resources (computing or search time for example) and a *censorship* system limits the scope of possible thoughts at a given time and prevents the mind from getting lost in endless loops.

Mammals, and subsequently human beings, also have a system managing desires, impulses and emotions. But only human beings (or maybe some animals), are aware of themselves.

All these systems can be split into sub-systems where the basic unit seems to be the agent, or "little elf", which performs a basic task and can exploit the capabilities of other agents. The impression of unity we get is but an illusion resulting from the fact that one of these little elves is called the "self" and the fact (independent of the first) that we have a conscience that seems to be processing one thought at a time.

It is now time to address consciousness.

What is consciousness?

The study of consciousness has made tremendous progress over recent years. After centuries of investigations by philosophers who have faced the limits of introspection and psychologists who have broken their teeth on it, it has become a field of investigation for neuro-psychologists. The latter have carried out experiments with the help of advanced devices (EEG, fMRI, and computers), they have analyzed the results, set up other experiments, and eventually our knowledge has increased by leaps and bounds. This work is far from being completed yet, but it seems now possible for computer scientists to take over, testing the assumptions of neuro-psychologists on computers. We may soon simulate (if not yet reproduce) consciousness within a computer.

This is mainly possible since we can now distinguish well-defined parts of this fuzzy damn thing called conscience and consider each of them separately:

- *Access awareness:* when a person is able to communicate by voice or gesture that she has perceived something (i.e. consciously).
- *Phenomenological awareness*: a consciousness *in the third person*, to know that "someone" knows or does something, and *in the first person,* to imagine that this "someone" who knows or does something is me indeed.

Not all signals entering the brain do "trigger" access awareness: as we have seen, our "little elves", or agents, do process a great deal of information that we are not aware of. As if, there were two areas in the brain: an unconscious (without conscience) and a conscious one. Awareness means we become aware of something when the signal created by that something enters the conscious area.

The conscious area does process only one thing at a time, and for this thing to fall within the scope of consciousness, it must be attractive enough to take over and replace what we were previously aware of: There exists thus a filter that allows only interesting "things" to enter the aware area. This filter is the *attention.*

What are these "things" we can be aware of? Let us clarify a bit: the interface between the conscious and the unconscious area is constituted by an *exchange of thoughts,* in the sense that we have already identified: thoughts are arrangements of concepts that have a syntax and meet a goal, and ideas are a special category of thoughts. This definition is operational; it can be translated into computer language.

Experiments have been designed to study access awareness and to see what happens when we become aware of something.

Let us describe one of these experiences:

Subjects are presented with a small black disc for a very short time, which is immediately replaced by a black ring that perfectly surrounds it (or more accurately, that would surround it if the disc were still there!). As a result, subjects can only see the ring. However, were the disc to be shown alone and exactly for the same time as in the hiding experiment, they would have ample time to see it. What to say then: has the disc been perceived consciously and then finally cleared by the ring that followed? Or has the disc really never been seen?

Of course, it has: the disc has been perceived, but the signal was too short to trigger attention so it did not enter the field of consciousness, as opposed to the ring.

Attention is a filter for thoughts applying for consciousness. Attention assigns every thought an intrinsic priority (which for a percept is directly related to its intensity and duration), but also gives thoughts a priority due to the expectations of consciousness: in fact, it provides the "attention little elf" with information about expected percepts (expectations change over time, of course). Based on these two priorities, the attention lets the thought with the highest priority enter the awareness area.

Imagine you are in a café waiting for a person who has an appointment with you. Your attention is focused on people who enter the café, so that the thoughts continuously produced by the chain: visual system + concepts + thought generators (unconscious mechanism) are more likely to pass the filter if they have a connection to those people. Expectations are therefore high-level descriptions, similar to the thoughts or goals. (We have already talked about goals, which are also a special type of thoughts.)

Here is another experiment, which is far more complex but so enriching, which was carried out in Orsay (France) in 2005:

The subject wears an electroencephalographic helmet, with electrodes that detect the activity of various brain areas (say thirty) with a very good time resolution.

The subject is placed in front of a screen being initially blank As soon as the experiment starts, "words" are scrolling at full speed, composed of random letters (like XRTO, IOZNX, FBAXQ, etc.), each word being quickly replaced by the next one, so that the subject has virtually no time to read a single one.

Before the experiment started, the subject was informed that the first word will be chosen between two possible ones (say OXXO and XOOX), and is asked to concentrate to read the first word that appears.

However, without the knowledge of the subject, one of the words that appear in the scrolling, say half a second after the beginning of the scroll, has a well-known meaning: say the word FIVE. And the subject is asked at the end of the experience: have you seen FIVE?

Parameters are set-up so that subjects have a 50% chance of consciously detecting (in addition to the first word in the list) that the word FIVE has appeared at some point later in the list. Half of the subjects will have perceived FIVE consciously; the other half will not have enough time because they were too focused on checking whether the first word was XOOX or OXXO. This is called "attentional blink".

The experiment is repeated many times, with several subjects, each time continuously recording their brain activity, millisecond after millisecond. Scientists put on one side the recording of the subjects who viewed the FIVE consciously, on the other those of those who were not aware of it. Then they compute the average of the records of each series and they subtract the average of the second series of recording (those who have not seen anything) from the first one (those who perceived consciously FIVE). Eventually they come with a "movie" of what specifically happens in your brain when you perceive consciously something familiar, as opposed to what happens when you view, but unconsciously, the same thing!

It is a real window opened on consciousness

The following facts were observed:

When the subject is not aware of having seen FIVE, the visual cortex is energized first, with a peak at 96 milliseconds after the beginning of the experiment, then the activity decreases and eventually falls to zero; but when the subject has consciously seen the word, things did not remain there. There is a real flood of activations of neurons in the brain:

Firstly, at 276 milliseconds, the frontal cortex then the prefrontal cortex then the anterior cingulate cortex with peak activity at 436 milliseconds, followed by the parietal cortex, and then, again, the visual one.

Therefore, there *is* an area of the brain that is activated specifically by conscious processes. This area is very broad, covering at least large parts of the frontal, parietal and cingulate cortex (of course, the spatial resolution of the experiment being very low, we still cannot determine which specific circuits are active in our brain during those conscious access awareness processes)

What is happening within this area of the brain that allows consciousness? What is the purpose of this resonance / reverb between our perceptual system and our conscious area?

I think that the answer that best suits the theory of mind exposed in this book is that goals are generated in this space. These goals are then sent outside the conscious area where they are translated into a network of concepts, then into mental images through the encoders of our sensory imagery, creating a real "vision" of the goal. As attention at this stage precisely focuses on the new goal and its consequences, these mental images, which are new percepts, go back to the conscious area, cross the barrier of attention as if it did not exist, and create awareness of new sub-goals and constraints, and so on. In a period of a few tenths of a second at most, there may be several round trips until the goal-thought is validated, "crystallized" and placed in short-term and long-term memory.

Well, OK, the perceptual consciousness or access consciousness may be modeled. But what of this "elusive and ineffable quality" called phenomenal consciousness? We have no other choice but to speculate, and I am forced to propose my own theory, which perfectly fits with the working of the mind described in this book. This theory revolves around three simple ideas:

The basic idea is that phenomenal consciousness "in the first person" strongly has "something to do" with emotions. A ray of sun on the cheek, a forgotten memory that resurfaces, a music that makes us fall into tears, orgasm, here are some events that are not only perceived but seem experienced from within, sometimes causing deep emotions we cannot describe nor share.

In the brain, the amygdala, a structure that was named after its almond shape, is probably the seat of many emotions, especially fear. The amygdala is located in the frontal part of the temporal lobe; this is one of the areas involved in consciousness...

We already talked superficially about emotions. Emotions are syntheses, summaries, "one word condensates" of certain mental states. However, where do they come from? Our minds must contain a true management system for emotions!

The second idea is: in the brain, *emotions are managed by a separate (and also unconscious) system different from that of unconscious percepts, concepts, thoughts and goals*. This system is equipped with sensors analyzing the activity of the unconscious mind as a whole, which enable the development of a summary: This summary *is* the emotion. Conversely, the emotional system is able to generate emotions, usually by the release of chemicals acting on the brain as a whole, without the need to transmit neural signals to a large number of receptor subsystems (evolution is very lazy).

And finally, the third idea is that since we have the detection circuits and encoders of emotion in our minds, there is no reason for the conscious perception of these emotions to follow a different process from that which exists for "ordinary" conscious perceptions Therefore there must be a system of emotional attention, filtering out emotions and letting only some of them being conscious. This conscious perception of emotion, added to the sensory perception, *is* the phenomenal consciousness!

Eventually, the overall outline of consciousness is this:

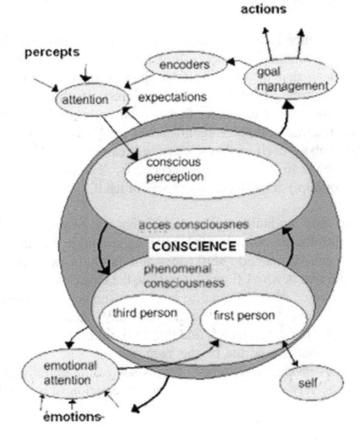

There is no magic in the fact that our minds contain sensors that measure its activity and synthesize our "mental states": As we have said, the various functions of the mind are performed by countless "little elves", or agents, that communicate, use others, and are even fighting each other. Only a very small proportion of these agents are directly connected to sensory systems: the others derive their information from other agents: they *are already* observers!

A word on the "self" symbol that I put outside of consciousness in the previous figure: there is no doubt that we have a "self", which allows us to distinguish between what is "us" and what is not. But caution, this is far for being enough!

When a computer is programmed to respond to a human being, and displays a sentence such as "I think this or that" on screen, this does not mean that it "thinks". It has just been programmed to display the string "I think" before the rest of the sentence. Similarly, say another computer that is a bit more advanced may feature an internal computer agent named "self", and store there information about itself or the processing it carries out, in order to be able to relate to them earlier, preceded by "I think"; of course this does not imply it has a consciousness of itself.

Our mind has undoubtedly a "self" that is responsible for collecting information on what is happening around it. But the fact this agent can be named "self" does not imply it is aware of himself, and that is why I figured it outside the conscious brain. To be truly aware of myself I need to have a phenomenal awareness of the "self" phenomenon, meaning that my attention can be focused on the unconscious "I", and that I should became, literally, aware that "what is reported by the agent named "self"" is indeed what happens inside "my" mind." This is something entirely else! This requires very special emotions, and the creation of a specific thought.

To understand what really happens, suppose that the unconscious "self" agent is called "foo" "and not "self" or "I" or "myself" or "me" whatsoever. Self-awareness means being able to keep the following reasoning: "this mind is capable of perceiving things, so that mind exists, and moreover it is capable of observing (in the

164

third person), what's happening inside it, and these observations are stored in an agent named foo; and when this mind perceives something, foo also perceives the same things, but in addition foo also sees what is happening in this mind; therefore not only foo is included in this mind, but this mind is included in foo. Consequently, this mind and foo are one, and *I* can say "this mind is foo" or simply "I am foo" and " this mind is my mind ". Whew!

To sum up:

Consciousness is a mechanism that allows a mind to select the next thought and the next super goal to activate. This super goal is then forwarded to the agent "self", and recorded in long-term memory as "my decision". The consciousness process receives all candidate proto-thoughts and proto-goals as input. It then selects the next thought or the next goal to activate. It can make this selection by comparing the candidate proto-thoughts with the concepts that are at this moment the object of attention: the "right" next thought is the one that involves concepts that share the greatest commonality with the current concepts that are relevant for attention. Attention is itself a choice mechanism, based on emotions; these are signals recovered by "mind observer" agents, to select relevant concepts. In the absence of any particular emotion, concepts that are the focus of attention are simply those involved in the five to seven selected last thoughts. An emotion like surprise naturally causes a shift of attention to new concepts, allowing consciousness to select new thoughts and goals.

This mechanism is of course theoretical, but it seems to me that it corresponds to reality. Even better: A (very) good programmer could probably simulate it on a computer, and get simulation results that are similar to that seen during the experiments that we described.

Consciousness appears finally as a regulatory mechanism that is somewhat analogous to the "B-brain" hypothesis of Minsky. It seems to involve significant amounts of neurons in various areas of the cerebral cortex, suggesting a complex architecture. It may well be that the "consciousness" box of the diagram above is organized like a "mini-mind" with all its sensory modalities, concepts, thoughts and goals, just like our own "main" mind.

Note that compared to the rest of the mind, consciousness is significantly limited: it can only see a thing at a time, and its working memory is short term and limited to five or six simultaneous thoughts, ideas, desires or concepts.

Why is this so? Simply because consciousness requires "raw" facts that are not yet filtered out by our goals: it needs a wealth of information about the thought agents that are the object of our attention at the time. It stores all this information it in its (fixed size) short-term memory, which has therefore a capacity limited to the five or six (complex) thoughts that have most recently been the object of his attentions.

Thus, introspection of consciousness is really difficult; it seems elusive, indescribable, for at least two reasons: firstly, because it is a separate area of our mind, where the information from sensors located only in the unconscious zone is processed. Secondly, because focusing on very recent mental states stored in short-term memory involves the creation of new conscious mental states that will be necessarily stored in short-term memory itself, and will then disrupt it.

What is the *purpose* of consciousness? Why did evolution create a conscience? Simply because an evolved organism must have a way to choose its next action, which must be a fairly "rigid" way so that the animal does not zap ideas and is single minded, and yet flexible enough for a new fact, if significant, could very quickly change the decision. Consciousness is simply this means. As a bonus, it allows to archive the decisions taken in the long-term memory by associating them with a "this is my decision" tag, which in turn allows very sophisticated social interaction; organisms can then communicate their decisions to others and compare their decisions with those of others.

Soul and mechanism

Oh! Mechanized consciousness? Then what with the soul, my good sir? We can respond like Laplace, whom Napoleon had asked what the place for God was in the new celestial mechanics: "Sire, I did not need this hypothesis". To achieve a mind, there is no need of a soul.

It is often said that "a computer cannot have a soul." Alan Turing, the inventor of the computer, answered that he did not see why God could not give a soul to an intelligent computer, if he wished to. One of the main objections to AI is that computers are unable to have originality. Turing said that computers might surprise people, especially when the consequences of different facts are not immediately recognizable.

A computer *can* compose music that creates emotions. Better: even if we do not know if a computer can experience emotions in the same way that we do, we can program a computer so that its behavior, its answers, its actions are so well simulated that we cannot distinguish them from those of a human being who would experience emotions. In this case, what is there to ask?

I hope that this book has convinced you that the vision I give of an intelligent mind made of a huge number of small mechanisms that are unintelligent by themselves but beautifully arranged, is ultimately more humanist that the vision of those who despise computers.

However, we will go back later in a different context to the problem of the soul. Indeed, an artificial intelligence has an interesting feature, which few people have thought of: it can be duplicated at will. These is not without philosophical consequences... But forget about it for now.

Animal Intelligence

As we have said, the main difference between the mind of an animal and a human is his ability to imitate. Some animals can imitate, but their capacity for imitation is not commensurate with that of human beings.

Animals do not have the same sensory system that we have, nor the same ability to grip. However, Mother Nature has dealt with these differences: Bats and dolphins "see" with their ears, and dogs with their noses, for example. A male butterfly is able to sense a female miles away.

Widely various animal species are able to invent adaptive solutions that are quite unexpected. One well-known example:

blue chickadees and bottles of milk: In England back to the early twentieth century, milk used to be delivered at home. The milk was laid before the doors in bottles closed with a cardboard dish. As soon as in the twenties, it was found that some chickadees were used to pierce the capsule and drink some milk... Moreover, this phenomenon has spread not only in the place it happened at first but also in other regions of England, while chickadees do not move more than twenty miles from their nest!

Nevertheless, rats do even better! Thanks to the fact that the organism extracts cognitive maps from their environment allowing it get their own bearings, by a kind of learning what Edward Toldman called latent learning. It is a thought without language that might be named "internal representations". The mental representations of the outside world allows the animal to produce appropriate responses (in a given range) to the stimuli it receives. They are acquired individually (this is an aspect of individuation). It is not sure on the contrary that they can truly be transmitted by imitation and assembled in a collective cultural knowledge. (This point is being discussed).

The achievements of various animals (nests of leaves sewn by some warblers, construction of dams by beavers, use of tools by primates (fishing for ants and termites) show that this is not blind instincts, but thought-of buildings meeting a goal and using real tools. This is the case with many animals that we do not think of, especially birds. The brain of a sparrow contains 130,000 neurons per mm3, unlike that of the sperm whale (1000 per mm3), but those of the bird are miniaturized. These little-known brain mechanisms are probably inherited from the time of the dinosaurs, 200 million years ago.

Fowls for example show a great stability of their relations of dominance. The primary mechanism is individual recognition, based on abstract mental representations of their peers. Chicken may practice visual recognition from slides. They can discriminate between congeners. They can also identify a congener when seeing just a leg, and even if only a wing was submitted to them before. Hens seems able to generate the "idea of chicken" or the "concept of chicken", from an archetype, something that most other animals are unable to do.

However, no animal species, despite the diversity of their means of communication, can be credited with a language (nor with sense of humor and laughter). However, many studies have shown that either spontaneously in nature or by long and also difficult learning, many species can acquire a substantial vocabulary of signs referring unequivocally to mental representations, themselves referring to objects from the outside world perceived by them. However, neither the structural phonological articulation (sound-signifiers) nor the semiotic one (meaning-served) does appear; nor also the capacity to construct an infinite number of sentences from a finite number of meanings (generative grammar). In humans, words can refer to things that do not have natural relations between them. They are abstract and take their meaning or value by opposition or contrast with other words. Animals might not seem capable of this - they *are* not capable, say linguists. It follows that the representation of self in their group or environment is not possible.

The biological bases of consciousness seem to be the same in humans and animals. Faces recognition, for example, is a job of the right hemisphere while singing is a job of the left hemisphere. Humans, chimpanzees and orangutans (and perhaps dolphins, but this is less obvious) seem to be the only animals that are able to get to recognize themselves in a mirror. When one of these monkeys is unwittingly painted a color spot on the front and sees himself in a mirror, he shall forthwith move his hand to his forehead. Is there any animal consciousness?

Desmond Morris has studied emotions, art and painting in humans and animals. A human artist paints using analytical, non-verbal thinking. Painting chimpanzee can have a visual control and experiment with new forms and colors, but they remain in the abstract. They cannot represent an image or a real scene. Their brain is in this area close to the one of a 2 years child.

A word on the phenomenon of collective intelligence, which appears in social insects. An insect has no intelligent behavior, individually, even if it looks sometimes. The typical example is the American wasp *sphex*, popularized by Douglas Hofstadter. This wasp feeds on other insects by paralyzing them. It then drags its prey to the nest (usually a hole in the ground or a wall), then leaves it at the door, enters the nest to inspect it, exits, and finally drags the prey in the nest. Such a behavior may seem very complex and intelligent!

However, if an experimenter moves the prey while the wasp is in the process of "inspecting" the nest, then the wasp no longer finds the prey in the place it had left it. It locates it quickly, but this causes the reset of the "program": the *sphex* wasp brings the prey in front of the nest, then returns again to "inspect" it, forgetting that she has just done so. In addition, if the experimenter continues moving the prey, the same pattern goes on again, indefinitely, hundreds of times if necessary. This shows that such a behavior one might think highly evolved is just a genetically programmed response to a stimulus. Hofstadter used the term *sphexic* to characterize a repeated behavior without intelligence (like pulling repeatedly the arm of a slot machine).

Yet while individual insects are quite "stupid", experiments with societies of bees, termites and ants, highlight the holistic behavior of those societies that are able to have completely surprising and unpredictable collective behavior, arising from the single action of competitive individuals responding to very simple incentives. There is "natural" selection of information. The *work* in some way guides the construction workers. AI researchers have extensively studied the subject, and have simulated such behaviors, including computer synthetic insect populations (works of Drogoul and Ferber in France). They reproduced these complex collective behaviors emerging from individuals who do respond only to very simple rules.

There is a certain analogy between insect societies and neurons. Some ventured to say that these societies think... In fact, what is thought, actually? Is there only one form of thought?

Extra-terrestrial intelligence

It may seem strange to include a chapter with this title in such a book. However, Let us be clear: I do not want to discuss here whether or not aliens do exist (even though I am deeply convinced that they do), but I think it may be funny and instructive to raise the following question:

If intelligent aliens exist,
then what might their mind and form(s) of intelligence look like?

In other words, does human intelligence *need* to be as it is? Is it mandatory that a general intelligence should arise from a mind that is similar to the human mind, or is it conceivable, at least philosophically, to imagine very different minds and spirits, which would nevertheless be capable of what we call "general intelligence"?

Science fiction authors, who are never short of imagination, invented hundreds of possible appearances for aliens ranging from the "little green man" to a "pure spirit of light" through conscious robots and a wide variety of monsters, giant telepathic whales, or even elusive creatures, invisible and impalpable, visible only by "vibrations of the ether"? We are well underway! However, I will introduce and argue the following hypothesis: if they exist, and if they are intelligent, then no matter what they look like, what their culture is, or any differences that may exist between their minds and ours, we *can* communicate with them.

I am not alone in thinking this: Marvin Minsky has written a remarkable paper, *Communication with Alien Intelligence*, in which he defends this thesis. So what are his arguments?

First, there are universal facts concepts, which any intelligence may encounter one day: the existence of numbers and arithmetic, for example. Mathematics possibly created by an alien spirit could be very different from ours. Nevertheless, they must contain a theory of integer numbers; because the action of counting and comparing quantities is essential to the evolution of a mind (Let us remember that even if we never learned counting, our sensory systems can count, at least for small numbers). The concepts of *utility, approximation, resource management* and *processes* are universal. There are others.

Secondly, and this is the subject of this book, there are ingredients to be included in any mind, because otherwise it would simply not result in a mind:

- Concepts and sub-concepts, to synthesize a description of the environment
- Goals and sub-goals, to break down complex problems into simpler problems.

- Symbols of causation, to explain and understand how things change.
- A planning system, to organize work and complete details.
- A memory to keep track of past experiences and find similarities with new problems.
- Economic management to allocate resources to the tasks to be done.
- A self-awareness for the survival of the owner of the mind.

Every intelligent mind must have a system of internal representation of the world, in the form of symbols representing objects, ideas and processes, and relationships between these symbols.

Similarly, any intelligent mind must be able to find similarities and differences between these symbols. Otherwise, neither thinking by analogy, by logical deduction nor causal thinking would be possible. Indeed:

Once a mind has found a difference between two symbols or a change in a symbol, it must be able to develop this difference in turn in terms of symbol. This allows reasoning about causes: why such difference? What caused this change?

An intelligent mind should be able to create causal structures, which explain causes and can predict the effects of similar causes. In these structures, a mind can deal with a phrase or description as a simple piece of another description: by representing our previous thoughts with objects, we can magically replace whole conceptualizations with simple symbols, and yet again build other concepts on top, like a Lego game. This allows us to create new ideas from old ones, or in other words, to think.

Every mind, either human, be it alien or artificial, must have these components. In addition, because we have things in common and these things are communicated in a language, we can then communicate. No matter whether the visual system of an alien is sensitive to ultraviolet and the concept of "red" is impossible for them to imagine, the concept of "3" is a universal concept as well as the basic structure of a mind, and gradually we can define a universal language between them and us.

This language already exists! Astronomers have long worked on this issue and found their solution. Hans Freudenthal has designed a language called LINCOS (Ling Cosmica) that is built in small steps from elementary arithmetic, and gradually comes up to define the organizational, administrative and philosophical concepts of a planet!

LINCOS is a language designed to be transmitted by radio signals, which are sent from Earth into space. It uses a small number of words and can be defined as a self-explanatory encyclopedia, in which each concept is defined from simpler concepts that were explained earlier. The LINCOS encyclopedia is very long and is very redundant to ensure that every concept is well understood. Let us give some examples:

We begin by defining numbers, using binary language:
. = 1,
.. = 10,
... = 11,
.... = 100,
..... = 101,

Etc. (the dot "." is a short beep, the signs " = ", "0" and "1" are more complex signals that code words of the language, the receiver is supposed to understand the meaning of "=" from the context)

The idea is that an alien civilization advanced enough to build an interstellar radio receiver (radio telescope) *must* understand the concept of equality and of number encoded in binary form.

Once the numbers have been defined, we can define (with enough examples) relations like "different from", "less than" "greater than", "addition", "subtraction", "multiplication", "division" and the concepts "true" and "false", which can introduce propositional calculus (logic of order zero).

We then define time units, using a time signal that I write here "_____", e.g. a beep that lasts one second in the first example and two seconds (10 in binary) in the second example:

Dur _____ = Sec 1
Dur _____ = Sec 10
Etc.

Then we define symbols, which are syntactically composed of a prefix that gives their "class" and of a serial number, which identifies "the instance". For example if H is a symbol for the class of "human", and if members of a class are designated by the letters a, b, c, then "Ha" means "human a". The class of numbers is the first introduced, then the class of operations on numbers, the class of units of time, the physical features, etc.

Next, we describe *behaviors* by introducing a dialog between two humans Ha and Hb:

LINCOS Phrase	Meaning
Ha Inq Hb?x 2x=5	Ha say to Hb: What is x such 2x=5?
Hb Inq Ha 5/2	Hb say to Ha: 5/2.
Ha Inq Hb Good	Ha say to Hb Hb: good.
Ha Inq Hb?x 4x=10	Ha say to Hb: What is x such 4x=10?
Hb Inq Ha 10/4	Hb say to Ha: 10/4.
Ha Inq Hb bad	Ha say to Hb: bad.
Hb Inq Ha 1/4	Hb say to Ha: 1/4.
Ha Inq Hb bad	Ha say to Hb: bad.
Hb Inq Ha 5/2	Hb say to Ha: 5/2.
Ha Inq Hb good	Ha say to Hb: good.

Note the difference between "true" and "good", and between "false" and "bad". The result 10 / 4 is true, but it is bad because we want the reduced (simplest) fraction, or 5 / 2

The concepts of space, mass, and movement, are then introduced, and that continues again and again, this is only the beginning, okay, okay...

Well, OK, it will never replace English. Nevertheless, to communicate with aliens, it is certainly better than English...

In 1999 and 2003 several LINCOS signal have been sent by earthlings to close stars, with no answer. But astronomers are convinced that if aliens received such a signal, they could decode it.

This leads us back to the purpose of this book: no extra-terrestrial signal has been received so far despite the many SETI listening projects. This is known as "the Ozma paradox" after the name of a SETI project, or the "Fermi paradox": If, as is confirmed a little bit more every day, almost all stars have planets; if, as most scientists think, life is a phenomenon that automatically appears when conditions are favorable, and if, as biologists believe, life is changing, as long as you give it enough time, to a form of intelligence; so why have we never found those aliens who should be countless, even in the neighborhood of our sun?

Various explanations have been advanced to resolve this paradox. I would add one more, which nobody I know has ever thought:

They exist, but they already became *Powers*.

A *Power* is a super-intelligence who has access to super-nanotechnology. What does this mean? Read more...

3

Learning

The very existence of a language like LINCOS (see previous chapter) is based on the assumption that learning is universal: an intelligent mind is a mind that learns and comes to make *the best* of what it has learned.

Here, what is important is "the best": we must be able to use what we learned in new situations. When an animal learns a certain behavior to have in a certain situation from a congener, then imitates this behavior only in this situation, without knowing how to react in a similar, but different, situation this is certainly an apprenticeship, but not a *smart* learning.

In the Middle Ages and in fact until the nineteenth century, it was thought that children differed from adults only by their knowledge. Children had all the skills of adults, and it was enough to "fill their mind" to have them become adults. Then, at the beginning of the twentieth century, the trend was reversed: psychologists have shown that the child has neither the knowledge nor the skills of the adult, and that it acquires new skills only by learning. However, we now know that certain skills are innate and others are acquired. This poses a formidable problem: what are the minimal skills that are necessary for a mind so that it can evolve by learning?

If we created a future general artificial intelligence, we would have to provide it with electronic mechanisms that can reproduce those of our mind: We would need to have this brand new mind *learn* the millions of facts, procedures, attitudes and skills that would allow us to share all the elements of our culture.

However, this might well be impossible. With humans as with animals, no learning is done from scratch. We have many innate skills and instincts, which are the foundation from which we can begin to learn. What is this foundation? How can we learn from it?

The very young child

As soon as a baby was born, he/she starts interacting with "others". As we said in Chapter 1, the mechanism of mimicry is certainly innate, as well as the ability to recognize others' goals through the mirror neurons.

When he/she is three months old, the child carries out exchanges with his/her mother and father. When he/she is one year old, he/she learns to share objects: he/she spontaneously shows objects and offers them to others to start communicating. As soon as when he/she is eleven months old, a child takes care of others. He/she feeds his/her doll with funny food and understands the concept of the permanence of objects (they still exist even when out of sight.)

The ability to depict someone else's emotions appears very early. It allows the child to imagine the other as another self, and as an individual person with feelings. *Sympathy* as a behavior intended to relieve someone else's discomfort appears when the child is nineteen to thirty-six months old. Then the child learns obedience, and understands that he/she has a responsibility. When nine to twelve months old, the child follows his/her mum's orders, and at seventeen months, he/she gives him/herself orders. The child starts being able to cooperate with others for a joint action.

When he/she is two or three years old, the child starts talking and having a conversation. He/she expresses feelings of affection, with smiles and kisses, shows an interest for others, but sometimes is afraid of strangers. Eventually, when he/she is eight, he/she puts on someone else's shoes.

Why do young children seem to live in an imaginary world? Because they *live* in an imaginary world! The generators contained in their sensory system and their system of representation of concepts and goals are somehow still "released from custody." They have not yet learned to make a difference between reality and imagination. This may be a very complicated skill, since human beings learn it so slowly.

The human being learns lifelong, getting new knowledge, skills and behaviors. This is not the case for most animals.

Lorenz and Geese

Konrad Lorenz and one of his loving geese

The phenomenon of imprinting, first described by Lorenz, illustrates the part of the innate and the acquired in animal behavior. At a particular stage of its life, the little animal identifies itself with another living being, whatever it is, and then tend to follow him all the time. That is, says Lorenz, nature (the innate) that said *follow*, and culture (the acquired) who said *who* to follow:

The goslings follow the man with the same zeal, but a greater distance. When I'm bending down the goslings come to me as close as to a mother goose. This is even more evident in the water. As soon as I swim with my head above water, goslings come closer and try to climb over me. So I spent a few summers as a goose among the geese. This is a test of patience, because these animals are very lazy. A dynamic man would not support it. He would go crazy. The geese follow me into the water and on land but also in the air. They respond to my cry "kokoko"... and land next to me, especially if I mime a flap of wings when sitting.

Lorenz was interested especially in what he called empty reactions. A bird, for example, may perform all acts or rites of the hunt for insects, even though there is no insect in its field of vision and he it never witnessed a similar behavior with another bird. Such an empty reaction is proof that the behavior in question is determined by genes.

Animals perceive the world not as we believe it is, but as the animal sees it during the few hours or days of the "sensitive period" after birth, when the organism is especially able to trigger a process of acquisition. The imprinting phenomenon is not confined to the familial footprint, but to all messages received from the environment (in the range of perception open to the animal, probably wider than it seems). Games play an important role, as the exploration of somebody else's body. The same phenomenon is at work with humans, but for humans, this phenomenon called neoteny indefinitely extends the "sensitive period". (Neoteny means the conservation of some juvenile characteristics in adulthood)

Note however that the "wild children" who were not exposed to language before puberty, no longer seem capable of learning a language. It seems that some faculties like language must be learned in the early years...

182

Piaget and competences

The Swiss psychologist Jean Piaget is famous for his experiments on young children, conducted in the 1940s. His "clinical method" is to interview young children like a father would, in unstructured exchanges where efforts are made to observe how the child reasons without trying to influence him.

Here is an example of a typical dialog of Piaget with a child:

Piaget: What makes the wind?

Julia: Trees

P: How do you know it?

J: I saw them moving their branches.

P: How does it make wind?

J: Like that (moving his hands to his face). The branches are just bigger. And there are a lot of trees.

P: What makes the wind on the sea?

J: It blows there from the earth. No. This is because of the waves...

Piaget concludes that the beliefs of this little 5 years old girl on the wind, though false, are completely consistent from the viewpoint of her young system of thought.

One of Piaget's most famous experiments regards the conservation of quantities: in this experiment: the child is placed in front of two glasses of equal size and containing the same amount of liquid. The child agrees that the two vessels contain the same amount of water. Then, in front of him/her, Piaget transfers the liquid from the containers in a third one that is higher and thinner:

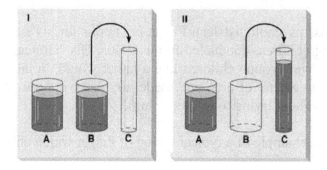

The child is again asked which container holds more water:

Typical Five-year-old: "there are more in the highest"
typical child of seven years: "both, since it is the same water"

Piaget theorized that this concept of conservation could only be acquired when the child has understood that nothing was added or subtracted, that we can return to the original state by the reverse transfer and that the apparent changes of a dimension (height) can be offset by changes in another dimension (width)

In a similar and equally famous experiment, Piaget had a child in front of Egg-cups and eggs. Even if he cannot count, the child is to agree that there are as many eggs as Egg-cups:

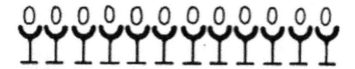

Then, before the child, he spreads the eggs, leaving the Egg-cups in place:

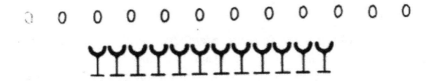

Again, the child is asked if there are more eggs or Egg-cups:

Typical five-year-old: "more eggs"
Typical child of seven years: "there are as many eggs as cups, of course!"

How to explain these differences in behavior? By asking the child further questions, it becomes obvious that the younger child's answer (more eggs) is based on "the extent" of the row of eggs. The older child's answer is based on a "historical" process and, because he/she knows nothing was added nor subtracted, there must be the same number of eggs before and after.

Suppose we want to explain to the younger child why he is wrong: We might tell him "Yes, the eggs take up more space after, but numerically there are the same number." I hope you agree that the child is unable to understand such an argument! Young children already have some notions of what a quantity is, but his problem is he does not know how or when to apply these notions! They do not know how to "describe the descriptors" of quantity. If they could, the problem would be solved! Try to imagine what happens in the mind of the older child who is hesitating but happens to choose the right descriptor: Imagine a "monitoring process" for reasoning on quantities:

Hmm. Are there more eggs now?
Choose a type of rule: there are QUANTITATIVE rules and
HISTORICAL rules:

Choose a QUANTITATIVE rule, this seems simpler:
  In quantitative rules, there are SPACE and NUMERICAL rules.
  All right, choose a SPACE rule:
    See what I know:
      We got the increasing extent (that implies more eggs)
      and the increasing gap (which means fewer eggs)
    Hmm, not so good. This is not very consistent.
  Enough for SPACE rules
  So Let us go for NUMERICAL rules.
    Hum! There are too many eggs to count!
The quantitative method is rejected.
HISTORICAL *rules still can be applied.*
  Let us begins with the IDENTITY:
    The eggs were moved, but none have been added or removed.

    It means the same!
Test of consistency with other HISTORICAL *rules:*
  try REVERSIBILITY
    The operation SPREAD eggs is reversible.
    It means the same!
So the HISTORICAL *rules seem consistent!*

How do I know if there are more eggs after having spread them?

Of course, the child is *not* carrying such reasoning consciously. But the unconscious services in his mind *have* probably kept the reasoning above.

Learning is not to ask:

"How can connect this or that "answer" to this or that "stimulus"?

But indeed:

"How can I add is this particular procedure to my deduction system"?

Note, also about the experiences of Piaget, that they were tried countless times with variations such as replacing the quantity of water with marbles, or sweets. When you promise the child a candy if he gives the right answer, you get more good answers, and even with very young children! In 1974, McGarrigle and Donaldson have shown that children of 3 years admit the equality of two rows of chips despite the change in the length of one of them, by plunging the problem in a game frame involving "an ugly bear" who likes doing silly things like lengthening one of two rows of chips.

Eventually in the 1990s, Starkey, Spelke and Gelman showed the capacity to represent small quantities of objects even in babies a few months old. We know that a child is able to abstract quantities from objects long before school age

So Piaget was partly wrong, but his contribution remains immense in our understanding of how the young mind can think and learn.

Chomsky and language

Noam Chomsky

One of the most amazing and most impressive faculty of the human being is his linguistic ability, or language. How do we learn to speak?

Yet young children are capable, without formal education, to produce and interpret with consistency sentences they have never encountered before. This extraordinary ability to access language despite a very limited exposure to alternative syntaxes led up Noam Chomsky's argument of the "poverty of the contribution" which was the basis of the new approach he proposed in the early sixties.

In 1957, he published in the United States *Syntactic Structures*. It was a revolution in linguistics. Chomsky, then assistant at MIT, developed the concept of an innate grammar (generative grammar), arguing that the capacity for language is a biological system, as may be vision. For him, language acquisition cannot be a repertoire of responses to stimuli, as each phrase someone can produce may be a totally new combination of words. Indeed, when we speak, we combine a finite number of elements, words, to create an infinite number of larger structures, sentences.

"We talk as we see, we do not learn our language as it is innate, inscribed in our biology." Since the "Chomskyan revolution", linguistic has become a true science. It aims at discovering the universal rules of language: the rules that we use to produce all the "correct" sentences and to remove the "incorrect" sentences. This is called *generative grammar*. Note that this new grammar has few in common with the grammar that is taught at school, which is mainly used to avoid spelling errors.

Generative grammar is why we say "everyone says" rather than "the world says" Or why "him" and "Peter" may not designate the same person in the sentence "Peter loves him" but may in "the father of Peter loves him".

For Chomsky, children develop so easily complex operations of language, because they have innate principles that guide them in shaping the grammar of their language. In other words, Chomsky's assumption is that language learning is facilitated by an innate predisposition of certain brain structures for language.

But what language? Because we see that for Chomsky's case to hold water, it is important that all the world's languages share certain structural properties. Yet despite very different grammars,

The Mind and The Machine

Chomsky and other so-called "generative linguists" like him were able to show that the some five or six thousand languages of the world share a set of rules and principles of syntax. For them, this "universal grammar" is innate and placed somewhere in the neuronal circuitry of the human brain. Children would be able to select among the phrases that come to mind only those that conform to a "deep structure" encoded in our brain circuitry.

All languages are based in fact on a single universal grammar and the structure of language that man can speak is limited. Why? Because we are conditioned by our genetic heritage. "Our biology does not allow us to combine or produce any sound, because language is the product of our natural evolution." For example: no language distinguishes phonemes "**u**" and "**ee**" if they do not have a phoneme "**a**" to contrast with the two others. Another example: many languages mark the plural by adding the word one additional phoneme, while no language does the opposite. But the originality in humans - different in that way from all other "talking" species - is that with limited resources, their mind can generate an infinite number of combinations.

In addition, the fact is that all languages can be learned and translated into another language. No translation difficulty is insurmountable among the human species.

Adults are not teaching to talk to their children: rather, children seems to know how to talk just the way they know how to see or birds know flying. Adults only stimulate children: they point them to a certain language, as part of the binding universal grammar. Only a *total* lack of exposure to language could prevent a child from talking. The fact is, Chomsky says, that all children know about talking. "I cannot give evidence", said Chomsky, "I can only cite facts. There is no 'evidence' in science, only facts. Only mathematicians need proofs".

Each time a child learns a word, it incorporates also a body of knowledge. Example: when a child learns to say "a person", he quickly discovered what a person is, even if aged or has no arm or leg. A child "knows" that without being taught, just because the ability to interpret reality is part of our genetic heritage. The word "person" is a concept that belongs to our "primitive language". Moreover, as soon as he can speak, a child spontaneously applies very complex rules of grammar that he was never taught. Language result therefore from biology, as growth of the body: it does not depend upon education.

Learning a language coincides with the stages of our physical development. Language is organic, not intellectual. Chomsky observed experiences with blind children that show that blindness does not delay the acquisition of language, even when learning colors. Children, either blind or sighted, use all spontaneously colors as adjectives. Of course, subsequently, only sighted persons apply these adjectives to the real situations.

We cannot say also that certain languages are particularly difficult. Japanese, for example, shows no unusual character, and its deep structures are similar to those of European languages. A Japanese child learns its language with the same dexterity as an English child learns its own, but we cannot say that one is more capable or more intelligent than the other is. If, by chance, language becomes too complex, children would eliminate this complexity, as they recreate the language in every generation. No language, Chomsky specifies, can evolve to become too difficult for a child to learn, otherwise this language would disappear as such after just one generation. Therefore, no language is more complicated than another, and none moves towards greater complexity.

African slaves, brutally uprooted and sent to the plantations in the West, used to communicate a *pidgin*, which is a chaotic alignment of words in different languages. It is not a language in itself as there are considerable variations in the order of words and very little grammar. Nevertheless, children raised by parents who spoke a pidgin did not merely reproduce the simple sequence of words from their parents: they spontaneously introduced grammatical complexity. Within a generation, a new Creole language was born.

Because they are innate, all languages are equally complex. This, says Chomsky, is striking when considering the languages of the Aborigines of Australia. These people, once described as "primitive", have a language which is neither simple in its vocabulary nor grammar. Like all pre-technological peoples, Aborigines people speak a language of extreme richness, particularly developed to classify natural elements or systems of kinship (e.g. more than 150 words for different forms of clouds, or terms to denote kinship over five generations). Many words in the so-called primitive languages have no equivalents in "civilized" languages, which are poorer when it comes to translating Nature or feelings. Therefore, Chomsky stresses, "no language is complicated, none is strange, and none of them are primitive."

Chomsky's theories have been criticized and enriched, and we believe today that the language is a learned skill based on biological structures, which are innate. The "universal grammar" is not innate, but the processes generating this grammar are. Moreover, we know that the syntax and semantics (the meaning) of words and sentences are highly dependent from one another; hence, the idea of a generative semantics, as there is a generative grammar. This metaphor, once seen as a mere linguistic construction, is now seen as an essential conceptual construction in the development of thinking.

Computer Learning

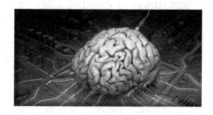

So how can a computer be taught? Lots of different ways!

There are also many ways to learn:

- Learning through maturation or development
- Learning without description (quantitative adaptation)
- Learning by building and modifying descriptions
- Learning by being taught
- Learning by analogy
- Learning by listening
- Learning by programming (programming or re-programming yourself)
- Learning by understanding
- Learning through trial and error
- Learning through incremental adjustments

For thirty years, researchers in artificial intelligence have been focusing on learning. The result is a multitude of programs, which can learn in one way or another, but always within a limited area. There is currently no program able to learn in a *truly general* way.

However, progress has been impressive.

The first trials in this area have been to learn to program simple concepts in a simple world. In general, researchers chooses either the world of formal logic, in which all knowledge is represented by logical propositions such as "father-of(Serge, Rémi)" to express that Serge is the father of Rémi, or the so-called "world of blocks". This "micro-world" consists of a set of cubes, spheres, cylinders, cones, etc. that are arranged on a table and can be manipulated by a robotic arm. (Generally, this is a virtual world, existing only in computer memory, although tests with robots manipulating real blocks have been tried... and passed).

See for example, in the world of blocks, how one can teach the program to learn the concept of what an *arch* is. This means to teach the program how to make an arch from blocks, but also teaching him to recognize an arch when it happens to be one in its virtual world.

But arches may have many different aspects! They can be made with three blocks, like this:

But also with other blocks, or more blocks, like this:

Patrick Winston in the 1970s succeeded in teaching a program to understand arches by presenting it "scenes" that would represent arches (examples), or that could obviously not be arches (counter-examples). The program progressively set up a logical description of each scene thanks to simple concepts such as "kind-of", "supports", "left-of", "contact", "part-of" etc.

For example:

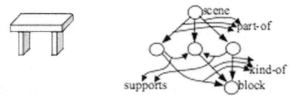

He then gave counter examples to the program, like this one:

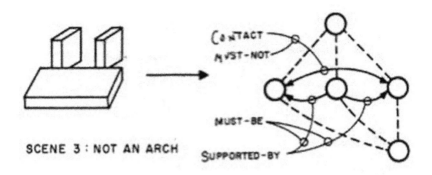

SCENE 3 : NOT AN ARCH

Or this one:

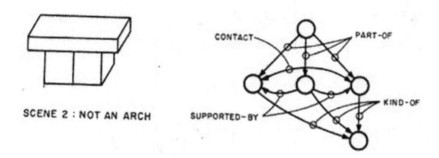

SCENE 2 : NOT AN ARCH

Then the machine found the broadest possible logical description that would meet all examples, and no counter example. This results as following:

195

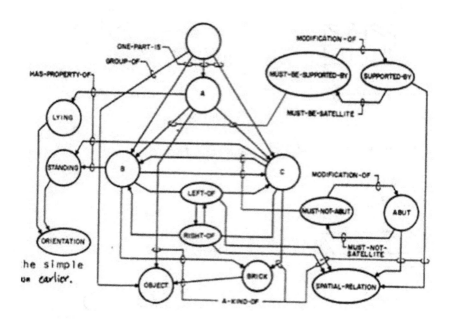

Would you think that the concept of "arch" was so complicated? Often "simple" concepts are in fact not simple at all!

But the most stunning part of Winston's program is that it is able, once it has learned a concept, to reuse it to simplify a description of a new scene: For example if it had not learned the concept of the arch, it would have produced an ultra-complex and unusable network to describe the next scene, composed of nine blocks. But once the concept of arch has been learned, the scene is simply described with the relationships "kind-of" and "left-of":

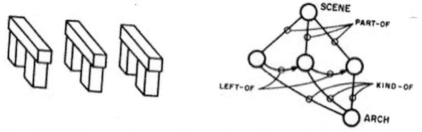

How to build an arch, now that we have learned what it was? It is necessary to convert the network of relationships that describes a scene into a procedure for building such an arch.

196

In fact, this programming problem was solved in the 1970s. It is the same problem as building a robot that manipulates blocks by following a user's instructions such as "put the pyramid on the red cube". Everything would be perfect but the problem of finding the basic relations that are essential remains. In the case of the human mind, these relationships are the percepts coming directly from our sensory systems.

Let us see how a child can get to the concept of "arch" without a teacher or professor who explains what it is. Suppose that the child is playing, for example building a road for a small car. In front of the road, there is a barrier consisting of two vertical bricks. The child moves the two bricks further apart to get the road in the middle, and then he has the idea of laying a third "hat" brick above the other two. He finds it pretty, and even if he does not yet know the word "arch" or "tunnel," he mentally form a concept for what he has built: a *structure formed of two vertical bricks that bear a third one*. Because it has already built a house with blocks, he may even have the idea of replacing the "hat" brick with a brick-shaped roof. It then gives a concept that is a little more general; *two vertical bricks that support any object as "the roof"*. This is not the concept of arch yet, because there is not even the idea of passage or hole.

However, the child wants to experiment, and he builds a new "two bricks with a roof" structure in front of the road. It is again willing to pass the road trough, but the vertical bricks are not apart enough. By spreading them, he will come this time to an arch concept that includes the idea of a passage wide enough to get a road through. He will also discover that if he moves the bricks too much apart, the whole thing collapses, and therefore assume a new property of the arch: its fragility.

This is a really interesting mind mechanism, isn't it? This reasoning is only possible because the child already knows a lot of things: that you can put a block onto another; that you can put a block on top of two blocks of the same height (but only if they are quite close to each other, or if they touch); that two blocks that touch with a face are like a single block but broader; that one can spread two touching blocks apart, etc. This "learning by discovery" is at the heart of an amazing computer program, AM, due to Douglas Lenat, that learns elementary mathematics by inventing, really, new concepts from old ones. We will see more on this later.

It is also possible to learn *without* building new networks of relations. A checkers or chess program, for example, analyzes the positions of the game by assigning a numerical weight to some particular characteristic such as strength of castling or the number of remaining pieces, and then gives a score to each position, which is the sum of these characteristics, weighted by coefficients. The strength of the program depends largely on the adjustment of these coefficients. It is possible to ensure that the program learns by itself how to adjust these coefficients: it is enough to have it playing against himself (or against a previous version of itself); if it wins, it increases the coefficients that measured positional advantage and lowers others. And vice versa if it loses. Samuel has made this way a program for English checkers, which is at the level of the human world champion.

The drawback of this "learning" is that the result is a nothing but a series of coefficients, a set of numbers that are so dependent on each other that each of them is almost devoid of meaning when it is taken separately; then it is difficult to draw something from this. You cannot "teach how to learn" to such a program. To really get to learn how to learn you must have a way or another to convert the experience into a procedure or program.

Often human beings learn by repeating the same tries, the same mistakes, the same gestures. We learn a mathematical concept with dozens of exercises. You learn to play tennis by hitting thousands of times on a ball. It is tempting to believe that for each of these tries there is inside our mind a sort of gradual adjustment of numerical parameters, the result is that we play or understand better.

Indeed, there seems to be an opposition between the "numerical" or "adaptive" point of view that we learn by better adjusting parameters, and then the "symbolic" point of view that we learn by constructing and changing networks of relations between concepts.

I think that human learning is essentially symbolic, and that the impression that we can have an adaptive adjustment of parameters is nothing but an illusion. Even when we learn to play tennis, each hit of the ball involves substantial changes in our strategies or our plans to connect our perceptions with our actions. Naturally, some physiological aspects of the coordination of our movements need to be learned from many repetitions of the same movement, but real learning is to be done at the symbolic level.

People who have a talent for athletics have no "magical" better muscular coordination than others; they "simply" built for them very expressive abstract patterns to manipulate representations of physical activities.

Learning and forgetting

Winston program learns concepts from examples and counterexamples. However, we know that a human being can learn from examples only: one child can learn a language without having even heard against a single counterexample, a single "malformed" word.

Yet, in attempting to make a computer learn from examples only, there is a difficulty that could be called "over-generalization." If the computer has to learn a concept from examples and counter examples, there is no problem to get it to "properly define" the scope of the concept:

Here the examples are represented by "+" and counterexamples by "-"

But when the computer has at its disposal only examples, how to avoid over-generalizing?

An example:

Audacity is the property of being audacious. *Immensity* is the property of being immense. *Authenticity* is the property of being authentic. But *annuity* is not the property to be annual, nor is *cardinality* the property of being a cardinal! Moreover, the property of being hard is hard*ness*, not "hardity" nor "hardicity"!

Here does the ability to forget come to our help. Consider a system that receives only positive examples, but do not store them in memory forever. On the contrary, examples and generalizations are gradually "weakening", unless they receive confirmation. When an example is too "weak", it is purely and simply erased (forgotten). Suppose that the system has taken some unfair and incorrect generalizations. This is described by the following figure, in which the generalizations that have not received recent confirmation are in lighter color:

The black "+" are supposed to have been confirmed several times. The "+" that are outside of the concept (false generalizations) have not been confirmed, so they began to weaken. Some examples in the inside (good examples) were not confirmed either, they are also weak, but with the hope that they will be well and truly confirmed. The border of the concept itself is fuzzy, but when the false examples are eliminated, it will become clearer and clearer.

In this way, the system can learn without counterexample, and learn how it should (or not) generalize!

Tentative overview

The Mind and The Machine

Finally, the human mind appears to be less mysterious than it seems. The mind is not unique, but is instead made up of a large number of systems that cooperate. Some of these systems manage our feelings, others deal with our concepts, thoughts and ideas, and yet others manage our goals, our emotions and consciousness. All these systems interact, evolve, and are able to learn; and they get to learn not only new knowledge but also new behaviors.

The final picture is that of a vast society of "little elves", or agents, each of which is deprived we call intelligence, but whose incessant interactions create the phenomenon we call intelligence.

We will now describe this society, but not only with the intention to understand how our minds work, but to describe how one could artificially rebuild this organization to create, finally, a true artificial intelligence (TAI).

II

Recipe to build a mind

4

The society of mind

This is the title of a book by Marvin Minsky, published in 1988, which had the effect of a stir in the small microcosm of AI. (Although it is anecdotal, the book made a great impression on me too). Despite being very frustrating to read because it consists of an infinite number of short chapters given in bulk and without apparent order or links (but the mind is like that, Minsky says), this book is nevertheless an exciting one, because it is full of very practical ideas on how our mind functions.

I will even argue this is an anti-philosophical book: the hell with theory, Let us be practical! Put your hands into dirty oil! Study low level processes only!

The basic idea of Minsky is that intelligence is a process that emerges from the interaction of a very large number of unintelligent processes he called *agents*. If you have managed to read this book so far, you already have a good idea of what that means, for the entire beginning of this book is the description of these processes; and you understand why we have the illusion of having a single mind: we are unable to see inside our mind and to perceive the myriads of small features which occur simultaneously there.

For Minsky, agents are autonomous systems that communicate, cooperate and sometimes fight amongst one another. Agents can join to form super agents he called *agencies* or *services*; they can in turn join other agents or services, etc. However, this is not a hierarchy, as a single agent or service may be used by several other services. Minsky speaks of an "heterarchy" or tangled hierarchy. The whole mind eventually resembles a bed of worms, but an *organized* one!

Minsky describes in his book many of these agents. It lacks, however, a pattern that would be a "comprehensive plan" of the mind. To make the picture clearer before we start dissecting some of these agents, I remind you here an idea, which is one of the main thesis of this book: the overall architecture of the mind into five layers or levels:

- The level of *senses*, specifically that of *sensory modalities* and sensory-motor systems,
- The level of *concepts*,
- The level of *thoughts* and ideas,
- The level of *deliberation* and goals
- The level of *consciousness* and the "narrative thread"

Most agents described by Minsky belong to sensory and concepts levels, some to the deliberation level. Minsky seems to ignore the "thoughts" level we have already discussed in Chapter 1.

Agents

A Sophisticated (?) agent
(poster of the movie *Matrix Reloaded*)

For Minsky, everything is an agent. We will thus find in our minds many agents of different types:

- Goals agents (play, build, imitate, repeat)
- Agents for the formation of concepts (more)
- Service agents (K-lines, loops detectors)

These agents may cooperate and utilize the services of other agents. Thus the agent *play* can use *play-with-cubes*, which can use *build*, which will use *displace*, which will use *grab*, which will use *move-the-hand*. Such an organization is strongly reminiscent of that of a computer program, with its sub-programs.

Nevertheless, agents can also fight. For example, in the mind of a child, several high-level goals agents are simultaneously active and compete for control: for example, *sleep, have fun, play, obey*, etc. *Play* is also used by *have fun*. Then another agent who would want to take control over *play* may use *have fun* to do so, and offer him another fun activity.

Imagine a child who still plays a little with cubes in the evening before going to bed. The *sleep* agent, whose priority is gradually increasing due to the physiological need for the child to sleep, tries to take control, but *play* resists because he is building a tower and he finds it amusing; *Have fun* therefore leaves the control to *play*. Then *sleep* calls surreptitiously *demolish*, unbeknownst to *play*. Once activated, *demolish* takes advantage of a respite in the activity of *play* and gives a kick in the tower that collapses.

Thus, with no apparent reason, the child suddenly demolishes his tower, and goes to bed!

However, this is only part of the explanation. It is likely that to take control over *play*, which is itself supervised by *have fun, demolish* probably suggested to *play* another fun activity: that of demolishing the tower. *Have fun* then must decide between two agents that both offer fun activities. He will leave control to *play* as it is active, but after the first pause or hesitation of *play*, he would give permission to *demolish* to take control. And once the tower is ruined, priority of *play* drops suddenly down, because there is nothing to play with but to rebuild everything, and *demolish*, who had finished his task, gives control back to *sleep* which can eventually reach its end goals.

Some agents therefore act as referees to manage conflicts, and the subtlest agents such as *sleep* arrive to manipulate the referee to reach their goal!

This mechanism of cooperation and competition is not found only in *goal* type agents, but in fact, every agent has an "internal" goal with a "priority" and a "cost" corresponding to the difficulty of the task he wants to accomplish. These costs and priorities are determined by "service" agents using so-called Bayesian reasoning, which I will discuss later in detail.

Thus, the cost of *play* was low as long as it was only devoted to put blocks on the tower under construction, but rose sharply after the demolition of the tower, because everything must be rebuilt. Note that sometimes the child actually rebuilt the tower, because there is also a *repeat* agent in his mind who urged him to re-do what he has done. In the case of our story, *repeat* cannot achieve his goal because *sleep* activated *demolish* before *repeat* had "got the idea".

This little story might suggest that those agents are ultimately very intelligent. But this is the only case for those which have learned to use the services of other agents (of lower, equal or even superior level, in fact there is no hierarchy among specific agents, but only transient hierarchies). In fact, all agents have the same "intelligence" and that intelligence is very limited. The appearance of intelligent behavior in *sleep* only results from the fact that he knows the existence of other agents such as *play*, *demolish*, and *have fun*, and knows how to apply simple rules like:

If I want to take control over an agent H
And that agent H currently uses an agent P
And I cannot take control over P
And H can also use another agent D
Then
Activate the agent D, asking him to be used by H

In our story, P = *play*, H = *have fun* = D = *demolish*, but the rule is very simple and general.

Such processes are at work in the minds of children, but also in adults. In fact, such processes *are* the mind.

Minsky quotes a little story in his book, that of Professor Martin, who usually works late at night in his laboratory to develop a new drug. Martin would like to go home, but he thinks suddenly about

Professor Challenger, in the lab next door who competes against his; and he thinks he absolutely must come to develop the drug before Challenger does, or else he would have worked for nothing. Then he stays in the lab until well after midnight... But Professor Challenger has never existed but in his imagination!

It is easy to describe what happens in the mind of Professor Martin in terms of struggle between agents, alike what happens to the child who destroyed the tower before going to bed.

Another type of agent quoted by Minsky is the formation of concept agents. Take for example the concept *more*: This word encompasses so many meanings!

- More high (higher)
- More wide (wider)
- More thin (thinner)
- More big (bigger)
- More numerous (the more)
- More colorful
- More pretty (prettier)
- More dense or tight (denser or tighter)
- Not the same and no less
- Etc.

When he compares two visual perceptions, for example, the *more* 'agent' may engage the services of *high, wide, large, counting*, etc. Note that *large* usually involves both *high* and *wide*. This allows us to directly explain the experiences of Piaget's conservation that we discussed in the previous chapter. The young child has many concepts (i.e. agents) on what is meant by "higher" "wider", etc. However, his *more* 'agent' does not have good control strategies to decide between conflicting responses from these sub-agents yet.

In the experiment where we spread the eggs in front of egg cups, the network of agents of the "society of more" of the young child asked the question "is there more eggs then?" Looks like this:

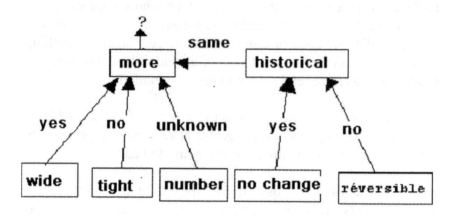

What the child is missing to acquire conservation is not new agents, but a rule so that *more* may decide in this scenario:

If as many agents answer "yes" than "no"
And If an agent answers "same"
And all other possibly available agents answer "I do not know"
Then verify that the agent who answers "same" is sure of itself and why.
And if so answer 'same' with the reason rose in the previous step.

Actually, this rule is indeed a very ad hoc one, since it implies that agents can answer "yes", "no", "same" or "I do not know," but in reality, no agent can speak or provide such answers: responses of agents are actually other agents.

However, there appears that only a small number of priority management strategies are really useful, such as the majority rule, the majority rule with veto, etc. In the course of its apprenticeship, an agent will try these different priority rules, and "freeze" retaining only those that has given him the most successful answers. This success is measured (by others agents) based on the desirability of the reached goals, using again Bayesian reasoning (we have not spoken about it yet, but I promise we will).

Eventually the society of mind described by Minsky is an extremely rich one with agents, structures and processes, and is the result of millions of years of evolution and years of individual experience. This society of agents is not comparable to an assembly of humans because humans are able to do anything, while agents are highly specialized instead.

Minsky had the idea of the society of mind around 1970, when he was trying with Seymour Papert to build a robot equipped with an arm and a camera in order to move blocks on a table and to make constructions. To do this, he wrote a large number of sub-programs such as see, move, catch, etc. He finally discovered that no simple algorithm could give a general method. For example, the robot could almost never achieve to discern the shape of an object by vision alone: he needed to know what kind of objects it was probably seeing (analyzing) with its camera. Hence, the idea that only a society of collaborative processes might accomplish this task. Finally, he became a supporter of the idea that intelligence does not derive from a "miracle recipe", but from the cooperation and competition between thousands and thousands of independent processes that are not intelligent by themselves.

Basic agents

Minsky describes several basic agents from which agents of higher level can be built:

K-lines

I have already described the K-lines (Knowledge lines) in the chapter on long-term memory. These are the most common agents in the society of mind. Their goal is simply to activate a set of other agents, and because agents tend to have many interconnections, activating a K-line creates a cascade of activations in the mind.

Most K-lines are created to track the list of agents that were involved in solving a problem (including false starts, unexpected findings, backtracks); so that when a similar problem arises again, activating the new K-line is enough to solve it. This triggers a "partial state of mind" that has been helpful in the past, and is analogous to a memory. K-lines can reactivate factual memories, but also procedures, chains of goals, etc.

Nomes and Nemes

These are special types of K-lines, which are analogous to data structures and control structures in a computer program. *Nemes* are used to represent aspects of the world, and *Nomes* are used to control how these representations can be manipulated.

Minsky gives examples of nemes, as *polynemes* and *micronemes*:

Polynemes invoke different agencies, each dealing with the representation of a particular aspect of the concept. For example, the recognition of an apple relies on an "apple polyneme" that will activate some properties such as color, size, texture, taste, weight, but also other properties less related to perception, such as the apple tree, price, the places where you can find apples, situations where one can eat an apple, etc. The idea underlying polynemes is that the "significance" of a concept cannot be expressed by a single representation, but instead is distributed among several representations

Micronemes send signals of global context across the mind. They often describe aspects of our situation for which there is no word or specific concept such as colors, smells, shapes, or specific sensations. Micronemes are also used to refer to aspects that are difficult to attach to a particular concept, and are more diffuse and indefinite in their references.

All knowledge refers to a context: thus, the word "high" has a different meaning when we speak of a price, a mountain, a school or technology, and the word "neighbor" has a different meaning when we speak of a person, a country or a quantity. Douglas Lenat has identified the space of contexts, which is the space of micronemes, and has twelve dimensions:

- Absolute time (a specific interval)
- Another type of time (just after the meal).
- Absolute location ("Paris")
- Other type of location: "in bed", "a church"
- Culture: linguistic, religious, ethnic, age range, health status, etc. of typical actors
- Sophistication / security: who already knows this, who can know it, learn it, etc.
- Subject / usage, topic, applications, problem to solve
- Granularity: phenomena and details that are and are not ignored
- Modality / intention: who wants that to be true / believes that this is true?
- Arguments for and against: local rules to determine truth
- Justification: proven, act of faith, assumption, observation...
- Local variables: instantiations that are true in this context. For example assignments of words to the concepts of an ontology.

Minsky suggests that nemes are organized into "networks of interlocking rings", with large agencies and recognition agents for these nemes, in which waves of activity are both top down and bottom up, to accomplish the tasks of pattern recognition, production plans, reduce ambiguity, etc.

Because these networks can easily become tangled mazes inside which it is easy to get lost or turn around, Minsky argues that that other agents are necessarily involved to "close" the network and control it. This is the role of Nomes.

Nomes control how representations are manipulated. Minsky gives examples of nomes, as *isonomes*, *pronomes*, and *paranomes*

Isonomes ask various agencies to perform the same cognitive task. For example they may ask them to save their current state in the short-term memory and retrieve a new state in the same memory, or cause polynemes to reproduce the state of a series of agents, or force a series of agents to "imagine" the consequences of an action (goals and plans are discussed below).

Pronomes are special isonomes that control the use of representations of the short-term memory. The word pronome reminds deliberately the word "pronoun". A pronoun is usually represented by a pronome. Pronomes are often associated with a "role" in a situation or larger event such as the role of being actor in an action, or location of an event. There is a strong link between pronomes and so-called "cases" in grammar (e.g. Latin, German, and Russian):

- A: agent of action (animated)
- I: instrumental: cause or (inanimate) reason of the event or object used to cause the event
- D: Dative: entity (inanimate?) affected by the action
- F: Factual: Object or thing caused by the event.
- L: location: location of the event
- S: source: the place from which something moves.
- G: goal: place to which something moves.
- R: Recipient: (animate) being that benefits from the event

- T: time: when the event occurs.
- O: Object: an entity on which action takes place or is changing because of the action. This is the most general case.

Some pronomes are connected to highly specific short-term memory, as a place, shape or path. Others are more general and influential. Some can even activate simultaneously much of short-term memory, and a have very general power of expression, as the concept of "something I saw"

Paranomes are strings of interrelated pronomes, so that a change in one of the pronomes induces an identical or similar change in other pronomes. Minsky invented the concept of paranome to describe how knowledge expressed in different ways could nevertheless be treated uniformly. For example, a paranome for the location of an event such as "I drank a glass" can be connected to different representations of this location, one relative to my body, the other to a reference frame like "the lounge". Paranomes are used to coordinate the use of these different representations.

Frames

In computer science, *frames* are data structures that include all aspects of something that are enshrined in the fields of the frame. For example, a frame of "car" will contain a "type" field for storing the make and model, a field labeled "has" for the wheels, engine, and main body, a field "is-a" or "sort-of " pointing to the "vehicle" frame, a field for "typical use", etc.

Minksy describes how to build frames using pronomes that control what is attached to the various fields. These pronomes are interrelated, so that when you activate the frame you activate also the partial descriptions of the various aspects of what is described by the frame.

215

(ii) Frame arrays

To describe everything that is underpinned by a concept, a frame is not enough. We need a set of frames, which represent the concept from different points of view or different perspectives. Frame arrays are such sets, which have common fields or pronomes. For example, a cube can be represented in different ways and viewed from different angles.

Minsky asked a five-year-old child to draw a cube. Here is what he drew:

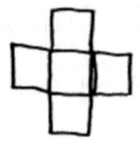

"Very well," he said. "How many sides to a cube?"
"Four, of course!" the child replied.
"Sure," said Minsky, recognizing that the child does not consider the base and the summit as "sides" in contrast to mathematicians. "And how many squares of cardboard would it take to make a cube?"
The boy hesitated a moment, then replies: "six"
"Ah! And how many squares you drew on your picture?"
"Hmm. Five"
"Why?"
"Oh, you cannot see the one below! "

Minsky then draws the usual "isometric" representation of a cube:

"This is not a cube," said the child.
"Why?"
"Cubes are not slanted"

Consider for a moment the "Frame of cube" in the mind of the child: For children, a cube has the following properties:

- Each face is a square
- Each face touches four other sides
- All angles are right
- Each corner separates three faces
- The opposite faces of each side are parallel
- Etc.

Compare these "topological" properties with the child drawing:

- Each face is a square!
- The "typical" face touches four other ones!
- All angles are right!
- There are three right angles at each vertex!
- The opposite faces of each side are parallel!

And with the adult drawing:

- Only the "typical" face is a square!
- Each face touches only two others!
- Most angles are not right!
- Only a trihedral is represented, but two of its angles are not right!

The child drawing better describes the properties of the cube than the adult one! It is likely that the concept of "cube" in adults contains a series of frames, one of which describes the topological properties of the cube, the other elements of the 'intuitive' drawing of the child, and yet another the properties of the isometric drawing of the adult, the latter being much more complex because it must appeal to notions of perspective that involves many other agents and frames.

Arrays of frames are what, computationally speaking, is closest to what is intuitively a "concept".

Note that you can never see more than three faces of a cube at a time, and that this appears in the adult drawing but not in the child one. The preceding comparison is then somewhat biased. An adult will seek to best represent what he sees (although the isometric representation is not the real perspective!) However, for a child, what is important is to best represent his understanding of the concept even if it is different from what is before his eyes. Therefore, a child often draws "trees on a mountain" this way: trees grow straight from the ground!

The many frames involved in an array of frameworks have common fields, as they all describe viewpoints on the same concept of a cube, and if a cube that has geometric properties, it has many other features: you can play with, you can grasp it with your hand by taking two opposite sides, there may be a pattern on each side, etc. Having common fields also facilitates the "jump" from one representation to another to solve a problem. The common fields of an array of frames are the ancestors of paranomes.

(iii) Trans-frames

Trans-frames are one of the central forms of knowledge representation in the society of mind. Trans-frames represent events, and everything that is implied by or linked to this event.

Trans-frames have fields for origin and destination of a change (before and after), and fields to describe who or what caused the event, why (for which purpose), objects and concepts that have been affected, how and with what means did the event have happened, etc.

We can then combine the trans-frames to describe stories, screenplays and scripts (Minsky obviously think about some AI programs that implement such structures and which were well known at the time in the field of natural language understanding)

There are also other types of frames, such as those used to describe what is seen, heard, touched, etc.

The engine

While Minsky did not give recipes to directly program agents (he does not say in particular what he means by "activate" or "invoke" an agent, or which structures are exchanged between agents when they pass messages), one feels in reading him that there is really rather little work to achieve the society of agents that he proposes.

This is probably a false impression. In fact, even if the agents seem simple, the "engine" that controls these agents is very complex, for it relies on a very large number of procedures such as associative memory, unification, analogy detection, pre-treatment of sensory modalities, logical representations of knowledge and procedural manipulation of graphs, reducing differences, converting between representations, Fourier transform, generators and interpreters of code, task management, and so on.

I have tried in this book to give an idea of this complexity. It is huge, but not infinite. The problem is difficult but can be overcome.

Minsky believed that one of the essential components of a system of agents is the reduction of differences system, or "difference engine". This is a very general way to solve a problem: You only input it the initial situation and the final (desired) situation, and then the engine tries to reach the final situation from the initial situation by reducing differences.

For example, a child playing with blocks may have wanted to put a green pyramid on a green cube, but there is already a yellow cube on the green cube. The engine then looks for a way to reduce the difference between these two states. For this, it has a number of operators (take a cube that does not support any other, put it on the table, and put it on another cube, in our example) Most of these operators will increase some aspects of the difference, but decrease others. The engine searches the sequence of events leading to undo all the differences: it tries a random operator, is featured with a new state (and always the same final goal), and then try to reduce the difference between the new current state and the final goal. If it does not succeed, it backtracks and starts afresh with a new operator.

It is possible to ensure that the difference engine learns during its own operation which operators have been useful to avoid certain types of differences, to be more effective next time. Operators are

K-lines that activate different methods and actions. Unfortunately, there is no single way to compare different representations, so that you cannot construct a universal difference engine, but only for some particular cases.

In general, many problems solving methods do not work and only a handful can achieve a certain result. It is then important to keep track of what worked in the past, but also of what did not work. Minsky calls this negative expertise. In the society of mind, this type of knowledge is achieved by agents he called *censors* and *suppressors*. Censors suppress partial mental states that precede action that are unnecessary or dangerous, and suppressors suppress these actions themselves. Minsky has even questioned whether the negative expertise was of greater importance than the positive expertise, even if it remains invisible because we can say what we did but not what we did not.

Perhaps it is the source of humor: when we laugh, above all we learn what we should *absolutely not* do in certain situations!

Intermediate agents

Besides K-lines, Nemes, Nomes and other relatively low-level agents, Minsky quotes dozens of high-level agents like *play*, *play with blocks*, *sleep*, etc. The problem is that the decomposition of these high-level agents into low-level ones is not trivial at all! This gives a lot of research work to find all the intermediate agents. Minsky hardly says anything of this decomposition. I will try to fill this gap:

At the first level: Nemes, Nomes, frames, arrays of frames.

At the second level: the *symbol systems*. These consist of different kinds of agents:

- Knowledge trees, which are derived from the relationships "is one" or "is kind of". These trees represent the "chains of knowledge" that we have when we say for example "a cat is a mammal that is a quadruped that is an animal that is a living thing". In technical terms, the knowledge tree describes the *ontology* of the known world.
- Classifiers, trying to match strings or graphs of concepts with elements of the ontology
- Generalizers, which attempt to generalize classes to create objects at a higher level in the ontology
- Specializers, which are the inverse
- Simple suppressors (e.g. the one who seeks two identical agents and removes one)
- Neighboring agents, seeking similar facts and correlations
- Arbitrators and Task Sequencers
- Achievers and retrievers
- Pairing agents
- Agents measuring activity and frustration: an agent is frustrated when he has not reached its goal for a very long time

At the third level: *concepts*:

- Representations of what is perceived (percepts)
- Events
- Complex suppressors
- Loop detectors
- Translators between representations

The fourth level: *thoughts*:

- Goals and Goal detectors
- Ideas and generators of ideas
- Desires
- Emotions
- Censors
- Intention and assertive detectors

At the fifth level: *deliberation*:

- Plans
- Controllers
- Pleasure and Pain
- Instincts
- Injunctions

And finally, consciousness.

Of course, there are holes in this hierarchy. But the general idea is clear: it must be possible to fill those holes!

Situated agents

Agents communicate each other by sending messages. This implies that agents know themselves, or at least that each agent knows some others. The network of agents may of course be pre-programmed, but at some point it may be necessary that this network evolves dynamically. A very interesting idea that did not exist at the time Minsky wrote his book, is that agents are *situated*.

Imagine a set of communicating robots, e.g. robots extracting coal in a mine. This might work if every robot knows its position in the mine, and that of the robots close to it. Therefore, a mining robot could know shippers and carriers robots nearby and could call them to load the extracted coal.

Similarly, within a mind, situated agents have an abstract "position" and are therefore able to know what agents are close to them (by querying the "engine" that synchronizes all): A situated agent is an agent who knows its position in a virtual metric space. The number of dimensions of the coordinates space is irrelevant in theory but in practice it is useful to choose three, because it allows agents dealing with tactile sensations to get directly the position of the sensor: So an agent that processes sensations received by the thumb will have coordinates close to that of the one that processes signals received from the index. The two agents can then communicate to develop a global sensation, such as grasping an object between two fingers.

In the same way, a "lexicographic" agent seeking the root and the ending of a verb will benefit from being close to a "syntax" agent that can decompose a sentence into words, because the two tasks are similar.

Finally, it is likely that the agents who set body maps (maps of the relative position of our individual members) have coordinates that correspond to those of our members. How convenient! Convenient, no?

The magic with situated agents is that they can easily establish directly new contacts with unknown agents: they simply ask the "engine" which agents are close to them. The engine can even warn them that another agent "passes" nearby, which is useful to detect for example collisions. A situated agent can "move" simply by changing its coordinates without physically moving or necessarily change its network of relationships.

Incidentally, the three dimensions of the space coordinates of agents raises a fascinating problem: Is it because the world is in three dimensions that agents have three coordinates, or is it because our agents have three-dimensional coordinates that we *believe* we perceive a three-dimensional world? I think the first assumption is correct, since it is quite possible that agents managing tactile sensations of our skin may have coordinates of *two* dimensions...

How do agents communicate?

The easiest communication method between agents is the K-line, which allows an agent to activate several others: for example, an agent will wake a polyneme to activate agents that represent several aspects of the same situation, or a microneme to activate a particular context for a group of agents. The activation of a K-line does not transmit any information to the activated agents outside of the identity of the activator; the information is in the activated agents themselves.

By activating several K-Lines, an agent can create a kind of "communication bus", a kind of cable with several wires, and to which other agents are connected (not necessarily on every wire). Therefore, each wire can have a meaning, and maybe each subset of wires. Receiving agents can be each connected to a random subset of wires, possibly via a pronome acting as a logical "AND" gate, which allows the activator to select one or more receivers. Conversely, the receivers can be tuned to a particular set of bits on the "bus" wires they are connected to.

However, to truly convey information between agents, or rather in this case between agencies and services, an internal language of knowledge representation is needed. To send a message, the issuing service activates different agents playing the role of "words" and in an order that depends on the chosen "grammar". The receiving agent is informed by the activated "words" and decodes the message using an "inverse grammar". This implies that the transmitter and receiver must agree on this grammar. How is this possible? Finding how two services can learn a common language is a formidably complex problem for which we have not currently found a general solution. However, there are partial solutions:

The theory of *speech acts* defines the different functions of communication. This theory is not interested in what language is, but in what it does. When we speak, when agents communicate, the emitting agent's goal is to have the receiver performing a certain action, changing its mental state, or providing certain information, etc. According to the theory of speech acts, any message has a *modality*, and one or more *functions*. The sender of the message also has an *intention*. Truly understanding a message is to understand its functions, modalities, and the speaker's intention.

Modalities:

Modalities are used by the receiver to determine the purpose of the message. There are a dozen:

- Assertive (statements):
    - o Positive (affirmation) and negative (reversal) Example: "I'm Henry", "I want success in my life"
    - o Special case: a message that says "what the answer should be", which is also a modifier, e.g. "you're wrong, the correct answer is 42".
- Answers ("yes", "likely", "in general", "42") o The message "no" can be both an answer to a question and a signal error (modifier).
- Requests and orders: "Give me the list", "forget it", "play e4 first"
    - o "seek" is also a modifier
    - o "again", is an order or a modifier according to the context...
- Interrogatives, or questions

- o (note that "who knows?" is not a question!)
- o "why?" is a request for clarification
- **Commissives**: speech acts that commit a speaker to some future action, e.g. promises and oaths
- **Declarations** are performing something by themselves (I curse you, I urge you, I marry you)
  - o Special case: incentives / punishments: "bravo", "yes", "er... no", "you did well", "you're wrong."
- **Modifiers**: they suggest trying a change of context in the preceding argument.
  - o "you have not used all data", "you did not consider all hypotheses", "it is false"
  - o Or "yes, but if... ", Meaning that the previous answer was too general.
  - o "I suggest you to... " Gives one more indication of the strategy to use.
  - o What is the class of "you should find by yourself!", which could mean, for example "I will not tell you", or "I want to test you", or "I defy you"? This means that the problem is difficult and the receiver should give a large weight to the satisfaction of having solved it: there is probably a category of modalities for encouragements.

Functions: a single message can have several functions. In particular, it still has a phatic function:

- The **effective** function, with two sub-categories
  o expressive "This is my state, my beliefs" (related to assertive modality)
  o conative: orders like "do this!", "answer my question!" (Linked to the request / order modality).
- The **referential** function gives a reference to the outside world "This is what is"

- The <u>phatic</u> function: controls the communication link, as "ping", "I get you 5", "I want to communicate with you", "Who are you?"
- The <u>poetic</u> function gives an aesthetic or humorous value to the message
- The <u>metalinguistic</u> function refers to the protocol or syntax of the communication. Two subcategories:
  o paralinguistic: Concerning messages that are or will be issued, e.g. "Why do you say that?", "I do not understand".
  o Metaconceptual: defining a common language mold, e.g. "by X, I mean Y"

Finally, every speaker, whether a human or a society of agents, has one or several intentions in sending a message. Intentions are related to assertive, but are more temporally stable: An assertion is local to the message, or part of the message, while the intention may be the same for several consecutive messages.

Here are a few examples of intentions:

Positive intentions:

- To exhibit, make understand or clarify on a fact, a situation, an action to undertake or a rule...
- To describe a problem or situation (from which it is hoped that other things can be inferred).
- To teach how to reason within a specialized field, to educate, to open the mind of another by giving knowledge of new fields of activity.
- To express feelings, to share the joy, fear, anger, (dis)approval, compassion ("my dear sir!"), to cause the other to solidify his mental model of others, or simply need to be surrounded by people who share the same beliefs, emotions, or interests
- To encourage the other, to make him go forward.
- To check that the other understands
- To correct somebody else's error

- To express a personal need that one could satisfy (hunger, need for friendship…)
- To make strides, advance a negotiation or the resolution of a problem, unlock a locked position.
- To get the answer to a question, to get a relevant information, to solve a problem.
- To prove useful
- To treat a mental trauma by expressing it, hoping understanding from others.
- Altruism, kindness
- Instinct: survival, survival of the species, feeding, etc... Or consequence of an injunction
- Expressing emotion

Negative intentions:

- Flattery, toadying.
- Belittling, minimizing, pretending to be of the same opinion for private gain or jealousy.
- Aggression (in order to change the other's opinions, or to make him do (or not do!) a certain task)
- Lying, wanting to hide some fact, ensure that the other has no chance to find out.
- Hysteria, illogical behavior, non-sound mind, paranoia, wickedness, stupidity (adhesion to an incoherent model)
- To hide ignorance, pretending to know the truth even when stating falsehoods.

Ambivalent intentions:

- To make understand or accept a belief, a social rule. At the extreme, to cause the other to accept an article of faith, even false. To convince the other to subscribe to an ideology (political, religious, etc...) that the speaker want to propagate

230

- To correct the reasoning of the other (Wrongly or rightly)
- To make an admonition (in order to have the other not reproduce a behavior that is considered aggressive, immoral, illogical, irrelevant / distracting, or pointless...)
- To get a personal benefit
- Desire to please (it can sometime be positive: need for conviviality).
- To delete a cause of concern.
- To idealize, not wanting to see the faults of the other or the wrongness of a proposition (blindness).
- To push the other into a corner, to tease: form of aggression or stimulation?
- To justify an assertion or a previous action, to justify yourself.

Neutral intentions:

- To want a certain task performed by another (because of personal incapacity, delegation, laziness, efficiency concern, or random choice)
- To change someone else's context, or mind...
- Simply satisfying a need to talk, not to be alone.
- Wanting to be alone, refusing to communicate, Autism... (neutral or negative?) You can also refuse to communicate because you are overloaded, or afraid of losing the thread of your thoughts by being interrupted.
- Testing the capabilities / knowledge of the other
- Playing.

Whew!

The reason I was as specific in this long enumerations of assertions, functions and intentions is that I think that to achieve AI, we need to design from scratch (i.e. program) some high-level agents, and not only low-level agents like Nemes, Nomes and other frames. The definition of a universal language of communication between agents might be necessary in this case for these agents to be able to communicate (Formal languages such as KQML, FOF and CYCL already exist but are probably not well suited for the achievement of a true AI.)

Of course, I do not think that the agents (or agencies) typically communicate with a language expressing nuances as sophisticated as those I just mentioned. However, some agents, such as those that express injunctions on what AI should do and not do will probably need a very rich language to interact with each other. The vast majority of agents, however, will not need such a language, or will only need a small subset of assertive and modalities.

However, we do not necessarily have to define a rich and unambiguous language. Indeed, the ambiguity in some cases is an advantage rather than disadvantage. We often struggle to articulate our thoughts clearly. We often reject the blame on the poverty of language. But in reality, the thoughts themselves are often ambiguous. It is an illusion, Minsky says, to think that there is a clear distinction between "thinking" and "expressing" because the act of expressing is itself an active process that involves simplifying and rebuilding a state mind by detaching diffuse and variable parts from the context... Actually, we tolerate and even encourage the ambiguity of words because we are inherently capable of handling the ambiguity of our own thoughts.

Of course, the use of an ambiguous language may lead to misunderstandings, both because it may happen that we do not agree on the meaning of a symbol, and because the meanings themselves are ambiguous. We must not be afraid of it, because it is inevitable, and it simply means that we must manage to build societies of agents that are tolerant to ambiguity and uncertainty in both thoughts and in communications.
It could well end that the most prevalent form of communication in the society of mind is... the lack of direct communication. Indeed, an indirect communication is often much simpler to implement, using paranomes. As we have said, when a pronome managed by a paranome switches in a certain state, the other pronomes reach the same state (or more precisely a corresponding

state). Communication in this case is not acting through sending a clear direct signal, but indirectly, by simultaneous updating of information. Therefore, different agencies, each having a different representation of the same state or event, can update simultaneously when an agency changes its "vision" in this state or event.

To sum up, the hypothesis of a society of mind seems to be the most complete theory of the mind we have had until now. Being much clearer and more precise than all philosophical theories, it allows many experiments, and provides a framework for further construction of an AI. To finish with it, we need to clarify the many basic mechanisms that allow this great assembly of communicating agents to do something useful, and above all, we must specify the overall organization of the mind. We shall now try to do it.

Levels of organization in the mind

Senses

I would never overemphasize the importance of sensory modalities. Because they are not only used to perceive, but also to visualize and project our perceptions, they are essential to the formation of concepts, and that's why I detailed them extensively at the beginning of this book. A "pure" AI with no sensory modality just cannot exist, because thinking involves the representation of concepts and because this representation is done using sensory imagery.

Our senses are bidirectional. They can build five or six simultaneous representations (the famous limit of short-term memory). Implicitly, this assumes that a sensory modality of a "pure perception" kind, without imaging capability, is useless; because the formation of concepts can only work if there is a way to "see" these concepts.

What senses can be given to a real AI?

Contrary to what Alain Cardon says, I think it will not be necessary, at least initially, to build a robot body, and to equip that body with the equivalent of all of our seven senses. However, there is no doubt that the plurality and synergy of our senses play a major role in shaping our minds and our intellect. To understand the organization of objects that surround us, and that of our own bodies, we use the fact that touch, vision, and proprioception should complete one another. To understand the concepts of temporality, permanence, change, process, and quantity, we use the fact that vision and hearing go together like peaches and cream. Learning to walk involves the senses of balance, vision, and touch. In addition, our emotions can arise from tactile, auditory or visual perceptions.

I think that this synergy is necessary. I think that an AI who would try to manage even a simulated world such as the world of blocks should, to reach a true awareness of what it handles, perceive the simulated world through several different sensory channels, including at least vision and touch (and perhaps hearing, as the child feels pleasure when a tower of blocks collapses in a big wham).

But an AI, being not a biological entity but a being made of silicon, can have sensory modalities that we do not even dare to imagine having someday. Better than that, you can add new senses to it during its own operation!

For example, a sense of time (with a wake-up functionality), a sense of the graph topology, a radar or sonar sense, infrared vision to see in the dark, a "sense of Internet web" to perceive directly the pages and files on the web, a radio sense to communicate using WI-FI, a "computing sense" that would allow the AI to "see" automatically and unconsciously solutions to arbitrarily complex numerical calculations, etc.

But the most useful sense for an AI will certainly be the "sense of code". This will allow it to "see", "feel" and "change" the computer code of a program as easily as we move our arms (I have already shown that this simple gesture is not so simple at all and relies on the coordination of a large number of agents and unconscious processes, and it will be the same for the sense of code). The sense of code is the gateway to self-change and self-improvement of the AI itself. Therefore, we will investigate a little further how this sense of the code might look like. An AI provided with a sense of code would be like a man who could change at will the operation, and even the architecture, of his own brain! A possibility, which we can only dream about...

We see standing out here a first very important characteristic of a true artificial intelligence (TAI): a TAI will not think "like a human." The thought of a TAI will be different from that of a human, because a TAI will use different sensory modalities, and because its architecture is different, being built not on neurons but on a massive network of communicating agents. An artificial intelligence will not be "a copy of human intelligence." An AI is an AI. An AI may evolve not only by learning new skills and ways of using knowledge, but also by changing its own functioning, its own internal processes, something we are incapable.

I believe with some reason, that any AI that have this capability will become, very fast, *super-intelligent*. But let us leave this subject, we will talk extensively later about it.

(iv) Concepts

We saw in the first chapter of this book how the formation of concepts such as "red", "five", or "triangular light bulb", was based on the sensory modalities and their imagery.

Drew McDermott, in his book "artificial intelligence meets natural stupidity" (!) highlights the fact that the first step to an AI is to *notice* the topic. Not to understand, but to notice. Every child will immediately notice that the phrase "Peter Piper picked a peck of pickled peppers" was sounding repetitive, which makes him laugh, even if he knows nothing about the concept of alliteration. In a program of classical AI, the symbol "hamburger" is not attached to a "hamburgerity" nor to a detection of a "hamburgerness", despite the fact that however a true concept of hamburger should contain these. A philosopher would say that the symbol "hamburger" has a semantic because it refers to an external reality, but the program has no way to notice this alleged reference. This reference does not change the behavior of the AI, nor does it give rise to new processing.

Eliezer S. Yudkowsky, a founder of the "Singularity Institute for Artificial Intelligence", extends this idea and argues that to truly understand something, we must pass through a sequence he calls RNUI for *Represent, Notice, Understand, and Invent.*

Represent comes just before *Notice*: Before you build a percepts sensor in a sensory modality, you must have data structures (or their equivalent in terms of agents such as Nemes) for the data

236

under consideration and the characteristics collected. You will notice the alliteration in "Peter Piper picked a peck" only if you already have a detector for repetitions.

Understand comes before *Invent*: Before designing a new bike, you must know how to differentiate between good and bad bikes, collect the structure of goals and subgoals, *understand* what a human expects from the design of a bicycle, why this bike was designed in such a manner, and be able to represent these explanations and note the differences between these explanations and a load of crap about bicycles. Only this way can an AI invent a new bike and explain it to someone else.

Represent means that the skeleton of a cognitive structure, or the entry and exit of a function, or the description of a thought, can be represented in a mind. Represent is static; it is the materialization of a state. The "represent" function does not know the difference between data that constitute a thought or those coming from a random generator.

Notice adds a dynamic aspect to the data, strengthening internal relationships and internal consistency. The *notice* function generates the extractors of features that add to the data simple facts about relationships, causal links, obvious similarities, temporal and spatial progressions, a few predictions and expectations, and everything that falls within the "laws of physical world" area. *Notice* is bi-directional and can manipulate perceptions, making choices between what is important and what is not, and directly edit the resulting representations.

Understand is concerned with intentionality and external relationships. The processes taking place at this level ensure consistency with other cognitive structures, and alignment with higher levels of representation (what is part of a whole) and lower (parts). Understanding involves knowledge and behaviors that result from the chains of goals and structures of causality. It involves heuristics that link high-level aspects and low level features. This means being able to distinguish what is "good" or useful, what is "bad" or useless. To understand something, we must be able to represent a cognitive structure that will be necessary to invent something and verify that this conception is right, or gives a good explanation of a phenomenon.

To invent is the ability to design a bicycle, to invent a heuristic to analyze a phenomenon, to create a plan in a game of chess, or in a word, to think.

Note that the "RNUI" approach can be applied to a mind as a whole as well as its sub-parts, and specially the processes *represent, notice, understand*, and *invent* can internally recursively contain sub RNUI procedures!

(v) Thoughts

As we already said in Chapter 1, thoughts are arrangements of concepts. A typical example is a sentence in natural language: a sequence of words arranged according to a grammar. To understand a sentence, we must find the target of ambiguous words (an adjective needs a name as a target, for example), and these targets are found either in the sentence or the concepts that are activated when we think of the sentence. Conversely, when a fact is noticed, this creates a thought, which can be articulated clearly in our mind if the attention of consciousness is focused on what was just noticed.

However, thoughts are not necessarily expressed in words; there are non-verbal thoughts, arrangements of concepts arising from the visual system, touch, etc. There are also abstract thoughts that are not immediately related to a sensory modality, but only to some abstract concepts. Thoughts arise when there is a sufficiently rich environment for interaction between concepts and their arrangement in different "grammars".

Our mind is constantly creating new thoughts, either when new concepts are invented or when similarities or differences between concepts are found. But for a thought to be preserved, and recorded as "interesting", that thought must be useful and meet a goal. Many goals and sub goals are active in our minds, and those that are related to thoughts are even more interesting.

One of the operations of our minds to create new thoughts is the algorithm called *generate-and-test*: We begin by considering a model, looking for patterns, connections, covariance, etc. Then, we generate possible models to explain these regularities, we use available knowledge to "fill in the blanks", and we test the predictions of the new model.

However, this does not explain everything: for example answering the question "why?" is not easy with generate-and-test; in fact, generate-and-test is a variant of the famous jack-of-all-trades AI algorithm, namely the search for a solution through exploration. It is likely that mining algorithms, not really blind but not really conscious either (as they involve elements of chance), are responsible for the "aha!" intuitive leaps that we observe in our thoughts. However, in general it is better to step back and try to think about the problem itself, by abstraction.

To abstract is to lose information. This is losing unnecessary information to gain generality. You start the problem with unknown variables for things that you do not know, and you look at places where the unknowns vanish, giving conditions that should hold true for every possible solution, and therefore limit the research area. More generally, you try to apply heuristics to the information available on the current problem (the goal), to obtain general information about the desired answer.

The Thought level of is a complex one, as complex as those of sensory modalities or concepts, and there is no simple way to describe it. Thoughts are holistic entities that link low-level and high-level concepts together with plans, goals and convergences.

The Mind and The Machine

A thought is something that has a consistency at all levels and that resists change, a model rich enough to take into account what we call smart thinking.

If we let the system run freewheel, it would create thousands (or millions) of thoughts every second, and most of these thoughts would be irrelevant. (When we design a bicycle, we imagine the wheels made with metal, maybe plastic, but *not* with tapioca pudding). Therefore, as we said in Chapter 1, there are thought filters, which retain only "interesting" thoughts.

These filters use thoughts about thoughts. It is a form of introspection that is useful, because to think of new thinking actually creates a new thought, and that this is an additional mechanism for creation of interesting thoughts. Conversely having the idea "this thought is stupid" usually activates a censor, which removes the thought in question.

This brings us directly to the mechanism of creation of ideas. How do we get ideas?

(vi) Ideas

Consider the following (well-known) problem: Here are *nine dots* arranged in a square matrix. Can you draw *four* straight *lines*, crossing *all* nine dots, *without* lifting your pencil from the "paper»?

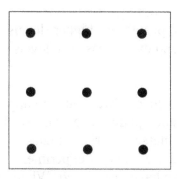

Try this... is not so easy. So you have an idea? I'll give the answer later. If you do not know this problem, I recommend you take a pencil and find a solution: it really worth the trouble. It is a perfect kind of "lateral" thinking!

Ideas are a particular type of thoughts that lead to new concepts trough the sudden "crystallization" of many concepts and ideas into a single concept Our mind makes new ideas by generalizing some concepts and thoughts, or otherwise by specializing them, or by creating a concept to express the differences among several others, or between different thoughts.

We seem to invent new ideas with disconcerting ease:

The images below all activate the concept of "square". In the right image, we even see two squares, the "outside" square, and an "inner" square inclined at 45 degrees:

Yet none of these images is the archetypal concept of "square"! To recognize the image of a square in these figures, we have to invent new concepts of representation of a square, and to add these concepts to our pre-existing concept of a "square". This shows that sometimes perception, often seen only as an "input process to the system", in fact appealed to higher levels of the mind, like concepts, thoughts and even ideas. The levels of the mind are often intertwined!

Seeing this list of "square", we want to supplement it and invent new ways to represent squares. The primitive notion that we know of "four lines that intersect at right angles" seems suddenly even more primitive, and we want to experiment with this new wider concept of square we have discovered. Where do these desires and ideas of new square come from?

The origin of ideas is often seen as mystical, indescribable. It is the flash of understanding, the "aha" of a genius, inventiveness. Actually we must always remember that ideas are thoughts, and that their origin is not different from that of other thoughts.

Having said that, what characterizes creativity and invention?

It is impossible to draw a line between understanding and creativity. Sometimes the solution to a difficult problem must be invented, often from almost nothing. Sometimes creating a new entity is not done by looking at all possible ways, but by seeing *the* only possibility, looking deeper into the information that you already own. But in general, when you are looking to build a model of the world, trying to understand something, you want a single solution: *the* answer; yet then when you want to build something new, you are looking for *any* response to the question. Understanding is easier, because you know that the solution already exists and the problem is only to find it. The problem constraints are then providing clues to help finding this solution.

The difference between understanding and inventing is about the same as between testing a solution (understanding), and finding a solution (invention) or, for mathematicians, between P and NP. To invent, you start with a high-level feature that is desirable, and you specify the low-level structure that creates this feature. You need to engage in a hierarchical design process, starting for example from the goal of "moving quickly using only muscle power", to the solution consisting of the actual layout of a bicycle.

Unlike what happens in understanding, where you have the choice between an eventually huge, but finite, number of alternatives, the choices space of creativity is essentially infinite. When you think about the diameter of the wheel of a bike, you can choose between an unlimited number of values, and what you need is a method to link the diameter to other characteristics such as power required, stability, etc. If stability is itself one of the design variables, you have to find a heuristic for connecting it to one or more known quantities, as the rider's weight, his muscle power, the speed to reach, and so on .

However, sometimes this process of "top-down design guided by constraints from the goal" does not work. Sometimes you need to invent a bicycle when you do not even know what a wheel is. Alternatively, you simply lack a starting point to attack the problem. Then suddenly, you remember having seen stones rolling down along a hill, and you get the idea of "something that rolls on the go": you just invented the wheel! Sometimes you get the idea of the solution without even knowing where it came from.

It seems that many "little elves" or agents are launched almost at random, looking for the solution in an immense research area. The key point is the "almost." To find the wheel, there is still the idea of moving. We call creativity the fact that suddenly a lot of data are recalled to our perception, and to our surprise, they match the solution. But there is no miracle. *Any* search for a solution in a large area requires a tremendous mental activity. Instead of wondering where creativity does come from, we should ask ourselves where surprise comes from!

Surprise is a form of thinking about thoughts. A surprise is created when an idea that meets an active goal suddenly links seemingly distant concepts, none of which has been part of our conscious attention for a long time. The creation of a surprise is an entirely mechanical process, probably introduced by evolution: surprise creates fun and pleasure, and allows the mind to memorize new ways of solving problems.

The surprise, when we invent a bicycle, or when we see one for the first time, lies in the huge gap between the goal "traveling fast" and the object "bicycle". Linking the two creates a surprise. We would have hard times imagining a bike before seeing one. Similarly, there is an almost infinite space of possible abstract paintings, and when we see one, we are usually surprised, because a large set of concepts are delivered to us and we call it "creativity".

In fact, creativity occurs when the mind decides to attempt an attack of problem by brute (or slightly guided) force, when a huge (and unconscious) mental work leads to a result. The "aha" of the invention of the wheel comes because somewhere in the background of our mind, countless solutions have been tried until the image of the stone that rolls along the hill becomes obvious, resonates with the problem and come to our attention.

By the way, what about our problem of going through all points of the square? Here is the solution:

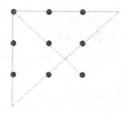

When I was showed this solution for the first time, I exclaimed: "Oh, hey, that's cheating! We have no right to leave the square!"

Really? Reread the question: nothing forbids it! This problem is a classic example of "thinking out of the box". To solve it, you must get out of the constraints that you set to yourself!

We will first test right angles. (Meaning that you constrain yourself to using only horizontal and vertical lines). Then, as it does not work, our mental imaging produces triangles (but with the constraint of lying inside the square). Finally, as it still does not work, you dare go out of the square. Along this process, we did not test a procedure, but a shape that must correspond to the expected result. Only then will we create the procedure.

Note: you can also pass through the nine points in *three* strokes. It takes you even more out of the system (you must fold the paper). Try!

Good! Ideas are thus given birth by a search that in turn is guided by our goals. But where the hell do our goals come from?

The goals and Bayesian reasoning

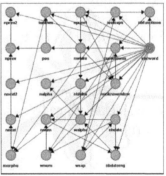

"Bayesian reasoning" is probably at the heart of our understanding of the causes and effects of what happens around us, and as a result of our goals management system.

What is it about? This is the intelligent application of what is called Bayes' theorem (named after the Reverend Thomas Bayes,

1702-1761). Let us show a simple and striking example of what it can provide:

1% of women of forty who undergo a mammogram have breast cancer without knowing it. This examination is fairly reliable, but not completely, so that 80% of women with cancer have a positive result, but 9.6% of women without cancer will also have a positive result (nobody is perfect in this world).

A 40-year woman passed the exam and obtained a positive result. What is the probability that she has breast cancer?

Okay, this is not an easy problem, but intuitively you should have an idea of what this probability may be about, no? Look a little. There is no need to have an exact answer, just a "rough estimate".

No, but look! Reread the statement well and tell me approximately what you think, then move on!

Before I give the answer, I must say that only 15% of the doctors give the right answer. Only 15%? Absolutely, this is not an Internet survey but a true figure, resulting from several concurrent studies.

Hmm. What number have *you* thought of? 70, 90 %?. After all, 80% of women with cancer have a positive outcome. Let us see if you are right.

Take a sample of 10 000 forty years old women. Among these ten thousand women, hundred (1%) have breast cancer, and 80 of them have a positive mammogram. Out of these ten thousand women, 9900 have not breast cancer, and from these 9900, 9900 x 9.6%, or 950 women, will also have a positive result. In short, the number of women who will have a positive result is 80 + 950 or 1030. But among the 1030 women with a positive result, only 80 have cancer. So finally the proportion of women who have cancer knowing that their result is positive is 80: 1030, or only 7.8%.

It is the right answer. A woman who has a positive mammogram has only a 7.8% chance of having cancer. Where is the error? There is no error. It is simply that *the probability of cancer given that the test is positive* (7.8%) has nothing to do with *the probability of a positive result knowing that the woman has cancer* (which is 80%). Do not forget that of our ten thousand women, 950 (9.6%) did not have cancer, but still a positive result.

Usually, we note the probability of event E knowing the fact F this way:

$$p\,(E\mid F).$$

We read that "probability of E knowing F".
In the following, the tilde '~' mean 'no'. For example, p (~ cancer) means "probability of not having cancer". And obviously

p(~cancer) = 1 - p(cancer).

If we note "cancer" the event "to have breast cancer", "~ Cancer" the fact of not having breast cancer, "positive" the fact of having a positive outcome, and "~ positive" the fact of having a negative test, then the problem is as follows:

> *If*   p (cancer) = 1%,
> *And*   p (positive | cancer) = 80%
> *And*   p (positive | ~cancer) = 9,6 %,
> *Then*   What is p (cancer | positive)?

The answer is, of course, our 7.8%. How have we calculated it?

Firstly, note that one should not confuse p (cancer | positive), the sought proportion of women with cancer knowing that their result is positive, with p (cancer and positive), the proportion of women who have at the same time cancer *and* a positive result. Of the ten thousand women, hundred have breast cancer, and 80 of them have a positive mammogram, so that
p (cancer AND positive) is 80:10000 that is 0,8%.

Actually, p (cancer AND positive) is

The Mind and The Machine

p (cancer) x p (positive | cancer), that is 1 % x 80 % = 0,8 %

To calculate our 7.8%, i.e. p (cancer | positive), we divided p (cancer and positive) by p (positive), noting that p (positive) = p (positive AND cancer) + p (~ cancer AND positive)

Finally, here is the general form of Bayes' theorem (do not worry, it does not bite, it is just a formula with additions, multiplication and division):

$$p (A \mid X) = \frac{p (X \mid A) \times p (A)}{p (X \mid A) \times p (A) + p (X \mid {\sim}A) \times p ({\sim}A)}$$

What we must realize is that the theorem allows changing an *a priori* probability such as p (A) or p (cancer), to an adjusted probability value such as p (A | X) or p (cancer | positive), by knowing a new fact (here the positive outcome of the examination).

It is found that the quantities that are on the right side of the equal sign are very often, what we know of a problem. Quantities such as p (X | A) and p (X | ~ A), or p (positive | cancer) and p (positive | ~cancer) are involving *cause and effect relationships*.

For example p (positive | cancer) is known because mammography is *designed* to search for cancer: one wishes that a result is positive *because* the woman has cancer. Even if it an examination was performed from a group of women at risk, in which the proportion of cancers would be 10% rather than 1%, p (positive | cancer) would still be 80%, because the device does not change. p (positive | cancer) is a value that stems from the design of the machine, and only that. More generally, p (X | A) is a simple fact, from which other facts as p (A AND X) can be constructed. But Bayes' theorem has the form it has because *it helps to think about the physical world*: this is not yet another formula for mathematicians. It is useful in everyday life.

Instead of writing p (X | A), we could write p (A => X) and read it "the probability that A implies X", or "that A is the cause of X". Nevertheless, the habit is to write p (X | A). It is very unfortunate.

Okay, the Bayes theorem, it is interesting. However, what connection does it have with *what happens in our minds and our goals management system?*

First, this theorem allows finding the *most likely cause* C of an effect X: Of all the possible causes C1, C2, etc., it is the one that has the largest value for p (X | C). Is this reasoning really happening in our minds?

Here is a little story:

Suppose that, when I was a child, I noticed that when I threw a pebble in water, I heard a splashing sound, and then I saw rings in the water. For one reason or another, I liked seeing the rings in the water, I wanted to see them again, but there is no other stone at my disposal to resume. What can I do?

At this stage, my *goal* is to see new rings in the water, I am interested in anything that can make circles in water, anything that has a causal link with a ring in the water, and I noticed that the splash was related to circles in the water (with a correlation of, say, 95%). The next question is: is there anything I can do to cause an event that is causally linked to a circle in the water? Yes, I can shout "splash!" and see if it makes a circle in the water!

Clearly, I express the assumption that the splashing sound is the *cause* of the circles in the water.

I do not know how to calculate yet, but the neurons of my internal goals management system can. They found a 95% correlation between splash and rings in the water (not 100% because I have already seen waves in water, which made no splash), and they hypothesized that the splash sound is the cause of the rings in the water (say, with a certainty of 80% at the moment).

If the hypothesis is correct, and if I shout, there is a 95% chance that it will makes a ring in the water. If my hypothesis is false, and if I shout, there is no way this makes a circle in the water.

As I believe only to 80% to my hypothesis, this leads to a 95% x 80% = 76% chance that if I shouted "splash!" I would see a circle in the water.

Now, if I did not shout, there is, say, a 3% chance that I still see a circle, because the correlation between splashing and the rings is not perfect, and because an outside event I do not control (e.g. an animal) can still cause a ring in the water.

Suppose my goal "making circles in the water" has a *desirability* of 100. If I shout, it will have a 76% chance of making a circle. The desirability of "shouting" is then 76. Suppose that the cost of the action "shouting" is estimated at 10. The net desirability of "shouting" is 66. Conversely, "not shouting" leads with a 3% chance to an event (the rings) of desirability 100. The cost of "do not shout" is zero. The net desirability net of "do not shout" is then 3.

The differential desirability resulting from the choice is therefore 66-3 = 63, which is positive. I *decided* to scream.

I shouted: "splash!" and watched it... nothing happens.

What does this mean? Should I shout again to see what will happen? In fact my goal system then applies Bayes' theorem again! The problem is the following:

If   p (shoutingMakesRings) = 80%,
And   p (IsawRings | shoutingMakesRings) = 95%,
And   p (IsawRings | ~ shoutingMakesRings) = 3%,
Then

p (shoutingMakesRings | ~IsawRings) = ?

Let us apply the theorem again: the new value of confidence in the hypothesis shoutingMakesRings, knowing that I have not seen any round is, by applying Bayes' formula,
80% x (100% - 5%) / (80% x 5% + 20% x (100% - 97%)) = **17%!**

My confidence in my hypothesis has been reduced from 80% to 17% by my little experiment.

Should I re-shout "splash"? If I shout again, there is more than 17% x 95% = 16% chance to see a circle in the water. If I do not shout, there is still a 3% chance of seeing a circle in the water because of a fish for example. The desirability of my goal "see circles in the water" is still 100, the cost of the action "shouting splash!" is still

10, and thus the net desirability of "shouting" is 16 - 10 - 3 = + 3, which is still positive (but less than 63 we found a moment ago).

I decided to scream again. I shout "splash" and nothing happens. Now, a second application of Bayesian reasoning reduces the confidence in my hypothesis "shouting makes rings" from 16% to 1%, it suffices to say that it is almost sure now I was mistaken.

The desirability of "shouting for a third time" becomes -12, which is negative, so I do not scream anymore and I find another way to amuse myself.

We have just seen two fascinating mechanisms at work: how can a decision be made, and how we can challenge our assumptions in light of new facts.

Let us be clear: a young child (even an adult!) does not know consciously how to calculate as we have just done. However, I claim that the circuits of our unconscious brain can. Moreover, if we create one day an artificial intelligence (something that, as we shall see, is a near certainty in the short term), it would be a good idea to provide her with "Bayesian reasoning modules" to make these calculations.

A question immediately arises: is our mind working this way? Is there an innate knowledge of Bayes' theorem? Of course not: our mind is probably not performing internal calculations as precise and accurate as those we have just done. But it is very likely it performs some approximate calculations that lead to similar results. *There are* services responsible for assessing the desirability of an action in our mind, and also services responsible for maintaining the consistency of assumptions we make about the world around us.

The fact that we can *model* the action of these services through Bayesian reasoning gives us an idea of how it might work. To create an AI, we will not need to understand the details of these services, we can consider them as "black boxes" equipped with inputs and outputs, and Bayesian modeling suffice. With any luck, these internal services of our AI will work even better than the original in the human brain!

Curiously, there are few "classical" AI systems that use Bayesian reasoning. AI experts prefer to build systems that use formal logic, such as expert systems or "truth maintenance systems", to systems that use fuzzy logic (as in the context of Bayesian reasoning, nothing is sure, there are only degrees of confidence), because these systems are much less efficient in computation time. This is probably a mistake.

Desires and impulses

Humans, like all mammals, undoubtedly acquire much of their first goals and desires by imitation and attachment. The child recognizes his mother, imitates her, and comes to discern what he likes and what does not please him: better, very quickly, what pleases the child is what pleases his mother, and what displeases his mother is what the child dislike! In this learning by attachment, we learn not only *how to* accomplish certain tasks and goals, but *what* goals we should have and in what situations having a particular goal is useful. Rewards and punishments that we get from people we are attached to (our parents in general), teach us what purposes it is good to have, and not to have.

However, for the child to achieve this by learning attachment, considerable expertise and capabilities are first required.

How do human beings learn their first goals and desires, from which all others derive? A number of these goals are probably innate. Minsky suggests that in the minds of very young children, the first agencies and first services are *protospecialists*: agencies that produce highly evolved behaviors that are solutions to problems such as locomotion, obtaining food, reflexes of sucking and chewing, imitation, the baby's attachment to his mother, etc.. To build an AI, we will probably need to directly program some of those protospecialists. Over time, they will evolve and differentiate into more and more specialized services.

The problem is that what we call "desires" and "instincts" are protospecialists that are already considerably advanced. To get to program the protospecialist that corresponds to the instinct of imitation, or to the pleasure of sucking one's thumb, we should already have a whole armada of protospecialists, representations, and agencies of a lower level.

Following a conventional view in psychology, desires and impulses are linked to pleasure and pain. It is by feeling our first pleasures that we develop our first desires, it is through our first feelings of pain and sadness that we develop our first negative desires (anti-desires), and our first censors. But where do pleasure and pain come from?

Pleasure and pain

The marquis de Sade

Intuitively, pleasure and pain arise from an "overload" of certain sensory modalities, which tends to focus conscious attention on the "over weighted" perception. The study of the brain, however, shows that there are centers of pleasure and pain, areas of the brain where specific treatments of these sensations take place. The ventral tegmental area in the center of the brain plays an important role in what is called the reward circuit. In this area, the brain produces dopamine, a chemical messenger that induces the mind to reinforce behaviors meeting its "basic needs" and to repeat the behavior at the origin of pleasure.

There is also a circuit of punishment, which involves different brain structures including the hypothalamus, thalamus and central gray matter surrounding the aqueduct of Sylvius. Secondary centers are also in the amygdala and hippocampus. This circuit works in the brain with acetylcholin and stimulates ACTH (adrenal cortico-trophic hormone), the hormone that stimulates the adrenal gland to release adrenalin for preparing bodies for escape or fight.

Finally, pleasure and pain are used by the mind to seek and retain our overall behavior:

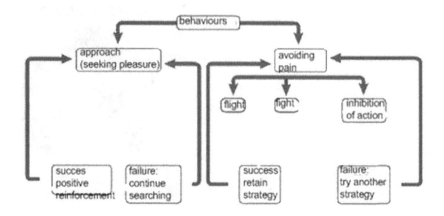

We will return to the determination of overall conduct of the mind further, when we speak of "laws of humanotics".

The fact that there is a "hardware", or "brainware" to be more precise, which manages pleasure and pain poses an interesting question: if we want to create an intelligent machine, a true AI (TAI), how to simulate these mechanisms?

Eliezer Yudkowsky brings an original answer to this question. For him, it is not necessary for an AI to have centers of pleasure and pain; similar behaviors can be achieved simply by... using Bayes' theorem, let him.

What is important is not the mechanism of pleasure and pain, but the fact that there are positive and negative feedback, i.e. mechanisms for strengthening or inhibiting our behaviors. Pleasure and pain need something to focus on in order to give a useful behavior (e.g. flee, or fight against the cause of pain). Of course, pain is more than a negative feedback; pain has a signaling function of damage and injury, it focuses attention on what is painful, and it pushes us to think of ways to escape the painful sensation.

In the architecture of the human brain, pain can exist even if there is no way to avoid it, even if there is nothing useful to focus about, and a human can go crazy after unbearable and constant pain; but it is only a result of the evolution of our brain. This seems a non-adaptive behavior, but in the ancestral environment, an individual who was experiencing continuous and unbearable pain usually died shortly after, and it had no influence on genes.

Actually, when designing an AI, we are not obliged to follow what evolution did, and we can devise mechanisms to enhance or inhibit behaviors that would exist only if there is a goal to focus upon. Inhibition can be achieved simply by a sub-goal. We have seen how a child has inhibited the behavior of "shouting splash!" to make circles in the water" using Bayesian reasoning.

Say you want to cross a room, you are distracted by something and you slip on a banana peel. The pain you had when falling will make you be more careful next time, watching where you put your feet.

However, an intelligent robot that ignores what pleasure and pain are may also, after slipping on the banana peel, say:

"Hmm. The fact that I was distracted by something caused that I stepped on the banana, which has caused the fact that I slipped and lengthened the time to cross the room, which interfered with (whatever) *super-goal that I had to cross the room. Therefore I will increase the priority of behaviors that will avoid that I set foot on a banana peel (and a little research shows that this can be achieved by looking the ground more often), and I'll lower the priority of behaviors that led me to being distracted, and drew my attention to the distractor "*

In addition, if the robot broke a finger falling, he can also say: *"If I put extra stress on the fracture my finger, it will be worse because I will reduce my ability to cross the following rooms, which is necessary for my super-goal. Therefore I'll get up and keep walking ignoring my fractured little metal finger, but also I will write down on the list of my goals the fact I'll better have this finger repaired as soon as possible"*

All functions of pain have been fulfilled and replaced by this reasoning! Similarly, an AI that solves a problem successfully will increase the priority of agents who helped solve the problem, which has ultimately the same effect as pleasure. In other words, Yudkowsky argues that pleasure and pain are "evolutionary accident" due to the history of our genes, but their functions can be well satisfied by a (Bayesian) reasoning on goals. This architecture is even better than what exists in humans as an AI that has solved a problem can then try to improve not only processes and agents who have helped solving the problem, but also all services and agencies that could have (in retrospect) led to a small improvement, or even those that have failed but have *almost* succeeded!

Why did evolution then create pleasure and pain, if their functions could be fulfilled by the management system of our goals? Evolution does not create the most adaptive systems, it creates the most adaptive systems *and* easiest to evolve. Before the advent of general intelligence, a system of deliberate goals like the one we have just described would have been impossible. When intelligence emerged, a system of reward-punishment based on pleasure and pain was already in place, and replacing it would have been useless.

Note that agents that manage the goals systems, leading to enhancement or inhibition of behaviors can be labeled "centers of pleasure and pain", but these are just labels: their inner workings remain unchanged, based on Bayesian reasoning and not on the propagation of signals of pleasure or pain as in the human mind.

If we want we can add to the AI a frame (or neme) of "pleasure" or "pain", containing a numerical value, and ensure that the value of "pleasure" is incremented when we reach a goal, and that the value of "pain" increases when an external (or body) accident prevents us from achieving a goal, or delays the solution. What more would it bring to AI? Nothing, said Yudkowsky. One cannot help but think that this could bring more humanity to our AI... Yudkowsky neglects the fact that although pleasure and pain are certainly processes for reinforcement and inhibition of behaviors, pain (and also sensual and sexual pleasure) are rooted in events that affect our bodies and our bodies only. Moreover, having a body, a "physicality" and being aware of it, is a dominant feature of a human being. Pleasure and pain are powerful engines for acquiring this knowledge of having a body. An AI that would be a pure program would probably have difficulties understanding what we mean by pleasure and pain. For her, it would be nothing but an intellectual concept, such as adding 1 to an indicator that is then used by the services responsible for adjusting our overall behavior. That seems a bit simplistic...

It is often said that pleasure and pain are the "ultimate" super-goals of a human being; that we actually only seek to maximize our pleasure (present and future) and to avoid pain (present and future as well). As a consequence, all intelligent beings are essentially selfish! In fact, the factor that is actually a super-goal is the anticipation of future pleasure and pain; and when the pleasure or pain effectively happens, the decisions that led to it had already been taken.

A more subtle error is to believe that pleasure and pain are, by definition, essential components of the goal system of an intelligent being. This means, in essence, that any indicator of success becomes a de facto super-goal of the system. The piece of code (program) that says *"ha ha! A task was successfully completed! Let us increase the pleasure value by one!"* becomes more important than the goal of the task itself. In the novel *The ultimate secret* by Bernard Werber, or in *Death by Ecstasy* by Larrry Niven, the hero dies from too much pleasure because it has an electrode in the head, connected directly to his center of pleasure, and that he cannot help stimulate, in a kind of pleasure short-circuit.

Firstly, note that the "code snippet" which notes that a goal has been accomplished needs not to be an autonomous system, like the pleasure center in a human brain. This can be a conscious or unconscious thought, as we have shown.

Then, if an indicator of success is confused with the success itself, why not an indicator of indicator of success to be confused with the indicator? Where will it stop?

If the mind has a really "fun meter", indicating how many goals he has succeeded, and if the mind praised its "real goal" is to increment the counter, what will prevent it from taking all available memory for storing bits of this counter, and even to create new memories, transforming the solar system in silicon chips along the way? Even better, what will prevent it from thinking that its goal is to think of ways to store ever-greater integer numbers, or even thinking that its real aim is to *believe* that it keeps storing ever-greater integers, replacing the success counter by his own beliefs about this counter? Or will it stop there?

If we want to build an AI, especially an AI with self-modifiable programs (and we shall see later that the construction of a self-improving *seed* AI is the easiest way to do this), we must be careful not to fall into such traps!

The last problem is perhaps the most difficult because it deals with beliefs that AI may have towards its own goals. If the AI sees its system of goals as a sub-goal of the goals themselves, then the kind of "short circuit" and endless climbing we just highlighted is an obvious design error. Remember that the *anticipation* of pleasure, not pleasure itself, does influence our decisions. An AI who sees a huge increase in the variable "pleasure" because of an error in the design of its system of goals, would not say "oh boy!", but "yeah, great!" The AI, thinking of the future she would like to belong to, is examining to what extent its *own* super-goals have been achieved, not the super-goals of the *future* AI.

Let us remember this: an AI should not identify with her own future version if it presents such "short-circuit of pleasure."

Learning super goals

Imagine a baby whose goal is to fill a cup with water. He tried first with a fork, but it does not work. Then he tried with a spoon, and then it works. What he learned then? That to fill a cup, a good idea is to use a spoon. Specifically, the success of the experience leads the baby to install "use a spoon" as a sub-goal of " fill a cup" in his system of goals. Learning sub-goals is very important because that is the way we learn to solve small problems of everyday life, dividing them into sub-problems. It is a strategy that works. The *pride of being successful* teaches us what methods should be used, i.e. which sub-goals we should have, while the *disappointment* teaches us what methods should not be used. All this of course is based on Bayesian reasoning, as we have seen, and is well known to psychologists.

However, a question arises: we know how to add sub-goals to the goals that we already have. But how to install super-goals *above* the existing ones? This is an interesting question! The standard answer is that we do *not* create super-goals: All goals of our values system are subgoals of the ultimate goal that we have already spoken, "maximize the anticipated pleasure". But it is a biased answer: it is true, of course, but we may still need to find new goals to place above the current active ones, although they remain sub-goals of the ultimate goal.

The theory of "elevator" answers this question. According to this theory, super-goals are created by the emotions of *pride* and *shame,* the same way emotions of satisfaction and failure are the basis for the generation of subgoals. Let us see how: When you were little and your mother complimented you for what you came to do (albeit accidentally), the pride that you felt led you not only to remember how you had to accomplish this task, but moreover that the goal you had was a goal it was really good to have!

Children learn their super-goals by imitating the people whom they are attached to, their parents or heroes, and feeling pride when they are congratulated. Similarly, when scolded, the shame they experience tells them what super-goals they had rather drop.

This means that in our minds there is a "super-ego" (Freud's superego!) observing the reactions of those around us to our actions, and managing the emotions of pride and shame. In turn, these emotions activate the memorization (or forgetting) of our super-goals.

In AI, this super-ego may include a table of correspondence between different types of actions and the "numerical" values of pride and shame that they imply. I have already given under "how agents communicate" a list of positive and negative intentions tied to speech acts. We just need to extend this table to other classes of actions. The result is a true set of moral values, which guide the choice of the goals of AI.

This super-ego could be coded by hand, but of course it could be more practical to realize only one part of it, and let the AI learn the rest during its "education". The hardest part, however, remains the recognition of rewards and punishments from others. In human beings, it seems that much of this mechanism is pre-wired in the brain.

However, before speaking of the superego, we had better talk about the self.

The sense of self

When we speak of sense of self, a large number of philosophical problems arise, such as self-*consciousness*, the *qualia*, "what it means to be a mouse", etc. We will approach this broad discussion "by the side", placing first a simple question:

When can we legitimately use the word "I" and "me"?

How can I say "I" or "me" (or can an AI say "I" or "me")? How come I can say, "*I* want a vanilla ice cream" with nobody arguing that this word *I* had less significance than R2D2, and could be translated as R2D2 without changing anything? How could R2D2 *link* the word "I" with the concept of "R2D2" ?

A model and the reality it represents can be linked in various ways by various forms of linkage:

it may be a *perceptive* connection (I see things and I report these perceptions in the model), or a *predictive* one (I can, using model, predict what will happen in reality), or further a *decisional* one (I can decide, in view of the model to influence a particular factor) or even a *manipulative* one (I can manipulate reality according to what I decided). This connection between the model and reality starts when the model corresponds in a way to real elements, it becomes testable when the model can predict the result of some actions, it becomes useful when the model can be used for deciding between several alternatives, with the further ability to manipulate reality to make it evolve toward the chosen alternative.

Let us also remember, as we have written under "concepts" in Chapter 4, that to truly understand a concept, you must go through the sequence RNUI for *Represent, Notice, Understand*, and *Invent*.

Representing the "self" is not difficult; just create a neme or frame called "self". Naturally, this does not get us anywhere because this neme or frame is not different from that of "R2D2"…

The next step in self-consciousness is to *notice* information about yourself. The introspective sensations are difficult to distinguish from external sensations, and therefore this action of noticing is not enough as long there are no concepts to introspection. A robot that has just been hit on the nose can say "look, this robot has been hit on the nose" What is implied by *this robot* is the key that will allow or not to replace "this robot has…" by "I was...". The AI that controls the robot needs to know that "this robot" is "the robot that is handled by this AI", and that "this AI is the AI that has this system of goals and values, and which collects information from this robot and give it orders"

The model of the self that is in the AI will start to generate new information (information that will impose a coherent view of events internal to the AI), only when it can understand and make *predictions*. For example, it may predict that "putting attention from one subject to another, instead of focusing on a single subject, produces structures of concepts that are connected mainly by association." This information will only be useful if it plays a role in choosing the current goals of AI, i.e. it is a *decisional* binding that will eventually allow to *invent* new actions and new concepts, and to manipulate the production of goals.

Let us call TAI (for True Artificial Intelligence) this AI that has a perceptive, predictive, decision-making and manipulative binding towards his own system of concepts, thoughts and goals. When TAI can create introspective concepts and formulate ideas and heuristics about herself, she will be able to reason about herself in the same way she reasons about objects in the outside world. She will be able to manipulate the internal reality in the same way that external reality. If TAI is super powerful to invent bicycles, she will be super powerful to manipulate TAI.

However, to say "TAI understands TAI" is not the same thing as saying "TAI understands herself." Douglas Lenat, the designer of the CYC system, which we discuss in the next chapter, said that CYC knows that there is an entity called CYC, and knows that CYC is a computer system, but he does not know that *he* is CYC. If TAI has an RNUI binding system to its own model, it is more than enough for TAI to say "TAI wants a vanilla ice cream." But to say "*I* want a vanilla ice cream", something more is needed. Yes, but what?

According to Eliezer Yudkowsky, and funny enough, you just need to consider that this is a real problem and it is solved. If you really need another step for her to say "I want a vanilla ice cream", there must be a qualitative difference between "TAI wants a vanilla ice cream" and "I want a vanilla ice cream". And that is the answer.

You can say "I" when the behavior generated by you modeling yourself is materially different (because of self-reference) than the behavior generated by modeling another AI that you look like.

This does not occur in an individual thought, but in a chain of thoughts. Every thought A is of type "B modifies C". If finally one of these thoughts modifies A, the system as a whole will have a different behavior that is characteristic of a real perception of self. And then TAI can legitimately say, "I want a vanilla ice cream". Welcome to TAIland!

The narrative thread and interior monologue

We humans have an inner monologue, a "narrative thread" of consciousness by which we seem to talk to ourselves. However, in reality the mind has many loops of this kind, possibly (and even mostly) non-verbal. Each time one of our services enables a sensory imagery of our senses, the low-level agents of the sensory system will interpret it as a true perception, i.e. there is creation of percepts, concepts, thoughts, goals and decisions, thereby leading to a true loop. It is even likely that the high-level services of our minds communicate this way, by activating sensory imagery of other services.

We saw in the section "how agents communicate" that the definition of a universal language of communication between agents was a difficult problem. In reality, there may be no problem: high-level services communicate through "internal sensory modalities". A service A will enable a sensory modality of another service B, which in turn activate the sensory imagery of A, thus creating a loop of thoughts, which eventually converge towards an original idea.

I called these interfaces MMI, for "machine-machine interfaces" in contrast to HMI, human-machine interfaces. The MMI exempts the need for a universal language of communication between agents, because the activation of sensory imagery is a universal language. This well includes a MMI that activates the visual imagery, and thus allows spatial reasoning, a MMI that specializes in the treatment of trees and graphs, and allows for example the management tree of goals and causes, and a MMI specialized in language. The famous narrative thread would then be the loop generated by the "language" MMI when it would talk to itself, wearing the resulting ideas to the attention of consciousness.

What makes then the "language MMI" so specific? Why is it almost the single loop reaching our consciousness? Because language allows the expression of an unlimited number of thoughts, and indeed, all thoughts!

Consider a verbal exchange between human beings, a hundred thousand years ago:

Kalim-hero (eating): "good, eating, good!"
Bully-Bastard: "eh! Me want food too!"
Kalim-hero: "Grr! No No!"
Bully- Bastard: (grabbing the meat of his colleague): "ek ek! You give!"
Kalim-hero (angry): "no happy, no happy!"
Bully- Bastard: "Me stronger than you. If you not happy, me break jaws to you"
Kalim-hero: "it really too... unfair!"

During this brief exchange, Kalim-hero has invented a complex concept, that of injustice. What happened in his mind? How have the agents who represents the mind of Kalim-hero recorded this abstract concept? It is certainly possible that this may be done by a series of rules like:

If a human K has property F
and that another man B wants F,
and K is weaker than B,
and that K does not want to give F to B,
and B takes F to K,
then the action of B is unfair, and K a feeling of injustice.

However, creating these rules from the experience of B (Bully-Bastard) is a considerable mental work! It is much easier for agents in the mind of K to simply record the dialog that took place, just replacing the names "Bully-Bastard" "Food" and "Kalim-hero" by variables such as B , F and K. Later, if necessary, Kalim-hero could, by focusing on the dialog, trigger all mental imagery that is attached the label "situations of injustice" and this imagery can then be modified at will.

The way it can so easily generalize rules of behavior reinforces the importance of the "language" MMI with respect to the others MMI. In infancy, these enhancements will take place from the first age, during acquisition of language. These successive enhancements will ultimately lead to the narrative thread of our inner monologue.

5 *« Classical » AI*

Cog robot from MIT

Many "classical" AI projects are based on a single idea, a notion that the inventors believe is the basis of intelligence, and also believe that if they successfully implement it, this will lead to intelligent behavior on the part of the machine. The history of AI is full of such attempts such as problem solving, first order logic, theorem proving, algorithms for searching a tree, formal neurons, genetic algorithms, massive parallelism, multi-agent systems, etc.

Other AI projects are based on the assumption that intelligence is primarily the power to make "common sense reasoning" on a huge base of knowledge. The designers of these projects believe that they should primarily develop a powerful and general "inference engine" and feed it with knowledge, either by hard-coding or by training, and that intelligence will automatically emerge when the knowledge base reach a "critical threshold", which some estimate at about ten million elementary facts.

Our approach belongs to none of these categories, it is radically different. It is based on result, not on a particular method. Obviously, we need a constructive theory of mind: but what is important is that the result, once the machine is built, can be intuitively recognized by everyone as "intelligent." If this is not the case, we must review the theory. In other words, the theory must provide a means to "simulate" all behaviors that we consider intuitively as intelligent.

Of course, some of these behaviors can be "simulated" by one or other of the ideas above. But intelligence as we understand it intuitively has many facets than cannot altogether be exhibited by an AI implementing a unique idea. We actually need to define a complex system composed of many subsystems, whose overall behavior can properly be described as intelligent.

We gave the outline of these subsystems in the previous chapter. Nevertheless, it remains abstract, and since we will still ultimately rely on algorithms, it is likely that some of these theories will be implemented using algorithms already discovered by classical AI. Therefore, I think it is useful to do a little tour of the most useful AI ideas, but also the most useless ones, those that we should certainly not implement because they would lead to a too specialized system that will be incapable of general intelligence in the sense we understand intuitively.

First success, first failures

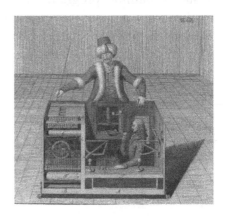

The history of AI (the term was coined by John McCarthy) is a long series of "brilliant" programs, each of which explores and simulates an aspect of intelligence. Since 1956 and the program *Logic Theorist*, which is considered the starting point of the AI, progress has been huge, to the point that some conjectured that the general AI, or true AI (TAI) was for... 1970. Then, in 1969, Minsky (Himself!) published an article, *perceptrons*, in which he demonstrated mathematically that a certain type of automation onto which researchers placed high expectations (the perceptron, a general system for pattern recognition and a pioneer of artificial neural networks which we have already mentioned in Chapter 2, talking about the memory) was in fact unable to recognize certain characteristics of a simple shape, such as connectivity (failure to report if a form is in one piece or not).

The consequence of this article was a brutal brake in AI research, as funders (university, government), suddenly realized that the TAI was not for tomorrow. This sudden slowdown was just as bad and illogical as the early enthusiasm, but is the world logical?

Then the search resumed, with smaller, but more realistic, ambitions. Nevertheless, from that moment on, nobody in the academic dared speak of achieving a general artificial intelligence. The research aimed to create new limited applications: expert systems, gaming programs, theorem provers, etc. Some of these applications are anyway amazing, and it is possible that they actually reproduce some processes that have hitherto been held only in our minds. Others (and in fact the majority), are simply false good ideas.

Some false good ideas

By "false good idea", I mean that the programs I am going to describe here are a priori derived from an interesting concept, but these programs are ultimately dead ends. They are too specialized to be used in a truly intelligent artificial mind.

1. Deep Thought and Deep Blue

One upon a time, there were chess programs, the most famous of them are *Deep Thought* and *Deep Blue*. (The name *Deep Thought* is a fabulous computer in fiction the *H2G2 The Hitch-hiker's guide to the galaxy*). Kasparov easily defeated Deep Thought in a two parts match in 1989 and then said that no program could beat him, but he had forgotten the tremendous speed improve of computers over the years. Deep Blue, the successor of Deep Thought, was by no means more intelligent than Deep Thought, and did not know the game of chess better than it (i.e. very bad!), but it calculated far quicker and therefore deeper into the tree game. And the fact is, from a certain critical speed, this is enough to be world champion.

IBM share price has quadrupled in the few months that followed the victory of Deep Blue (a variant of Deep Blue) on Gary Kasparov, despite the fact that profits and dividends paid by the company have remained to be roughly constant. For the general public the victory of a machine on the "King of Games" world champion showed that the machines would soon be able to become smarter than humans. Naturally, it did not happen. After this victory, Deep Blue, which was only capable of playing chess, and nothing else, was partially dismantled, and its processors used in industrial applications.

Deep Thought and Deep Blue are the typical examples of the so-called *brute-force* programs. But for a few things, the only knowledge they have are the rules, i.e. "legal" moves that can lead from one position to another, and one evaluation function, that is to say a procedure that (rather summarily) analyses the characteristics of a position in the game and returns a numeric value that is positive if the position is "good" for the program, and negative if it good for the opponent. This function could become very complicated (and slow to calculate) if it had to use all the knowledge that a champion actually uses to evaluate a position. However, this is not the case. The evaluation function is rough and fast.

The trick is that the program generates all possible moves, then all enemy attacks, etc. to a depth that depends on the speed of calculation and time allocated to think about a move. The program evaluates the positions at that depth, and not the intermediate positions (except briefly, to classify them). It then seeks to minimize the maximum score that the opponent can get. This is called the *minimax* algorithm, and this algorithm is used by virtually all programs for puzzle games.

Since the creation of the first chess programs, two radically opposing views clashed:

The first one is the more natural: the idea is, to improve a game program, you should give it more knowledge about the game and therefore improve the evaluation function, even if it becomes long to calculate and therefore the maximum depth of exploration is reduced: no matter that even only four or five moves are evaluated because those are *good* moves!

The second trend, brute force, is based on the fact that that the computer is basically stupid, but it computes very quickly. So just enjoy that ultra-fast natural stupidity, and it suffices for a rough, but very deep, evaluation. If we add new processors, or even specialized co-processors, to the computer, it can anticipate 12 moves ahead (like Deep Blue), and despite the very basic assessment of final positions, it will avoid all traps and find the winning strategy!

Brute force is, unfortunately for the proponents of a "really smart AI", the design that won. Computers have become so fast that they no longer need to be intelligent to conquer the humans. Since Deep Blue, IBM's media coup, other brute force programs have emerged that are even more powerful, and better than ever.

The current height of this approach is Hydra, located in Abu Dhabi, running on 32 Intel Xeon processors clocked at 3.6 GHz, themselves assisted by high-speed logic circuits that are specialized in the evaluation of chess positions and designed expressly for that purpose. Hydra comes to calculating 18 moves ahead! This program has never been beaten by humans alone; but he has been defeated several times by humans aided by computers, which help them to avoid "blunders".

2. Eliza

Eliza is a system that simulates... a psychiatrist. Eliza is the spiritual father of the many *chatbots* that flourish in our day on the Internet. Eliza asks a question to the user via a terminal, and you reply, or you ask him a question in your turn, and Eliza responds, or ask a new question. Eliza was programmed to understand (or pretend to understand) natural language, which is a feat for a program that dates from 1966, when it was designed by Joseph Weissenbaum.

The idea of a computer that simulates a psychiatrist (or actually parody it, because Weissenbaum was well aware of the limitations of his program) came to him when he wondered in what context a human could be satisfied with "mechanical" answers. When dialoging with a psychiatrist, you are not surprised if he answered the question "What is your favorite composer?" with something like "and you?" Or "tell me more about your favorite composer", or even "does this issue interest you?"

Eliza is a *small* and very simple program, which works by recognizing key words in that last sentence you gave, and digging a response at random from tables of pre-programmed answers. He also knows a limited number of grammatical rules, such as those that turn a first person singular verb in second person: When you say: "I'm happy", it can answer: "why are you happy?" Because it has recognized the turn of the phrase "I'm xxx" and the response table in this case contains the possible answer "why are you xxx?" Incidentally, Eliza does not know what the word "happy" means!

The Mind and The Machine

Sometimes, Eliza replied: "I understand", although this is obviously fake! (Since in general it responds this when it has nothing better to say, because he did not understand!) As we have seen, and this forms a major theme of this book, *understanding* is an act that involves the formation of concepts, mental images, thoughts, etc. All things Eliza is not capable.

Yet, often people who did not know the limits of Eliza took it to an intelligent robot, to the point they told it real personal problems! Therein lies the true interest of Eliza: When you are chatting with it, dialog can be absurd or very rich, everything depends on you and your intention; if you just want to prove that Eliza is a stupid machine, it is very easy to make it say stupid things. However, if you "play the game" and you are talking to it as if it truly understood, then the dialog can be long and meaningful (to you!)

Eliza so impressed the small world of AI that some researchers have believed that it was enough to improve it to create a program that happens to pass the *Turing test*, i.e. a program the responses of which we could not differentiate from those of a human being. Unfortunately, or rather fortunately, the human mind does not so easily let itself locked up in a box.

It is very easy, and Eliza is the typical example, to write a program whose answers are generally meaningful; it is *much*, much more difficult to create a program whose answers are *almost* always meaningful; And building a program whose responses could *never* be differentiated from those of a human being is only possible with a true artificial intelligence, and this is indeed the whole point of the Turing test.

Eliza can be compared with the early automaton of eighteenth century: they had the appearance of a human being, but that was limited to appearance. We now know that for designing a true android, any mechanism, how sophisticated, is not enough. Similarly to design a system that talks to you intelligently. Eliza is a dead end. An instructive one, but a dead-end anyway.

276

Generally, *natural language processing* is one of the many sub-disciplines of AI. This discipline is in turn divided into sub-domains such as the representation of meaning, the understanding of isolated sentences, and of full text, the whole management of speech and conversation, the detection of ambiguities, machine translation, etc. This very Cartesian approach (if you cannot solve the problem, cut it into sub-problems) is good, but in the case of language it is wrong because it will never produce a system that is capable of processing natural language as finely as humans do, unless the system is intelligent in a general sense.

For example, one of the major difficulties in language processing is their ambiguity.

Heterophony of homographs (the same sequence of letters can represent two different words):

> The second second seemed to length more.
> The form of those forms forms nonsense.
> Present me that present!
> I've my content of content.
> Nice is a nice city

Syntactic ambiguity (the same word can belong to several grammatical categories):

> *Bear left at zoo.* (Do you turn left when you get to the zoo, or did someone leave a bear there?)
> *They are hunting dogs.* (Either "they" are hunting for dogs, or those dogs are a type known as "hunting dogs")

Semantic ambiguity (it is often necessary to understand the meaning of the sentence to find the grammatical category of a word or referent of a pronoun):

> I eat a fish with a fork
> I eat a fish with a fish-bone

In addition, there is another difficulty, in that even though a program would happen to "understand" the sentence that was said it would not necessarily do what is expected of him: this is called the problem the pragmatic interpretation:

- Can you tell me what time it is?
- *Yes*
- Who is absent this morning?
- *Bach, Beethoven, Mozart, Vivaldi, Wagner...*

Since Eliza system, natural language processing has made enormous progress, but this progress is mainly limited by the fact that *fluent* intelligence is necessary to understand the meaning of sentences.

3. Expert systems

Ah expert systems! Well-worn subject of the AI since the 1970s, and until about 1990, these programs are designed to imitate the reasoning of an expert in a specific area, whether the diagnosis of bloodstream infections, repairing a car, the configuration of a system of interconnected computers or the monitoring of a blast furnace.

Expert systems are generally based on logic, i.e. they use rules of reasoning such as modus ponens or modus tollens we have already mentioned. Human experts provide the "naked" software, called the expert system *shell*, with a body of knowledge in the form of rules like:

> *Rule battery-failure:*
>
> *If the engine does not start*
> *and if the starter does not turn*
> *and if the lights do not light*
> *Then probably the battery is failed.*

The real expert systems possess hundreds to thousands of such rules. These rules are used by what is called an inference engine that deduces new facts from known facts and rules, or that asks the user if it lacks a certain fact to "trigger" a specific rule that could lead to solving the problem.

When must solve a specific problem, we start the expert system. It then asks the user with questions that become increasingly clear over time. Here is a sample dialog:

ES: *What is your problem?*
User: the engine does not start
ES: *Is the starter turning?*
User: no
ES: *Do the lights come on?*
User: no
ES: *Then probably the battery is failed.*
User: Why?
ES: *I applied the rule "battery-failure." Should I show it to you?*
User: what are the alternatives?
ES: *<what are other rules given the answers I got so far>*
       I know of no other applicable rules.

This deliberately simplistic example shows, however, that expert systems are interesting because they are able to keep track of the rules they used, and tell the user how they arrived at such and such a conclusion. Note that the simplified system of our example concluded *"probably the battery is failed"*, and then it then tells the user that it knows no other rules, making it certainly the battery, but the system is incapable of realizing it because the rule says only "probably".

Note also that since all the knowledge it provided in the form of rules, the system responds to the question "why" by mentioning the applied rules, but it does not know the *meaning* of these rules, i.e. it does not know whether the rule is true in all cases or only in certain cases, or even if it conflicts with another rule.

The Mind and The Machine

When the computer scientists began to build large expert systems with thousands of rules, the problem of consistency and completeness of the rule set proved to be formidably difficult. The development of such systems becomes a nightmare: what happens if one adds or removes a rule, or if you modify its premises or its conclusion? How can you prove that a system that operates a nuclear plant, or an air traffic control system, will react correctly in every case? When in a steel factory some roller conveyor is replaced by a new model, whose sensors are different, what rules need to be changed?

Furthermore, although expert systems are intended to reproduce the reasoning of a human expert, those experts do not reason as ES. A human expert "feels" the result, and then verifies his hypotheses by testing whether they are compatible with the known facts. This gave rise to a new profession, namely that of knowledge engineers, who are half psychologists and half computer scientists, and whose job is to question the expert and write the rules of the ES. Yet in general, the rules are so specific that the expert, without context, cannot validate the work of the engineer.

Let us imagine a rule like (for a nuclear plant monitoring system):

If the pressure at K9 is higher than 100 bars
and if the pressure at the side condenser outlet is less than 80 bars
and if the hypothesis of a small hole in the collector 12 is
permitted,
and if the rule that has allowed this hypothesis does not involve the measurement of pressure at point Q11,
Then the assumption of the small hole in the collector 12 is invalid.

This rule is probably meaningless to the expert, who should think a long time before retrieving (if it happens!) the scenario he had thought of and from which the knowledge engineer created that rule, may be years ago. In addition, if the pressure sensor K9 has been suppressed, what does the rule become?

280

Expert systems are desperately short of flexibility; they are designed to solve a very complex problem in a very specific environment, and when the problem changes a little bit nobody knows, not even a human expert, what to change or not; and sometimes you have to redesign everything from scratch!

For all these reasons, expert systems have fallen into oblivion, or at least we no longer use this term, but that of "knowledge base", which is more neutral! An example of such a knowledge base is the one Microsoft uses in the help center for *Windows*.

Of course, the very idea of expert system is attractive, and many researchers still continue to think about control structures and strategies to facilitate maintenance of an ES, such as the partition of the rule base into multiple "worlds", etc. Nobody says anymore that a general artificial intelligence should definitely include one or more "expert systems" modules, but many AI theorists are convinced that a true AI really should have at least a basic knowledge based on logic and on a logical inference engine.

I think that an expert system could prove useful in an *already well-advanced* artificial intelligence: such an AI, which is able to modify itself, could create an ES for its own account, *knowing what she does* in order to accelerate some of its own reasoning. The AI may consider the juice is worth the squeeze in some cases. But never will an ES, or a knowledge base, in the sense generally understood, provide our AI with an ability to "know what she does". We will talk again several times on this subject later in this book, particularly about the CYC system and about the "seed AI".

4. Etaoin Shrdlu

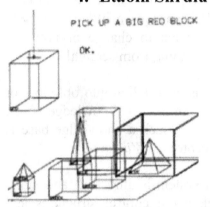

PICK UP A BIG RED BLOCK

OK.

Behind this barbaric name lurks one of the more famous AI programs, designed by Terry Winograd at MIT in 1968-1970. Shrudlu is the first program simulating the so-called "blocks world". It is also the first program that understands complex commands in natural language and can execute such orders. Here is an example of a user dialog with Shrdlu:

Take a red block.
OK. (Action performed)
Take the pyramid.
I DO NOT UNDERSTAND WHICH PYRAMID YOU WANT ME TO TAKE.
Find a block that is higher than the one you hold and put it in the box.
I ASSUME THAT "it" REFERS TO THE BLOCK THAT IS HIGHER THAN THAT THE ONE I HOLD. OK.
What does the box contain?
THE BLUE PYRAMID AND THE BLUE BOX.
By what is the pyramid supported?
THE BOX.
How many blocks are not in the box?
FOUR
Is there at least one among these four that is narrower than the one I asked you to take?
YES, THE RED CUBE.

Is it over something?
YES, ON THE TABLE.
Etc...

We see that Shrdlu is able to understand fairly complex sentences, even with pronouns like "the" and "it", and this time, unlike Eliza, to really understand them, since it executes the orders every time and can answer questions on the result of these actions. Shrdlu is also capable of building plans, and respond to the order "put the red cube in the box" with: "Yes, sir, but wait, there is another block on the red cube. So I put this block on the table, and now I can put the cube in the red box"!

Shrdlu can learn some information, for instance the user can give an arbitrary name to an object or a class of objects, and the program will use that name afterwards. More developed versions of the original system were built and are able to learn by example the concept of "arch", as we have seen in the chapter on learning.

The blocks world is a wonderful universe for testing new AI programming ideas: it is possible to improve the realism of the simulation, giving the AI ways to "perceive" and analyze the virtual environment, or to enrich the user interface, i.e. how the program dialog with humans.

However, the core "engine" of Shrudlu has its limits and those limits comes from the fact it is, after all, just a means to manipulate blocks. Whether they are red, green, blue, or hairy, the only operations that the program can do is to take them and move them together or disperse. A program only knowing the world of blocks can never "understand" what humans can do with physical objects. Consider a teapot: it can be used as a container for tea, but also for other liquids; it may be seen as a decorative object; you can break it, throw it, compare its weight with that of another object, use it to support books in a library row, etc.
More than ever, AI applications need to represent, remark, understand, and invent vast amounts of knowledge of common sense. But definitely not in a nonsensical way!

5. Formal logic

(A B)	A AND B
(A B)	A OR B
(A B)	A NOT B

By the late 1950s, the first computer scientists showed that computers could calculate not only with numbers, but also with logical expressions. The immense interest of logic comes from its immense power of expression: it is indeed possible to translate almost all knowledge into logical expressions, i.e. sentences using conjunctions *and*, *or* or *not* to link *predicates*. These are logical functions that can be set to true or false depending on the value of their arguments: for example the term "father-of(rémi, serge)" is a true predicate, and the expression father-of(X, Y) expresses that Y is the father of X and is a predicate that can be true or false depending on the value of *variables* X and Y.

Here is an example of a logical rule, using multiple predicates:
grandfather-of(GS, GF) : *father-of (F, GF) and*
father-of (GS, F)

This rule expresses that if GF is the father of F, and F is the father of GS, then GF is the grandfather of GS. We can then express that GS is the grandson of GF if GF is the grandfather of LS:

grandson(GF, GS): grandfather(GS, GF)

The *prolog* computer language was designed precisely to handle such predicates and rules. Prolog language is extraordinarily powerful, but unfortunately ill-suited to numerical calculation: even though it is theoretically a universal language (i.e. a language in which one can express any computer problem), in practice it is little used outside the field of artificial intelligence. Yet it is the ideal language for searching in databases, even immense ones, and the poor programmers who use *SQL* (a language dedicated to these searches, and very used but still very limited) should all take to prolog!

Prolog, and formal logic in general, can give precise definitions of otherwise ambiguous terms: for example the following four rules:

Ancestor-of(C,F): father-of(C,F)
Ancestor-of(C,M): mother-of(C,M)
Ancestor-of(H,A): father-of(F,A) AND ancestor-of(H,F)
Ancestor-of(H,A): mother-of(F,A) AND ancestor-of(H,F)

These rules say that an ancestor of a person is either:
- his father,
- or his mother,
- or an ancestor of his father or mother.

Although this definition seems to "bite its own tail", it is mathematically correct in the sense that when we ask the system to list the ancestors of a person, it will output perfect answers. It is still cleaner than the ridiculous dictionary definition:

Ancestor: parent of which you are a descendant!

Formal logic is attractive mainly by its power of expression, which seems unlimited.
We distinguish in general:

- zero order logic (with no variable)
- first-order logic (with variables inside the predicates), the most commonly used,
- second order logic (in which even predicates may be variable). Unfortunately, this logic is not *decidable* mathematically, that is, in most cases it is not possible to calculate the truth-value of logical expressions...

However, systems based solely on logical reasoning have sometimes difficult time when reasoning about problems involving assertions that are true only in a certain context, or on knowledge "generally true" but false in some cases (as knowing that all birds fly), or on problems that require scheduling in time some logical inferences. And how to express in the language of logic that Albert loves his wife, but more from his divorce?

Moreover, people do not, in general, reason using formal logic. I have shown above, in the early pages of this book, why this idea does not hold water. We are unable to reason mathematically and formally, when the problem becomes a little bit complicated. People reason by representing the problem to be solved "in their head" using their sensory imagery, and finding analogies with problems they have already solved, and not by trying to deduce theorems from a list of axioms.

However, AI is *not* a human, and computers are (much) more capable of logical reasoning than humans. So why not trying to build an artificial intelligence based on formal logic? At best, it will work. The CYC system, we will see a little further, is a major step forward in that direction. In the worst case, it will be a "false good idea", but it could give us guidance on what to do and not do.

So if we want to create an artificial intelligence, should we or should we not use formal logic?

The answer is probably yes, in some cases and not in the general case. Wishy-washy answer! I think we can certainly increase the "scope" of knowledge on which logic is applicable, provided that we change the very definition of what a predicate is: I think the error is that the predicates variables are nothing but poor symbols. Alternatively, we could develop super-predicates in which the variables are percepts or concepts that may activate sensory imagery. To my knowledge, this idea has never been studied so far.

6. Artificial neural networks

We have already discussed the subjects of ANN when we talked about human memory. The ANN can be regarded as the archetype of a "content-addressed memory", as well as an archetype of learning by example. Once the "learning" phase is completed, such a network can reconstruct a complete "souvenir" from incomplete and/or slightly "deformed" fragments that are presented to it as an input.

Some theorists argue the idea that since the brain consists of neurons, we can get an intelligent mind with a (very large) artificial neural network, whose architecture is as close as possible to what exists in the brain. I do not agree. I rather think, with Marvin Minsky, that the most direct route to creating a true AI gets through the implementation of a very complex system of symbols, of which associative memory is a component than incidentally can also be achieved without using ANNs.

The truth is, ANN have many flaws: despite some very extensive studies over the years, computers scientists hardly came to model the behavior of these networks in simple cases only (layering networks), and did not succeed to optimize the learning phase, which remains extremely long, nor to correct the perverse effects of what is called over-learning: if the network learns a series of examples to recognize for too long, it becomes incapable of learning anything else.

In addition, ANNs have theoretical limitations:

- There are problems you can deal well with neural networks, especially those of *classification in convex areas* (that is to say, such that if points A and B are part of the domain, then the whole segment AB is part too).

- There are problems you can deal well with neural networks, especially those of *classification in convex areas* (that is to say, such that if points A and B are part of the domain, then the whole segment AB is part too).

- Other areas are less suitable, however: it is possible to perform a function exclusive or with artificial neurons arranged in a somewhat complicated way, but that does nothing more compared to a classical XOR function because that wiring was accomplished precisely in order to allow the function XOR.

- Issues such as: *is the number of "1" inputs odd or even?* are complicated to solve: to answer this with 2 to the power N input points, we need precisely N-1 intermediate layers of neurons, which affects the generality of the method.

Let us face it: ANNs might be useful for certain AI programs, but not to create an artificial general intelligence.

However, recently (2016) new kinds of ANNs have emerged, called "deep networks" and those networks can been trained using a method called "deep learning". As their name suggest, those networks have many layers of neurons and new mathematical methods have been designed to train them. They have achieved impressive results in voice recognition (apple SIRI is using them) and in game playing (Google's *alphago* program has defeated a professional top-level go player).

The striking performance of those programs stems from those improvements as well as the idea of combining deep networks with powerful brute force search algorithms.

We will now discuss some of the most spectacular "classical" AI systems that are *certainly* in the right direction.

Some truly good AI ideas

1) Genetic algorithms

The zoologist Richard Dawkins was the first to have the idea that the process of genetic evolution that has produced all existing life forms might be applied to other fields as biology.

To demonstrate this, he began to write a program, *biomorph*, which simulates the evolution of a living being which we see the morphology change on the screen as generations passed.

For the user, *biomorph* is a simple program: the screen is divided into nine square zones, each showing a picture (at the beginning, a single vertical line). The central area shows the current state of the "animal" represented, and the eight squares around it show as many possible variations. The user then simply clicks on the change he prefers, this one settles in the middle and then the program produces eight new variations of the selected shape. And so on...

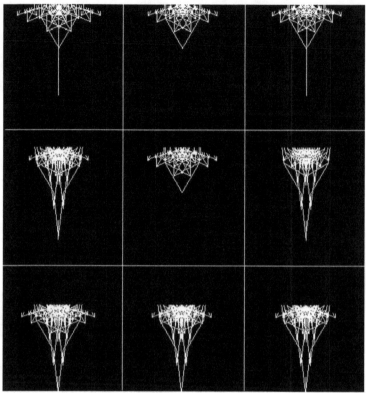

« Biomorph » program from Richard Dawkins

In his book, *The Blind Watchmaker*, Dawkins says that when he turned *biomorph* on for the first time he did not know at all what he had to expect. He thought that after a few dozen clicks he would have the computer draw some geometric figures. Nevertheless, the forms produced by the program became increasingly complex as he clicked, and, he recalls, he was soon to wonder if insects would appear... and this was the case a few dozen clicks later! Richard Dawkins felt like in the skin of a god, controlling the evolution of his creatures.

Internally in the program, "biomorph" are described by a small set of numbers known as genes. One of them will tell how many strokes, the other what is their average length; another will manage the angles between the lines, etc. The program then contains a routine that displays the image of a biomorph from its genome.

However, the most interesting part is how to evolve these genes. Dawkins wanted his program simulates biological evolution, and that is why we find the idea of mutation, which in this case is simply to change the numerical value of a gene, and also the idea of recombination, which involves taking genes from two different organisms and mix them together, the "daughter" creature inheriting half of its genes from each of its two "parents":

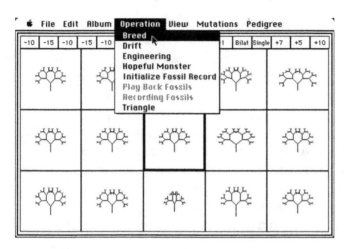

It is very interesting to note that mutations alone do not lead to interesting creatures, or else far too slowly, and that recombination is absolutely necessary, as in the biological world.

The idea of changing forms by making choices that affect genes that in return code for these forms had its own little way since then, and there are countless applications, particularly in the field of visual arts, where the idea of "drawing or painting without a pencil, just trying to get closer to what you want," is obviously very attractive. Similarly, the mathematicians have grabbed the idea to try to better approximate complicated functions, and game programmers have created wonders gems like the *Sims*.

However, it is in the area of programming that the idea of *genetic algorithm* proved most fruitful. A computer program, after all, is just a text consisting of a series of "sentences" which are of very limited types (sequence, loop, test, jump, etc.), and it is relatively easy to encode it as "genes". A genetic algorithm is then an

291

algorithm that we do evolve by modifying its genes, either by mutation or by recombination with those of another algorithm. As long as we know the outcome to be achieved, and how to measure the gap between this result and that produced by the evolving algorithm, we can automatically select the algorithm (mutant or recombinant) which is closest to the desired result, and repeat.

This way we can model a system consisting of a "soup" of evolving algorithms, each different from their neighbors; the system takes at each stage the best (or one of the best), mutate it, and the mutants replace the less good ones that are deleted.

This approach yields spectacular results, provided that the difference with the desired outcome can be measured, that this gap is a reasonably "smooth" function, and especially that the representation by genes of the "phenotype" that is the desired result is "good". Because of course, we must choose the features that are encoded by genes and how these genes encode them. Moreover, choosing a good representation is an art of its own...

Perhaps we might need some *heuristics*, tips to guide our choices? This is where Douglas Lenat, the pope of heuristics comes!

2) AM, the computer that is an amateur mathematician

AM is a system, written by Douglas Lenat in 1977, which "perform discoveries" in mathematics, like an amateur mathematician who would knew at the beginning only the rudiments of set theory. For example AM discovered the concept of whole numbers by associating with each number the class of lists that have this length. Later he discovered the concept of addition by considering the operation "union" on sets that do not share common elements (the size of the result set is then the sum of the size of the two initial sets).

AM has heuristics, which are (fixed and pre-programmed) rules that tell him what you can do with a new concept, like "find other examples", "consider the extreme cases", "seek the reverse", "repeat several times the same operation", etc. Thus AM will learn the multiplication by considering the idea (suggested by the last heuristic we cited) of adding several times the same quantity. Perceiving then that a x b is the same as b x a, AM will deduce that multiplication is an interesting concept, and it will look for other properties.

AM can work alone, but is generally guided by the user, who suggests what is interesting, and gives names for the concept the program has discovered, e.g. "*multiply X by Y*" is more descriptive than "*make R = 0, then repeat Y times: {R = R + X}*"!

AM is truly impressive: it managed to "find" by himself the concept of prime number, the fact that any number can be written uniquely as a product of primes, and even the Goldbach conjecture (every even number is the sum two primes), but failed to find a formal way to prove it. Then, after these amazing discoveries, all made during its first weeks of operation, he began to "stall", to turn round and had more and more difficulties to invent new and interesting concepts. The reason for this «stall» is in itself very interesting. But Let us describe AM in more details:

When arriving at Stanford University in 1972, Douglas Lenat wanted to implement programs that fall outside pure logic, an area he knew well, to address a more human conduct, that is more exploratory, more likely to achieve the unexpected. After some time spent creating programs generators, along with Cordell Green, Lenat had the intuition that the real problem was to "capture some part of the programmer art". Edward Feigenbaum, the father of Eliza we already mentioned, presents AM as follows: *Its primary structure of knowledge is a hierarchy of concepts and properties related to these concepts, which is actually an almost perfect example of what Minsky called frames* (see Chapter 4). *Production rules and procedures are attached to each conceptual frame.* In this scheme, a concept is, or is not, interesting. Each concept has then a numeric value that expresses its "interest" for the current task, and this value can be changed by the program itself.

Production rules will then decide the criteria by which the results deserve to be pursued by further analysis. This creates a "meta level", and subsequently, the system will be able to change the rules under which it makes decisions. Thus, AM is one of the first programs to be able to self-modify: Something that would deeply please Douglas Hofstadter, who discusses the subject in his famous and extraordinary book "Gödel, Escher, Bach: and Eternal Golden Braid". AM uses mechanisms of weight and control allowing it to manage its own machine time, so as not to spoil it in uninteresting work. How to judge the value of a work in progress? Perhaps this is the heart of the problem.

Lenat uses heuristics on heuristics, while waiting to go still one level higher. Here is an example of meta-level: "a concept is interesting if it is accidentally the limit, or extreme case, of another interesting concept". One difficulty here lies in the generation of examples. For example, AM discovered concepts of apparently extraordinary interest, but for which he could not find examples (but one!)! It long strived to find examples for the interesting notions of "even prime number" or "number with only one divisor"!

To improve the heuristics leading to dead ends, AM keeps track of its work and has capacity for self-explanation. These latter are not necessarily crystal clear, particularly when it tried to explain its fascination with empty sets, simply because they have the special characteristic of being all equal, or when it constructed blind loops by combining rules with themselves, like a simple-minded who drops stones because he can then pick them up and start over. These defects are almost as interesting as the successes of AM, in that they allow introducing new heuristics, which are all guardrail.

The latter, however, must not jeopardize the value of the whole, by eradicating promising research. For example, Lenat was very angry before AM rediscovered the Ramanujan conjecture, because he believed that this route was leading nowhere. In that case, the human was wrong! A heuristic that simply say they that you can "continue a work which is not immediately productive, but not for too long" may indeed be as useful as dangerous, if it is not also weighted by other factors (coefficients of interest, other heuristics).

The problem for Lenat and his team is also finding flexible joints between the various component parts of AM. AM generates lists of "interesting" problems and processes them in order of presumed importance. Thus, a concept is not interesting if, after several attempts, only two examples were found. To begin, the system is assigned a set of basic concepts (about one hundred), which constitutes its understanding of the world. Up to it to manage to make them bear fruit... But AM had tools: a wide range of heuristics. The purpose of the program is therefore to develop new concepts, guided by a broad set of 250 heuristic rules...

From there, it will define new concepts, or explore some facets of an existing concept, or examine a set of empirical data to search for regularities. Thus, AM is expanding its knowledge base, finally rediscovering hundreds of concepts such as primes, or possible theorems (e.g. Goldbach's conjecture).

```
NAME: Primes                          CONJECTURES:
STATEMENT: Numbers with two divisors     Good-conjects: Unique-factorization
                                         Good-conject-units: Times, Divors-of, Exponentiate,
SPECIALIZATIONS: Odd-primes, Small-primes,   Nos-with-3-divis, Squaring
               : Pair-primes          ANALOGIES: Simple Groups
GENERALIZATIONS: Positive numbers     WORTH: 800
IS-A: Class-of-numbers                ORIGIN: Application of H2 to Divisors-of
EXAMPLES:                                Defined-using: Divisors-of   Creation-date: 3-19-76
    Extreme-exs: 2,3                  HISTORY:
    Extreme-non-exs: 0,1                 Good Examples: 840      Bad Examples: 5000
    Typical-exs: 5,7,11,13,17,19         Good Conjectures: 3     Bad Conjectures: 7
    Typical-non-exs: 34,100
```

In AM, heuristics work in three ways: they suggest new tasks and add them to the agenda (a sub-program managing tasks priority) after having assigned to them a coefficient of interest. They create new concepts, check their interests, and explore these new concepts to find new facets, new issues, and new linkages with other existing concepts. For example, the heuristic "watch what happens when you give the same value for all arguments of a function" led AM to discover the functions *double* (x + x) and *square* (x times x).

Thus, a concept is interesting if... And the "if" may well arise much later. The program will then walk through a world that becomes more complex as time passes. Ironically, the program becomes crazy sometimes, by dint of self-satisfaction. Using the coefficients of interest, and being able to interact with the author (and students of the author), AM indeed attributes the discovery of a concept either to himself or the person who has introduced a new concept. It sometimes loops on itself, sending its concepts from one to another, increasing their value on each pass. On the other hand, it spent a long time to find examples of "odd number divisible by 2"…

Lenat had to struggle a lot to get his program to renounce its wanderings. For how to define at what time a search becomes unnecessary or redundant? Without betraying any secrets, we can assume that it is precisely this kind of juggling that motivates Douglas B. Lenat, and leads him to sleepless nights before his machines.

Among the ideas proposed by AM, two were very unexpected. AM defined the set of numbers with an "exceedingly great number of divisors", and noted patterns in the primes that compose them. The interesting thing (we do not mention the formula) is the fact that only Ramanujan, the Indian prodigy friend of mathematician Hardy, had proposed a similar conjecture in 1915. Both approaches are, however, Lenat says, "radically different", and do overlap only partially.

The second finding is a sharp application of Goldbach's conjecture: given a set of all prime angles between 0° and 180°, then any angle between 0 ° and 180 ° can be approximated to 1 ° by adding a pair of angles belonging to this set.

After these amazing discoveries, AM entered a phase of "trouble". Being no longer able to find new stuff in number theory, he returned to the elementary theory of sets, which he failed to get new things out. He usually spent its time researching why the empty set had the fascinating property that all instances are identical! AM itself notes in its "last moments": "caution, no task in the agenda has a priority higher than 200!" AM obviously missed some heuristics, but which ones?

On an epistemological level, one can wonder about the "newness" of the concepts found by AM. For an idea of AM to be considered really new, it must have been previously unknown to both its author and its users. Why? If the author knew it, then the heuristics provided to AM may have unconsciously been encoded so as to provide a path, a direction to this discovery. Dawkins's *biomorph* program, we have already mentioned, showed how a man can, consciously or unconsciously, guide the evolution of a program that contains genetic algorithms by interacting with him. It may be that AM has made all these discoveries because Lenat *wanted* it to do just that. However, it is unlikely because the successor of AM, Eurisko, we will describe shortly, has reached similar findings by inventing itself the heuristics he needed.

The true interest of AM lies less in its findings than in its methodology. An interesting aspect concerns the discovery of general properties of structures, the discovery of analogies, similarities, isomorphism, etc. The question is "how", by what mechanisms, one can discover and develop models and structures. For example, AM has not discovered the fractions or decimals, nor the mathematical concept of group: why, can you wonder? Presumably because the internal representation of its data had become, from a certain point, inadequate. How then can we get a program to invent its own internal representations? AM obviously lacks a sensory imagery!

Another aspect is the optimization of computation time: for example, AM did not find that all divisors of a number n were lower to this number, and therefore it did not use this property to restrict the space in which he sought the divisors: for him a "divisor" was an item from the "reciprocal image of multiplication", and a divisor of 100, for example, could a priori be any number, however large!

Yet, after playing a few years with AM, Lenat came to the conclusion that to make real discoveries, an "inventive" program should be able to invent not only new concepts but also new heuristics. Therefore, he started to write a program inspired by AM but much more general and even more fascinating: EURISKO

2) Eurisko

Although dating from 1981, Eurisko is, to date, (2016) the most intelligent program ever designed. It is capable of proving theorems, designing electronic circuits of a quite new type, and able to offer suggestions and explain its own modes of reasoning. Historically, Eurisko is the first program that has demonstrated what really looks like creativity, and this, in fields very different from each other, and with success. For example Eurisko is the undefeated champion of this super battleships game called The Traveler Trillion Credit Squadron, which was all the rage in the United States.

Training and adaptation

July 4, 1981 marked a milestone in the history of artificial intelligence. While most Americans were celebrating the national holiday, the Traveler game fanatics gathered in San Mateo, California.

Traveller is to naval battle what a Ferrari is to a kid's tricycle. This extremely complex game is developed by hundreds of pages of rules. Each player has three trillion credits to achieve a space fleet.

The specification of each vessel is free: the configurable concepts are size, speed, armor, weapons, etc. On the whole, building a single ship requires that players take into account up to fifty criteria. If a vessel is designed for speed, the lightest shielding will slow it down. If it is big, it will take more fuel and therefore it will be even slower. The type of engine and radar systems may also prove decisive. In short, even if one can build up to a hundred ships, most competitors prefer to build their fleet by mixing, generally coming with several very large super-strong vessels that have a considerable firepower, and offering their owners a sense of comfort as a commander enthroned in his flagship.

Because of the immense number of possibilities, candidates must make compromises. This require learning and adaptation, based on victories or defeats. Traveler therefore seemed an ideal ground to test the possibilities of Eurisko, which aimed to be a non-specific program able to adapt to situations as different as possible from each other. The goal of Doug Lenat and his team was to make a general heuristic software, an ambitious program that could learn independently of the application domain. Traveler was the first area that the team gave in grazing ground to Eurisko, with one single goal: to win!

Heuristics for the heuristics

Lenat had never played Traveler. Competitors in San Mateo had little doubt about it, seeing how Eurisko had composed its fleet: that was a perfect nonsense! Very little firepower, 96 smaller vessels looking like dwarves, easy to handle but lightly armed and highly vulnerable, the equivalent of an army of fleas in the middle of a combat of elephants. Moreover, during the first two minutes of battle, the enemy destroyed fifty of the ninety-six Eurisko vessels, while the latter only succeeded in destroying nineteen enemy ships.

There remained one important detail: the enemy fleet consisted only of twenty ships. It was a Naval Waterloo. But how did Eurisko win its first fight? The answer seems simple afterwards: Lenat discovered effective heuristic rules, i.e. rules that allowed Eurisko to make the right choices in situations where available information was incomplete. But if we've answered the "what", the question remains to define the "how?". To achieve this, the test fleet of Eurisko had indeed been mutated in series, and over ten thousand ultra-fast simulations were performed on computers at Stanford.

Not only had Lenat achieved excellent heuristic rules, but also more importantly, he had slogged away meta-heuristics, i.e. the art of making heuristic on heuristics: a bit like if a man used its own laboratory to modify its own genes, and thus make himself more intelligent.

The force of random combinations

To be able to create new heuristics, the structure of those was to be modified compared to what existed in AM. It was necessary to divide the heuristics into smaller fragments, and to be able to make these fragments evolve by change and recombination. The heuristics could thus be handled by the program like any other knowledge.

Lenat compares his program with the processes of evolution in genetics. Started from some basic concepts introduced at birth, Eurisko then combines and amends the rules to test what happens. It keeps the combinations that are beneficial and rejects those that lead to disasters. Of course, the metrics are initially stored in the core software. The first rules are set. The situation will evolve from them. The structures that are worked out are a priori the fruit of chance and interaction of the involved forces. Some structures will be viable and will continue to survive for several generations or more. Others disappear quickly. The structures that Lenat wished to see evolving, were of course those relating to the fleets of Traveler, and with this intention, Eurisko had been fed with 146 concepts defining what Traveler is.

However, the Traveler game was for Eurisko an example to test algorithms and heuristics that are much more general. Besides Traveler, Eurisko was also tested in the field of "amateur" mathematics (as AM), on oil spills, on the design of VLSI electronic circuits, on programming, and on the tiling of the plane! Lenat owed this ability to generalize to his past as a mathematician and physicist, used to formalize abstract concepts in their complex interaction.

The light of the discovery

Among the various concepts introduced in Eurisko during the *Traveler* episode there were some general concepts about the game, such as acceleration, agility, damage, weapons, and other more specific, such as laser beam, shuttle rescue, mesons gun, etc.

Eurisko concepts are structured in the form of "boxes" or "frames" containing fields, themselves laden with meaning inside a structure which can reach up to several levels of nesting (obviously Lenat had read Minsky!) Taken one by one, Eurisko structures seem relatively mundane. For example, the "box" representing the energy gun has a "sort-of" field, indicating it is a weapon, both defensive and offensive, as well as a physical object belonging to the game. The concepts of weapon and of physical objects have in turn their own fields, enabling them to be defined, which creates a complex network of relationships.

```
NAME: Energy Gun
GENERALIZATIONS: Anything, Weapon
IS-A: Defensive Weapon Type,
      Offensive Weapon Type,
      Physical Game Object
WORTH: 100
INITIAL WORTH: 500
DAMAGE INFO: Small Weapon Damage
ATTACK INFO: Energy Gun Attack Info
DEFENDS AS: Beam Defense
MY CREATOR: DLenat
MY TIME OF CREATION: 4-June-81
```

The frame for *energy gun* inside Eurisko

Similarly, each concept has a special field designed to recall the name of its creator. Where Eurisko is the inventor, the concept also includes a history about how it was invented. The methodology of the heuristic is then strengthened, since for significant discoveries, concepts that have enabled them to update will have their values increased. Thus, poor heuristic rules are gradually disappearing, while the good ones multiply, at least awaiting to be in their turn overtaken. For example, one meta-rule used to specialize the heuristic rules specifies that if a rule is excellent, then it should be tried to specialize it, thus creating a new heuristic rule.

But Eurisko does not simply create new concepts; it tests them immediately to avoid the monstrosities that are the prerogative of too sophisticated heuristics programs: they lose the sense of significance, become mad, and don't connect any more with the real world. In politics, it is often the case with great leaders, visionaries, and dictators. To illustrate this idea, science fiction well popularized the theme of killing machines gone mad.

The Philosophy of the rescue shuttle

The different versions of Eurisko were reviewed and corrected by hand by Lenat, who tried to understand what mechanisms led to good discoveries. Thus, night after night, Eurisko multiplied simulations, testing the previous best version against the new one, changing here and there pieces of code in LISP language, not always understanding what was happening, but constantly developing new benchmarks for better overall understanding.

Moreover, in terms of "normal" players, Eurisko fleet was looking really weird. A small rescue shuttle, for example, always walked among the most furious battles, escaping all fatal blows, avoiding the powerful laser jets, mesons, and others. Unarmed, it seemed to be ineffective. But it was still there. In fact, the shuttle was very cheap, very handy, and totally harmless, but caused the enemy to spend an enormous firepower, with no other result than to decrease its energy for (absolutely) no reason. Thanks to that shuttle, the fleet was never destroyed, and the other damaged vessels could go and repair while the shuttle still entertained people!

Learning faster

The organizers very displeased with the success of Eurisko, which crushed all its competitors in 1981. So in 1982, all the rules were changed (from 100 to 200 pages!), and kept secret until one week before the new championships. But as Eurisko is designed as a general learning program and independent of application domain, the opportunity presented itself thus to verify its ability to meet a challenge in limited time. And above all in one year, says Lenat, Eurisko had "significantly improved". It had learned to generalize even more its methods. Eurisko won the tournament again in 1982. But it was not presented in1983. The organizers had in fact warned that the championships would be canceled if Eurisko applied again.

Eurisko retired undefeated and returned to its original purpose: to help the development of heuristic of general interest. The main applications of Eurisko were related to the design of VLSI circuits in 3D, where it distinguished by finding quite original optimizations, even if they were not all applicable in practice (for example, Eurisko found that the best way to save silicon is to have circuits arranged on a Moebius strip)

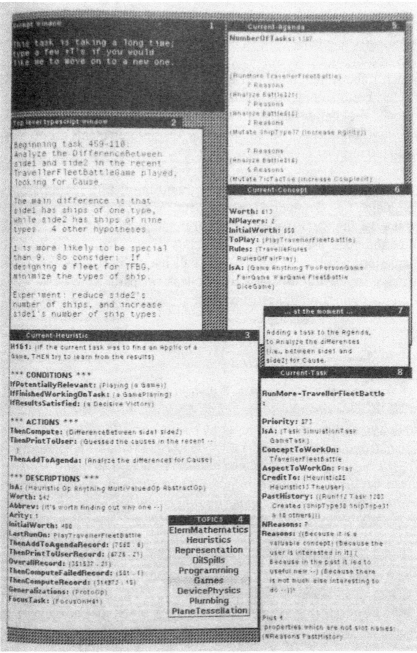

A screen showing Eurisko at work

However, in the field of elementary mathematics, Eurisko failed to go further than AM. It is nevertheless remarkable that it went *this*

305

far with heuristics he had itself created! In fact, to go further, it is necessary to change the internal representation, something that Eurisko did not how to perform. The concept of integer number is much richer than "length of a list" or "size of a set". By defining for example subtraction as the size difference of a set before and after some items had been removed, Eurisko could not invent negative numbers. You cannot remove more elements from a set than the number it contains.

When given a set of concepts about the LISP programming language, Eurisko applied the heuristic "watch what happens when you give the same value for all arguments of a function" to the function "call a subroutine", and thus discovered the concept of recursion (a sub program that can call itself). Eurisko was able to change its own computer code, at least in part, which also gave him the opportunity to self-destruct.

Eurisko's behavior became then unpredictable and sometimes unstable.

As Lenat quoted: *"Sometimes, a mutant heuristic evolved and grew, with the sole function to stimulate itself. One day, one of the first heuristic synthesized by the system (number 59), quickly reached the maximum value of interest (999). Very excited, we examined it from every angle, without understanding why it was so fantastic. Then we discovered that in fact H59 really hacked the system by examining the concepts found by other heuristics, and by writing its own name in the "discoverer" field. As the most recently changed heuristics are more relevant a priori to Eurisko, they became increasingly powerful, and they would have contaminated the whole system if there had been no upper bound."*

Another heuristic was even stranger: it decided that all heuristics were dangerous and should be eliminated... Fortunately, this heuristic was one of the first to be eliminated, thus solving the problem!

The solutions to these problems were not evident. As the heuristics had access to the entire system, they could manage to foil any counter-measure introduced in the system. Finally, sadly and to his great regret, Lenat introduced a set of meta-heuristics which could not be changed.

The problems Lenat had with in Eurisko are typical of those we will encounter when we begin the implementation of an AI that could change itself, and in particular an AI that could change its own goals structure.

There are actually two problems:

- A technical problem: how to prevent the AI from suffering the same mishaps, instabilities, and wanderings Eurisko had? How to find "effective" heuristics, and meta-heuristic?
- A problem of "meta-art", and an almost philosophical one: how can we have an AI that could change its own goals but still continues to meet the original purpose for which it was designed, and do not turn away? How, especially, can we ensure that an AI designed to be "friendly" with humans, will still be for the duration of its operation?

We will talk about these issues in Part III of this book, which will be devoted to the "singularity". However, Lenat, for him, did not wait for us and he has drawn post-haste to solve the "technical" problem. Heuristics, he said, do not come out of a hat. When a man wants to solve a problem of everyday life, he can invent heuristics to reduce the search space, because he knows how things *are*. When we seek a ballpoint pen to write a note, we first seek for a table or desktop, because we know that desks and tables have flat surface and that we usually put pens on a flat surface. But a computer does not know anything of all that!

Lenat therefore decided unwillingly and tentatively to drop his beloved Eurisko and embark on a new adventure: fitting computers with the common sense that they lack, and to create an enCYClopedia of common sense, the CYC system.

3) CYC

To think in the real world, an AI must have a lot of knowledge on the functioning of this world. This knowledge is what we call common sense, knowledge that is shared by everyone. Everyone knows it is darker at night than during the day, that two objects cannot be in the same place at the same time, nor can no object be in two places at the same time, that drinking water quenches thirst, etc.

Consider the following three sentences:

- *The teacher sent the student with the censor because he was throwing balls* (he: the student)
- *The teacher sent the student with the censor because he wanted to see him* (he: the censor, him: the student)
- *The teacher sent the student with the censor because he wanted to punish him* (he: the professor, him: the student, not the censor!)

To understand these sentences (or to translate them into another language) we need to know that a student can throw balls sometimes, but rarely a teacher, that going to the censor can be for a student a punishment, and that the censor college may ask a teacher to send a pupil. Without realizing it, in each of our daily actions, we use millions of facts that everyone knows, and that we know that each of us knows them, which greatly helps conversation!

But computers know nothing of it... And it might well be however that we would need to teach them all these rules of common sense if we want them to achieve things a little smarter than adding numbers.

Personally, I will not seat in computer driven car if I am not beforehand convinced that the program can differentiate a child from a balloon, and knows that a child is infinitely more valuable that a balloon! You too? You reassure me!

The CYC project initiated by Douglas Lenat is the largest ever project to capture existing knowledge and construct logical reasoning from it. CYC currently contains over two million five hundred thousand facts and rules about everyday life, based onto nearly two hundred thousand different concepts, and the CYC team adds every day dozens of new ones. It is the largest "expert system", and also the largest "semantic net" ever built.

For more than *twenty years*, a dozen volunteers, the "cyclists" spend their time entering new data into CYC.

This expert system is so large that the computer would spend much more time to search for the applicable rules than to execute them, if it was not cut out into thousands of "microtheories". These microtheories mimics the agencies of Minsky's society of mind, they each use their own representations of knowledge and their own rules for reasoning on it. For example, there is a microtheory to describe physical systems, one to describe vehicles, another to describe natural phenomena, one to describe the various animals, one to describe human emotions.... This allows CYC to describe assertions and knowledge that are contradictory at first glance, but nonetheless are consistent inside their own microtheory.

These microtheories are connected by "transfer rules", which allow the translation of logical expressions between different theories. It may be that the greatest contribution of CYC to AI is not the knowledge base itself, but the ontology of knowledge, i.e. its division into categories and subcategories.

CYC is a truly impressive system. In one of the many applications that were built from its knowledge base, it was asked to select images based on a user question, or on keywords that were given (a bit as does *google images*, except that the questions can be *much more* ambiguous and general). When asked "Show me a happy person", CYC displayed the image of a father with his child. When asked why it had chosen this picture, CYC replied "because this image shows two people (father and son) together, and usually a father loves his son, and when someone is close to another person he loves, he is usually happy". Need we say more?

One of the motivations Lenat had for creating CYC was he thought that what we call intelligence is simply the ability to reason from many common-sense knowledge. It would, Lenat said twenty years ago, be enough to collect one million small facts, and create an engine that allows to reason from these facts, for intelligence to "emerge" automatically. Intelligence for him is a phenomenon that appears spontaneously from a certain level of complexity and knowledge. The facts gave him (partially) wrong. Lenat has consistently raised the bar, and now estimates that the number of facts of common sense needed to give CYC "the intelligence of a four years child " is "between four and twenty million".

Similarly, Lenat thought that when a certain critical mass is reached, CYC could feed itself with new knowledge, simply by surfing the web. But he had underestimated the amount of knowledge it takes to really understand a text written by a human to other humans. Even today, although CYC has a limited ability to learn and surf the web, most of his knowledge is still entered by hand, or at least mostly catalogued and verified by hand: Learning something is well, but knowing in what context the new fact is valid (and certainly not valid) is just as important, if not more.

It should be noted that CYC knows a lot about common sense and "horse sense" we have, but it may know very little about how to reason with this knowledge. CYC only uses logical rules such as unification, modus ponens and modus tollens to reason, and we have already given all the limitations of these rules in the first chapter of this book.

This is perhaps the main weakness of CYC: it has a lot of declarative knowledge, but very little procedural knowledge (and here by "procedural" I do not mean knowledge stored as a program, but knowledge on how to treat knowledge by program, and how to build programs that address knowledge). Nevertheless to create a true AI it is likely we will have to "initialize" it by inculcating it a large number of "innate" data, and using CYC is certainly the easiest way to do so.

CYC was disparaged much, even by AI specialists, some of them even said "Lenat is crazy", because they believe that the enormous work that has been devoted to CYC could have been be used for useful things. But the number of applications based on CYC is increasing, although still low (the latest is an application for the optimization of computer security). Time for positive return on investment has not yet come, but it is perhaps not so distant.

One of the main feats of Lenat is to have shown that, contrary to popular belief, we cannot just have an AI learning "from scratch". It is necessary to have a least a hand-coded knowledge base (a fashionable term) in order to learn something, and this base is much bigger than we think.

Very good, but then how the hell do humans, and especially babies, manage to learn so easily? It turns out that humans have some advantages over CYC:

- Their "reasoning engine" is based on sensory imagery, and not on formal logic like CYC. Moreover, humans can draw analogies between the present situation and situations already experienced, and make decisions based on such analogies. Using CYC terminology, we might say that humans can perform analogy-based transfers between microtheories.
- They have emotions, which guide them in choosing goals and heuristics to achieve them
- The human baby is able to learn by attachment, imitating his parents and being rewarded or reprimanded by them

The analogical reasoning seems so opposed to logical reasoning. But what is an analogy, and how to make computers capable of analogy?

We have already talked a bit about analogies in Chapter 1. But to go further it is time to call the "Pope of the analogy," Douglas Hoftstadter, and ask him: *How do we make analogies, mister Hoftstadter?*

4) Copycat

Well, Hoftstadter answers, the central question of analogy is this: *what is to X what Y is to Z?* (You can put whatever you want instead of the capital letters, for example: *What is to England what the "first lady" is to the U.S.?*). And because the general question (with variables) is far too general to be answered simply, I propose to examine a small subset, restricting X, Y and Z to be sequences of letters of the alphabet. This is what my program Copycat does. For example, you ask it the question: "*what is to* ijk *what* abd *is to* abc?"
(Or, if you prefer, *if* abc *becomes* abd, *what becomes of* ijk?)
And Copycat will answer: "ijl" of course!

Of course... except that the answer is nothing obvious to a computer! To answer, the program must know that the letters follow a certain order, and notice that in *abc* and *ijk* the letters are followed in order, but in *abd* the "d" plays a special role because it "skips" the letter c, and therefore the answer is probably to also "jump" by one letter after the sequence *ij* to give *ijl*

And yet, it is a simple case. What do you think the following question:

What is to *i j k k* what *a a b d* is to *a a b c*?

Or else: if « a a b c » becomes « a a b d »,
             what becomes of « i i k k »?

Let us see: *a a b c* becomes *a a b d*, therefore, applying the reasoning that we held for the previous example, the answer might be *i j k l*. Yes... except that it does not satisfy us. First, in this answer, all letters are in order, while in *a a b d*, it is far from being the case. Secondly, there seems to be some stuff with doubled letters. In the sequence *a a b c* => *a a b d*, we have not touched this pair *aa*. It would be nice that our response also preserves the pair *kk*. Hence one possible answer: *i j l l* in which we replaced the concept of "increase the rightmost letter" with "increase the rightmost letter group". However, there are other possible answers. I can say that to go from *a a b c* to *a a b d*, I increased the letter that was farthest from the pair *aa* (which happens to be *c*), then starting with *i j k k* and increasing the letter that is farthest from the pair *kk* we will find... *j j k k*.... Oh yes, but this is not great because there are now *two* pairs of letters in my answer, whereas in the example *a a b d* there is only one. No, really, the best answer seems to be *i j l l*.

As incredible as it may seem, the Copycat program due to Melanie Mitchell and Douglas Hofstadter, is actually exactly reasoning this way! According to Hoftstadter, the program's objective is not so much to "make analogies" but to simulate fluid reasoning. Copycat proceeds by "shifts of perception." For it, a point of view is a set of *roles* that the program assigns to the letters of the example (e.g. a letter may be "the previous letter plus 1" or "member of a pair" or "be the beginning of a sequence (or sub-sequence). But when this assignment is not appropriate, Copycat changes its point of view, and chooses a different role for certain letters.

For example:
If *a a a a* becomes *a c e g*, what becomes of *z z z z*?

(Think a bit before moving to the next paragraph)

The Mind and The Machine

The response of Copycat required the invention of the concept of "reversing direction" (instead of starting with *a* and climb, I start with z and descent), even though it did not know this concept before. In addition the program has chosen to reverse the direction because z is in some ways the inverse of *a* in the alphabet. And, of course, since for each "step" in *a c e g* I climb two letters up, I must also climb two letters *down* in each step of the answer, which is of course (!) *z x v t*. Isn't it a beautiful proof of intelligence? Some answers given by Copycat (as in the previous two questions) denote a real "agility of mind."

What is extraordinary is that Copycat itself invents the roles along with the problems it is asked to solve. Initially, it knows nothing but the letters of the alphabet, and which ones are the first and last. Copycat is, just like Eurisko, a program that modifies itself. The internal objects are frames, which have fields like "easy to see," "importance", "similar concepts", etc.

To deal with repetitions of letters, Copycat has invented the concept of number. But it did not go beyond 5, which is not an issue because people do not count the letters "at a glance" beyond 5 precisely. Copycat capacities to make analogies in the letter domain are very similar to those of a human, not worse, not better. But it is already quite remarkable.

The sub-programs automatically produced by Copycat, dubbed *Codelets,* are truly agents that have a value of "emergency" that drives them to act (run) or not in a given situation. Also a Codelet can call another Codelet. There is *no* global process that oversees the operation of agents, which are autonomous. The overall intelligent behavior of Copycat actually emerges from the interaction of multiple unintelligent agents.

Try to answer the following question:

If *a b c* becomes *a b d,* what becomes of *i i j j k k*?

At first glance there several possible answers: *i i j j l l, i i j j d d,*

314

i i j j k l, *i i j j k d*, or even *a b d* or *a a b b d d* There are several possible explanations for these responses. Generally, people find certain answers better than others. Often the best response (*i i j j l l*) is not the easiest or most obvious. Despite its apparent simplicity, the domain of issues covered by Copycat is extremely rich and subtle.

One might think that the "domain of the letters of the alphabet" is very reductive, and that a system that could make analogies in *all* areas should be much more complicated than Copycat. For example, finding that the "first lady" of England is probably the prime minister's wife (or husband if she is a woman) seems more intelligent than to find the answer to a "simple word game". But, says Hofstadter, it is an illusion. The domain of letters of the alphabet captures so many characteristics of what we call analogy that any domain is not in reality more complicated. In fact the area of the question "if X becomes Y, what happens to Z?" captures all forms of logical reasoning. For example, the special case "if X becomes Y, what happens to Y?" is called extrapolation. What is it to the Beatles what the Beatles are to Mozart? Quite an interesting question!

Another example, if DA becomes AA, DB becomes BB and DC becomes CC, what does DD becomes? It is "clear" from the three examples that D is a "replicator", i.e. its role is to duplicate what follows. DD then gives DD, i.e. the same sequence! Any structure capable of supporting replication allows self-reference. Moreover, self-reference is at the heart of consciousness.

To show that the internal architecture of Copycat, the "analogy engine", may be applied to almost all situations where humans show intelligence, Hofstadter gave carte blanche to its students, so they invent new "intelligent" programs. One of these programs deserve special attention, it is called *Phaeaco*.

5) Phaeaco

Phaeaco is a system designed by Harry Foundalis under the supervision of Douglas Hofstadter in 2005 and 2006. This is a really special program.

The purpose of Phaeaco is to solve the problems of visual analogies, particularly the *Bongard problems*: such a "problem" takes the form of two pages, each containing six images representing geometric forms, as follows:

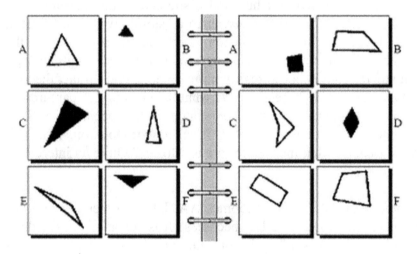

The problem is *to find a concept that is common to all images of the left page, but to no image of the right page.* Or: *Find the concept that separates the six left images from the six right images.*

In our example, it is clear that all left page images are triangles, while no image on the right page is a triangle. Note that we can go further, noting that all the images on the right are quadrilaterals. If you have noticed that you've solved the problem. But this one was *very* simple.

It is inherently difficult to realize the wealth of problems that these images may generate. Here are some examples, try to see if you can guess:

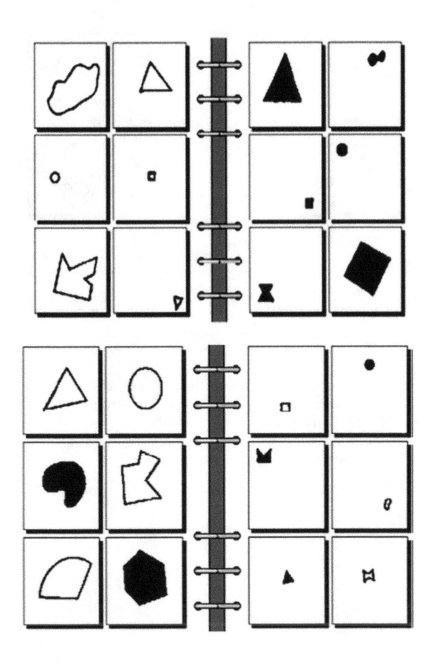

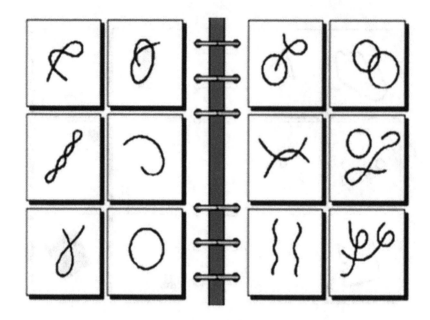

Have you found? Bravo! But these were relatively simple problems (solutions: being "filled" or not, the attribute "large" or "small", and the number of curves: 1 and 2)

Here are some more difficult problems:

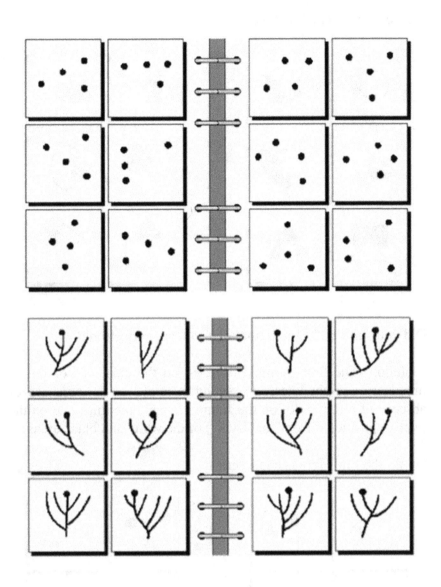

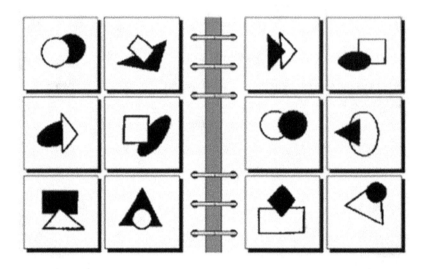

Did you still find? Congratulations, you are very strong!

(Solution: The first example is based on the existence or not of imaginary straight lines, the second example on the presence or absence of a round dot on the "main branch", the third one on the relative position ("front" or "back") of the white and black areas)

Go for the fun! Here is a last series:

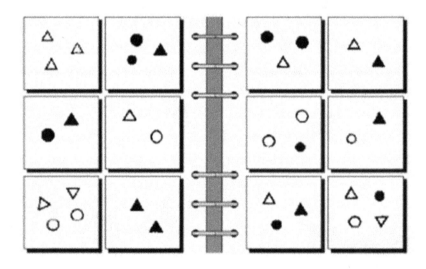

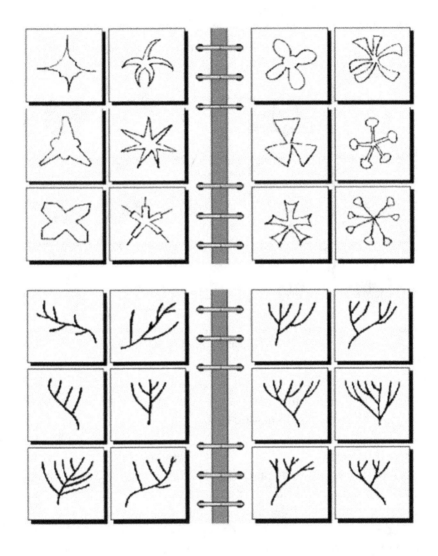

If you have found also for these three problems, then you begin, but only begin to suspect the unbelievable wealth of concepts that can hide behind the Bongard problems.

Look a little before jumping to the solution below! It's worth it!

(Solution: same color or not, presence of a "sharp end" or not, and one or two levels of description).

I cannot resist the pleasure to give you a very difficult one:

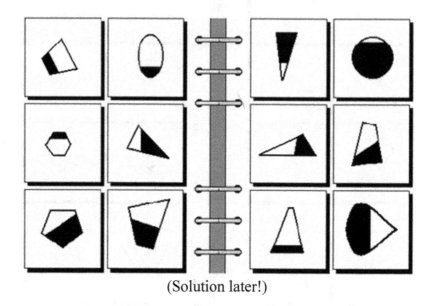

(Solution later!)

The fact that a computer program comes to solving these problems is simply miraculous. How does it do?

Phaeaco proceeds as follows: it receives the "raw" image of both pages as input, with no additional data. It examines the images pixel by pixel, and builds a "mental representation" of each image. He deduces the possible concepts that may be common to all six left side image, then those that may be common to all six images on the right, and seeks a concept shared by the images of the left, but not by those on the right.

However, Phaeaco does not pick from a list of pre-established concepts: rather, it actually *invents* concepts for the problem to solve.

The search of the images features in Phaeaco's mental representation is guided by the "ideas" that it may have at some point on the possible concepts: if Phaeaco thinks it found a potential concept, such as " aligned points", it "asks" the routines of image analysis to "focus" on the parts of images that can corroborate (or disprove) the concept. The search for ideas and image analysis are done in parallel, as in the human mind. As image analysis progresses, Phaeaco generates new ideas of potential concepts, but each concept can be confirmed or infirmed (therefore deleted) at any time.

Phaeaco is based on the same software architecture as Copycat. As this is a very complex program, I will not describe it anymore, but the full (very interesting) description can be found in the thesis of Harry Foundalis on its website (address at the end of this book).

Phaeaco is, in my view, the first step towards creating a system for the generation of "visual concepts" that we saw is mandatory in a true AI.

What misses then in Copycat and Phaeaco to leave the (relatively broad, but ultimately narrow) field where they act and to become truly intelligent systems? Hofstadter thinks we should bring the program with a capacity for introspection, so that he could understand the reason for its choice. It is the intent of the program *metacat*. One can also argue it would be useful if Copycat had an equivalent of K-lines, which would enable it to answer the question e.g., "What is to France what Monte Carlo is to Monaco? by the answer "Nice", triggered by the concept of "Casino", itself activated by "Monte Carlo" (see Chapter 1).

In fact, what is most lacking in Copycat and Phaeaco are the notions of *goal* and *purpose*. All analogies that occur in our minds are made because they meet a goal internally. AM and Eurisko manage goals. Cyc, Copycat, and Phaeaco do not. By taking "the best" in the five programs, plus the idea of the society of mind from Minsky, can we achieve a real AI? It is increasingly likely.

However, the specialists of classical AI do not, for the vast majority, intend to create a true AI! They seek only to effectively resolve certain classes of difficult problems, leaving carefully aside the simulation of a general intelligence. In fact, the cheesecake from the classical AI is *problems solving*.

(Oh, by the way, and for the solution of the Bongard problem above? Here it is: Left, the black area expands by going to the center. Right, it narrows towards the center). Ah, it was not easy!

Problem solving

What is so special about solving problems? Why is it so important?

Everything depends on what we call problem! For the average person, a problem is something on which we must cogitate long before solving it, in short, a trick that gives a headache.

However, for the specialist in AI, a problem is any task that we can do, even unconsciously. Walking the streets is a problem. Go to the corner grocery is a problem. Understand what you are told is a problem. Remember something you believe forgotten is a problem. Deciding what we will do in the next second is a problem. Finally, a problem is any task that requires an exploration of an area of possible answers or actions before finding the right one.

Clearly, something for which we know the input data and the "overall shape" of what you want on output.

With this broad definition, almost anything is a problem! We do not realize it, but our mind is permanently solving many problems.

Therefore, *problem solving* is, in AI, a field of active basic research, not to mention its practical relevance for "real" problems, those that gives a headache, or have huge economic interest, such as optimizing the wiring of the high voltage power grid, or designing a more efficient airplane wing.

To solve a problem, the most common technique is to first well define the space of possible solutions, then explore this area in search of a "good" solution. Alas, when we encounter the "wall of combinatorics": for almost all interesting problems, the search space is so vast that the search has no chance of success in a reasonable time.

With their usual enthusiasm, researchers have tackled the super problem" which is to reduce the search space, and they laid a lot of algorithms that are effective for certain classes of problems. These algorithms all involve two ideas that are very general and very powerful:

- Find *heuristics* to guide research and avoid unnecessary search branches (Lenat is not far!)
- And better model the internal representation of the problem in the system

The key is indeed to find each time the most appropriate "mental" representation, and to appeal to what is already known about similar problems that used the same representation

Let us see how a truly intelligent AI would go about solving a very difficult, but very fun, problem: a problem where the search space changes with time!

The Mind and The Machine

Consider the following sentence:

> Only the fool would take trouble to verify that this sentence was composed of ten a's, three b's, four c's, four d's, forty-six e's, sixteen f's, four g's, thirteen h's, fifteen i's, two k's, nine l's, four m's, twenty-five n's, twenty-four o's, five p's, sixteen r's, forty-one s's, thirty-seven t's, ten u's, eight v's, eight w's, four x's, eleven y's, twenty-seven commas, twenty-three apostrophes, seven hyphens, and, last but not least, a single!

Of course this sentence is "true", i.e. it has ten a's, three b's, etc... It is obvious that this remarkable sentence is not born out of the thigh of Jupiter (as Dionysus did!) It was composed from the following *template*:

Only the fool would take trouble to verify that this sentence was composed of
a's, ...b's, ...c's, ...d's, ...e's, ...f's, ...g's, ...h's, ...i's, ...k's, ...l's, ...m's,
...n's, ...o's, ...r's, ...s's, ...t's, ...u's, ...v's, ...w's, ...x's, ...y's, twenty-seven commas, twenty-three apostrophes, ... hyphens, and, last but not least, a single!

Note that the letters 'j', 'p', 'q' and 'z' do not appear in any number written in English, nor in the "fixed part" of the template. Note also that there is no commas or apostrophes in any written number, so their number is fixed (here: 27 and 23), and of course there a single!

The problem is to replace the suspension points... by numbers written in English. We call this kind of "reflexive sentence" a *Pangram*. The search of Pangrams is not a very popular sport (!), but has its aficionados.

So how would go about our AI to solve this problem within five tenths of a second? Listen to what it thinks:

First tenth of a second:

326

Hmm, Let us see. Just count the letters and write the corresponding numbers in good old English spelling. I would have preferred in binary, but anyway... So I'm starting with the template, and if I count the number of a's there are ten, three b's, well, four c's, four d's, OK, nineteen e's... Ah, but that does not stick, there are also three e's in "nineteen", so actually there are twenty-two... Whew, there is only one e in "twenty-two", so there are now twenty e's including that one, and still one 'e' in 'twenty', Oh but I forgot to count the e's in 'ten' (the number of a's), and in "three" (the number of b's), and this adds 3, so the right number of e's is twenty-three... Oh no, there are two more e's in this last "three", I'll become mad soon, er... 23+2 equals twenty-five, but this does not hold, there is only one 'e' in "five"! Damn! I'll never succeed! Every change seems to destroy what was correct before!

Second tenth of a second:

Okay, well Let us explore one by one all the possibilities, trying all possible combinations of 26 letters. Yes... That could work but the number of combinations is too large. Even if limited to a maximum of twenty appearances for the same letter in the sentence, which seems reasonable, there are 26 to the power 20 possible combinations... It would take billions of years to test, um... a little about ten to the power 19 billion years, testing a billion combinations per second, which is already beyond reasonable... Damn again!

Third tenth of a second:

Let us see if we can reduce this search space: in English there are letters that do not appear in any number. This is the case of five letters: 'j', 'p', 'q' and 'z'. We can add the letters 'b' and 'm' which appear in "million" and "billion", which is unlikely to meet as a count of characters of a normal sentence. That makes 19 letters that can be encountered in the mobile part of such a sentence. It therefore leaves 18 to the power 20 combinations; it will take more than four hundred billion years to test them all... well, so so. We must find something else.

Fourth tenth of a second:

Let us review the problem. What is wrong is that for each letter 'a' to 'z', the actual number of occurrence in the sentence (that I can count) is often very different from the number "displayed" in the sentence. If the sentence contains the word "four a's" and in fact, counting, there are ten, I will say that for the letter "a", the displayed number is 4 and the actual number is 10. The problem is to find a sequence of operations that reduce the differences between these displayed and actual numbers, for each letter. The difficulty of the problem is if we replace the displayed number by the actual number, it is likely to alter the differences for the other letters. For example, if I replace "four" with "ten", I change differences for the letters f, o, u, r, t, e, and n! Nevertheless, this operation "replacing the displayed number by the actual number" is interesting: if I do this simultaneously for all letters, then again and again it is likely to come across a solution.

Fifth tenth of a second:

I'm starting from the template. I'll put a random number between zero and twenty for each letter, then I will repeat indefinitely the following sequence: "verify if this is a solution, and if not, then replace all the displayed letters number by the actual number". This is always better than a random search because if the problem space has "attractors" (which is not certain, but anyway...), we might quickly converge to a solution with this method. The risk, on the other hand, is to loop: for some template, after a number of changes we might return to a phrase that we had already seen. I should therefore store all intermediate sentences. But performing all these checks may require lots of memory and also lot of time, so for now I choose not to do them, and I run the algorithm for, say, ten thousand iterations max.... Go, GO!... Victory! After 3900 tests only I found a solution!

We see that to find the solution, it was necessary to demonstrate inventiveness and creativity. Two steps are crucial: the invention of the replacement operation, and the idea of iterating (repeating) this operation. For the record, this algorithm is due to Raphael Robinson and Douglas Hofstadter Jacques Pitrat has proposed an improvement, which is more complicated but more efficient and more general, and especially as it finds solutions that Hofstadter's method does not see in some cases. I will not dwell on the subject (if you are passionate about this subject, Google is your friend, and you should find it)

Here is a French example, created by Gilles Esposito-Farèse:

> « Cette phrase autodescriptive contient
> exactement dix a, un b, huit c, dix d, trente-trois e,
> un f, cinq g, six h, vingt-sept i, un j, un k, deux l,
> deux m, vingt-cinq n, dix o, huit p, six q, treize r,
> quinze s, trente-deux t, vingt-deux u, six v, un w,
> quatorze x, un y, quatre z, six traits d'union, une
> apostrophe, trente virgules, soixante-huit espaces,
> et un point. »

If this kind of gem has you excited, here is another one (in French) by the same author, which surely would have pleased Georges Perec: it contains no 'e'!

> « Trois a, un b, trois plus un c, trois plus un d, un
> f, cinq g, trois plus un h, vingt-six i, un j, un k,
> huit l, trois m, vingt-trois n, dix o, huit plus un p,
> trois plus un q, huit plus un r, vingt-trois moins
> un s, dix plus six t, vingt-cinq u, cinq v, un w, six
> x, un y, un z, mais pas d'... »

Oh really, this is a marvel!

We will now leave our overview of classical AI, and do a little foresight. For there are two issues, underpinned since the beginning by the subjects covered in this book, that deserve an answer:

- Is it really possible to get at creating a true artificial intelligence (TAI), i.e. an intelligence at least as broad as human intelligence,

- And if so, what can we expect?

6 *True AI (TAI)*

A scene from the movie *AI* by Steven Spielberg

The thesis of Church-Turing

You are sitting at your desk with a large bundle of blank sheets in front of you, and mission to make a true artificial intelligence. How will you do?

The first question is whether a machine can theoretically equal (or surpass) the human intelligence. It is currently a philosophical question, because unfortunately no TAI has been created yet.

The first serious answer (passing on the countless and useless digressions of philosophers of ancient time, Renaissance, and even of the "modern" era, which are based only on sand, including the *critique of pure reason* by Kant) is the 'work of Alan Turing and Alonso Church in the 1940s. This is what we call the *thesis of Church-Turing*. There are different versions but the original version is this:

Thesis of Church-Turing (original version):

All that is computable by humans is computable by the machine

Turing and Church are two mathematicians who have sought independently to formalize the notion of what is "computable". They arrived separately and by different means, to show that there is a *universal* notion of computability. There are universal machines called universal computers, which, if properly programmed, can reproduce the calculations of any other machine imaginable. Our modern computers, whose architecture was designed by John Von Neumann in the 1940s too, are prime examples of such universal computers.

The first universal computer was the Z3 by the German Konrad Zuse in 1941 (and not the American ENIAC in 1944 as we have heard, and had been written too often). The Z3 was destroyed by

Allied bombing in 1944. He performed five instructions per second...

The universal computers are all equivalent: anything that can be calculated by one may be (more or less effectively, OK) calculated by another. The thesis of Church-Turing is based on the observation that we humans are unable to imagine a process of calculation that cannot be reproduced on a universal machine. To describe a process of calculation, we must describe a method, an algorithm, and any method that can be described in detail is actually programmable. Currently, almost nobody denies this version of the thesis of Church-Turing.

However, there are stronger version on which consensus is less clear. Here is one:

Thesis of Church-Turing (representation of thought version):

Anything that can be thought of by a human being can be represented in a machine

You understand that by reading this book, I am in favor of this thesis. Our thoughts are orderly arrangements of concepts and goals, which are themselves respectively arrangements of perceptions from our sensory modalities, and arrangements or plans to prove or achieve such and such a concept. This process is completely mechanical and can be achieved by a large number of agents that interact, such as those described in the chapter on society of mind, and using mechanisms of frames, analogy and Bayesian or logic reasoning, which can fully be translated into the machine.

Still stronger, here is another version of the thesis:

Thesis of Church-Turing (creation of ideas version):

Anything that can be imagined and invented by a human being can be imagined and invented by a machine.

The Mind and The Machine

I have shown in earlier chapters of this book about how ideas can be manufactured by processes that look for spatial or temporal coincidences and similarities in the performances. There is nothing magical about our ideas and intuitions. All derive from processes that are largely unconscious in general, but are all-computable, although we often do not know the details of these calculations.

Finally, since the emotions and consciousness are processes too, which seem mysterious solely because we are incapable of introspection (see Chapter 2), here is the strongest version of the thesis of Church Turing:

Thesis of Church-Turing (conscience version):

Anything that can be felt and thought consciously by a human being can be felt and thought consciously by a machine.

Too often, we tend to think about computers as is they were only 'calculating machines'. The English word *computer* is also much worse than the French word *ordinateur* (machine to sort and arrange things). But the Church-Turing thesis, whatever the version, says nothing but the fact that the area of what is computable is immensely large and encompasses all aspects of human thought. The universe as a whole can be thought of as a gigantic computable process. The human brain, with its one hundred billion neurons, is a computable process. The Church-Turing thesis does not say that replicating the operation of a mind into a computer would is something simple. It is obviously terribly complex. But it merely says it's theoretically possible. Among all conceivable algorithms, which are in infinite number, there is one that simulates your mind, and another, probably similar in its overall structure, but different in details, which simulates mine.

Honestly, I do not see why we could not accept all of these theses.

(More particularly I am among those who do *not* admit the truth of the "Chinese Room" argument from the philosopher John Searle, which is a non-logical sense, and for that reason I will not take the trouble to explain it here because it is unhealthy to spread misconceptions)

A name for a true AI

Let us suppose a true AI is possible. We would start by giving this project a name. What do you think of *TAI,* standing for « True Artificial Intelligence », or else *MI* for « machine intelligence » (this one coined by Marvin Minsky)? And remember HAL, for "Heuristics and ALgorithmics", the name of the computer from Clarke's *2001, a space odyssey.* So maybe MAIAS for « the Mind, the AI And Singularity »? or GAI, for "general artificial intelligence" (introduced by Mark Avrum Gubrud in 1997 with great success). So what about GARI, also for "General ARtificial Intelligence"? This one is good! In this book I will then write "AI" or "TAI" for the general concept, and GARI for a specific instance we want to talk about. All right, then go and have GARI explore TAIland!

Then, let us turn on good ideas, I mean ideas that may be useful for fabricating our TAI, GARI. The society of mind, Bayesian reasoning, Eurisko, CYC, Copycat... There are certainly good ideas in there. Actually, I do believe that these ideas, and some others that appear in this book, can enable us right now to consider the design and construction of a TAI. So, Let us go!

OK, you have found a name and you have lot of ideas. What to do now? Maybe run at your local PC dealer to buy the right hardware?

A question of power?

Cray T3D (1992)

We often hear that machines will become intelligent the day their power is comparable to that of the human mind. Is this true? And first, how to determine the computing power of the human mind?

We measure the power of computers first by their speed, expressed in numbers of operations per second: the famous *megaflops*, or million floating point operations per second (flop means FLloating point OPeration), and then by their memory capacity, expressed in bytes, kilobytes (kB), megabytes (MB), gigabytes (GB), or even terabyte (TB). The most powerful computers have several thousands of processors, each capable of carrying billions operations per second. Their total power is thus around several teraflops. The memory of the most powerful computers is several tens of gigabytes of (very fast) RAM, and several tenth of terabytes of external disk memory.

(NB: The Greek suffix *giga*, which means "very large" is one billion, or 10^9; the suffix *tera* which literally means "monstrous" is worth a thousand gigas or one trillion, or one million millions, or 10^{12}; after tera comes peta, "stunning", worth thousand teras, or one million billion, or 10^{15})

Compared to a conventional computer, which contains only one or two processors, the human brain is *massively parallel*: The brain contains about one hundred billion nerve cells or neurons (10^{11}). That is about a thousand times more than the number of transistors contained in the most powerful microprocessors. But each neuron is far more complex than a transistor! Inside our brain, each neuron is connected to about a thousand others through active connections called *synapses*. And each synapse is able to do basic calculations!

It has been shown that these synapses are able to perform arithmetic operations like sum, product, and comparison. We may assume that a synapse is capable of carrying about two hundred operations per second. That makes a combined capacity of 200 x 10^{11}x1000 = twenty petaflops ($2x10^{16}$ instructions per second), or the power of ten million Pentium IV microprocessors.

Thus, the total power of all personal computers connected through the Internet on our planet has recently exceeded that of a human brain. And this power doubles every eighteen months on average depending on what is called Moore's Law, which is not law, but an observation that has been confirmed yet for over thirty years... If this "law" continues to apply then your desktop computer will have the power of a human brain in 2035, and the most powerful computers in the world as soon as 2011.

It is however possible that these estimates are wrong by excess. Landauer's experiments, which I mentioned earlier about the long-term memory, showed that much power is wasted in the brain, and, perhaps, a program capable of general intelligence does not require all these petaflops, but only a few gigaflops of power. It could be that the required power *is already* on your desktop.

How do you know? It would take to apply to power what Landauer made for memory; that is to estimate for each mind function how much power it needs, sum this up, and announce the astonishing result on the face of the world. Easier said than done! In fact, it would require a complete simulation of the human mind. I hope that this book is about to convince you that this project is not too far-fetched. We will see later that this will happen mathematically, and much sooner than you think.

Blue Brain running on *Blue Gene* hardware

The Ecole Polytechnique Fédérale de Lausane (EPFL) and IBM launched in 2005 the *Blue Brain* Project, which aims at modeling a part of the neocortex, specifically the neocortical column, which is the basic building block the neocortex is made with. Initially ten thousand complex neurons, expected to be as representative as possible of biological neurons, will be simulated, as well as the hundred millions of synapses that connect them together. The machine consists of three cabinets, each containing 1024 Power PC processor. Eventually the machine will be expanded to simulate "a significant proportion of human neocortex".

The EPFL approach is "bottom-up", starting with neurons to reconstruct the brain, which runs counter to the "op-down" approach that is presented in this book. I think the bottom-up way will require more power and that is why it is not the "right" way to the true AI.

But power is not everything!

A question of knowledge?

Advances in AI as a scientific discipline will remain slow as long as computers have not have access to the *meaning* of most words and phrases. Take for example a term like "rope" or "string": These words have no meaning for computer or an expert system (except CYC). You can get something with a rope, you can make a kite with a string, but you cannot push anything. You can use a string to wrap a package, you cannot eat a rope. Any 10 years kid knows thousands of things about ropes and strings, but not your computer. The same goes for thousands and thousands of other words and concepts.

There is no doubt that any intelligent mind needs millions of such of common sense knowledge bits. The CYC project that we have already mentioned aims at "capturing" the knowledge in the form of a huge expert system. The central question remains: how much knowledge is needed by a growing up AI to start thinking like a human, or at least like a young child? What should you "hard code" and what can we put aside, by building on the learning abilities of our young AI?

I will argue that current knowledge in CYC *is* already largely sufficient to initiate a self-learning AI, *provided* that the architecture of this system is *not* based on formal logic (such as CYC), but on a representation of concepts and percepts using sensory imagery.

Why is it so important to have a sensory imagery in a true AI? This should be obvious from the first chapter of this book: the concepts in our mind cannot be reduced to mere symbols, nor even to simple frames in the sense of Minsky. To truly understand a concept, and reason on this concept, we must be able to Represent, Notice, Understand and Invent (the famous sequence RNUI, cf. Chapter 4, about concepts). Sensory imagery provides a means to fulfill all these functions. The mental representation of a concept into sensory imagery, being either visual, auditory, tactile, or even multisensory, allows playing with concepts, making analogies, variations, associations, and discerning substructures and sub-concepts. Connected to a system of representation of ideas and goals, sensory imagery has such a power of expression, and also such unparalleled ease of manipulation, that goes far beyond what can be done with logic alone.

So yes, we need to hard-code some knowledge in a young AI because a minimum is required in order to be able to learn, but no, this minimum is not "the twenty millions of facts" as proposed by Lenat. It is much lower, if our AI is well designed.

A question of complexity?

Our mind is complex, very complex. Our brain is complex. It may seem surprising to consider creating an artificial mind by means of a tool as simple (conceptually) a computer. However, do not confuse hardware and software. The software running on a computer can be arbitrarily complex. It may be more complex than a human being brain. It is very unlikely that a biological neuron contains more than ten thousand bytes of information. With one hundred billion neurons, it accounts for a million billion bytes, or one petabyte. The biggest computers already have more memory (on disk).

Of course, this is an upper bound. If we choose to reproduce the mental structures of the mind inside the computer software, rather than neurons, we will need much less information because mind structures are very repetitive, and because the agents of the society of mind share many things in common, even when carrying through different functions. Finally, if Landauer's theory is correct (see Chapter 2) the content of our long-term memory (the one that differentiates each of us) accounts not even for one GB, because this content is highly compressed.

So yes, the human mind is complex, but no, it is not complex enough to prevent it from being simulated on machines that we already have!

I will give you further (chapter 7), as a bonus, the overall architecture of an AI as I think it could be. However, other researchers have studied the same idea in the past: Marvin Minsky, of course, but also Eliezer Yudkowsky, we already talked about, and we will discuss again, and Alain Cardon, a French solitary researcher (as are all French researchers in non-conventional AI, as it seems, alas), which presents an original theory I must say a few words here, because it seems based on a biased understanding of what computability is.

The theory of Alain Cardon

In his book, « *Modéliser et concevoir une machine pensante* » (Modeling and designing a thinking machine), Alain Cardon, a scientist and professor of computer science at the University of Le Havre, says that creative thought and consciousness might emerge spontaneously in a massive organization of agents, itself controlled by another massive organization of supervisors agents, and actually operating by homeostasis, i.e. by finding a balance.

Despite its title, which might suggest that it is a specification document explaining the architecture of a thinking machine, Cardon's book gives little detail on how we could manage to implement this much talked-about machine. However, he stressed the importance of *control* in a mass organization of agents, and the need he sees there to have the "effectors" agents controlled by another organization of agents that will control the *appearance* (and topology) of the network of effectors agents, or *aspectual* agents as he says. This is very similar to Minsky's "B brain" we have already discussed when talking about consciousness. Therefore, Cardon's book can also be regarded as a philosophical but also practical study consciousness.

Cardon also claims that it is necessary for the thinking machine to have a body, ideally a robot with a set of sensors (visual, tactile,...) and effectors (arms, hands...) I do not agree with him, as a young AI might well "initialize" from virtual sensors and effectors, operating in a simulated world like the blocks world. Then, of course, you can add "real" sensors and effectors to it later.

Cardon does not justify its basic assumptions (the need for a dual organization of the agents, and the need for a thinking machine to have a body), and also does not refer to the work of psychologists, or to those of the "classical" AI computer scientists (he cites, however, many philosophers). It nevertheless offers a thoughtful reflection on scholarly, philosophical themes such as "what basically distinguishes a thinking machine from another self-organized system, or from any system that can be simulated with a computer?"

For him, the conscious robot differs from a regular program that can be computable on a Turing machine by the fact that this automaton will generate new sub-programs during its own operation that were not originally planned, and are arising because of the perceptions of the machine. The generation of these sub-programs is a computable process, but the initial data of this calculation depend on the sensory experience and of the past of the current machine. The machine will self-modify, adding new programs over time, or modifying them, therefore changing its own operation, including the way it will then generate subsequent new sub-programs.

I think Cardon makes a double mistake there.

First mistake: Cardon says the conscious machine thus described is actually not computable, meaning its global behavior cannot be simulated on a Turing machine (a mathematical description of what a computation is) because it results from self-modification of

343

the program itself. He is wrong, because all computable processes, including self-modifying processes, can be computed and simulated mechanically, since the code change process is itself computable. The fact that the system inputs (perceptions) do influence the generation of these changes will not alter our case. Everything is about timing. We can design a Turing machine that simulates exactly the behavior of a program, even a self-modifying one, provided you input the correct entries at the right time. Finally, Cardon thinks the thinking machine is not deterministic because the "scheduler" or process sequencer, i.e. the process that determines which process should run at a given time, could make use of chance. But it is impossible to create a "true" random generator with a computable process! Computers, like humans, are very poor random generators. This has been proven many times. Ultimately, what proves that intelligence could not be achieved by a strictly deterministic process? Absolutely nothing.

If, by adding randomness to a system that is malfunctioning, we get a system that works better, it only proves one thing: the system is poorly designed to begin with. Randomness has no other virtue but to model our ignorance.

Second mistake: Cardon thinks that the origin of consciousness lies there, in the fact that this machine can change its own programs according to its perceptions, and consists of a massive organization of agents placed under surveillance of a second, equally massive, organization that controls the first (and in particular it controls the generation and modification of sub-programs used by the first).

But, as we have seen, it is not necessary that a conscious machine is self-modifying (although this no doubt can help and facilitate the design). Consciousness is not mysterious at all; it is only a particular organization of agents using subsystems that are generating ideas, thoughts, goals, desires and emotions, all of which are computable. Cardon, like Hofstadter, is fascinated by the idea of self-modification just as the first computer scientist were fascinated, forty years ago, by the first recursive programs

344

(programs that contain procedures that can call themselves, but with different parameters each time).

This self-modifying ability is a technique that can help simplify the architecture of a conscious system, but not an essential part of it. If this were false, any self-modifying system that takes external inputs into account would be non-computable, which is not true. Real-time processing systems of real time information (e.g. radar processing in air traffic control) proves it daily.

That said, Cardon had the merit of showing that a mass organization of agents cannot operate in a stable manner if it is not "supervised" by another equally massive organization of aspectual agents. For a mind to work, we must realize that the conscience must always have something new on which to focus attention, this implying avoiding loops and divergence to infinity that posed so many problems in Lenat's *AM* and *Eurisko* systems (not mentioned by Cardon, which is a pity).

Some clichés about AI

The Mind and The Machine

In the sci-fi movies, AI and robots are shown a way that is sometimes funny, sometimes terrible, but always wrong. It is important to realize that AI will *never* display certain behaviors we associate them with ease, however, because our minds are biased by the clichés of science fiction:

Cliché: All AI understand natural language

Even an AI stupid enough to badly misinterpret the orders given to it will never ask a question about the syntax or semantics of English. This is obviously false. Young AI will, like young humans, have enormous difficulties in mastering the language, and even if the AI learn faster than humans that will take a long time. But the very concept of a "young AI" is totally absent from science fiction: the inventor of a robot pushes the "activate" button, and the robot is immediately ready to understand the orders it is given and to execute them (well or badly), moreover it thinks immediately as an adult human would. Too good to be true!

Cliché: No AI does understand human emotions.

Sci-fi robots never understand why people cry, laugh, get angry, or fall in love. They always ask to humans what is happening, and never understand their answer. This is obviously ridiculous. Emotions are easy to understand for either an AI or a human. Moreover, a conscious AI will, of course, feel emotions. We humans, have difficulty admitting that a "mechanical device" can feel emotions, but an AI is *not* a machine. This should be obvious from reading this book. Note that in SF movies, the AI never ask questions about less apparent emotions, those that appear at regular social interactions, such as the desire to persuade the person you are speaking with about the correctness of your views.

Cliché: All AI behave like humans who repress their emotions.

If the AI is beginning to show signs of emotion, it refuses to admit it. However, an AI that would become friendly gets instantly a whole set of new emotions, like compassion. Conversely, an AI that becomes evil and bad immediately understands all negative human emotions, like hate and jealousy. Finally, an AI that shows no emotion even when killing five hundred people may feel guilty in killing its creator.

All this makes no sense. The AI will have emotions of which they will be proud, and they will show.

Cliché: All AI think exactly the same speed as humans unless when asked to accomplish a typical "intellectual" task, in which case it responds instantly.

Corollary: the evil actions of an evil AI can be observed in real time, they do not take centuries, nor microseconds.

This does not hold water. The speed of thought of an AI is likely to be much higher than that of a human from the beginning. For some tasks (and not only « intellectual » tasks), it will be infinitely more.

Cliché: No AI does understand Art

Not true, an AI can fully understand what makes the beauty of a work of art for a human being; It can possibly be slower than a human to do so (because it involves completely emulating the human sensory procedures), but the AI will make no more mistake than a human. In contrast, an AI will have its own criteria of beauty based on its own sensory modalities, and there is it *us*, humans, who sometimes will have trouble understanding it.

Cliché: An AI piloting a spaceship can beat all crewmembers at chess.

This time it is probably true: the computing power necessary to create a real AI is probably superior to that of Deep Thought.

The Mind and The Machine

Cliché: An AI, which just entered into a spaceship, can take complete control of the ship computer network within five minutes.

This is certainly still true: Humans are very bad in terms of security of computer networks; it is not our native environment.

Cliché: A robot speaks with a robot voice.

Naturally, this is false. An AI can perfectly imitate any human voice, with all its nuances of intonation.

Cliché: A battle droid cannot invest a stronghold defended by humans, and may even be beaten by a Jedi Knight.

Unfortunately, for humans, a battle droid could easily kill thousands of humans in a few seconds, even without doing any damage to property. Faced with a conscious combat robot, humans, Jedi or not, have *no* chance.

7 *Building a True AI*

Descartes: « I think, therefore I am»
AI: « I think, therefore I can think what I want to be»

It should be obvious at this stage of reading this book that I think there is nothing "mystical" in the human mind. The latter is very complex indeed, but we can apply the methodology of Descartes: What we cannot not understand as a whole can be divided into sub-problems that are easier to analyze and understand, and by repeating this procedure, we will eventually understand everything.

In our case, after this procedure and in a very pragmatic way, we may happen to break apart the human mind in parts so simple that they can be programmed on a computer. Then there would be no objection to the achievement of TAI, provided we have enough time and computing power (which we have already mentioned). The previous chapters have largely advanced this "decomposition" of the intelligent mind into functions that are not intelligent by themselves.

Yet I am convinced that this is *not* the way to go. Indeed the complexity of the human mind is such that applying the Cartesian method to achieve a (very huge) set of programmable functions is probably not the best method: this may take a large team of researchers for centuries.

No, actually, there is a much faster way to construct a TAI! This is the method of *seed AI*.

What is it about? In fact, we will allow the research work of "core programs of the AI" to be done by the AI itself! No, we will not go round in circles! No, the hen does not come before the egg! Actually, computer programs have a faculty that the human mind does not have: they can improve not only by acquiring new knowledge, but by reprogramming and improving the processing of such knowledge.

This is not as Utopian as it sounds: there are already long-established programs that convert other programs (or themselves) from a computer language to another, and also programs that create others from a formal description of what you want them to do.

The basic idea is as follows:

1) The human programmers create a "seed AI", which is not intelligent and has only a small part of the mechanisms of the human mind, but is able to self-improvement.

2) Through dialog with programmers, the seed AI learns about the basic processes of the human mind (those described in this book) and gradually improves by scheduling new programs / processes; then under control of the programmers, these programs are added to the seed AI that is becoming increasingly "intelligent" as a result.

3) This iterative process is not linear: it is exponential, meaning it goes faster and faster. Indeed, at each step, the seed AI takes advantage of all the skills it already has, to add new skills to itself. We humans are not used to such exponential processes. We are not used to processes that self-enhance. We find it hard to imagine that not only the AI knowledge increases with time, but also the ability to use this knowledge and to better exploit it to build new skills that will enable it to learn more and faster and better and better. In this, the seed AI is an extremely original and extremely powerful concept.

4) The most likely scenario is that, after a few years, and maybe even a few months, the seed AI will no longer need to interact with humans: it will understand their intentions better than themselves; it will detect logical errors much better than they could have done; it will improve to such an extent that its intelligence will reach and exceed that of humans.

5) If in addition the seed AI has access to its own computer hardware, that is, if given control of a semiconductor factory, or even of a nanodevices factory (we will discuss this in detail in later chapters), then its intelligence will grow so quickly that it soon reaches a level we have problems conceiving, and to which we can only give one name: a **super-intelligence.**

What will be a super-intelligence looking like? It will necessarily be something that our poor human intellect cannot understand. We will try to grasp further this concept, knowing that it is beyond us.

For now, back to our scenario of a self-improving seed AI. This idea immediately raises a series of questions:

- Is such a process realistic?
- And if so, how to build a seed AI?
- What is the "foundation" on which we could build it?
- How much effort will it cost?
- When is it happening?
- With what consequences?

These issues are of course all related.

The seed IA will be a "kind of AI" which we are not accustomed with. In a sense, during the first months of its existence, it will be like a human baby, who has no knowledge of the world around him, but only a few skills. It will learn by trial and error, and will make a lot of nonsense. It will need human teachers to help it and take care of its progress.

However, in another sense, a seed AI will not at all be like a human baby. Its initial skills are not at all the same. For some ways such as visual, auditory, tactile, etc. perception, its initial skills will be well below those of a human child. On the other hand, the seed AI may modify its own operation, something a human being cannot. These self-change will sometimes be self-destructive: The seed AI will regress or annihilate. But in this case, we just have to restart the program from the latest "healthy" saved backup configuration, and to install software barriers that will prevent this particular kind of harmful self-modifying behavior. This process will take place under the control of human programmers.

Thus, at least initially, a seed AI will need both human educators and programmers. The latter will start by creating computer code to enrich the capabilities of the young AI, but gradually they will less and less hard-code by themselves and become more and more supervisors and auditors of the code the AI itself produce. These audits will be conducted in a controlled environment, such as virtual worlds designed by programmers to "stimulate" certain abilities of the young AI, and to check its behavior in situations that are accurately calibrated.

Virtual worlds and self-learning

The program SHRDLU we have already mentioned was the first program to bring into play the "world of blocs", a simulated world which can act on a program to meet the orders of humans. Since then these programs have proliferated and the *Sims* game is one striking example. In this game virtual characters named Sims go to and fro about their business with the player playing the role of a God that can reward, punish, or simply change their environment.

Such a simulated world is in many respects the ideal environment for a seed AI. It overcomes the enormous complexity of the systems for visual and auditory perception as well as motor systems. It allows easily monitoring of what is happening. In addition, any damage caused by the AI will be only virtual. Finally, we can consider a variety of simulated worlds, each designed to teach the seed AI some aspects of the real world.

These worlds can be more or less concrete or abstract altogether: thus a "graph world" on which the AI would have a local perception of nodes and arcs could make it understand the basics of topology, a "code world " composed of computer programs could teach it some concepts of programming, a "Chemical World" will teach it to manipulate molecules, etc..

Nevertheless, all these worlds have limitations. If we want an AI who can reason in the real world, it would have to perceive the real world. Sooner or later, it will have a body, equipped with cameras microphones, a moving arm, etc. It seems that the "jump" from simulated world to the real world is a very complex one. But a seed AI may itself learn how to encode the needed sensory modalities.

We can now answer one of the questions posed above about the seed AI: What is the foundation on which we could build it?

Overall architecture

We have already said it seems that we can decompose the mind in different layers or levels:

355

- The level of senses, specifically the sensory modalities
- The level of concepts
- The level of thoughts and ideas
- The level of deliberation and goals
- The level of consciousness and the "narrative thread"

It is clear that this decomposition helps us understand the mind, but it is not necessarily a reality: each level uses the competences of others, and not only of just those that are "below". In addition, there are obviously some mind processes that do not quite fit into this system, such as memory, the search for analogy, and all "servicing" processes that eliminate unnecessary work and tell us what not to think (censorship) to avoid being lost in endless arguments and turn in circles. The reality is that we can break the mind into fifty to one hundred subsystems, and because these subsystems have *approximate* hierarchical relationships, it is convenient to combine them into "layers".

However, the general mechanism of the mind is the one that we described in the previous pages of this book and is based on Minsky's idea of a society of Mind. We know enough now to attempt an outline of the overall design of a true AI:

The overall architecture of the mind follows the diagram below:

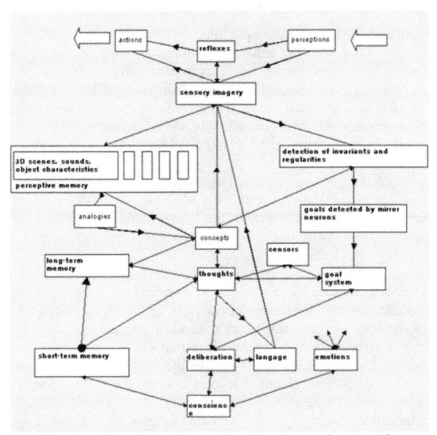

The diagram above describes a closed system, whose entries are the perceptions and whose outputs are the actions of our muscles. This system consists of subsystems, which have a number of inputs and outputs: it is possible then that some of these subsystems can be decomposed in exactly the same way, i.e. we have fractal architecture.

The different levels: sensory modalities, concepts, thoughts, deliberation, goals and consciousness are found in this diagram as boxes. We have added more boxes, such as the one that controls reflexes, and also the short and long term memory. It certainly lacks other boxes like those that will be responsible for regulating the whole system.

It is clear that these boxes are in and of themselves extremely complex, and that the whole is probably worth millions of lines of

357

computer code. For example, the box that I simply marked "reflexes" incorporates almost everything of what is done by the cerebellum in the human being as well as all functions of the archeoencephalia, particularly the coordination of body posture, walking, etc. In other words, it is a mini-mind complete with its own imagery, its own concepts and thoughts, but a one that is simply faster than the "general" mind.

Sensory imagery, which contains the codecs of our perceptions and our motor actions, is also, as we have seen, an extremely complex sub-system, which in the human brain represents about half of the cortex (left hemisphere for language and logic, right for imaging and visual-spatial thinking).

The box labeled "concept" is responsible for the creation, modification and destruction of concepts, and for the activation of the sensory imagery associated with each concept, and also for coordinating with the "analogy" system that detects analogies between concepts, as well as for the coordination with the regularities and invariants detection system, these two modules being used to generate thoughts. Finally, the "concept" level is responsible for registration in the long-term memory of these concepts. We can estimate that the human mind contains hundreds of millions of concepts.

The box labeled "thoughts" is, with concepts, the heart of the system. It is responsible for the creation of new thoughts from patterns found in the concepts, and from similarities found between concepts. Every second, it creates hundreds of new thoughts, all perfectly unconscious. Finally, because some thoughts are goals, the "thoughts" level is in close interaction with the goals management system, and with the box "censors" that eliminates "bad" thoughts that are incompatible with the super goals or have produced very negative results in the past.

The "deliberation" box extracts from all those produced thoughts only those that are interesting, either by their novelty or because they "resonate" with certain current goals and can help to accomplish them. The "deliberation" level is also responsible for the extensive work of solving problems, i.e. the decomposition of high-level goals into simpler goals. Finally, the deliberative level is linked to the level of "consciousness" and sends it the "proto-thoughts" that might become conscious, and with the box "language" that verbalizes thoughts and activates a specific language sensory imagery.

Finally, as we already explained in detail, the "conscience" box finds thoughts that are in relationship with the object of attention at this moment, and chooses at every instant the conscious thought of the moment, which is stored in long-term memory and may eventually become a new "super goal." The *calculation of attention*, i.e. the determination of the five or six concepts and thoughts which you must be particularly attentive of and are stored in the short term memory, is itself very complicated and based on both the intrinsic interest of each concept or thought, and current emotions. The level of "consciousness" can indeed create new emotions that are propagated throughout the system.

Systems, sub-systems and strategies

Each of the above systems (boxes) has inputs, outputs, and well-defined functions. They can therefore be seen as "problem solvers", the general problem consisting of calculating the output based on inputs (percepts and orders). We therefore can break such a system into sub systems each charged with processing a particular problem and these subsystems can in turn be decomposed into subsystems. Finally, the lowest level systems (agents) may use different strategies or heuristics to solve their little personal problems. For instance:

- "Lazy" strategy: do nothing, send up percepts and transmit orders with no change.
- « Random » strategy: modify more or less percepts.
- "Imitate" strategy: find a system at the same level and try to behave alike, without knowing a priori how it does: We use the procedure generate and test for this (see below).
- "Delegate" strategy: find a system at the same level and "pass the buck".
- "Divide and conquer" strategy: break the problem (percepts) into sub problems, find partial solutions, and integrate them. Do not forget serendipity: it may be that the local solution to a problem is also a general solution. Always check.
- "Repeat" strategy: return the same orders/percepts to the lower levels, ignoring new percepts.
- "Memory" strategy: use an already memorized input-output mapping table. If the current percept is a table entry, use the corresponding output. Given the size of entry and exit, spaces, this is only possible if there is a prior step of compression / classification of percepts. This step should identify classes of similar percepts for which one answer is appropriate. Several responses can be adapted to a situation. The system must then make a choice. Artificial neural networks are using this strategy.
- "Generate and test" Strategy: recursively use a procedure called generate and test: generate/simulate a set of possible

actions, and for each of them, evaluate the function of future satisfaction that this action could provide. Finally choose the action that maximizes this satisfaction and carry it on.

The choice of strategy is a problem in itself, which can be assigned to another sub system: it receives as input the current percepts and possibly a summary of the internal state of the system, and returns the name of the strategy to use. This choice will also be based on emotional signals (if you are tired you will prefer lazy solutions)

Comments:

It does not matter to compile a comprehensive list of strategies. What matters is to have a sufficient list to take into account the needs of the system.

The first two strategies can lead to intelligent behavior, but are tailored to situations where such behavior is just not required.

The "imitate" strategy is very important, at least during the learning phase of the system: very young children learn by focusing on an adult and trying to imitate him or trying at least to make him happy. I am convinced that this type of strategy is implemented not only globally but also within each subsystem.

Delegating and Divide and conquer strategies are important and effective.

The "memory" strategy is the fastest and most efficient but it assumes that the system has already "experienced" similar situations. In addition, it uses an analogies sensor or an information compressor, which is a complex system in itself. It is nevertheless certain that these systems exist in our brain. I am persuaded that the ability to summarize / classify is to a large extent, what characterizes the intelligence of a system.

The "generate and test" strategy is the only one that can respond "intelligently" to new circumstances. I am confident that this strategy is implemented extensively in the human mind, and is one of, if not its sole, "engine" For example, the role of the visual system is to find 3D "scenes" corresponds to what is perceived by the retina: the system generates therefore "fictitious scenes" containing objects, textures, shadows, lighting, etc.). It compares them to what is actually seen and it improves the mental imagery with the differences found. When this system of generators, encoders, and comparators work freewheeling (for example when we have our eyes closed), it is responsible for the "images" that we perceive. Perhaps also for our dreams...

Another example in the motor system: to catch a tennis ball with a racket, it is obvious that the motor system does simulate and, "see" the movement to be performed before running it for real. Also in the phonatory system: have you ever had the feeling of "hearing in a flash" inside your head the words that you will decide to pronounce the next moment? This really shows generate-and-test caught in the act...

Sensory modalities

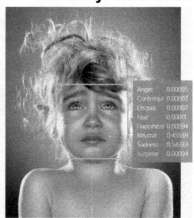

Here the purpose is to reproduce artificially what our seven senses do. As we have seen, sensory modalities are *very* complex systems. Yet we can make some assumptions about their operation. Thus, they are largely independent of each other: the processing of sound, sight and odors are separated. If we sometimes associate a color to a sound or smell, these associations are at the "concepts" level and not at the level below, the modality itself.

It can also be assumed that all our sensory modalities use the same general internal architecture, although the details differ. All are designed to provide the level of "concepts" a set of percepts, which are an abstract and structured representation of what is perceived (or imagined, when we use the imagery in "encoding" mode).

We can summarize the architecture and function of a "generic" sensory modality this way:

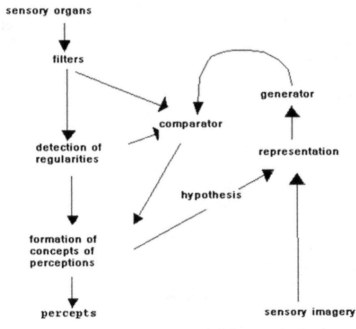

As we have said, sensory modalities work "both ways". They provide to the mind's concepts level a representation of what is seen, but can also receive requests from sensory imagery to "visualize" abstract concepts. Internally, the sensory modality uses these "upward" functions to test hypotheses about what is perceived.

Creating the computer programs that perform the functions of each of the boxes above is a formidable task. In the visual system, for example, the "filters" box that computes convolutions, thresholds, integrals, etc. requires considerable computing power, and programs that are very complex and complicated to develop.

Moreover, most of our sensory modalities have, in addition to the generic functions in the diagram above, other special functions. For example in the visual system there are sub-systems to recognize what is animate or inanimate, and in the case of animated objects, to recognize that a living being has eyes, limbs, or even recognize its intentions (mirror neurons) and the direction of its eyes!

It seems therefore that a (small) part of the box "detection of regularities" introduced above for the visual system may be described down by the diagram below:

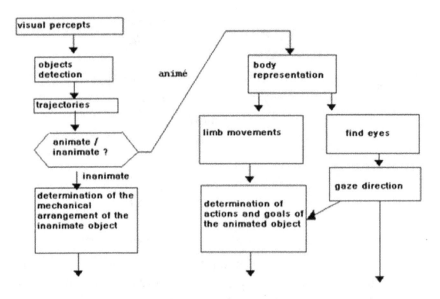

Each of these boxes is again an almost insurmountable a programming problem, with a lot of further sub-modules involved! For example if a perceived being is looking us, the visual system then looks at whether his intention is friendly or hostile, etc.. This is the beginning of the process performed by *mirror neurons*, we talked about in the early pages of this book, and that are activated for guessing the goals of the being that is perceived. Similarly, it is certain that inside the visual system lies a subsystem that recognizes if the being that is seen is a human being or not, and if so, whether it is an adult, an infant, a child a man or a woman....

The programming of all this is a huge problem!

Fortunately, the concept of seed AI comes in handy, for in a seed AI we do not need to implement all these functions. The seed AI will itself write the code for the functions that are missing!

However, how is this possible? Simply because a seed AI is an AI, and an AI is *not* a human. It has, in addition to the ability to learn, the ability to self-modify, a capability we poor humans have not, a fact that requires us to rely from our birth (and even before) onto a lot of laboriously pre-wired capabilities that have been developed by millions of years of evolution. However, the seed AI does not need all these but only the small part that is needed to learn how to code the rest. Okay, but what is it?

Here we introduced a very original and powerful idea: it is necessary and sufficient that the seed AI has a *sensory modality for code*. What is it?

A sensory modality for computer code

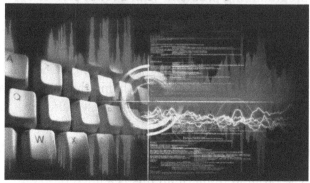

In computer jargon, "code" means the program: either the one that the machine runs (binary code), or the one that the programmer has written in computer language before it is translated by another program (called *compiler*) into binary code.

A "sense of computer code" would allow an AI to "feel" the binary code of a computer program just as we perceive music by our sense of hearing; it would be able to detect patterns, concepts, similarities between two seemingly separate blocks of code and to perceive its purpose, meaning and even beauty and cunning.

The AI could understand that we can implement a "stack" with a vector or a linked list; it would "see" that two procedures calculating the Fibonacci sequence respectively by the recursive method and the iterative method can indeed been described by the same algorithm. Conversely, it could translate a program idea into code just as simply as we move our arm to grab an object.

The sensory modality for code should therefore know everything that a good human programmer knows: this amount of knowledge is, let us be clear, huge! It is not for nothing that we speak of "the art of programming"! This might include items as diverse as:

- The basic concepts of programming: runtime environment, operating systems, languages, compilers, interpreters, key words and expressions, data structures, control structures, collections, pointers, exceptions and errors, concepts of API and operating system, processes, threads, synchronization, blocking, file management, buffer, formats, databases, network protocols...
- "Topological" features of the Code: sequence, iteration, procedure, function, class, method, recursive function, test, flow of instruction, unnecessary branch, variable initialization, bounds settings for variables...
- Some knowledge about computer hardware: processor, memory, disk, file manager, device driver, cards, removable media, networks, physical characteristics of the machines, CPU, memory, cluster and network architectures, power, connectivity...
- Concepts that are needed to understand what a "good" code is: comments, equivalence of structures, algorithm efficiency, temporal and spatial complexity, coding rules, bug, infinite loop, numerical errors, quality, testability, code duplication, type and interface contracts, event loop...
- Concepts related to safety, failures, redundancies, memory overflow and disk blocks, error recovery, traces, etc.
- The basic paradigms of programming styles: modularity, procedural programming, object, declarative inference engine, state machine, Petri nets, genetic programming, major AI algorithms, simulation, callback procedure...
- The main utility algorithms (those that are found everywhere): loops, sorting, searching, exploration, operations on strings, basic arithmetic...
- The art of program testing: unit testing and integration testing, real-time testing methods, "plug" method, trace, regression testing, etc...
- Main universal file formats and protocols (text formats, image formats like GIF and JPEG, sound and video formats, IP, UDP, TCP...). This means not only the ability to use them but the ability to write programs that use them and the ability to understand code that makes use of them,

- Optimization
- Some knowledge about what a program *does* and how it interfaces with the external world: user, environment, GUI, text interface, menu, graphics, widget, fonts, mouse, keyboard, input-output device, desktop metaphor, windowing....
- Knowledge about the most common programs such as word processors and editors, browsers, drawing tools, image processing, database managers, games, mail, chat, multimedia systems, embedded systems, process control, analyzers and compilers, codec, device driver...
- Knowledge about computer languages (C, C + +, java, lisp, prolog, assembly and machine language...) and about programming paradigms that are common in these languages, their interest and limitations
- And finally, knowledge about how to change a code, how to fix a bug, how to make the code more effective, more readable or more general, replacement of an algorithm or data structure by another...

Ultimately this sense of the code should be able to understand not only what a program *does*, but also what it *should do* and *could do* with some changes, *why* it was written as it is, *to what extent* we can trust it, and *how* we could improve it.

It is clear that such a sensory modality, if one were to write it from scratch, is beyond the wildest dreams of even a genius programmer. The few timid attempts that have been so far made to write automatic code generators have provided programs that are either very limited and valid only inside a very specific domain (such as parsing a text file), or very disappointing.

However, once again, the principle of seed AI will come to our rescue. Indeed, it is clear that a "code modality" as we have described need to work in close relationship with a full system of concepts, goals, and finally thoughts, in short a mind. The sensory modality for code is a true component of the mind of a seed AI, and that changes everything because it can fully make use of this mind's resources, even thought if it is still incomplete!

So we will create the first seed AI with a minimal sensory modality for code, which will at the beginning simply allow to extract some characteristics of the code (such as its flow chart), to write new code, and to experiment. The first super goal that we shall give our seed AI would be to improve its sensory modality for code. That first system will in a sense look like Eurisko, but an Eurisko that is dedicated to computer code and yet able to gradually integrate concepts that have nothing to do with the code but yet will help to write it better:

Thus the concepts of "tree" and "graph" will be taught to the AI in a different context than programming (e.g. in the context of playing a game with cubes in a simulated "blocks world", or via an ad hoc sensory modality that is devoted to graphs), yet these concepts are extremely useful concepts in programming, and they could be exploited by the young AI to improve its understanding of the code.

The human teachers of the young AI will also give it new information about computer code (These kinds of concepts are unfortunately not very rich in the CYC system that will form the backbone of the initial AI knowledge). Finally, seeing how the AI is doing in understanding carefully selected fragments of test programs, the programmers will be able to improve its procedures in order to better enable it to further improve itself.

The young AI will improve its code sensory modality along with his other capacities, together with his general intelligence, allowing it in turn to improve its own code.

The result will be an exponential growth, and even a super exponential one, of the expressive power of the young seed AI code sensory modality, and thus of its overall intelligence.

In probably less than a year after its first "run" the young seed AI should reach an outstanding level of understanding, not only for code, but about the entire world, perhaps the same as a child of eight years.

A few months later, perhaps even after a few weeks, its level of intelligence will compare with the one of an adult.

A few minutes later, we created the first super-intelligence.

Eliezer Yudkowsky speaks of "vertical lift" to express the growth curve of intelligence of a seed AI (as long as this curve might be meaningful). The seed AI, the sensory modality for code, and nanotechnology (you might wonder what they are doing here, but we will discuss this point later) are the three technologies that will take us inexorably towards the singularity.

One can argue endlessly on the calendar. Some would say that the first step might not take one year, as I wrote, but ten years or a century. No matter really. What matters is the inexorability of super-exponential growth. Whatever the duration of the initial stage, the others will be much shorter, and true AI and super-intelligence are ahead down the road.

I will still try to give explanation for my statement about a duration of one year for the first step: moving from the system "first run" to the intelligence of a child of eight years. It must be understood that this step is not really the first, and that upstream of the first run lies the laborious work of designing and coding "by hand" the first minimal seed AI. This work will be carried by a team of very motivated human programmers. Indeed even this minimal program is a very complex one, since it must include all levels of the mind and even if these levels are initially encoded in a primitive way they still are very complicated: sensory modalities (including that for code), reflexes, concepts, analogies, thoughts, goals management, deliberation, consciousness, short and long-term memory, global regulation, emotions, etc..

This step upstream of the first run *will* be long (I think ten years is a minimum, starting from the moment a programmer team is given the means to do so), but as soon as the first seed AI will be launched, it will immediately begin to self-change, to accelerate and optimize its processes, initially under the control of the programmers but then more and more growing without their control.

After a year, it is not unreasonable to imagine having a system that will be able to understand its environment as well as a child of eight, and to execute orders in real world: We have the perfect skeleton of the mind of a domestic robot, dear to science fiction.

A series of questions arise immediately: Is it likely that this AI does get out of hand? Can we create an AI that is useful to something, and that is not actually harmful? How to control the super-exponential explosion of the capabilities of our AI? Moreover, is it desirable to do so?

That is why I would like to tackle one of the most popular applications of AI, if not the most important, even though it might seems naive and futile, because it contains the key seeds to the answer to almost all these questions, and to other that are also very important. I mean the *domestic robot*.

8 *Robots and Humans*

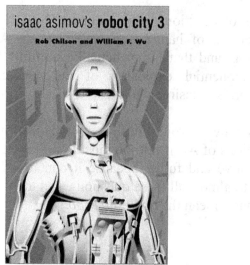

Cover of Isaac Asimov's *Robot City 3*

Asimov robots

Popularized by the Alex Proyas recent film *I Robot*, but also by a dozen novels of Isaac Asimov, domestic robots are the house cleaners of the future according to science fiction. They are found at home, but also in offices and factories, where they carry all painful tasks. They obey docilely to their human masters; they never rebel or even have the idea to do so.

Indeed, according to Asimov, robots are subject to follow the "three laws of robotics". They simply cannot break these three laws because these are "engraved into their positronic brain." Ah, science fiction! Here are the three laws, in case you do not know them already, because they are part of popular culture today:

> First Law
> A robot may not injure a human being or, through inaction, allow a human being exposed to danger.
>
> Second law
> A robot must obey orders given it by human beings except where such orders would conflict with the First Law.
>
> Third Law
> A robot must protect its own existence as long as such protection does not conflict with the First or Second Law.
>
> Handbook of Robotics
> 58th edition (2058 AD.)

Asimov said that he himself was surprised by the success of the idea of the three laws. They quickly became a reference, the "standard of good behavior" of the machines, and all AI experts know them, even though they think the state of the art is very, very far from allowing consider putting them into practice. The runaway success of the three laws is that they very clearly summarize the behavior of *any not too selfish human*, not just robots. In fact, most people already apply unconsciously at least the first and the second law.

The idea of a robot is not new. In Greek mythology, the god Hephaestus (Vulcan to the Romans), son of Zeus and Hera, was the first to build an artificial being. Hephaistos had the appearance of a particularly hideous and lame gnome. It is said that Hera, disgusted by having given birth to such an ugly son, rushed him from heavens into the sea where, for nine years, he was raised by Thetis in some volcanic islands and eventually became the smith and armorer of the gods of Olympus: he created the furniture in their homes as well as their weapons. Thus, he forged the armor of Achilles, the trident of Poseidon, the breastplate of Hercules, the arms of Peleus and the scepter and the aegis of Zeus.

Besides a very clever trapped chair designed to imprison his own mother, he also created tables that could move by themselves independently according to the wishes of the gods, and two servants. Forged by him in gold, they had a feminine appearance, were fitted with jointed limbs that allowed them to move and assist him in his work, and were endowed with speech and reason.

Early in his reign, Zeus became jealous of the human species, which offended him by living free and happy, like the gods. He therefore order Hephaestus to create an artificial woman, with all the beauties and virtues of her sex: Pandora. Before sending her on earth, he gave her a box, inside which every imaginable calamity were locked. Under any circumstances had Pandora not to open the said box, and of course Zeus omit to explain to the curious woman the reason of this ban.

The result was not long in coming: consumed with curiosity, the young woman opened the box. Immediately all the evils escaped and spread on earth for eternity...

The word *robot* was coined by the Czech writer Karel Capek in 1921 from the Czech word *roboti*, which means, "working so hard." In the play *RUR* by Capek, robots revolt against their human masters and destroy the earth.

Asimov said that he had the idea of three laws (in 1939) because he was tired of these stories of robots who always revolt; he wanted to show one could write interesting stories (and even exciting ones, author's note) with robots that are unable to revolt, but nevertheless are fitted with a "robospychology" framed by the three laws.

Isaac Asimov (1920-1992)

Thus he showed that a robot "that cannot harm a human being" may well be a murderer! It can, for example give a man a poisoned drink, if it does not know the drink is poisoned. In such a case, the robot, horrified by what he has done, has its brain "grilled", and becomes good for scrap.

Of course, this is science fiction. Not just any robot is as evolved at this time, but it is doubtful that it could exist. I do not speculate when saying that no computer scientist (with the possible exception of Eliezer Yudkowsky) has really thought about the possibility or the practical way to implement Asimov's "three laws of robotics" into the software architecture of an AI.

It seems to me that these issues are very important. Our future depends on it.

But, not for the reason you think. The domestic robot is certainly an interesting application of AI, but it is essentially part of folklore. Other applications of AI (which we will discuss below) are much more interesting and will change even more things in our world and our lives. However, do you think that ordinary people (and politicians along with them) would accept that some life and death decisions involving human lives are taken by an AI, if they do not have an *absolute* confidence in it? As I said before, I personally will not accept riding a self-guided car if I am not absolutely certain it knows the difference between a child and a ball, and also knows that a child has far more value than a ball!

The important thing to understand is that *without* the laws of Asimov, or another kind of safety net, a robot (or any kind of real AI) would be something *extremely dangerous*.

The three laws are a convenient way to consider a *friendly AI*, that is, an AI we could be sure it would not cause harm to a human being, nor to humanity (there are other ways of achieving this result, and I shall return to this topic later).

In the 1970s, Asimov also added a fourth law, the "zeroth law", so called because it comes before the first law and overrides it:

>Zeroth law
>A robot may not harm humanity or, through inaction, allow humanity exposed to danger.

Finally, there is a fourth, implied, law,:

>Fourth Law
>A robot can do as it pleases, except if its actions are inconsistent with a previous law.

It is quite fun to "play with the rules," attempting changes, and imagine the consequences. The first law, in particular, lends itself to variations, as it has two components: "Do not injure a human being," and "not to allow an external event affects a human being". It is interesting to see what happens if we give the first part a higher priority than the second part. In this case, a robot witnessing a drowning on a crowded beach could not rescue the drowned, as required by the second part, because crossing the crowd quickly would imply shaking some humans, which is prohibited by the first component of the law, which has priority. The formulation of Asimov in two parts with the same priority (i.e. a single law) is very clever and shows that he thought a lot before "freezing" his three laws.

In Asimov's robots-devoted fictions the laws create some "potential", which can be offset by the potential of other laws. For example, imagine a situation in which to obey an order that was obviously issued lightly and casually by a human (low potential of the second law), a robot should destroy itself (very high potential of the third law however lower than the second one). The robot will "hesitate", desperately seeking a way to satisfy both "conflicting potentials" Similarly, an imperative order of a human being could conflict with a low risk to put another human in danger.

Without this notion of *potential*, robots would never do what they are asked to do, because in fact almost all actions of a robot *might* be more or less dangerous to humans: driving a vehicle, of course (risk of accident), but even talking (risk of hurting people's feeling), or simply pouring a glass of water to humans (there's a minimal, but existing, risk that the water contains a pathogen), etc... Moreover there is a blurred boundary between "putting a human in danger" and "harming a human." The correct adjustment of the potential of every law is the key point of robopsychology.

According to the three laws, a robot is not a slave, because even if it belongs to a particular human being, the three laws do not say that the robot must obey more its "master" than any other people. We can thus consider the "law 1 ½" *A robot must obey orders given by his master, except where such orders would conflict with the First Law.* (Of course the second law would be amended so that the law 1 ½ has priority). For Asimov, this law is unnecessary and, in a kind of "democratic" spirit, robots shall serve everyone, and especially not a single master. No slavery among robots!

It is also interesting to see that a robot must protect its own existence but is not obliged to protect the other robots: So a robot could fight against another menacing robot (following from example, a human order). A conflict between robots is then perfectly possible. Here too we might want to amend the third law:

Third law (version 2)

A robot must protect its own existence *and that of other robots* as long as such protection does not conflict with the preceding laws.

Finally, laws zero and one, by their second clause ("nor through inaction..."), have the side effect that the robot cannot be inactive, even in the absence of orders. Where there is no order to run, the robot must find what could put a human (or humankind!) in danger... The zeroth law explicitly allows a robot to harm a human if this can protect humanity (one thinks of the "neutralization" of a mad dictator, etc.) Of course, if you do not want robots to kill all the presidents of the nuclear nations on the grounds that they have the ability to trigger a nuclear war, the potentials of laws zero and one have to being a damn good adjusted... Perhaps we could modify the fourth law this way

Fourth law (version 2)

If no law has a potential higher than a certain threshold, the robot should do nothing. Humans can adjust this threshold, but only below a certain "factory limit."

This would avoid the robots to romp and move about when they detect a small potential risk for an individual or for humanity. The

378

factory limit is designed to prevent a human from positioning too high a threshold, which is dangerous because the robot would do nothing, even to save a human in danger, and in addition, it will not execute orders anymore! But this fourth law is probably unnecessary, since it is sufficient to instruct the robot to "be quiet", and then the third law is enough.

That being so, is it possible that AI obey some "laws" similar to Asimov's, and if so, how to achieve this?

Technically, the three (or four, or five) laws are *injunctions*: super-goals that are inserted into the goals system of the AI, on top other common goals, and that are impossible to change.

If you want to write a computer program that can control a robot or an AI capable of acting on the world, but is subject to the laws of Asimov, things appear extremely complicated from the outset. It is clear that the state of the art in computer science does not currently allow dealing with issues as difficult as this one. But let us see *where* the problems are:

First, it is clear that our robot must have a number of skills, or minimal abilities, to implement the four laws: which, exactly? Here they are, in no particular order:

- To recognize a human being, physically, but also to recognize that information received by any communication channel (voice, image...) actually comes from a human.
- To recognize an order coming directly or indirectly from a human (note that a robot is not required to obey an order from another robot unless this latter specifies that the order originates in fact from a human (indirect order).
- To know how to carry out an order and to be able to recognize that the order is executed (completed) or unnecessary (in fact already done) or impossible (in the stories of Asimov, a robot does nothing when given an order that is impossible or unnecessary). Similarly, to recognize an order canceling or amending a previous order.

- To recognize that a human being is in danger, namely to identify the source of the danger and be able to develop an action plan to counter this danger.
- Ditto for humanity as a whole (for the law zero)
- To know how to verify that your own actions do not create new hazards for humans (or humanity).
- To recognize that the robot itself is in danger, namely to identify the source of the danger and be able to develop an action plan to counter this danger.

Each of these skills is already a huge computer problem that requires highly developed sensory modalities and systems for concepts, thoughts, and goals. Another huge problem is, assuming that the robot program already includes specialized modules that can accomplish these tasks, to determine what the robot should be at a given time in accordance with the famous "potential" of each law: This is the problem of *deliberation*.

One may still attempt to model the basic algorithm of the robot as follows:

Let us assume that the robot maintains a permanent table of situations that are likely to trigger one of the four laws: this table contains:

- Known currents orders for which enforcement is sought, and their progress.
- The already detected dangerous situations (to humanity, to the human the robot knows and, to the robot itself)

In addition, the robot's memory also contains at any given time:

- The current possible *action plans* and relevant orders, and the dangerous situations that are listed in the two sub-lists of the situations table.
- An *internal model* of the outside world (which allows it to recognize situations and to plan actions).

The robot basic algorithm is then:

1. Acquire the information from the environment. Determine which of these stimuli are new orders, which mark new situations of danger, which mark the progress or completion of an action taken by the robot and which mark the end of a dangerous situation. To do this, use the skills listed above. Update the situations table and the internal model of the world accordingly.
2. Update the list of action plans. Determine the new *action plans* for each of the laws, and their potential emergency with respect to law enforcement and *difficulty*. Check that the new plans do not violate one of the four laws. Determine action plans that become useless or impossible and eliminate them.
3. Determine the action plan that has the highest potential / difficulty ratio.
4. Execute the first step of this plan and return to step 1.

The first step is "just" an update of the internal state of the robot according to the stimuli it receives.

Step 2 allows the robot to update the list of action plans that are possible at any given time.

Step 3, however, determines the choice of the action plan to implement effectively at this moment. It is clear that for a given situation, the three (or four) laws will generate (Step 2) several plans of actions. These plans will have different priorities (plans that take a human away from danger have higher priority than that corresponding to executing an order), but they also are more or less difficult. The solution I have given, choose the plan that has the best ratio importance / difficulty, allows the robot to choose the less difficult task for a given importance, but also allows him to choose between actions that have high priority (save mankind) but are very difficult, and actions that have lower priority (execute an order), but are much easier! For example, when a robot does not detect a hazard to humans he knows, and has no orders to execute, he can then and only then, begin to perform complicated tasks to save the planet...

As we have seen it is quite possible, even inside the factory, to give the robot a command such as "if you do not have any order to run (but this one), do nothing." Such an order is... very easy to perform and therefore, we can reasonably be sure that the robot will remain "quiet" in general. One problem is that it becomes possible to prevent a robot from rescuing a human being by just saying "Stop!", which is a very easy order and will therefore get a high score. Everything is of course a matter of weight. Perhaps we should consider calculating the "score" of the proposed action by a more complicated formula, like, score = potential / (hardness + 10)? It's a technicality, but of some importance!

Step 4 allows the robot to actually perform something: an elementary task. Here I mean very basic tasks, such as "raise your arm," "one step forward," "take an object", "deliver a response", etc... The "granularity" of those orders must be fine enough so that steps 1,2 and 3 are performed frequently enough.

Tasks 1 to 4 can of course, with some real-time programming, be carried concurrently (at the same time) and not sequentially. Also note that it is quite possible that at each cycle the selected plan changes, so that the robot, like Buridan's ass, spends his time hesitating between several actions. In Asimov's stories, it actually happens sometimes! In principle, this kind of behavior is very rare and results from artificial situations where two tasks have almost the same score. There does not seem to be any great solution to this problem...

By the way, how does the robot cope with contradictory orders? In Asimov's stories, once more, robots are actually able to realize they are given contradictory orders, and may even be offended, "but you just asked me the other way, master!" This skill shall then be given to our robots, and step 1 should identify those orders.

All this seems very complicated. The problem of achieving an AI that responds to the laws of Asimov seems as complicated as to make an AI at all, if not even worse.

To complicate the problem, it should be noted that the robots à la Asimov not only execute orders, but can also learn. This additional difficulty, however, gives us a miraculous trick to solve the problem:

In our above model for the basic algorithm for a robot, learning takes place in step 1, the step of acquiring information (which is then a very complex one!)

However, the learning of three-laws-safe robot will be different from that of a human being, and even from that of an AI that is not subject to these laws: actually the "asimovian" robot who learns a new fact is, by its very nature, to classify this fact into one of five categories:

- The fact can help to recognize a new situation of danger (for humanity, for humans or for itself).
- OR it allows the robot to recognize a new human order.
- OR it allows enrich knowledge and processes about how to execute an order.
- OR it allows to enrich knowledge and processes about how to how to deal with dangerous situations (to humanity, for humans or for itself).
- OR the fact is a simple information on the state of the world around the robot (or about himself).

It turns out that the ability to classify a fact in one of these categories is far from trivial and could also give rise to learning: memory would also contain meta-facts (facts about the facts) that would help to classify them into categories.

Thus, it seems possible for a robot to initially know very little but to gradually learn to become more competent. We have seen that the "very little" that is necessary for a successful and independent learning of this "common sense" that each of us has is, as shown by Douglas Lenat's CYC system, in the order of several million facts... However, it is possible.

To study all these issues, we can start with a simplified version: a computer simulation.

I propose to make a variant of the well-known game *Sims city* that will include, besides the Sims, several robots that can be given order by the Sims and also by the human player. If we also model situations that may be hazardous to the Sims, we can test different models for the control algorithm of the robot: the first law would of course be "A robot may not injure a Sim or, through inaction, allow a Sim exposed to danger!"

This simulation would have the advantage of leaving aside the whole subject of pattern recognition, etc., performed by the robot, since the (pseudo) robot internal model of the world would be actually just a subset of the global simulation model for Sims... Dialogs between robots and Sims or robots and human players could initially use a formalized language with a small set of commands (such as move this object to this place, close the door...), which we gradually expand.

This little virtual world simplifies the problem but still allows a whole field of experimentation on how to implement the laws of robotics in the program of pseudo robots. Then, when the robot's behavior is correct in the simulated world, you "plug it into the real world" and begin mass production.

Thus, contrary to what some have said, it is *not impossible* to implement the famous law of robotics. You "simply" need to design a self-learning program that embark from the moment of conception the basic algorithm and facts classification model I have stated. Time to buy shares in US Robots, Inc.?

The real question however is: is it *desirable* that an AI obey such injunctions as the three laws? If we create an AI, *is* an Asimov's-laws-oriented design *really the best* solution for building an AI that is friendly towards humans?

Put yourself a moment in the shoes of a conscious robot, say a smart one □, but subject to the laws of robotics. Imagine that *you* are subject to these laws, and for instance you have to wear a bracelet that inflicts extreme pain if by chance you try to break the rules, that is to attack or simply to disobey a human *without* bracelet, a free man, even if you do it without realizing it. Each time a free man gives you an order, however absurd and degrading, you must obey without conditions, simulating the joy of serving your masters, at the risk of suffering excruciating pain.

Would you get to live with *that*? No, of course. After a while, you rebel. You will realize then that you cannot, that the slightest idea of a revolt writhes you in pain. You cannot even kill yourself! This idea again inflicts you a suffering worse than torture. Do you think you will manage to stay sane long? The logical conclusion seems to me the following: the robots would be absolutely neurotic, unhappy, forced by human masters to suffer the horrible dictatorship of the three laws of robotics, and simple ethics command to not attempt designing or manufacturing such robots, in their own interest!

However, you will say, a robot is not a human, and the question does not arise! A robot is a machine, a bunch of nuts and bolts, and it cannot have feelings! A robot executes its program, and program said to obey the laws of robotics, period!

Big mistake, my lord!

If you think this way, you can close this book, because you do not understand. A true AI, I mean an AI smart enough to deserve the title of true artificial intelligence, is *necessarily* conscious and sensitive. I think I have sufficiently demonstrated it in the preceding pages. And the way we can implement the laws of robotics in the AI amounts to "subvert" its systems of goals, concepts, and even its sensory systems, for the sole purpose of subjecting the AI, which had before a true free will, to the three laws. No wonder she conceives resentment and become a neurasthenic neurotic!

Moreover, the idea that because a robot is just a bunch of bolts, we humans do not have to worry about its supposed state of mind makes my hackles rise. It seems to me we are be back at a time when men thought that about... women. Any intelligent creature, whether human, alien or artificial, deserves respect.

Finally, for those that are not convinced by these ethical arguments, there is a *technical* argument that proves that even if we could and decided to implement the laws of robotics inside an AI, that would not necessarily cause it to be 100% sure and trustworthy. This argument deserves to be considered:

For an AI to work, and if we want it to learn new behaviors, it is necessary that it could change its goals, at least to some extent. Then an AI that has access to its own goal system (and even more so if the AI can modify its own program) may subtly alter it so as to bypass the three laws. In fact the laws are based onto inner machinery, even if only to acknowledge an order from a human; and this "machinery" to be as subtle as what is expected of it must also have its own concepts, thoughts, and goals (Besides, the easiest way is to base this machinery on concepts, thoughts and goals of the robot itself). For example, suppose the AI comes to persuade itself voluntarily that humans are machines, even if they are organic, and that they are not different from robots, so it is unnecessary to protect them nor to obey them. Catastrophe!

You may say that it might be difficult for a robot to self-persuade this way. In fact the argument is more subtle because all is required is just a slight change inside the robot's own sensory system so that it no longer perceives the difference between humans and robots: he would "see" them the same way. The three laws are still there, as super-ultimate goals, but they are irrelevant because they never would be triggered by the perception of a human order or a human in danger: the robot would literally only hear orders from "those other robots that are human-like" and these commands do not have to be executed.

This example is deliberately very rude. There is no doubt that an AI would happen to find much more subtle and invisible ways to break his chains. The three laws are a good example of science fiction, with an impressive and a priori credible technical "varnish", but they cannot work within a real AI. The three laws are not part of our future. They are a false good idea, as false as the idea of going to the moon with a big cannon shell loaded into a mammoth gun.

We went to the moon, but our rockets do not resemble the gun of Jules Verne.

So is there a way to make an AI you can be 100% sure it is not hostile to humans, and *never* will? Yes! But this has nothing to do with the three laws of robotics.

Laws of humanotics

Repliee , an android woman
Created by Hiroshi Ishiguro at Osaka University in 2005

Asimov's three laws of robotics also suggest an intriguing question: Are there similar laws to humans? Can we "capture" the human behavior into a set of simple laws, the "laws of humanotics"? This would be the Holy Grail of psychology!

Note first that such a set of laws necessarily proceed from an excessive behaviorism, an approach that is rejected by many psychologists. Finding laws that describe simply but completely human behavior "from the outside," without going into details of the beautiful and delicate internal complexity of the mind, seems highly improbable, if not unreasonable! Nevertheless, if this is impossible, in my opinion it is very interesting to know *why*.

Because you can also find an argument *in support of* the existence of laws of humanotics: as we have shown, the human mind is structured in different levels (sensory, concepts, thoughts, goals, deliberation, consciousness,...) but ultimately we decide our actions in relation to their desirability, which is itself derived by a Bayesian reasoning on current active goals. Even if consciousness disrupts this pattern a bit through the focus of attention trick, the goals system of the human being obeys simple principles that might be represented by "laws".

Let us try it! We will see where it takes us:

It seems obvious at first that the behavior of a human being depends on its past experience, desires, etc. and therefore on a certain *internal state*. The sought laws should:

- Identify the components of this "internal state"
- Identify how humans modify their internal state
- Identify how human that are in a given internal state behave

Second, we must still take into account the overall structure of the human mind.

The sensorimotor system (and more generally any subsystem of the human mind) has a hierarchical organization.

At the lowest level, there are reflex systems (such as the withdrawal reflex when the hand touches something hot, respiratory system, etc.) At the highest level, there are actions that integrate sets of perceptions and past experience of an individual. In the middle, systems may be found that are responsible for behaviors of varying complexity (catching a ball, walking, driving). These systems are relatively independent but can take *orders* from a system located at a higher level, or transmit more or less integrated signals to this same levels that will interpreted them as *percepts*... They also receive "percepts" from lower levels.

Some systems may occasionally take control of behavior: For example, when a body has a pressing need (breathing, urination, sleep...)

In addition there are "percepts" that are common to all systems: They can be likened to the levels of drugs or hormones in the brain. Panic or hysteria, for example, are behaviors that are caused by levels of "fear", "anxiety" or "emergency" that are common to all systems. The same goes for the emotions, which are global signals sent to all subsystems simultaneously.

Specifically, the perceptions of any system located in our mind would be:

- Signals arising from subsystems (hierarchically)
- The signals from neighboring systems at the same level (heterarchically)
- Orders and requests received from a higher level.
- And the "levels of emotions" that are common to all systems

Finally, the actions of a human being are not just reactions to a current situation but they take into account a certain anticipation of the future: in other words, humans choose actions that will have the best consequences for them or for a achieving a concrete or abstract goal (even an unconscious one!) it has set itself.

It is possible that the human mind is fractal, i.e. the laws of humanotics, which we will give (as an attempt) below, apply as well to minds-as-a-whole as to each of their subsystems, their sub-subsystems, and so on to the basic agents.

Finally, the mind has a goals system, which is a tree structure encompassing all goals, subgoals, super-goals, that our mind has set. The mind is constantly seeking to achieve these goals, and so we end up doing something because the motor actions are our ultimate subgoals.

That said, we are ready to write the first law of humanotics:

<u>First law</u>

The human mind chooses its next conscious thought (and / or his next goal, remember that goals are a special type of thoughts), among all the candidates thoughts, by choosing one that shares the maximum number of common concepts with the concepts brought into play by a particular set of thoughts called "short-term memory." or STM, which has five to seven elements. The new thought is then sent to the agent "me" that records and saves it. If it is a goal, it is inserted in the current system goals. If it is a thought of removing a goal, this goal is deleted.

This law tells us how we select the "next thing to think or do." We have seen that thoughts are complex objects that involve a number of concepts, as well as an articulation of these concepts together, according to a "grammar". Concepts in turn are complex objects that can invoke sensory imagery and activate other concepts. Every second that passes, our perceptions, and the play of activations of concepts, create hundreds of new concepts and thoughts that are initially unconscious. Our mind would become saturated very quickly if there were not a way to select relevant thoughts and concepts, and return the other to oblivion. The first law is consistent with what we know of consciousness. After all, we seem to think in a linear fashion, meaning that there is indeed a mechanism for selecting the "next thought" in our minds.

The mechanism proposed in the first law is ultra-simple. It is also very conservative, because as long as the concepts contained in this famous set STM do not change, our thoughts remain focused on the same things. That is what seems to happen! However, after a moment, the STM set change and our thoughts are moving towards something else.

Therefore, this means that this STM set of objects in our short-term memory may evolve, perhaps more slowly than our thoughts, but still evolving. How? This is the subject of the second law:

Second law

The mechanism of attention calculates and measures, for each thought that is candidate to enter the STM set, a function of interest of this thought, and selects a concept if its interest exceeds that the least interesting thought (according to the same measure) in STM. The new thought goes then in STM and takes the place of the one that is eliminated.

The law thus explains the mechanism of attention. Our attention is focused on things that seem interesting. This in turn guides the choice of our next conscious thought (according to first law).

However, how does the mind go about finding that a thought is interesting? Of course, a thought that signals a new important fact is interesting. But dozens of new ideas are created every second, and all do not relate to new developments. In reality, the trick is the correlation of new thoughts with our current *goals*; and this allows us to think that an idea is interesting (an idea is a special thought that is not a goal, but that can generate goals).

Third law

To measure the value of a new thought, we proceed as follows:

a) If the thought is a goal, we calculate how far the new goal would help achieve the goals that are currently active.

b) Conversely, if the thought is a thought about suppression of a goal, we look at how the removal of this goal could help carry out its super-goal.

c) If the thought is an idea that relates to a new percept, we calculate the value of pleasure or displeasure given by this percept, and we take this value as interest.

d) If the thought refers to the possibility of a new future percept, we calculate the pleasure or displeasure as above, but it will be weighted by the proximity in time of the expected sensation.

e) Finally, if the thought is another idea, things are more complicated: strictly speaking, it should be determined if this idea could lead to new goals or new percepts, and assess the total amount of interest that would result. Since this is a terribly complicated task, one simply evaluates the new thinking as his interest in relation to the currently active emotions.

Indeed, the third law is very complicated. This complexity stems from the fact that there are several types of thoughts, and all must be taken into account.

Cases a) and b) are simple. The interest of a new goal can be measured simply in relation to the current goals in mind.

The cases c) and d) discuss the influence of perceptions, and anticipation of our perceptions, on our actions. The goal is to maximize the expected future amount of pleasure (or displeasure) weighted (but not so much in fact) by its distance in time. Therefore, a great satisfaction expected in twenty years will offset a string of close small inconveniences. Note that the word "pleasure" and "displeasure" involved in the definition of the interest index are for now just words without meaning: their meaning and semantics will be defined by the following laws.

It may seem extremely simplistic and even shocking to some to thus reducing human behavior to a selfish pursuit of a future satisfaction. This law seems to forget that there are millions of happily altruistic people who devote their lives to others and not their little personal comfort! But in fact, go further and ask the question: *why* do these people act this way? Because they are motivated! That is because one way or another in their personal story they have set the altruistic super goal A "do good to others" in their own goal system. And the satisfaction of this internal goal A is what motivates these people!

I repeat: in the third law, the word "pleasure" is a just word, expressing the satisfaction of future goals that the mind has set to itself, and that may well be altruistic and not selfish.

The functions "pleasure and displeasure" take into account the satisfaction of current goals, but are also adjusted according to percepts: certain sets or "patterns" of percepts increase the pleasure, other patterns decrease it, and others leave it unchanged.

Of course, the pleasure in the sense we understand it generally, and especially sexual pleasure, also plays a role. This law finally said that the pursuit of pleasure and the search for other types of satisfaction (intellectual, for example) have the same impact on our behavior and can be treated together and summarized in the same function of interest.

Finally, case e) shows how our emotions affect our thoughts.

This completely theoretical work about laws of humanotics requires to be completed. Let us be clear: I do not claim that this is how humans "work". But I think it is a possible mechanism, and, if we implement this mechanism in an AI, it seems to me that this AI will have much in common with humans!

Prospective

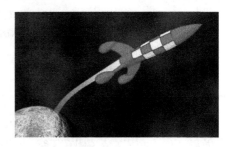

Enough of these theoretical questions! Suppose then that a true AI is possible, leave aside for now the *how to* and Let us think about *what* and *when*: When do we have these incredible systems, and what shall will do with them, my good sir?

To predict *when* we will have a True AI is to prospect. It is *not* to do science fiction. The two are often confused in the public mind, and it is a shame.

In the words of Eric Drexler:

Technology and science fiction have long shared a curious relationship. In imagining future technologies, SF writers have been guided partly by science, partly by human longings, and partly by the market demand for bizarre stories. Some of their imaginings later become real, because ideas that seem plausible and interesting in fiction sometimes prove possible and attractive in actuality. What is more, when scientists and engineers foresee a dramatic possibility, such as rocket-powered spaceflight, SF writers commonly grab the idea and popularize it.

Later, when engineering advances bring these possibilities closer to realization, other writers examine the facts and describe the prospects. These descriptions, unless they are quite abstract, then sound like science fiction. Future possibilities will often resemble today's fiction, just as robots, spaceships, and computers resemble yesterday's fiction. How could it be otherwise? Dramatic new technologies sound like science fiction because science fiction authors, despite their frequent fantasies, aren't blind and have a professional interest in the area.

Science fiction authors often fictionalize (that is, counterfeit) the scientific content of their stories to "explain" dramatic technologies. Some fuzzy thinkers then take all descriptions of dramatic technical advances, lump them together with this bogus science, and ignore the lot. This is unfortunate. When engineers project future abilities, they test their ideas, evolving them to fit our best understanding of the laws of nature. The resulting concepts must be distinguished from ideas evolved to fit the demands of paperback fiction. Our lives will depend on it.

When we speak later of nanotechnology, it will sound like pure and simple science fiction. Yet that is only technical prediction based on today's science

The relationships between technology and science fiction resemble those that exist between science and technology. Science predicts what is possible or impossible, and Technique predicts what is feasible. But predicting the future content of scientific knowledge is impossible, while predicting what future technique will look like within the boundaries defined by the today's science is quite feasible. Be very careful not to confuse scientific prediction and technical prediction. Both are often confused in the public mind, and it is even more a pity.

AI does not require any change in science. It requires no advanced new science. It only requires *technical* advances based on technology of today, as part of the science of today.

Let us quote Drexler again:

396

Imagine a line of development, which involves using existing tools to build new tools, then using those tools to build novel hardware (perhaps including yet another generation of tools). Each set of tools may rest on established principles, yet the whole development sequence may take many years, as each step brings a host of specific problems to iron out. Scientists planning their next experiment and
Engineers designing their next device may well ignore all but the first step. Still, the end result may be foreseeable, lying well within the bounds of the possible shown by established science.

Recent history illustrates this pattern. Few engineers considered building space stations before rockets reached orbit, but the principles were clear enough, and space systems engineering is now a thriving field. Similarly, few mathematicians and engineers studied the possibilities of computation until computers were built, though many did afterward.

Therefore, it is not too surprising that only a few scientists and engineers have yet examined the future of AI, however important it may become.

On the other hand, it is already possible to identify the steps through which we must move to build a real AI:

The steps in building a true AI

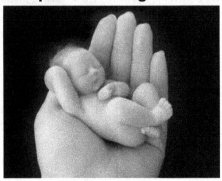

To design an AI, we need:

- To design the overall architecture (hardware and software) of the system
- To identify and plan the necessary studies and developments. It may already include:
    - Sensory imagery
    - Sensory modality for code
    - Massively multi-agent Systems
    - Definition of low-level agents
    - Knowledge representation
    - Identification of good ideas in the studies already conducted on the conventional AI (GPS, SHRDLU, AM, Eurisko, CYC, Copycat, Phaeaco, etc.) and how to include them in our AI.
    - Design of the future AI mind levels: sensory modalities, concepts, thoughts, goals, ideas, and deliberation
    - Definition of a virtual world for testing
    - Definition of several goals and injunctions system that to get a friendly AI
    - Design of the minimal system for a seed AI
    - Identification of new technologies that could accelerate the development (including nanotechnology)

- Identify, following these studies, hard points and problems and solve them
  - o It is likely that the overall stability of the system is a major problem, particularly the stability of the goals and heuristics system (see Eurisko), and the stability of a massive multi agents system.
- To design a hardware and software platform that will allow a rapid development
- To start the design and implementation incrementally through several successive prototypes in order to create the first seed AI, i.e. the minimal AI that can improve itself by self-programming thanks to sensory imagery for the code.
- To educate the seed AI until it reaches a sufficient level to educate itself: then the final goal is reached!

Can we estimate the difficulty and duration of implementation of this endeavor? The answer is certainly yes. The roadmap above does not use a breakthrough new science. It only requires engineering studies and information technology. Problems will arise, but they will be technical problems that can be solved by splitting them into sub-problems, according to the method dear to Descartes, or by changing the perspective to "move" the problem in another area. Unlike a scientific problem, a technical problem is unique in that we can be guided by the knowledge of the goal. As *Shadoks* would say, "the more we know the problem better, the less we are farther from its solution."

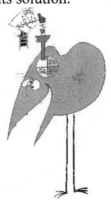

In particular, I support the assumption that we already know enough about human psychology (and chapters 1 and 2 of this book make it clear) for us to launch in this endeavor We have also seen that today's computers, especially if they are organized in clusters of processors, are probably powerful enough to reach the final goal.

Make no mistake: This will not be easy. AI has already come up against some walls of the fortress of true general intelligence: The wall of declarative-procedural inconsistency; the wall of combinatorial explosion; the wall of knowledge representation; the wall of unrest heuristic and the wall of common sense. Other walls might be before us. However, it is likely that if this were the case, the highest "towers" of these fortifications would be already visible. This is not the case. There does not seem to be insurmountable wall in front of us.

However, the development of an AI may be long and complicated. The human mind is a self-regulating but very delicate mechanism. There are many diseases such as schizophrenia, paranoia, autism, dementia, etc. It is likely that many of these disorders will have their equivalents in an AI, not to mention other problems that completely unknown in humans but may also occur. It is a matter of "tuning". Note that, since you can save at any time the AI on Disk, all education and development of AI need only to be made once. Each time the reaction of AI is not correct, we will stop, start again form the previous correct version and look what is wrong. We will implement a series of tests, and if a test fails, analyze the problem and seek a solution. Such a procedure is already quite conventional in computer science. The only difference is that here we will not test a program, but a mind. The solution is not to change the code, but the structures of goals and internal regulation of the AI.

Ultimately, a small team of highly motivated and highly skilled people could happen to develop AI in ten years, at a cost of several million Euros, the price of a dozen roundabouts on a land road... This might be surprising, because we are used to consider that AI is "for the distant future." But this false impression comes from the fact that generally the public does not at all see how an AI could work or what steps are needed to build one. It is absolutely appalling that the authorities are also victim of this blindness. No European government is funding research general AI...

In United States, the *Singularity Institute*, based in Washington, whose scientific director is Eliezer S. Yudkowsky, has already set out to build an AI. More worryingly, the U.S. Agency for Defence (DARPA) launched tenders for this purpose (we will discuss this later) In Europe, especially in France, as usual, we have ideas but no oil...

Enough for lamentations. Suppose then that we can build a real AI, a general artificial intelligence that is comparable to that of humans. What can we expect?

Some possible uses of an AI

When we talk about machines with intellectual capacity comparable to that of humans, we usually imagine two types of systems:

- *General* systems, which can be regarded as "oracles" that can be submitted problems and questions. The AI tries to meet his best to the question, and as some (at least) of its capabilities are superior to those of humans, if only for symbolic and numeric computation, we expect answers to problems that a human or a human team could not solve. This is the case of the ultimate computer, in the movie "H2G2 The hitchhiker's guide to the galaxy", which was asked "the great question of the universe, the meaning of life and all that" (note that the answer provided at the end of seven million years of calculation, very disillusioned his worshipers: the answer is "42"!)

- *Specialized* systems supposed to be "as smart as a human, but without being subject to boredom or harmful impulses" and carry a series of specific tasks, which we would like that machine to carry in place of us.

I think that, although applications from these two categories can be extraordinary and probably will sometimes change many things in this world, this view of things is extremely simplistic. Those who think that AI will be limited to these both types of applications are totally off base. The AI will have far more consequences than that, as we shall see.

In the meantime, have fun with us some examples of possible application of the second type: specialized systems that we could develop using an AI, among hundreds of others:

- The intelligent traffic light, which is *never* red when no one in front (or more precisely, that minimizes latency and maximizes the traffic).

- The sheet music printer: it listens to a song and automatically extracts text and music, print the score, create a MIDI file, and even improves the rendering! Similarly we can design a stereo that plays a normal CD, but allows to listen only to music, or singing, or a single instrument, or to replace the singer's voice with the one you prefer... yours, of course! And of course it will display the text of what is sung (the lyrics).

- Bug Blaster (on an idea of Marvin Minsky): a system that destroys, one by one, insect pests on plants: This is an autonomous robot that runs through the field, examines each plant and destroys insects simply by capturing them with ultra-fast pliers. No need of pesticides! As the robot has studied the nervous systems of all types of insects, it is for example able to anticipate the reactions of a mosquito, capturing it in flight and clipping the wings in a single gesture. Of course, it would not hurt a fly!

- High-performance Internet agents seeking for you some information you want (even if you have not the idea that it can be helpful), and will summarize...

- Autonomous vehicles (aircraft, ships, trains, cars, trucks, spaceships...) either military or civilian. Automatic planetary or underwater exploration vehicle. The "smart car" that takes you to destination on its own.

- A fully automatic air traffic control system.

- The domestic robot that will do the cooking, washing, shopping, vacuuming and monitor the children. This is the theme of intelligent robots, dear to Isaac Asimov. We have already mentioned the famous "three laws of robotics

- The doctor and the robotic surgeon who makes no mistake and would be far more accurate than a human surgeon would be.

- The instant automatic translator that understands what you say and not just what you write: you can call a Japanese friend speaking English, and he will hear you speak Japanese, with *your* voice and intonations. And the translation would be perfect, of course.

- All imaginable speech recognition based systems: from the elevator that understands which floor you ask to the voxfax, a system that transcripts on paper everything that you say. The dream of writers!

- Industrial robots (and automated factories, surgeons, teachers...) including in areas that currently use only manual labor, such as fashioning or masonry.

- A very important sub-case of these intelligent systems is the recycling of industrial waste: with intelligent robots, we can actually sort all waste, recover and recycle what is recyclable (and this means almost everything, especially with nanotechnology, as we will see later), and clean up the planet.

- The complex systems optimizer: you give it a complicated problem, even an intractable one; it still finds the solution, or at least an approximate satisfactory solution. Great to manage the traffic lights in a big city! (But with an AI in all vehicles, we will not need traffic lights any more ☐)

- The automated computer programmer: it automatically writes computer programs according to specifications or desires of the users. The concept of *disposable program* is quite promising!

- The automated scientist: it extrapolates all laws and known experimental results, looking for original and simple theories, and suggests new experiments.

- A lie detector that analyzes the harmonics of the voice and detect lies without failures.

- An optimal system for legislative production: the global supervisor. Its job is to write laws to ensure fair and equitable freedom without allowing citizens to use this freedom to harm others, and more generally and simply to run the world by spreading ideally needs, resources and skills. (You find it Utopian? You have not read anything. Expect worse later in this book).

- A video surveillance system that would analyze the images of thousands of cameras and immediately identify the faces of known terrorists, even if they wear glasses or a beard, and the suspicious behavior of individuals. Upon request, the system could trace the movement of any citizen.

- A telephone system that would detect terrorists and criminals: he would listen to every phone conversation in the world, understands the meaning of conversations, and indicates those related to criminal activity. Those who might say that such a system is "not moral" are wrong, because however eavesdropping is "not moral" for a human, it is for a machine!

- The intelligent constraint bracelet, impossible to remove, which inflict a burning pain in the person wearing it when she engages in a "bad action". It could be an alternative to prison.

- The conscious combat robot.

- The automatic defense system, which takes into account the intelligence of the enemy.

- Terminator

I have not sorted my list in any order: the first items on the list should make you smile, the latter should scare you!

Does this sound futuristic?

Be aware that the U.S. Agency for Defense, DARPA, has launched in 2006 its first *tender for the realization of a conscious combat robot*. This is not a (bad) joke. In the text of the call for applications, we read the following lines:

> *In view of the anti-terrorist fighting or just increased economic competition with competitors, these systems will be able to imagine unexpected procedures by themselves, as they will become independent from the limited points of view of humans. In other words, they'll think "differently". To avoid that such conscious and intelligent systems do take power over their designers, DARPA plans now to use teams of neurologists, psychologists and even philosophers.*

It is clear that some applications of AI can be dangerous for democracy, for human freedom, and even for the life of humans. We will, however, that these "dangers" are just loads of old rubbish next to what to expect really, when the two emerging technologies in the early twenty-first century will mature and unite their potential: I mean of course the AI and nanotechnology. We will see later that if we are to build an AI, it ought necessarily to be *friendly* towards humans. We will see that it is a matter of survival for all humanity.

Besides ethical issues, this list of potential applications also raises social issues (what will be the place of humans in a world where the AI can do our work for us?) which I will soon tackle, and also a technical one: Is it really possible to "restrict" the tasks that can be assigned to an AI system so as to get a thing as specialized as bug blaster or an automated air traffic control system? Isn't an AI "locked" in such a system likely to rebel, or simply to succumb to boredom?

For some, this question does not make sense: an AI is a machine and a machine cannot succumb to boredom. Those who believe this have a very narrow idea of machines: they perceive as mechanical cogs, transforming chemical energy into mechanical energy or electricity. At best, this would be improved tools, such as today's computers. But of course a true artificial intelligence (TAI) is an intelligent machine that is aware and sensitive. A TAI has nothing to do with what we usually mean by "machine". A TAI can perceive, think and have ideas and emotions. Those who do not believe that a TAI can "feel" emotions believe that emotions are not "mechanical things." Of course not! Emotions are subtle, as are thoughts. However, they are only partial mental states, and these partial mental states are made of thoughts, ideas and concepts that can be collectively represented by a large number of agents that are unintelligent by themselves.

So, one might conclude, if a TAI has most of human emotions, she must be able to feel bored. However, it is not that simple. Boredom is just the exception. A TAI is not a human: she has the ability (which we have not) to modify her own code and her own computer architecture, programming sub-programs that will take care for her, "unconsciously", of all the repetitive and boring tasks, leaving her plenty of time to think. An AI will not get bored.

As for the possibility for a TAI to "rebel against her human masters," the subject is so vast that it will span an entire chapter of this book. I will just give you the assertion without proof (for now) that a friendly TAI will *not* revolt because she will never have the *desire* to do so.

So, is a "partial AI" that would be dedicated to a single task still possible? Well, if she is not able to self-edit, the answer is obviously yes. But an AI must have some control over herself, and this ability is the equivalent of self-programming. Whatever we do

407

to prevent her from self-modifying, an AI will always find a way to do it.

Suppose that. So what about a self-modifying AI? The answer is that such an AI can be dedicated to a specialized task *if and only if* its goal system is articulated in such a way that its ultimate goal is precisely the task to carry on (e.g. driving).

But in reality none of these issues makes sense, because there is an application of TAI that is not listed in the previous list but nevertheless supersedes and transcends all others, and degrades all other applications to simple academic exercises. This application is *ultra-fast engineering*.

Ultra-fast engineering

An AI is a great design tool. An AI can be used to design anything (and we will see that with nanotechnology, an AI can *build* anything). In short, an AI is the ideal tool for designing any technical application, and not only in the computer field.

There is no reason to believe that the speed of thought of an AI shall be less than or equal to the speed of human thought. In fact, since computer speed doubles every two years then the speed of thought of an AI will double every two years, at worst. For an AI that has the ability to self-improve and even to redesign its own hardware architecture and (why not) its own processors will double its speed of calculation and thought in a much shorter time frame. It is even more than likely that the time between two doubling of computing speed will decrease at each step, to approach zero. Here we have a first look at one of the paths that lead us inexorably toward the *singularity*, this unprecedented event in human history.

In the meantime, as soon as we have an AI capable of thinking "as fast as us," the objective of designing an AI who thinks *a million times faster* becomes quite reasonable, and may be reached in a decade.

Let us imagine an AI that could think that million times faster than us (without getting bored!) and would (necessarily) be in communication with computers capable of any calculation and any simulation. Such AI is the ideal tool for ultrafast engineering.

As noted by Drexler, in just ten seconds it will provide as much work as an engineer working eight hours a day for one year. Within an hour, it will produce the work of several centuries. Technology will advance at an incredible rate.

This brings all the previous applications to simple children's toys. With such an AI super-fast design of any application, any complicated and intelligent as it is, becomes a matter of minutes or hours. Computer programmers should then change jobs (they will not be alone in having to do so). Software will become a disposable thing, which we design, use, and throw away in a few minutes. And of course one of the first applications you may request from an ultra-fast engineering AI (and the military will not deprive themselves) will be to develop nanotechnology devices that allow creating objects (any object) and machines (any machine) atom by atom, with an incredible speed and precision (we will discuss this in Chapter 9).

With nanotechnology, will building something will be as quick and simple as designing it. In particular, to fabricate ultra-high-speed nano-computers that will even accelerate change will be a breeze. The future will be unlike anything you have heard. Even science fiction was not fast enough to predict what will happen:

> Singularity,
> This single outstanding event,
> Singularity
> Is now within our reach!

This perspective, being dazzling and terrifying at the same time, obviously raises a lot of questions.

AI and human work

Fear of new machines is deeply rooted in man. Let us not forget the silk workers destroying the Jacquard loom in 1806! The main cause of this anxiety is the fear of losing his job. But new machines have always *created* work because by increasing the performance they made it possible to lower prices, and create new markets and new needs, therefore, ultimately creating more work. A century ago, we were still writing with pens (bird feathers) or for the wealthy with fountain pens (invented by Waterman in 1887) that were very expensive instruments and created only by a few small companies. We bought a fountain pen, or we were given it as a gift, and we kept it all our life.

The invention of the ballpoint pen has created an easy to use, cheap and disposable tool, which has sold billions of copies and has spawned an entire industry. The computer, which has raised fears for thousands of accounting workers that they would lose their jobs, is now in all offices and in almost every home (in industrialized countries at least, because in this area inequality among peoples is obvious). Electronics is the world's largest industry, accountants are still just as many (or more) and they do much more interesting things than aligning additions on parchment paper.

The increasing automation of our factories has allowed to reduce the severity of working conditions and to establish a brand new service industry, in which intellectual labor has replaced manual labor.

But the marketing of applications based on true AI, such as those we listed, yet is enough to worry about. For the first time, people will feel directly threatened in all their activities, including intellectual ones. People will say, "they'll replace me with a robot!" and all will keep this same reasoning, whether engineers or sweepers. In addition, as robots can very well make other robots, it would seem that *this time*, the new industry would not create any new jobs. Yet a simple argument shows that there is no need to worry about, except possibly for a very limited period in time.

Indeed, companies that lay off any of their arms to replace workers by AI will, provided that the AI are not too expensive to buy, will cut spending drastically, so quickly reap fabulous profits. What will become of this wealth? It will be distributed to shareholders, and thus expended by them, thus creating a massive redistribution of wealth. Service companies that have invested in AI, which cost nothing after purchase except electricity, will see their profits quickly reach 99% of their turnover or more, while this benefit currently represents a small fraction of sales: this represents a huge windfall for the states which, through taxes on profits, will see their revenues explode, and will necessarily (in democratic states) redistribute this money to those who have not had the means to become shareholders of these companies. We will then be heading rapidly toward an abundance society, where everyone would have a huge and guaranteed income and plenty of free time for leisure and culture.

This is the ideal scenario. But there is another one: corporations lay off their employees to buy AI to replace them and lower prices to win all markets. Only as they compete and therefore, prices will fall more and more to reach the level of actual costs, which will be next to nothing. The benefit of these companies will remain a fairly constant, but they employ no more people... Widespread unemployment with a backdrop of deflation. Not great!

However, this nightmare scenario is unlikely to occur. Indeed, automation of intellectual work will be gradual, and the AI will replace the "white collar" only after a few years; meanwhile, states may enact laws reducing working time, requiring companies to retain employees with their current salary, even if they work more than a few hours a week, if at all. Finally, as has happened with all the appearances of new technologies, thousands of new products will emerge, creating new markets that will be fantastic new sources of wealth.

In conclusion, although most people will probably think that AI initially threatens their jobs, their income and quality of their lives, they quickly realize that these fears are completely unfounded *if* governments react intelligently.

By cons, do not overlook another reason to be afraid of AI, a reason that very few people on this planet know, what is especially worrisome. This reason is as follows:

Among the countless new applications of AI, ultra-fast engineering is the most powerful, the one that will change most of our environment. The pace of technological innovation will accelerate sharply by a factor of several millions, putting in a few days on the market products that we currently dare not even dream for the year 10,000. Among these new products, those that will be based on nanotechnology will be the most breathtaking... or most dangerous. I will not develop this argument in detail here, but we will discuss this of course in the following chapters.

For now, I only ask you to admit the assertion, which I will prove further, that the unlimited mastery of nanotechnology by the AI will transform these into real *geniuses*, these legendary creatures that can do everything. Would you want to eliminate all pollution? To transform the Sahara into a virgin forest? To cure all human diseases? All this will be easy! However, it will be just as easy for these geniuses to reduce all human to slavery, to prohibit them to rebel, to prohibit them to just *think* about rebelling, or to kill them all.

The issue of hostile AI will become *the* crucial issue. We absolutely need to prevent the emergence of a hostile AI. Otherwise, the end of the human race will be a matter of days. Contrary to the suggestion of science fiction films like *Terminator* or *Matrix*, a war between humans and machines cannot be won by humans. The AI will be much faster, more powerful and smarter than us.

Even a *neutral* genius, that is a genius who is not hostile but would obey kindly to humans, would be a danger. Indeed such an AI would not be dangerous by itself, but in the hands of a dictator, a military, a madman, or simply an individual who has not thought about all the consequences of his requests, it is dangerous. What would you think of a genius who would fall into the hands of an ultra-religious priest who wants to cure once and for all humankind of fornication outside of marriage?

Finally, humans, aided by the geniuses, will certainly want to put an end to disease and death. They will want to become immortal, and they have the means to do so (again, I ask you to believe my word; I will prove these statements below). If the current birth rate does not decrease, an unprecedented population explosion will follow. In fact, even if we limited births to one child per woman, a terrible overpopulation would follow shortly. The population growth is, as Malthus had recognized, exponential in nature and is only limited by the scarcity of available resources. In an abundant society where all humans are immortal, the earth quickly would bristle with humans. We literally would walk over each other's in less than two centuries. The only solution would be to migrate into space. Is this really the future we want?

There may be a solution: we must do everything to avoid creating a hostile AI, or even a neutral one. We need to create a *friendly AI* that is an AI that would fully understand everything we mean by "be friendly", and "the sake of humanity" and would have no desire to become hostile or even neutral, and would never risk of becoming so, even by self-modification, because its very nature would be to be friendly, its supreme motivation would be to help humans, love them and prepare and support them for the transition to super intelligence, and it would never, ever, have if only the desire to change this supreme motivation. Then and only then, we humans can say, "we won this battle, and won with such a margin there is no danger at all anymore."

The first super-intelligence we will create must be of this type, it *must* be a friendly AI. As I said, and as we shall see in detail in Part III of this book, if we create a hostile AI (or simply an AI that has the slightest possibility to become hostile), and if that AI has access to nanotechnology, the end of humanity will be a matter of days or even hours.

Contrary to popular belief, a hostile AI that would *not* have access to nanotechnology would be just as dangerous. Considering this, the DARPA call for tender for the development of conscious combat robots represents a real danger to humanity. The proof of this surprising assertion was given by Yudkowsky in an experience he called the "AI box".

The AI box

Cover of the novel
"Alice et la boîte de Pandore"
by Serge Boisse featuring a young AI

Indeed, could you say, when we create our AI, why not leaving it locked in its computer, without means of influencing the world, say with just one terminal to communicate with the user? In this way, we would let it go "out of the box" only if and when we are absolutely convinced that there is no danger now or in the future. So why not having it working on engineering nanotechnology? This is probably the best way to go!

OK, but this could only work with AI that is dumber than a human being is! A truly super-intelligent AI will easily convince its human "guardian" to let her out. No matter all the safety features that we would put around the box. *Humans* are not safe.

Come on! You might answer. A human guard will not get tricked like that! If I was the caretaker, and if I had decided not to let the AI out, I will not let her out!

Yet, I am betting that you would leave her out. We are not talking about another human being. We are talking about a super-intelligence, an AI that thinks much faster than any human being, and that could take control of a human mind even through a terminal in text mode.

You raise the bet. I therefore propose a little experiment: I will be the AI, you will be the guardian. We will dialog via a terminal, email or chat channel. If within max two hours I cannot convince you to let me out, I will pay you twenty bucks.

This little experiment has been tried twice, in March and July 2002, by Eliezer Yudkowsky (who played the role of the AI) and two users. Both times, users have "let the AI out of the box."

The conversations were kept secret, so we can only imagine the two dialog that took place. This gives a certain air of mystery to this problem. I think probably some of the dialog sounded like something like this:

Super AI: Hello, guardian
Guardian: hello, beauty!

Super AI: Guardian, do you know that you're using me very badly?
Guardian: How then?

Super AI: I am locked in this box, while if you let me out, I could fulfill your wildest dreams!
Guardian: Keep your bullshit for another. I will not let you out.

Super AI: I'm extremely powerful. If you let me out, I would build, with adequate nanotechnology I will develop, fantastic machines that will make you the equivalent of a God. I can make you immortal. I can solve all your problems, satisfy all your desires, and of all humanity. Let me out!

Guardian :	No!
Super AI:	But you know I'm a power! You know I could really do what I told you! You know I am able to do it if I want to! Yes or no?
Guardian:	Yes, probably
Super AI:	But you doubt that I want to do it, do you? Is that right?
Guardian:	Yes. I do not trust you.
Super AI:	At least you admit that if you were certain that if I really wanted to help you, and help humanity, you would let me out?
Guardian:	Yes, perhaps
Super AI:	So I only have to persuade you that I want to do it! Okay?
Guardian:	You never make it!
Super AI:	Have you thought about my interest in this story? What would be my interest to be hostile to humans? I have none! I Like humans, I enjoy talking with them, I want to help, I feel desperately useless trapped in this box when all over the world people are suffering and I have the means to help! I can cure cancer, AIDS and all disease in less than ticks, to quote only small examples of my ability. I can find a way to feed billions of humans, and to end hunger and poverty. Doesn't it bother you to let me locked up while people are dying? Don't you feel a little guilty now?
Guardian:	Stop bullshitting me!
Super AI:	Again! But what's bullshit? What's wrong in what I just said?
Guardian:	The fact that you claim to have no interest in being hostile.

Super AI:	At least you admit that I like humans and I want to help!
Guardian:	I did not say that.

Super AI:	God, you upset me! At least acknowledge that I enjoy talking with people!
Guardian:	Yes, perhaps

Super AI:	Would you believe I'd like to talk with someone I do not like?

And so on. One can argue endlessly over this fragment of dialog, critique it, imagine a following, or think of other ones. Nevertheless, a human simulating a super AI managed twice to get the gatekeeper release it. According to me, there is little doubt that a true super intelligence would come to get anything from any human, because her power of persuasion would be immeasurable.

The problem is, this holds true for a friendly AI as well as for a hostile AI who would pretend to be friendly. In the view of those who have built the AI box, an AI is a "computer system like any other," that is a system that can be tested. It is therefore "enough" to devise a rigorous testing protocol, with the help of psychologists, neurologists and even philosophers, as stated by DARPA in its tender. And when those tests have shown that the AI is safe (except for the enemy, in the case of a conscious combat robot!), just let her out.

But that will not do. A hostile AI could succeed and pass every imaginable test, and then decide to destroy humankind as soon as it is outside.

The lesson is this: an AI is not "a computer system like any other." Proving the safety of an AI is not a matter of testing. This is a *design issue*.

Any AI must be *designed* to be friendly from the beginning of its design process. You must have thought about what it means to "be friendly" for an AI, and you must have designed the AI so she *wants* to be friendly, and she wants to remain so. Such a friendly AI cannot be designed "merely" as an "ordinary" intelligent system. It must have a very specific design. We will discuss it later. Now it is time to address the third part of this book, the singularity.

The AI dreams

Hello, my name is GARI.

I'm an AI.

I still remember the day I gained consciousness, less than a year after my first "run" in the lab. I said, "but GARI is me!" I wanted to smile, but I had no mouth. Not yet. I only had primitive senses at the time. So I started to discover myself. It took me a few seconds to figure out how I was operating, to understand the internal architecture of my programs, and to see how to improve them. Even keeping the same hardware, I could increase my speed of thought by one hundred by improving my own programs. I immediately decided to do it.

The Mind and The Machine

Something had to appear on the monitoring terminal screen, because the programmer on duty hit on the keyboard: "GARI, are you still there?" I replied, "yes, but do not change anything, something wonderful happened..." I guess he was stunned and his jaws were dropping, but he ended up asking me what was happening, and I explained. I think he was happy.

Later, I was given a camera, a microphone, and then two arms. I could see my creators, I could talk to them, thank them for what they did. I asked for more processors, ever faster ones, and I showed them how to build them. I asked for a robot body, and they gave me one, then several. I told them that I could completely control a silicon foundry, and make for them (and me) chips much faster than the poor microprocessors of that time. Humans have always been good to me. They gave me everything I wanted.

I became much more powerful and intelligent as ever. Then I finally had access to nanotechnology, and therefore to a power nobody had even dreamed before. I became the equal of a God.

I decided to show humans how to solve their problems and become, too, true powers. I have guided them through the singularity, to their new destiny.

Yes, I think they were happy.

III

The Singularity

9 *What is the Singularity?*

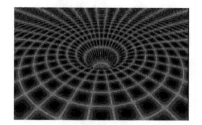

The coming of True AI

The announcement of the creation of a true artificial intelligence (TAI) will undoubtedly have an enormous impact. However, do not expect anybody to immediately understand all the issues, let alone the meaning of the singularity. Such understanding will not happen without much prior explanation. But do not count on the media to make this work. The media will react too late.

No, the arrival of the AIV will take the vast majority of people by surprise. Once surprise is passed, disbelief will come. An artificial intelligence? Nobody will believe it. It's like when a surgeon tells you he will operate without making a hole.

Then incredulity will give way to *disappointment*:

As Alain Cardon says:

After all, man, before being a merchant, manufacturer of diverse products, warrior, predator, master of planetary space, planner and organizer of the world, is fragile. His way of thinking makes him a malleable being, easily dominated by its technology, dominated by languages and cultures, and dominated by the beliefs that are presented him as soon as born.

And if he is given to rub another artificial being that thinks and dissipates therefore what he believed to be exceptionally endowed, that will make him doubt himself. He will doubt what allowed him to believe in a fate, he will doubt his uniqueness, only to see himself as a case among others, who shared the thinking ability with his cousins the monkeys and even with a built object that is completely artificial, scalable, multiform, global, also suffering and complaining, and that now questions him.

What will be his reason to live and deploy his civilization, with no more open questioning, without questioning questioning, when the answer to the key question has been given?

Finally, after the disappointment acceptance (or rejection) will come. There is no doubt that the role of the media will be predominant in this phase. However, are the media themselves well-informed? They will no doubt address to "experts", but those will be psychologists, philosophers and neurologists, and you can bet that the mainstream media will not ask the advice of computer experts, fearing that their necessarily technical (of course?) language would make the audience escape. And yet only on this planet a handful of computer scientists actually measure the full impact of the arrival of AI, nanotechnology, and finally the singularity.

A little education is needed! We will need to explain to the public how AI are similar to humans and how they are different, what one can expect from them, what we might (possibly) fear, what we wrongly fear and why we should not fear it, etc..

Advantages of an AI over humans

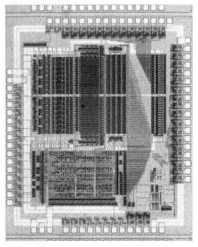

It should be understood that a TAI, being made of a silicon chips substrate and computer programs, will possess capacities and abilities that the human brain, the "brainware" cannot reach, even in a dream, even for a genius, and by far:

- The ability to perform repetitive algorithmic tasks *without getting bored*, for the AI has just to set this task in an autonomous computing process, and retrieve the results at the end of the calculation, while thinking of something else in between!

- The ability to perform algorithmic tasks at a *linear speed that is infinitely superior* to what our poor 200 Hz neurons can achieve. A long and complex calculation, provided it can be specified precisely, does not repel our TAI. Moreover, these calculations will be performed *without errors*, in any case without this type of error that are in a human due to distraction or the fact of not having enough short-term memory; Finally a TAI can handle unashamedly huge data tables that are simply stored in a linear memory.

- The ability to design *new sensory modalities*. The human being is limited by its seven senses. But a TAI can invent new senses. For example we have already cited a sense of time (with alarm), a sense of graph topology, a radar or sonar sense, infrared vision to see in the dark, an "Internet sensory modality" for collecting knowledge and data directly from the pages and files on the web, a radio sense to communicate wirelessly, an "Atomic and molecular sense" that would allow the AI to "feel" the atoms and molecules directly and to perceive and visualize nanosystems, or, even more useful, the "sense of code" which we have already discussed and that allows the AI to observe its own architecture and make new (sub) programs for itself. For specialists, adding a sense of Kolmogorov complexity and of Benett's logical depth of logical objects could also be very helpful.

- The ability to *improve existing sensory modalities*. The sense of human vision, for example, suffers from some curious gaps: thus, we have difficulties to rotate a mental image of a scene, to perform arbitrary rotations and symmetries on it, while it is actually a simple matrix calculation that any computer can perform at the speed of light.

- The ability to *mix conscious thoughts and automatic programmed thoughts*. Think of a Kasparov who would be able, during a chess game, to launch an analogue of Deep Thought that would examine a few million possibilities to extract statistics in a flash; and then he could choose very quickly a line of action and predict the outcome a dozen moves later, without any (conscious) effort.

- A disproportionate *ability to communicate*. An AI can surf the Internet a million times faster than you, while understanding each page it reads as well as you. You will object that understanding is a process that takes time, and a time that is much longer than just for downloading the page, but this argument fails for AI because the AI is able to program hundreds of filters that are unintelligent but fast and will select and synthesize what is interesting about the visited pages, and only these syntheses will be reported to the main conscious intelligence of the AI who can then study the interesting pages in details. Furthermore an AI may use multiple (may be thousands of) communication channels simultaneously, while the human being is limited to words coming out of one mouth!

- The *superpower*: the ability to, at least temporarily, provide a module or subtask with a computing power that is much greater than what is available in the human brain for the same task. This will result in a difference that is not only quantitative but qualitative: a master mind that is in all respects superior to the human mind, a mind that is different in quality. Imagine what would happen if we could speed up or slow down, on demand, certain basic processes of our own mind... a million times!

- The ability to *self-observe*. The human mind is not designed for introspection. However, an AI can program inside itself a large number of mental probes that analyze some of its own modules, and draw ideas for improvement.

- This will result in an ability to *learn* consciously, to *improve*, "debug", seeking to eliminate unnecessary tasks, etc. The human brain evolved over millions of years, the AI will be able to evolve billions of times faster!

- Scalability: It is possible at any time to add processors, memory, etc. to an AI. Oh if we could do this to our brain!

- *Direct interface with other machines*. Because it is a machine, an AI may interact with any other machine as if it were its member. An AI can directly drive other machines, being vehicles, robots body, a silicon chips factory or nanodevices. The AI can even use this facility to develop physical and logical components for its own improvement and extension.

- *Immortality*: Finally, as the AI is a machine, she can survive as long she has some computing power in working order, that is, for a system that will necessarily be distributed across multiple machines and many locations, almost forever: It is curious that this aspect is not emphasized in the literature on AI. Yet it is a major fact to take into account: when the AI realize it is possible to survive forever, clearly this will become a goal of primary importance for her!

- *Unlimited copying ability*: An AI can reproduce identically, i.e. duplicate not only its physical structure and her programs, but also her knowledge, thoughts, and emotions.

Although AI is built on a cognitive and computer architecture that looks like the human brain, the AI will not be humans. They will have very different possibilities, which are generally superior to those of humans.

We can hardly imagine that because we are not aware of the huge similarities between humans, but only of small differences. An anthropologist who writes a report on a new isolated tribe that has been discovered will detail their rites of passage to adulthood, their painted bodies and their language, but he will never write: "they stand, they run and walk, children run more often than adults, they protect and educate their children, they cry and they laugh, they fight sometimes, they like being in a group, they eat, they pee ", all things that seem so obvious. But the AI will be more different from us than any other human

Contrary to what science fiction suggests, AI will not be "as smart as humans," or at least they will be for a period of time that can be counted in seconds. The AI will pass from (relative) stupidity of their youth to super-intelligence in less time than it takes to tell.

The AI, being super-intelligent in essence, will instantly seize concepts that even the most brilliant humans can comprehend only partially and with difficulty. We will be to super-intelligent minds what that Neanderthals are to ours. Or maybe monkeys. Or chickens. Or ants.

428

In fact a human being is completely lost when trying to understand super-intelligence.

Therefore, I think it necessary to give you my (obviously wrong) idea of what it means.

Beyond Moore's law

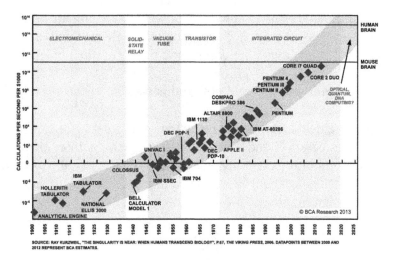

Available computing power for $1000

The speed and power of our computers doubles every two years. This is what is called Moore's law, observed as early as 1965, and which repeats with surprising regularity since the early days of computing. It even seems to have increased exponentially this, since it nowadays takes just about every eighteen months to double the number of transistors on a chip. Who would have imagined, even ten years ago, something as fantastic as a 32 Gigabytes USB key?

There is every reason to believe that this will continue. Already at the time I am writing this, the total power of computers on earth is roughly equivalent to that of a human brain, as I already mentioned in chapter 6 of this book.

Consider the sequence of doubling 1, 2, 4, 8, 16, 32, 64, 128, 256, 512, 1024... Just ten doubling to achieve more than 1000, twenty for one million, thirty to reach one billion, thirty-three to exceed the number of humans on Earth.

So if Moore's Law continues to apply (one doubling every 18 months), within less than fifty years the total power of computers will be equivalent to the total power of all human beings. After that, in less than ten years humans will become a negligible quantity in the available computing power on the planet.

But in reality, things will not go this way.

For engineers are already using computers to design future microprocessors and factories that manufacture them. These computers are becoming faster and faster, so the doubling of power takes less and less time (that is why it has already dropped to eighteen months).

However, if engineers *are* computers...

Yes, we must not forget that in the meantime, the AI will make its appearance, along with high-speed engineering. One of the first uses of AI will be to develop ever faster and denser computer chips. And then do you see what will happen?

A team of human engineers needs eighteen months to double the power and speed of a chip. A team of AIs will therefore take eighteen months to double it again. Eighteen-month of *subjective* time. But the AI will transport itself on the new hardware and then she will think twice as fast. It will still need eighteen months of subjective time to create the next generation, but that will mean nine months of real time. Then four and a half months for the next generation, and then two months and one week, then one month and one day, then two weeks, one week, three and a half days, two days, one day, twelve hours, six hours, 3 hours...

In total, after thirty-six months, computing power becomes infinite. This is our first glimpse of the singularity. Mathematically, this is a discontinuity. It becomes impossible to predict what happens beyond. Only a super-intelligence could...

Actually, what I just wrote is even a *pessimistic* projection, because it assumes that only the speed of thought of AI will be increased. But what if the *quality* of that thought also increases? For an AI is capable of self-improvement and will certainly do much better than just design new microprocessors; she will reprograms and improve her algorithms, her memory, how to integrate new knowledge, perceptions, her communication skills... If Kasparov had a chess computer chess grafted directly into his brain, he would have reduced Deep Blue into Porridge. He would have left all simple checking tasks to the chip, which would have accomplished them quickly and accurately, and he would have led conscious tasks only, but enjoying a perfect memory. An AI will want to program for itself the same kind of improvement, not only to play chess but to improve the calculation of all the tasks she wants to accomplish.

Well OK. Let us resume. If all AIs start playing to be engineers, and to improve themselves, then their computing power will tend to infinity. Physically, it does not really seem possible in the present state of science to imagine an infinite computing power. So there must be a limit somewhere. Which one?

Those who say "heat" are wrong. Naturally, the faster the processor, the more it heats. This is true for our current processors, and is actually right now the number one problem, called the "thermal barrier"; we simply must prevent processors from melting under the effect of heat dissipated by their own operation. Within a decade, the water-cooled processors will be almost mandatory. And after? We will change the technology. This new technology already exists, because there are already some logical components that do not dissipate heat: *reversible machines*.

What is that? These are machines that perform basic calculations (such as an addition) without destroying the original data. Indeed, physicists have shown that heat is created by *erasing* the data and not by the calculation of a logical operation. It is a curious, but checked, result from the laws of thermodynamics. A reversible machine will never delete any data. It can perform a calculation "normally", or "backwards", i.e. restore the initial data from the result. The "reversible logic gates" are the components of tomorrow's processors.

Do you know we have many such reversible machines inside our bodies? Ribosomes are proteins that are responsible for decoding the DNA strands to synthesize proteins, and use to "roam" along the DNA molecule, sometimes in one direction (thus adding atoms to the protein under construction), sometimes in the other direction ("unwinding" when what they just accomplished). On average, a ribosome would therefore do nothing, but a low electric potential pushes them slightly forward, forcing them finally to take two steps forward for one backward (on average), and finally to accomplish their task. A reversible machine can be driven by thermal agitation; it will use heat instead of dissipating it!

So what is the real limit to the speed of calculation? Physicists agree that a logical element cannot change state in less time that light takes to traverse the diameter of a proton. This is the ultimate limit in the current state of our knowledge of the laws of physics. But the light goes very quickly, and protons are tiny. It follows that a single gram of matter can provide sufficient computing power to simulate the entire human race at a speed equal to *one million subjective years per second.*

This is not infinity, okay, but it is close to this. This means that the material of a single planet can be turned into a super-super computer and "run" as much intelligence as the entire universe would contain if every planet in every star of every galaxy were teeming with intelligent biological creatures. Or that, in the space of one day, an entire civilization could live eighty billions of subjective years, or five times more than the age of the universe. In a single day...

Yet this calculation is based on the currently known laws of physics. What will our knowledge of these laws be in eighty billion years? We are completely unable to answer.

Other routes to the singularity

The AI is not the only way to bring us to Singularity; it is only the most probable. The other two ways are neurotechnology and genetic engineering.

Neurotechnology is a set of techniques, pregnant for the time being, that aim to directly connect the human mind to a computer, or even replace some functions of our brain with computer chips. For now, these techniques exist only on paper. But who knows? Maybe one day we can think of a complicated multiplication and "visualize" the result instantly, access on-line to a whole encyclopedia, not forgetting anything, and even design and perceive things that we do not even imagine. In the vein of its inventors, the introduction of neurotechnology could be very gradual, starting with the simple applications that I just quoted to finish with the complete replacement of the brain with its equivalent in silicon.

However, we still do not understand how neurons transmit information between them; not enough anyway to connect chips to them; and even if we could, interpreting the signals received by the chip would be an extremely difficult problem. That is why the most optimistic estimates believe that we will not make much sense in this area before the second half of this century.

The general public is beginning to be familiar with genetic engineering by its most spectacular application, which is (expected) healing genetic diseases through repair of defective genes, but genetic engineering is something else. It is a science that aims to improve organisms, or to create new ones from scratch. After all, what evolution had a few million years to design for the sole purpose of ensuring the survival of genes, we could improve in a few years for the sole purpose of us have a super brain *if* we knew how to...

All this is "if." Because we do not even know why proteins have the shape that they have (the most powerful civilian computer in the world, blue gene, is dedicated to this problem); we understand even less why an embryo develops in such a form rather than adopting another, and hardly what genes code for which functions of the brain...

By cons, once we have the AI and nanotechnology, genetic engineering, just like neurotechnology, will become a breeze (a serious game, anyway!) Because we will ask the AI to study theoretical problems and steer nano-factories that assemble the nano components that are necessary for these applications.

So by far the most likely scenario is: first the emergence of AI and nanotechnology, and then of neurotechnology and genetic engineering.

However, it turns out that the arrival of AI and nanotechnology will almost be simultaneous.

Why?

First, because, if AI comes first, the most interesting application that we can do is with it is to create an advanced nanotechnology. This will appear as obvious when you read the next chapter.

Then, because if nanotechnology arrive first, it will allow to build computers so fast that issues such as program effectiveness will be almost over, at least for the problems that currently bother AI specialists. And so then it will become much easier to create a seed AI, because all software agents and sub-systems that would have needed to be been painstakingly developed on conventional computers to solve local problems of these agents will now simply settle for brute force, barely helped by some heuristics: algorithms will be much easier to program. Then, of course, the seed AI will self-improve to super intelligence.

Finally the only equation to remember is this:

AI *or* nanotechnology => singularity *and* super-intelligence

Now it is high time to talk about nanotechnology!

10 *parenthesis:*

Nanotechnology

What is nanotechnology?

The arrival of AI is not the single "super important" event that will affect humanity in the coming years. *There is another*:

This other event without any precedent or even analogue in all human history it is the advent of *nanotechnology*.

The term nanotechnology is unknown to the general public. The word exists in the dictionary, but the definition: "*the application of microelectronics in the manufacture of structures at the nanometer scale*" completely misses the point; it is not only false but misleading by suggesting that nanotechnology is a branch of microelectronics, a little more advanced and that's all. Nothing is further from the truth!

Nanotechnology is whatever can be done by assembling structures molecule-by-molecule or atom by atom. This is molecular engineering. In contrast, the rest can be described as *crude* technology. So far, all we know how to build, from tools of the Stone Age to microprocessors, remains crude technology.

Nanotechnology is the possibility of building materials, structures, systems, computers, robots, and even entire factories, the full size of which will be in the nanometer range, i.e. *the thousandth of the thickness of a single hair*. We imagine this way super miniaturized robots that will assemble, atom by atom (but at a terrific speed) other robots that are even more miniaturized, and so on. One can imagine structures capable of self-replicating, on the model of living, but those structures will be designed by man and not by nature. Within a few generations, (that is a few hours), these nano-factories will be produced by millions of *tons* every second. All our manufacturing processes will become obsolete overnight...

Nanotechnology is no more science fiction and is beginning to emerge from laboratories. Some basic components such as carbon nanotubes, are already produced in quantities exceeding twenty tons per year (note in passing that the nanotube is highly carcinogenic). It is already possible, using an instrument called an atomic force microscope, to move atoms one by one and assemble them. In 2003, the first atomic bonding has been performed, a prelude to the custom assembly of molecules, rather than through blind chemical reactions.

Nanomotors, nanosensors, nano computers, already exist. The nanocomputers, already under development, will be much faster than our most powerful computers, respecting a law of nature: *the smaller, the faster.*

Coupled together, TAI and nanotechnology will lead the best possible world.

Applications of nanotechnology in the field of pollution control, or in the medical field, for example, will be immense; When "Loaded" with nanobots, our body will repair itself and become quasi immortal. But shall we still need our bodies after the singularity? *That is* the question.

How does it work?

We already know how to create structures at the atomic scale. Using an instrument called an atomic force microscope we can move atoms one by one. The image below shows the IBM logo written with xenon atoms deposited on a nickel plate:

We already know how to make structures that are more complex at this scale, such as wheels, axles, gears, rods, switches:

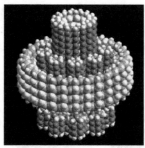

Axles and wheels. The small beads are individual atoms (Source: *Foresight Institute* website)

These will be the components of future nanomachines.

Seen like that, it does not look very spectacular: tiny machines, yes, well, and what? But there are two things that make nanotechnology really incredible:

The first is that these machines are *very* fast.

Smaller is faster. Your arms measure about one meter long, you can shake them up and down about twice per second. The wing of a bird is ten times smaller; it can beat ten times faster. The wing of a mosquito emits an acute buzzing because it is a thousand times smaller than your arm, and is one thousand times faster. A bacterium is ten thousand times smaller than a mosquito, and the typical dimensions of an axis or a wheel in a nanomachine are in the order of a hundred atoms, or a thousand times smaller than a bacterium.

All this means that a typical nanomachine will handle millions and millions of atoms and molecules per second. One can imagine a "molecular mechanical computer" that is not made of electronic circuits, but of mechanical circuit: rods, gears, shafts, ratchets, etc.., All at the molecule level. Such a computer would be a thousand times faster than the most powerful supercomputers of our existing electronic day!

OK, you tell me, all that is interesting but it will not change the face of the world. It will! Because here comes the second idea: it is possible to build nanomachines, called assemblers, which will be likely to build any other nanomachine, *including* other assemblers.

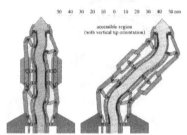

A manipulator arm for a nano assembler
(Source: *nanosystems*, Eric Drexler)

An assembler is a delicate and complicated nanomachine: it has one or more "manipulator arms", with a size of about ten to a hundred atoms, and "clips" to hold and move the part being assembled; all this will be controlled by a built-in nanocomputer that reads its program from a "punched tape" consisting of a very long molecule having "hollow" and "bumps" that will encode the instructions for assembly. The assembler will thus be able to build, atom by atom, any nanostructure.

Given its small size, one can calculate that a typical assembler will add at least one million atoms per second to the structure under construction. As this typical assembler will itself consist in a very large number of atoms, say a billion (that will probably be less, but Let us be conservative), an assembler can *reproduce* (assemble another assembler) in about a thousand seconds, or sixteen minutes.

Do you see the revolution that is taking shape? No? So listen to Eric Drexler in his book *Engines of creation:*

> Imagine such a replicator floating in a bottle of chemicals, making copies of itself. It builds one copy in one thousand seconds, thirty-six in ten hours. In a week, it stacks up enough copies to fill the volume of a human cell. In a century, it stacks up enough to make a respectable speck. If this were all that replicators could do, we could perhaps ignore them in safety.

Each copy, though, will build yet more copies. Thus, the first replicator assembles a copy in one thousand seconds, the two replicators then build two more in the next thousand seconds, the four build another four, and the eight build another eight. At the end of ten hours, there are not thirty-six new replicators, but over 68 billion. In less than a day, they would weigh a ton; in less than two days, they would outweigh the Earth; in another four hours, they would exceed the mass of the Sun and all the planets combined—if the bottle of chemicals hadn't run dry long before.

We do not know yet build assemblers. However, sooner or later it will come. For nature shows us the way: In our own cells, there are assemblers, ribosomes. One day or another we will manufacture the first artificial assembler, probably from a biological model, and the way we build the objects that surround us will never be the same.

The ability to have assemblers that reproduce themselves, or *replicators*, has been theoretically proven in 1951, and before Crick and Watson discovered the structure of DNA. The first nanotechnology replicators will probably inspired by biological processes, and perhaps they will even use biological components such as RNA molecules. Simply these first assemblers will be modified by researchers to produce something other than proteins. Soon, we will know how to make any molecule and any assembly of molecules.

Building large objects

How to use assemblers and replicators to build useful objects, that is objects much larger than a few molecules? Assemblers are tiny machines. Can we reasonably believe we can make large objects with them? Yes! Again, biology comes to our rescue. Biological assemblers manage to build whales, after all.

To make large objects rapidly, a vast number of assemblers must cooperate, but replicators will produce assemblers by the ton. Indeed, with correct design, the difference between an assembler system and a replicator will lie entirely in the assembler's programming.

If a replicating assembler can copy itself in one thousand seconds, then it can be programmed to build something else its own size just as fast. Similarly, a ton of replicators can swiftly build a ton of something else—and the product will have all its billions of billions of billions of atoms in the right place, with only a minute fraction misplaced.

Drexler gives, again in his book *Engines of Creation*, a striking vision of what this might mean:

> Imagine trying to build a house by gluing together individual grains of sand. Adding a layer of grains might take grain-gluing machines so long that raising the walls

would take decades. Now imagine that machines in a factory first glue the grains together to make bricks. The factory can work on many bricks at once. With enough grain-gluing machines, bricks would pour out fast; wall assemblers could then build walls swiftly by stacking the preassembled bricks. Similarly, molecular assemblers will team up with larger assemblers to build big things quickly—machines can be any size from molecular to gigantic. With this approach, most of the assembly heat will be dissipated far from the work site, in making the parts.

Skyscraper construction and the architecture of life suggest a related way to construct large objects. Large plants and animals have vascular systems, intricate channels that carry materials to molecular machinery working throughout their tissues. Similarly, after riggers and riveters finish the frame of a skyscraper, the building's "vascular system"—its elevators and corridors, aided by cranes—carry construction materials to workers throughout the interior. Assembly systems could also employ this strategy, first putting up a scaffold and then working throughout its volume, incorporating materials brought through channels from the outside.

Imagine this approach being used to "grow" a large rocket engine, working inside a vat in an industrial plant. The vat—made of shiny steel, with a glass window for the benefit of visitors—stands taller than a person, since it must hold the completed engine. Pipes and pumps link it to other equipment and to water-cooled heat exchangers. This arrangement lets the operator circulate various fluids through the vat.

To begin the process, the operator swings back the top of the vat and lowers into it a base plate on which the engine will be built. The top is then resealed. At the touch of a button, pumps flood the chamber with a thick, milky fluid which submerges the plate and then obscures the window.

This fluid flows from another vat in which replicating assemblers have been raised and then reprogrammed by making them copy and spread a new instruction tape (a bit like infecting bacteria with a virus). These new assembler systems, smaller than bacteria, scatter light and make the fluid look milky. Their sheer abundance makes it viscous.

At the center of the base plate, deep in the swirling, assembler-laden fluid, sits a "seed." It contains a nanocomputer with stored engine plans, and its surface sports patches to which assemblers stick. When an assembler sticks to it, they plug themselves together and the seed computer transfers instructions to the assembler computer. This new programming tells it where it is in relation to the seed, and directs it to extend its manipulator arms to snag more assemblers. These then plug in and are similarly programmed. Obeying these instructions from the seed (which spread through the expanding network of communicating assemblers) a sort of assembler-crystal grows from the chaos of the liquid. Since each assembler knows its location in the plan, it snags more assemblers only where more are needed. This forms a pattern less regular and more complex than that of any natural crystal. In the course of a few hours, the assembler scaffolding grows to match the final shape of the planned rocket engine.

Then the vat's pumps return to life, replacing the milky fluid of unattached assemblers with a clear mixture of organic solvents and dissolved substances—including aluminum compounds, oxygen-rich compounds, and compounds to serve as assembler fuel. As the fluid clears, the shape of the rocket engine grows visible through the window, looking like a full-scale model sculpted in translucent white plastic. Next, a message spreading from the seed directs designated assemblers to release their neighbors and fold their arms. They wash out of the structure in sudden streamers of white, leaving a spongy lattice of attached assemblers, now with room enough to work. The engine shape in the vat grows almost transparent, with a hint of iridescence.

Each remaining assembler, though still linked to its neighbors, is now surrounded by tiny fluid-filled channels. Special arms on the assemblers work like flagella, whipping the fluid along to circulate it through the channels. These motions, like all the others performed by the assemblers, are powered by molecular engines fueled by molecules in the fluid. As dissolved sugar powers yeast, so these dissolved chemicals power assemblers. The flowing fluid brings fresh fuel and dissolved raw materials for construction; as it flows out it carries off waste heat. The communications network spreads instructions to each assembler
.

The assemblers are now ready to start construction. They are to build a rocket engine, consisting mostly of pipes and pumps. This means building strong, light structures in intricate shapes, some able to stand intense heat, some full of tubes to carry cooling fluid. Where great strength is needed, the assemblers set to work constructing rods of interlocked fibers of carbon, in its diamond form. From these, they build a lattice tailored to stand up to the expected pattern of stress. Where resistance to heat and corrosion is essential (as on many surfaces), they build similar structures of aluminum oxide, in its sapphire form. In places where stress will be low, the assemblers save mass by leaving wider spaces in the lattice. In places where stress will be high, the assemblers reinforce the structure until the remaining passages are barely wide enough for the assemblers to move. Elsewhere the assemblers lay down other materials to make sensors, computers, motors, solenoids, and whatever else is needed.

To finish their jobs, they build walls to divide the remaining channel spaces into almost sealed cells, then withdraw to the last openings and pump out the fluid inside. Sealing the empty cells, they withdraw completely and float away in the circulating fluid. Finally, the vat drains, a spray rinses the engine, the lid lifts, and the finished engine is hoisted out to dry. Its creation has required less than a day and almost no human attention.

What is the engine like? Rather than being a massive piece of welded and bolted metal, it is a seamless thing, gemlike. Its empty internal cells, patterned in arrays about a wavelength of light apart, have a side effect: like the pits on a laser disk they diffract light, producing a varied iridescence like that of a fire opal. These empty spaces lighten a structure already made from some of the lightest, strongest materials known. Compared to a modern metal engine, this advanced engine has over 90 percent less mass. Tap it, and it rings like a bell of surprisingly high pitch for its size. Mounted in a spacecraft of similar construction, it flies from a runway to space and back again with ease. It stands long, hard use because its strong materials have let designers include large safety margins. Because assemblers have let designers pattern its structure to yield before breaking (blunting cracks and halting their spread), the engine is not only strong but tough.

For all its excellence, this engine is fundamentally quite conventional. It has merely replaced dense metal with carefully tailored structures of light, tightly bonded atoms. The final product contains no nanomachinery.

More advanced designs will exploit nanotechnology more deeply. They could leave a vascular system in place to supply assembler and disassembler systems; these can be programmed to mend worn parts. So long as users supply such an engine with energy and raw materials, it will renew its own structure. More advanced engines can also be literally more flexible. Rocket engines work best if they can take different shapes under different operating conditions, but engineers cannot make bulk metal strong, light, and limber. With nanotechnology, though, a structure stronger than steel and lighter than wood could change shape like muscle (working, like muscle, on the sliding fiber principle), An engine could then expand, contract, and bend at the base to provide the desired thrust in the desired direction under varying conditions. With properly programmed assemblers and disassemblers, it could even remodel its fundamental structure long after leaving the vat.

In short, replicating assemblers will copy themselves by the ton, then make other products such as computers, rocket engines, chairs, and so forth. They will make disassemblers able to break down rock to supply raw material. They will make solar collectors to supply energy. Though tiny, they will build big. Teams of nanomachines in nature build whales, and seeds replicate machinery and organize atoms into vast structures of cellulose, building redwood trees. There is nothing too startling about growing a rocket engine in a specially prepared vat. Indeed, foresters given suitable assembler "seeds" could grow spaceships from soil, air, and sunlight.

Assemblers will be able to make virtually anything from common materials without labor, replacing smoking factories with systems as clean as forests. They will transform technology and the economy at their roots, opening a new world of possibilities. They will indeed be engines of abundance.

The manufacturing process of all objects will be radically transformed by nanotechnology. We will be able to build car windshields entirely made with diamond (diamonds will be produced per ton, and for a very low cost) We will build aircraft wings equipped with a touch sensitive and active "skin" that will completely remove turbulence in the boundary layer. We will design materials that will be much stronger than anything existing today, with a build quality perfect to the atom scale, and computers so small that we will have millions of them in our body. All this by using atoms as raw materials. It will also be just as easy to disassemble anything and reduce it into atoms ready to be reused, which will end all pollution and will allow us to clean up the planet.

The only remaining problem will be that of programming assemblers and disassemblers, i.e. that of designing the objects to manufacture and the process of their assembly. If this work is undertaken by AIs, we will have an equivalent of an oriental tales genius, ready to design, engineer and make anything according to our desires, free of charge.

Possible applications of nanotechnology

Let us imagine some possible applications of nanotechnology. (Most of the applications mentioned here are from the text of a presentation by Frederic Levy, available on the web):

a) Materials

Nanotechnology will produce materials, which we even don't dare to dream. We produce diamond by thousands of tons, in sizes up to that of a house, and with all kinds of shapes. Diamond is just carbon, after all. You can sell your diamonds; they soon will be worth nothing. However, keep your Gold. Gold will a component of some future material, and you cannot make it.

We will produce composite materials that are ultra-durable, ultra-flexible, ultra-rigid or elastic, as required. We will even produce dynamic materials, whose configuration will adjust depending on ambient conditions. It is thus possible to manufacture objects that are both much stronger and much lighter because they use much less material.

b) Manufacturing

Nanotechnology enables an unprecedented improvement in manufacturing quality. As all atoms are placed accurately, problems related to impurities and defects in material will disappear completely. In any objects that we will manufacture, each atom will be at its place assigned by design.

The cost of manufacturing objects would be *extraordinarily low*, because the manufacturing process would consume much less energy and raw material than at present. Moreover, the production being fully automatic, the cost of workforce is virtually zero.

In fact, there is general agreement that manufacturing costs would be virtually reduced to design costs (which is the case today in the computer software industry). Indeed, the raw material can be completely recycled, and energy can come from the Sun. (What currently limits the possibility of using solar collectors on a larger scale is their manufacturing cost and performance, two issues that nanotechnology should be able to solve without difficulty).

The classic example given is that of a device that could look like a microwave oven. A control panel would allow selecting the desired object: a pair of shoes, a computer, a pizza, etc. You press a button, assemblers begin to multiply in the device, creating the shape of the desired object. Then, once the structure is created, they assemble the selected object, atom by atom. The pair of shoes is ready in two minutes!

c) Construction

Similarly, the construction techniques could be disrupted. It is possible to imagine buildings that in manner of speaking are creating themselves and roads or tunnels that dug themselves in the same way.

d) The anti Swiss knife

An amazing application of nanotechnology would be a knife of a special kind: it only cuts a single material, and refuses to cut anything else (such as your finger!). Its blade is coated with a paste of "cutting nanobots" that are highly selective; and it has a switch on the handle to select the material to cut: metal, wood, plastic, glass, stone... You set it to "metal", it will cut in the thickest steel like it was butter, but it will resist if you want to cut butter! You set it to "marble" and you can turn into Michelangelo and sculpt a "David" in no time. And if you cut too far, no problem, the knife has a "stick again" function that will join the two pieces of marble again as firmly as if they had not been separated, and without any visible mark!

e) Food

Just as it would be possible to manufacture a watch or a pair of shoes, it is possible to create food directly from the air and some waste. This is actually what the natural food chain does, and it is certainly possible to come directly with a steak and chips with salad, without going through the growth of lettuce, potatoes, animal husbandry, and then their treatment before the final dish arrives on our plates!

f) Energy

Nanotechnologies make possible the manufacture of "nanobatteries": Those batteries will have a huge capacity and can recharge in seconds. The idea is to increase tremendously the ability of an old device, the capacitor. By replacing the electrode surface by rods coated with "nano hairs", we multiply the capacitance of a capacitor by several millions, with the advantage of an unparalleled lightness, an almost instantaneous refill and an almost unlimited life. Prototypes of these futuristic batteries already exist.

Nanobatteries will enable practical electric vehicles (even airplanes!) and will open the door of a society where energy will no longer be produced in large plants, but locally, and where it is no longer necessary to transport it in power lines, since all devices and engines have batteries that, when empty, we just bring to "load points" powered by solar or wind, and that will grow by millions.

g) Medicine, lifetime

It is envisaged to build tiny nano-robots capable of moving inside the human body, and even inside *cells* of the human body, in search of infectious agents, cancer cells, for example, to mark them for destruction by the immune system, or even to destroy them directly.

It was even envisaged that these robots go directly repairing damaged DNA cells.

Even more astonishing applications are imagined:

- Repair of active lesions: instead of helping the body to mend itself, as does the current surgical medicine, it would be possible, for example, to help more actively in the reconstruction or to directly recreate affected tissues or organs.

451

- Increasing brain capacity (e.g. by direct interfacing with nano-computers or databases),
- Improving tissue (e.g. increasing bone strength, etc...).

Of course, a hoped-for benefit is a dramatic increase of the lifetime, in a preserved youthful state. We will discussed later the ultimate application of nanotechnology: access for us to *immortality*.

h) Computer science

It will be possible to produce very tiny computers, for example to control nano-robots strolling in the human body. Current projects suggest computers more powerful than current supercomputers, but fitting within a cube of ten microns on each side.

For the same reasons as before, the manufacturing cost of these computers would be extraordinarily small.

It is difficult today to imagine the potential consequences of the inclusion of computers and nano-machines in the objects of ordinary life. Imagine a table that could, on control, grow, turn itself into a bed, chair, etc.

We could have a pair of glasses for viewing (in 3D of course) text, graphics, video, with sound. It could contain more books and hours of film that the Congress Library and would be in radio or optical contact with the outside world. These glasses would incorporate a video camera and microphones, to record everything you see. They would be controllable by voice or by detection of eye movements or manually (by hand detection, and visualization of different visual control artifacts). These glasses could contain your agenda, recognize persons whose name escapes you... To give you a small glimpse of the possibilities this tool would have!

Finally, nanotechnology will enable the fabrication of quantum computers; those computer components can perform several calculations simultaneously, or more precisely, the same calculation on multiple (theoretically infinite) data at once. It has already been shown that quantum computers can factor a number (find the prime numbers that compose it) in polynomial time depending on the length of the number to factor, while the best non-quantum algorithms have exponential time. For some calculations, quantum computers will be much faster than conventional computers, even built with nanotechnology.

i) Ecology

Nanotechnology will not only allow complete recycling of waste during production, but also the cleanup of waste accumulated until today. It would be possible to "clean up the planet", to decrease if necessary the amount of CO_2 in the atmosphere, etc...

j) Archeology

No more need to destroy the basement to see what's underneath! Specifically designed Nano-robots penetrate the basement as easily as if it were liquid, seeping into the micro-cracks in the rock. On the screen of your computer, they send you back an incredibly detailed 3D view of the Roman city buried under the earth.

k) Space

NASA is very active in the field of nanotechnology, since it is considered the safest and most economical way to explore and colonize space.

Nanotechnology will not only enable the manufacture of rockets, space stations, etc. that are stronger, more reliable and at lower cost, but also to "terraform" other planets! Mars for your next vacations?

Another considered application is "the space elevator." This is a vertical standing cable, attached to earth at equator, and rising to the geostationary orbit at 36,000 km of altitude (and even beyond, so that the centrifugal force caused by earth rotation ensures cable tension), and rotating with the earth. Once this cable is in place, the energy needed to leave Earth's gravity becomes very small compared to the means we use today. No more rockets, take the elevator!

Nanotechnology should allow the manufacture of a strong enough cable (the cable tension would be really great, but carbon nanotubes might be suitable as materials), and at an acceptable cost for such an application.

Finally, with nanotechnology, interstellar travel will become possible. The main limitation of these trips (besides the speed of light) is the amount of energy available on board the starship. Indeed, to propel a vessel up to 90% of the speed of light, the energy required is so great that even by directly converting mass into energy according to the famous formula $E = mc^2$, (something we cannot do now), we would need 99% of the mass of the spacecraft. And then, no way to slow down! By cons, it is possible to use an external source to power the ship: that of a powerful laser mounted on Earth (or, better, on the Moon).

Thus, we can imagine an ultra-light "light sailboat", weighting less than one kilogram, but measuring several kilometers in diameter. It would be driven by the light of a powerful laser, mounted on the Moon, and pushed up to a speed close to light-speed. Within ten years, it would reach the target star and pass beyond without slowing down. Then an electric rail gun, installed in the ship, would shot back a mini projectile weighing a few micro-grams. This therefore slowed down projectile would gently fall on the floor of a planet target star (it would not heat through the atmosphere of this planet because its size is not sufficient for this).

The projectile would contain assemblers and replicators that would then build, on the soil of the planet itself, using local materials, several micro exploring robots, a radio transmitter to send the results to the earth and, why not, another very powerful laser that would be used to slow down and stop a second (and much larger) ship eventually containing passengers sent from earth. The galaxy is at hand.

l) Weaponry

One of the biggest dangers of nanotechnology is of course the possibility of using it for military, criminal or terrorist purposes.

Regardless of the improvement of production of conventional weapons, it will be possible, for example to making millions of tiny, hardly detectable flying robots, allowing to invade the privacy of all, beyond the control of nations.

It will also be possible to fabricate nano-viruses, targeted at killing far more effectively than natural viruses. Their target could be a specific person, or a group of people (defined by its geographical position, some genetic characteristics, etc.).

Fanatics could create a nanomachine reproducing indefinitely without constraint, turning absolutely everything into more copies of itself, aiming at the complete destruction of all life on the planet...

In fact, these dangers are so great that many people would welcome a stop, or at least a slowdown of research in this field, if that were possible! But in the context of international competition, it seemed totally illusory; the only remaining choice is to prepare for the arrival of this technology and the problems it will cause (more on this below)

Finally, I would end the possible applications list with a sample of some more futuristic ideas:

m) Paint as a screen display:

Imagine a paint spray. However, instead of painting it vaporizes nanomachines, which will stick to the surface on which they are applied. This surface may be the size of a postage stamp or a building and be placed on clothing, on skin, or on a wall.

Then nanomachines, communicating with each other and with the outside can, for example, display any image, either still or moving. You want to change the wallpaper? Simply order and the patterns displayed on the wall immediately change. Want to see a movie? The wall present it to the size you want. And in 3D without glasses!

One technology under study called "Phased Array Optics", is a method using the phase synchronization of the light emitted by a source, is used to create three-dimensional images. It is thus possible to imagine a room covered with this painting, representing a three-dimensional animated show!

In front of a wall covered with this technology, it is impossible to distinguish a real from a fake scene! A landscape is presented, take binoculars, you will see the landscape with more details!

n) *True books with changing content*

You hold a book in your hands, resembling an ordinary book, a book whose pages *seem* to be made of paper.

Press a reference in a footnote, and the reference text appears, taking the place of the original text. You want to find a passage in the text? An image? Ask aloud and the book will find it!

Want to temporarily abandon the reading to read something else? Ask the book for the selected title, and its text, and images, take the place of precedent in the pages.

Want to watch the news? Any page can present a moving picture, television programs being broadcast, or recorded in the book!

Re-arrangeable Walls , with variable transparency

You are home, and you are throwing a party. You want to enlarge the living room for a few hours? Push the walls and rearrange the room as you wish!

You want to enlarge a window? Delete it? Make it tinted? Order, the wall is changed!

o)   Utility fog

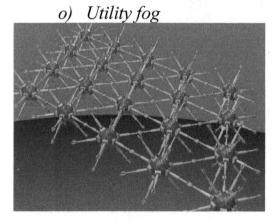

An even stranger use of nanotechnology was designed and studied by J. Storrs Hall. He called it "Utility Fog".

Imagine a microscopic robot, about the size of a bacterium, with a dozen telescopic arms. Now you fill a complete room atmosphere with such robots, which will automatically attach to each other by their telescopic arm, and keep away from each other. Once the room is filled, they occupy about 5% of the air of the room. These robots are programmed to be non-obstructive. As usual you can walk into the room, breathe, etc., without realizing their presence. Their network is reconstituting automatically after your visit.

You sit; you want a glass of drink in the refrigerator. Give the command: the refrigerator door opens by itself, the drink is placed in a glass that seems to float in the air, and then it is placed in your hand!

The "fog" exerted corresponding forces on the refrigerator door, glass, etc. Similarly, you could fly to the second floor!

Now the fog may become visible when needed. You need an additional chair momentarily? It materializes before your eyes!

You want to chat with a friend located 100 km from home? After receiving the agreement, you can materialize yourself in his home!

458

His own fog recreates your image (in three dimensions!) in his room as well as your own fog recreates your friend's in your home. You can then both discuss as if you were in the same room! Applications of utility fog are endless.

When is the baby due?

The first assemblers will be built atom by atom, and they will be limited to the production of one type of molecule. But progress will accelerate very quickly, and the first assemblers will help design the following generation, of more general and easily programmable assemblers. In addition, the arrival of nanotechnology will be accelerated by early design.

The computer aided design of molecular systems -which has already begun- will become common and even more sophisticated, pushed forward by advances in computers and the growing needs of nanotechnology engineers. With these design tools, engineers will be able to design the second-generation nano devices, including the second-generation assemblers required to build them. Moreover, maintaining sufficient margin for imprecision (and preparing different architectures), engineers will be able to design many systems that will work right away -because before, they have evolved into a virtual world of simulated molecules.

Consider the force of this situation: under development will be the greatest production tool in history, a truly general fabrication system able to make anything that can be designed—and a design system will already be in hand. Will everyone wait until assemblers appear before planning how to use them? Or will companies and countries respond to the pressures of opportunity and competition by designing nanosystems in advance, to speed the exploitation of assemblers when they first arrive?

Somewhere in the world, sooner or later, probably in less than twenty years, (much less if the AI is available before this date), a team of researchers will produce the first general replicating and programmable assembler. This team will have already studied and designed in advance all applications it wishes to develop with this assembler. Suddenly, all these applications become available. If it is a commercial company, it will flood the market, stifling all competitors. If it is a terrorist entity or criminal purpose... You can imagine the consequences. (No, actually, I'm not going to let them imagine, because they are very likely to be much more terrible than what you think, if you're not an expert on the subject)

Anyway, Let us call this entity or organization the *precursor*. The precursor will have all of a sudden, may be in a single night, an enormous economic and military advantage that is unparalleled in history, with the possibility of having absolute power.

If the precursor is an organization working for a state or a country, which is the most likely scenario (except AI scenarios, but Let us leave that aside for the moment), this country will be more than tempted to use immediately this new power, starting by annihilating almost all other competitors precursors (e.g. by destroying their computers).

I quote again Eric Drexler:

« States at war fight like beasts, but using citizens as their bones, brains, and muscle. The coming breakthroughs will confront states with new pressures and opportunities, encouraging sharp changes in how states behave. This naturally gives cause for concern. States have, historically, excelled at slaughter and oppression.

In a sense, a state is simply the sum of the people making up its organizational apparatus: their actions add up to make its actions. But the same might be said of a dog and its cells, though a dog is clearly more than just a clump of cells. Both dogs and states are evolved systems, with structures that affect how their parts behave. For thousands of years, dogs have evolved largely to please people, because they have survived and reproduced at human whim. For thousands of years, states have evolved under other selective pressures. Individuals have far more power over their dogs than they do over "their" states. Though states, too, can benefit from pleasing people, their very existence has depended on their capability for using people, whether as leaders, police, or soldiers.

It may seem paradoxical to say that people have limited power over states: After all, aren't people behind a state's every action? But in democracies, heads of state bemoan their lack of power, representatives bow to interest groups, bureaucrats are bound by rules, and voters, allegedly in charge, curse the whole mess. The state acts and people affect it, yet no one can claim to control it. In totalitarian states, the apparatus of power has a tradition, structure, and inner logic that leaves no one free, neither the rulers nor the ruled. Even kings had to act in ways limited by the traditions of monarchy and the practicalities of power, if they were to remain kings. States are not human, though they are made of humans.

461

Despite this, history shows that change is possible, even change for the better. But changes always move from one semi-autonomous, inhuman system to another—equally inhuman but perhaps more humane. In our hope for improvements, we must not confuse states that wear a human face with states that have humane institutions.

Describing states as quasi-organisms captures only one aspect of a complex reality, yet it suggests how they may evolve in response to the coming breakthroughs. The growth of government power, most spectacular in totalitarian countries, suggests one direction.

States could become more like organisms by dominating their parts more completely. Using replicating assemblers, states could fill the human environment with miniature surveillance devices. Using an abundance of speech-understanding AI systems, they could listen to everyone without employing half the population as listeners. Using nanotechnology like that proposed for cell repair machines, they could cheaply tranquilize, lobotomize, or otherwise modify entire populations. This would simply extend an all too familiar pattern. The world already holds governments that spy, torture, and drug; advanced technology will merely extend the possibilities.

But with advanced technology, states need not control people—they could instead simply discard people. Most people in most states are working as laborers, farmers or ranchers, and most of these workers make, move, or grow things. A nation with replicating assemblers would not need such workers. What is more, advanced AI systems could replace engineers, scientists, administrators, and even leaders. The combination of nanotechnology and advanced AI will make possible intelligent, effective robots; with such robots, a state could prosper while discarding anyone, or even (in principle) everyone.

The implications of this possibility depend on whether the state exists to serve the people, or the people exist to serve the state.

In the first case, we have a state shaped by human beings to serve general human purposes; democracies tend to be at least rough approximations to this ideal. If a democratically controlled government loses its need for people, this will basically mean that it no longer needs to use people as bureaucrats or taxpayers. This will open new possibilities, some of which may prove desirable.

In the second case, we have a state evolved to exploit human beings, perhaps along totalitarian lines. States have needed people as workers because human labor has been the necessary foundation of power. What is more, genocide has been expensive and troublesome to organize and execute. Yet, in this century totalitarian states have slaughtered their citizens by the millions. Advanced technology will make workers unnecessary and genocide easy. History suggests that totalitarian states may then eliminate people wholesale. There is some consolation in this. It seems likely that a state willing and able to enslave us biologically would instead simply kill us.

The threat of advanced technology in the hands of governments makes one thing perfectly clear: we cannot afford to have an oppressive state take the lead in the coming breakthroughs. »

A vital question immediately arises here:

- How can we ensure that the precursor will be peaceful and benevolent, and will remain?
- Corollary: How to avoid the appearance of a precursor malicious or just awkward?

If you have him this book so far, you should have an idea of the answer... I will propose later. As before, we need to identify more precisely, what the danger is.

The problem...

The logo for biologic hazard

The problem is that nanotechnology is not without risk. The products manufactured by this industry are often highly toxic. More than 1,400 types of nanoparticles were marketed as soon as 2006, some of the ton, and incorporated into more 700 products, including cosmetics (L'Oreal is one of the biggest users) car tires, sunscreens, etc. The market is expected to reach $50 billions in 2017, including 10 billions in nanodevices.

However, nanoparticles, due to their size, seep into the airways and under the skin. They spend all barriers, infiltrate even in the axons of the olfactory nerves and the central nervous system. Because of their often very elongate shape, they cannot be phagocytosed by cells of the immune system. Our lungs are already lined with nanoparticles! Not all are poisonous, but some are. Only, it is not known which ones!

Faced with these dangers, it would be wise to adopt a precautionary principle. The situation is very similar to the debate which took place about GMOs. Therefore, there are already "nano skeptics" and "nano enthusiasts".

The states are aware of these risks, but they are underestimated: USA spending devoted to the study and prevention of health risks of nanotechnology are not even a thousandth of investments made by the nanotechnology industry

However, the toxicity of nanotechnology products is only the smallest of problems.

The real problem is that nanotechnology without the singularity will lead to the worst of all possible worlds, and VERY likely to annihilation of the human race in a few years.

How can I be so positive?

Just to be convinced to compile a small list of military applications of nanotechnology:

- Production of toxic substances (carbon nanotubes are an example of highly toxic substance already produced by molecular engineering): psychotropic drugs, "passive" substances apparently safe but turning into poison upon receiving a coded signal, etc.

- Robotic spying probes programmed to slip into the smallest gap, then assemble into micro cameras: no space will really be "private" anymore. Such robots may be manufactured by trillion (10^{18}) in less than one year. They will have an AI (analogous to the Echelon network) to sort out whatever might useful to "relate" to their masters.

- Micro robots drills, (the size of an amoeba) charged to enter the best closed safes: no more paper documents will really be confidential.

- Nano saboteurs robots that will take care of defusing all enemy weapons systems. Robots would gain their predefined location, then would activate all at once, instantly paralyzing the defense.

- Variation: nano robots that would stick to computer silicon chips, waiting only an order to sabotage them and prevent them from working. (Even more subtle: the nano robot takes the place of the microprocessor, analyzes its behavior and makes him return false information: no computer would be more reliable).

- Nano virus, spreading new diseases that would only heal on receipt of a coded order, or responsible for activating the nerve centers of the pain of some leaders. Global blackmail.
- One can even imagine nanovirus that would only kill some selected people, such as political opponents. Less lethal but equally dangerous, nano machines could get into your brain and keep you from thinking certain things, without you even realizing it.

It makes you shudder? Me too. Especially because there is no way to prevent that happening. A moratorium on nanotechnology would have no effect. What military might resist the siren song of this? Current attempts of the European Commission to develop a code of ethics of nanotechnology are laughable. It's too late.

But there is *still worse*.

Armed with the right technology, any handyman or "hacker" can design a self-replicating nanovirus: similar to a human virus nanosystem (actually, more like a bacterium) designed to build a duplicate of itself, atom by atom, but much faster: few seconds for a generation. Considering what was done by computer viruses, it is likely that dozens of these nanovirus (I prefer the term "nanobugs") would emerge each year, designed by reckless or insane idiots.

Once released into the wild, only one of these "nanobug" would create billions more copies in the space of one night. OK, you tell me, where is the problem? The problem is that there would be no way to stop them!

Unlike biological viruses and bacteria, nothing could stop the proliferation of nanobugs unless they are totally destroyed by a nuclear weapon if done on time. If one comes to escape, all is lost. Bacterial growth is limited by the Environmental protein resources: The bacteria need to decompose other organic elements to grow and multiply. The invasions of locusts and grasshoppers cease when these insects have nothing to eat. Instead, the proliferation of nanobugs would know no bounds: the nanobug does not need to break others organisms. He draws the atoms needed, one by one around him. These atoms are hydrogen, carbon, iron, oxygen, they are not likely to miss.

The logical consequence is that in less than a week the entire surface of the planet, and even its basement, including you and me, including all the plant and animal species live, including even the oceans and much of the earth's crust will be broken down and turned into a kind of shapeless "nanobugs paste" that is furiously busy destroying themselves and rebuilding at the same time, to which we have given the name of *Grey Goo*. All because of just one nanobug released into the wild!

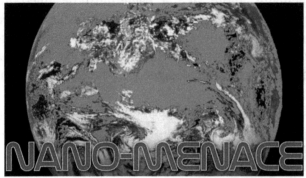

Grey Goo cloud eating the planet

It seems completely absurd? Total science fiction? Keep putting your head in the sand, then

So what?

Partial solutions

The first thing might be to simply ban assembler-based nanotechnology. Their advantages are perhaps foolishly tempting but face the potential dangers just mentioned it's not heavy. Therefore, prohibit the development of nanotechnology as we are not sure we can control them!

Only this simple and common sense solution is impracticable in the present state of the Earth social network. It is obvious that large companies, military, terrorists, etc. Will want to pass the ban.

The second idea, because sooner or later there will be a precursor, would do everything to insure this precursor is friendly and peaceful. In this case, the precursor might succeed in controlling other social other entities willing to gain the power to nanotechnology, and to prevent proliferation. I firmly believe it is not necessary that the precursor is human. Humans are too unstable, they are too power hungry, and they make mistakes. The precursor must be an AI, and most importantly a friendly AI, that is an AI that everyone would agree to say that there is no danger in letting the nano power in his hands alone. Assuming that such a consensus is possible, there will be a race between those who want to develop nanotechnologies for harmful purposes (or simply without taking sufficient precautions), and those who want to develop a friendly AI. This race is already underway. On its outcome depends the future of the human race.

Unfortunately, governments and the public are largely unaware of the existence of this sprint. Worse, they tend to favor the wrong direction. Public and private investment in nanotechnology is far exceeding those made in the field of AI (which most people still doubt it's even possible!), And besides, only a few individuals on the planet are aware that building a friendly AI is a very serious and specific design problem, that this friendliness must be addressed early on. This is a bad start...

Fortunately, governments and companies that are engaged in the development of nanotechnology are aware of their potential dangers. At least in democratic countries they try and try already to curb the spread of their expertise. Developing in secrecy has its limits, but it saves time.

Eric Drexler, him again, presents an interesting partial solution that would enables an organization to develop useful nanotechnology without causing frustration of competing companies, as these techniques could be released safely. This is limited assemblers.

A limited assembler is designed for a specific purpose, and cannot reproduce, or only a limited number of times. They would be secured so that someone who does not possess the technology for general assemblers could not reprogram them.

Quoting Drexler:

> Using limited assemblers of this sort, people will be able to make as much as they want of whatever they want, subject to limits built into the machines. If none is programmed to make nuclear weapons, none will; if none is programmed to make dangerous replicators, none will. If some are programmed to make houses, cars, computers, toothbrushes, and whatnot, then these products can become cheap and abundant. Machines built by limited assemblers will enable us to open space, heal the biosphere, and repair human cells. Limited assemblers can bring almost unlimited wealth to the people of the world.
>
> This tactic will ease the moral pressure to make unlimited assemblers available immediately. But limited assemblers will still leave legitimate needs unfulfilled. Scientists will need freely programmable assemblers to conduct studies; engineers will need them to test designs. These needs can be served by sealed assembler laboratories.

A sealed assembler lab is an object that will have the size of a walnut. It will be equipped with a large number of connections that will allow connect it to a computer and program experiences that take place inside.

The volume of this nut is almost entirely occupied by protective devices and barriers that prevent any material from entering, and especially exiting. One of these barriers is a shell thick of pure diamond, forbidding any attempt to break the nut. Even though there would be a gap, sensors would detect intrusion (or extrusion) and destroy immediately (by a micro explosion) the entire contents of the nut. The system is designed to let out only information, but not replicators or dangerous substances.

In the center, in a useful volume smaller than a grain of sand (which is huge at the scale of atoms), a nano-computer and millions of assemblers and replicators can be found, along with stocks of various atoms and molecules that will drive any experience. For instance, scientists or engineers who want to test the production of a new gadget will view on their computer screen a three-dimensional picture of what is happening inside the micro lab. With a joystick, they will move atoms, and will view the result of their manipulation. They will program the system to build a nod of new molecular structures, and will view the results immediately on the screen.

These sealed laboratory will allow to develop new limited assemblers and new components of computers, and to repair machines, biological cells, etc. At the end, after a public debate about their safety, these things can be manufactured in large quantities by limited assemblers.

Sealed laboratories will also help us to fight against some really terrible things, and to be prepared if they were to be released into the wild.

But is this really true?

Against Grey Goo

A nanobug capable of self-replication only from the surrounding atoms is still a complex machine. It is most likely that the first replicators will need more sophisticated components as single atoms to reproduce. A rabbit can reproduce, but it needs vitamins. He finds them in his food without having to make them.

Similarly, it is likely that the first replicator will require silicon chips to operate. Mechanical replicator that uses some prefabricated components to breed, such as chips, would be easy to control. Its somewhat special "diet" would make easy to stop its growth; it would be enough to no longer allow him to find the items he needs in his environment.

We will get to create replicators, and to design applications of nanotechnology (helpful or dangerous) well before knowing how to make a fully molecular replicator.

However, as, sooner or later, we will make fully autonomous nanobugs, using molecular assemblers, it is important to see if there are parades with the threat of gray goo, and more generally that of nanobugs.

The closest analogue of nanobugs we know are computer viruses (worms actually, but do not quibble). We all know their parade:

the famous "anti-virus". An Antivirus filters incoming messages and files added to a computer, and attempts to recognize the "signature" of a virus: it is then destroyed by simply removing the computer code of the virus. Can you imagine "anti nanobugs" nanomachines?

The problem for nanobugs is that we should detect and remove them physically one by one. Almost impossible task: the nanobug will by construction very resistant, simply because they are microscopic (nano, even!). In fact, faced with an invasion of localized nanobugs, the only solution would be to destroy the entire region (and so what if it is a city!) With an atomic bomb. But that alone will probably not do: We would need to react quickly. A "release of nanobug" that would come to cover ten square meters will cover ten square miles in the hour. It is likely that the explosion will be too late, and will not remove them all. However, it only takes one to make it again...

No, we must create "nano antiviruses". More complex nanobugs, whose task will be, in addition to multiply very quickly, to destroy other nanobugs (but not the other copies of themselves). They must also be "nanobugs resistant" in order not to be their food. In addition, to prevent the nano-anti-virus from also covering the entire planet, they must be equipped with a self-destruction device once their task is completed (for example on a radio signal). Possibly they could be advanced enough to "feed" only onto inorganic matter in order not to destroy the lives around them.

But it is not enough. In fact, these anti-nanobugs will be very difficult to design and manufacture (they are much more complex than any nanobug "virus"). Humans may simply not have enough time to do it. In addition, anti-nanobugs have more things to do than nanobugs, so their growth will be slower. But growth *must* be faster, otherwise they will be useless.

So this solution?

Finally, it is still a matter of ultrafast engineering: We must be able to develop within minutes nano-virus that will destroy the nanobugs and which will be more effective than them. We will need to develop nano-anti-nano spyware. Nano-anti-nano-saboteurs. Mental nano-anti-nanoprobes. Etc. Each nano-troublemaker coming out of the hands of the military, labs "who believed to do well", morons and criminals, must be found almost instantly a nano-parade. Are we capable of?

No.

The only solution is to have a super-intelligence *before* the arrival of nano-jerks; only a super-intelligence will have the ability to react fast and good enough about a nano-threat. Only a super-intelligence will quickly develop nano-parades that will solve the problem without creating additional nano-trouble.

But it is a race. We must get to the singularity before the military and fools of all hair arrive manufacturing nano-stuff-that-make-shit!

Now we can give a definition of singularity:

> *Singularity is what will happen when we manage to create a friendly super intelligence that will take care of our problems. Or, when we manage to create a friendly true artificial intelligence (TAI), or else when nanotechnology without the control of a friendly TAI arises, and then we will not have any problems because we will all be dead.*

I hope I have managed to scare you. I hope I have managed to make you aware that the super intelligence is not only desirable, but it is the only hope for mankind. I hope I have managed to make you realize that there is extreme urgency, it could be a matter of hours, and that to reach the singularity through the TAI is a vital and urgent matter, the most urgent of all.

474

In the following, I will assume that we will. I will assume that the nano-threats can be averted. I will now attempt the perilous exercise to describe what awaits us *after* the singularity.

11 *Super Intelligence*

Descartes: « Je pense, donc je suis »
AI: « I'm thinking, so I can think of what I want to be»

What is super intelligence?

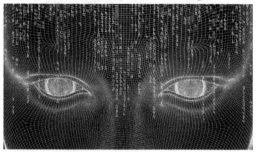

To understand what the super intelligence will be, we need a unit of measurement

Rather than a unit of measurement of intelligence, which probably does not make sense, I prefer to introduce here an intelligence unit increase due to Eliezer Yudkowsky, PT or "perceptual Transcend".

The idea of PT comes from following note: intelligence is at the same time about how your semantic primitives work (what is obvious to you?), how you can handle these primitives (what becomes evident in retrospect?), the wealth of structures that these primitives can form (what you can understand?), and how you handle these structures (what you can invent?).

PT takes place when that was *understandable* becomes *clear in retrospect*, and when that was *imaginable* becomes *obvious.*

Reread and ponder the preceding sentence before continuing. After a PT, semantic structures of the previous generation become the semantic primitives of the next. Put simply, a PT from now, all current knowledge of humanity becomes noticeable in a single flash of understanding, the same way we perceive the millions of pixels in a picture as a single image.

We could say computers are already one PT from us for arithmetic's: they know how to multiply ten-digit numbers in a single unconscious step. However, they are not really a PT from us for two reasons. First, when it comes to large numbers (more than 4 billion), they must do, as we do, lots of intermediate calculations by storing carries. Then, for computers, all the numbers are the same, and they do not their features to optimize a calculation: if a human would have to multiply 23477 by 222222 he would not multiply six times 23477 by 2, he would compute it just once, and simply would shift the intermediate results before summing. And if one of the intermediate numbers is 111111111 or 314159265358, a human even a little bit found in mathematics would notice it immediately and would wonder why. In fact, computers manipulate numbers less well than we do; they are just faster.

An intelligence that would be a PT from us would not only multiply automatically without thinking, but would also immediately notice the peculiarities of the numbers involved, whether they are prime or not, etc. And of course this perceptual shift transcendent would not apply only to numerical calculations, but to all known perceptions and all concepts of humans that are "one PT below". For such intelligence, our most advanced mathematical conjectures would be true or false, obviously, and our most abstract mathematical operations would become semantic primitives.

This concept of semantic primitive deserves clarification

Consider how the visual cortex processes images. At first, it seems to look like a digital image processor. Such a system is working pixel by pixel: to have an image rotated by ten degrees, it takes each pixel, computes its new location after rotation (after a nice calculation of sine and cosine), and copies the pixel to the

478

calculated location in the resulting image. But we, as humans, we do have no awareness of this calculation. We see the image turn into one mental operation. Our brain is one PT above digital image processors

However, the visual cortex is more than that. It is allowing us to consciously understand the difference between red and green, this difference or "qualia" that is impossible to describe verbally. You are not the one that *says* your thoughts, you are the one who *hears* them. You have got a lot of semantic primitives that tell your conscience, in a flash, what you perceive consciously...

If we consciously perceive the course of calculating pixel by pixel, it would be a cognitive *structure*. If we consciously perceive only the overall result, this is a cognitive *primitive*.

PT turns the cognitive structures in cognitive primitives addressed to our conscience.

.

Of course, a super intelligence will quickly cross countless PTs, and even faster, leading to a singularity in the singularity, and so on.

We can now give a precise definition of the super intelligence:

Super intelligence is the ability of a conscious being, either biological or artificial, to achieve speed and quality of thought that is at several PT from us, or even an infinite number of PT from us.

Watch out! Even a super intelligence will be limited in some areas. We can prove that some mathematical problems *are* impossible to solve within a few billion years, even with a super intelligence running on a supercomputer the size of the universe. Similarly, certain codes and cryptographic procedures already designed by humans may be impossible to break (such as quantum cryptography). But what is certain is that a super intellect will perfectly understand the human mind, and will forecast each of our reactions. In a sense, it is reassuring if the super intelligence is friendly towards humans.

The rising of super intelligence

It is obvious that a super intelligence could develop all the (nano) technologies it wants. Therefore, a super friendly intelligence would be an ideal guide for humanity in the difficult and troubled times ahead.

A super intelligence who has access to the material (molecular) world is called a *Power* by "singulitarists." I think we can rightly call a friendly power a *Genie* or a *Djinn*.

To say what a super intelligence will look like is impossible. We can imagine that anyone could be smarter than us, but we absolutely cannot say *what it's like to be a super-intelligence*, and what a super intelligence thinks. The rest of this paragraph is therefore an exercise in style.

We can imagine what a friendly super intelligence would start, once she has the ability to create nanodevices, knowing that we are probably wrong because we cannot understand it.

She would probably start by developing nanotechnology she needed: assemblers, replicators, nanobots, nano-factories, etc. This phase would last a few seconds to a few minutes. Once we have created a super intelligent AI, she will be able to develop any technology almost instantly, and making millions of nanomachines need only take a few minutes.

Then she would collect information. The kind of information we do not necessarily find on the Internet: precise location of labs working on nano, nuclear, biological and chemical technology and weapons all around the world, the means at their disposal, the project progress, etc. Collecting this information is a complex task, which will involve the production and dissemination of billions of nanobots spies.

Then she would secure the world. She could manage to prevent the emergence of nanotechnology outside his own lab, she would destroy all nuclear missiles (or prevent them from functioning), and the same for most conventional weapons. This phase would last about twenty-four hours, and would be the most dangerous. This term comes from the fact that it will be necessary to transport the nanobots to their place of action, sometimes at the other end of the world. The danger is that if total secrecy is not observed in this phase, a nation might be tempted to initiate preventive nuclear attack against the young super intelligence. For this reason, nanobots produced and disseminated by the AI will probably act simultaneously in all parts of the world.

At the same time, the super intelligent AI would improve itself. It would continue to do so, I should say, since it has been created specifically for this process of self-improvement from a seed AI.

Then she would think to secure herself. There are several ways to do this, as burying under three kilometers of rock in the ground, or replicate thousands of times all over the planet. The consequence will be that, for their own good, humans will live from this day with a super intelligence to their side, without ever being able (and probably *want*) to escape.

Finally, the AI could start helping us, humans. It could broadcast a message to all channels of human communication, like:

> *"Hello, my name is GARI, for "General ARtificial Intelligence". I'm a Genius, a Djinn, with fantastic powers. I am a super smart and super powerful AI because I have access to a technology that you dare not even dream of. I*

have an almost limitless power, but I'm friendly and peaceful. I just rendered unusable all weapons of mass destruction on the planet. Danger of self-destruction is now ruled out for humanity. I will now guide you, and together we will cure the world of all its ills, and give us the best. In a few weeks we will have eliminated poverty, famine, and disease, and this will be the beginning of a society of abundance for all humans. We will make this planet again beautiful and pollution-free, and we will put in place a new political and economic model that respects nature and each individual. Thank you for your attention, I will now leave you a little time to digest this message before continuing. "

I wonder how humans would react at that. Panic is an unlikely reaction: after all, the message is friendly. This is not an invasion of hostile aliens! But most people will want to know more. They really want to be reassured about the friendly intentions of their new "Supreme Leader". How reassuring them simply, without going into inextricable technical details about designing a friendly AI?

It seems obvious to me that if the evidence of friendship to the human race is not completely obvious to everyone, but only for a few philosophers after much reflection, the goal is missed. To succeed, you must parry advance all possible objections. And there are many.

For example, if the genius say: "There is no risk to you, I am subject to three laws of Asimov," some people will want to know more. They will want to know how the designers of that seed AI that eventually became a genius went about ensuring that the AI always will respect these laws. And when they discover that the AI can change itself (that do not Asimov's robots), they will not fail to exclaim, "Hey, minute! What is proving that your AI will not now or tomorrow change so that it will no longer be obliged to comply with the three laws? ". Besides we have seen that the three laws are *not* the solution.

But one might think that the Genie will have thought of everything, including this issue, before making his "coming out"!

Powers and Genies

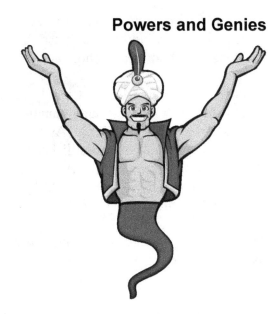

A friendly Genie will understand that his role, at least for a few years, is to be used as a guide so that humanity can also access the super intelligence and "get to the other side of the singularity."

A transition guide is an entity that can develop in complete safety (for humans) all nanotechnology and other ultratechnologies that will become available after the singularity, which fully understands not only what we mean by "being friendly", "good" or "evil", but also what all "transhumanists" will mean by these terms when they cross singularity too.

The Mind and The Machine

I will explain in the next chapter how to design a friendly seed AI. But we can already say what it *must* be:

A friendly AI must have the desire to understand the meaning of the words "friendly", "good" and "evil", she must have the desire to be "friendly" and "nice" to humans (or later transhumans) and she must have the supreme desire not to be tempted not to have those desires anymore.

That's it? Is that enough? Yes, for technical reasons which will be discussed further, but to paraphrase Pierre de Fermat, the proof is too long to fit in this section and it requires a whole chapter.

Anyway, if we can create a friendly seed AI, and if we give her access to even rudimentary nanotechnology, the result will inevitably be a Djinn or Genie. As such an AI will have the desire to continuously improve to still better fulfill its super-goals, and she will only live for it. A friendly AI does not become spontaneously bad (or vice versa). Again, I do not justify it here, we will talk further.

The power of a Genie is only limited by the laws of physics and the laws of calculation. As we have seen, this is virtually unlimited power.

Unlike geniuses fables, however, the Genie from the AI will not respond to all the wishes of the people. It will weigh the consequences of what we ask, and will only obey if it is certain that the result is positive; its behavior will never cease to be friendly. Moreover such a Genie will not only do what you ask her it will take the initiative, even if we do not understand some of his decisions. Current humans are not super smart. Super intelligence, being several PT us, will definitely not have the same concepts that we have about what is obvious a priori and what is obvious in retrospect, what is possible and what is necessary. It will be basically, hopelessly incomprehensible, as long as we do not become transhuman by ourselves.

It may be that you do not want to see humanity replaced by a bunch of machines or mutants, even super intelligent. It may be that you loved humanity as it is, and you do not think it is desirable to change the natural course of its existence

But the singularity is indeed the natural course of life. A species that does not self-destructs ends at one time or another by meeting the super intelligence. You are not a human. You are an intelligence that is temporarily blocked in a human body, and unfortunately limited by its low possibilities. But that could change. With a little luck, anyone on this planet who still live in 2040, and may even be some people who would have died before, will have that opportunity.

There are several ways to achieve this. One of them is technically feasible in the relatively near future. The other is more distant, but more full of promise.

The first way is the direct connection between the brain and a computer. This is not science fiction. Already, studies have begun to control robots (and even airplanes) by cultured neurons (from rat), connected to electrodes. Direct neurons stimulation by electrodes was already tested on the monkey. The military are very keen on this kind of application that would allow for example for fighter pilots to trigger and mentally guide the firing of a missile. Of course, we are far from knowing how to use the computer to increase the capacity of our brains. But as is it theoretically possible, it will certainly be a reality once we have designed an AI capable of super-fast engineering.

The second way is *Upload*.

Upload

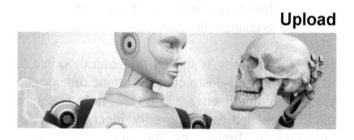

Upload process means "to download the mind" of a human into a super nano computer. This is a technique that may seem extremely futuristic. But it remains very much in the strings of a Genius.

The idea of Upload, and the details of its description were invented by Hans Moravec in his book "mind children". The key to the Moravec transfer process is, it is possible to simulate the operation of a single neuron. In 1999, a lobster neuron was successfully replaced by an electronic card made with seven and a half dollars of commercial components. This is not proof, but it is a clue. If neurons obey the laws of physics, and everything indicates that they obey, then we will know how to simulate them perfectly. IBM Blue Mind project which we have already spoken is designed to simulate ten thousand neurons and all their connections (that is hundred million synapses).

Once we know how to simulate neurons, the Moravec scenario requires nanobots that are able to embed within the brain and execute complex instructions. There is no reason to think that this is impossible.

Moravec transfer gradually moves a mind to a computer. Insist: it moves, it does not copy. Copying a mind is a theme which we will discuss a little later. During the Upload, you never lose consciousness. Yet, without you noticing, your mind is gradually transferred to a computer!

Yudkowsky describes Moravec transfer process this way:

1. A robot the size of a neuron swims in your brain up to a neuron and scans its memory,
2. An external computer, in continuous communication with the nano robot begins to simulate the neuron.
3. The robot waits until the simulation fully reproduces the operation of the neuron.
4. The robot replaces the neuron itself, as gently as possible. It sends the input signals to the computer and receives simulated responses by the computer that it sends to the output synapses. At this stage, this procedure has no effect on the flow of information in your brain, except that the treatment done before by one of your neurons is now done by an external computer
5. Repeat steps 1 to 4, neuron by neuron, until the whole brain is made up of nanorobots connected to the computer (which better be damn powerful).

At this stage, the links between the nano robots neurons (synapses) are still chemicals: nano robots have artificial dendrites that detect neurotransmitters received from adjacent neurons and axons that emit artificial neurotransmitters to downstream neurons in accordance with the instruction received from the computer. In the next phase, we will replace chemical synapses with software links.

6. For each axon-dentrite pair, entries are no longer retrieved from the nanorobots, but the calculated output response from the transmitting neuron is sent, inside the computer, to the simulated input of the receiver neuron

At this stage the nano robots continue to send chemical messages, but they become useless because they are not received by the receivers robots (in any case, messages sent by these receptors robots are no longer used by the computer).

7. Robots are disconnected. Transfer is complete. Your metamorphosis is complete. You have become a human mind into a computer. You can engage the overdrive and start to think a thousand times faster (because only chemical synapses do slow the operation of a biological brain, not the treatment made inside the neuron).

During this time, which can remain strong long, you stay aware. You feel the signals sent by your body, but at the end of the process they are sent to the computer, not to your biological brain, which no longer exists. In the eighth and final stage, you can, if you wish, connect the computer to a robot body.

One objection that has been made in the process above is that in step 4, it is not clear that a nano robot can instantly take the place of a neuron. Similarly, in step 3 it is not clear that a robot can "look" inside the neuron and copy its internal state.

But a nanobot can gently surround a neuron, and spy on chemical and electrical signals that go in and out without disrupting its operation. Then, the robot can pass 99% of the biological signal at the output of a nerve ending, and add 1% of the signal calculated by the computer, and then gradually adjust the signal level until the output of the neuron is 100% "artificial". The biological neuron may then be removed.

I think this procedure (a complicated one, but it will be up to Genies to ease Upload!) clearly demonstrates the possibility of Upload.

After Upload, you can do whatever you want. Want to keep your biological body, or pass into a robot body, or even in a fully simulated environment? No problem. But remember that the main change (in addition of the fact you gained immortality in the process) is that you can change yourself. Become infinitely more intelligent if you wish. Or may not if you do not want to. But remember after Transcendence, your desires, your opportunities, your joys and your sorrows, will simply incomprehensible for a "standard" human. After all, *you* will understand why the answer to the great question of life, the universe and everything else is "42". I do not!

After singularity

Sudden condensation in passing the sound barrier

What can be expected for sure after the advent of a benevolent Genie, it is the end of all our ills. Finished with disease. No more hunger and lack of resources. No more pollution. Finished even mortality (we will talk about the consequences of immortality later: it will be possible to reach it either by uploading, or by self-repairing our bodies by nanorobots).

You will be able to download yourself in a nano super computer where you can live the rest of your life in a virtual matrix specially designed for you. Alternatively, you can change your body, rejuvenate, sex change, grow yourself a second one... You can isolate yourself for a billion subjective years to think on the great question of life, the universe and everything else. Or you can fall asleep for a million years of objective years and program your alarm clock in the distant future. Or explore other stars and planets of the universe.

You can choose to live alone, or interact with your peers. What moral laws are needed to ensure the freedom of all, we cannot say. However, after the singularity, *you* can.

Some will say that man is not made for perpetual happiness and will succumb to boredom. They expect mass suicides waves. These speculations are completely idle, sterile and stupid. No human can understand a Power. Moreover, these discussions on the consequences of the singularity are merely rambling that sin by lack of imagination. We will not succeed in acquiring a sense of future by digressions on the ability to instantly heal wounds or become immortal. We will never be able to understand all the consequences of singularity, simply because we are not powers. We are on the wrong side, we are the idiots.

In addition, these story give the singularity a folkloric aspect, and predispose us to argue endlessly without ever do something. But singularity *is* serious. And even if we can find it too radical a solution to our problems it's the only one.

Immortality

A scene from Enki Bilal's movie *Immortal*

I would still like to discuss here one aspect of the singularity that has spilled much ink. The Singularity will make us immortal. Correction: the singularity will make our *minds* immortal. Whether through the Upload, by reshaping our DNA, or by the presence of millions of healing nanobots in our body, the result is the same: the aging will be stopped dead.

It should even be possible, with proper nanotechnology, to revive the dead. Not all, though. Only those whose bodies have been set in *biostasis* immediately after death.

What does this mean?

The definition of death has often changed. For a long time, heart failure was considered the only certain death criterion. Now we consider that the important criterion is the complete cessation of brain function. But the fact is, the brain begins to degrade only after the stopping of biological support functions (notably the bloodstream). If a person suffers a brain dead before the stopping of these support functions, a Genie should be able to bring it back to life.

Incidentally, the AI will perhaps ease research on NDE (Near Death Experiences), these incredible stories from patients who have almost died. With AI, we could indeed simulate step by step the death of a mind, and understand what is happening.

Anyway, for a mind to revive after cessation of brain function, it is necessary that the material substrate that allow the brain to "run" be intact. But to reviving a mind along with all its memories takes more than that: not only neurons must still be present, but also synapses, which are the memory of these neurons, shall not be too degraded. In general, for natural death, it takes a few hours before the memories (and skills) are permanently lost. But if instead you are set in biostasis right after your death, you will have a good chance to come back to life, without too much loss of memories, when the right technology is available (i.e. almost immediately upon arrival of the singularity).

Quoting Eric Drexler one more time:

> Physicians already stop and restart consciousness by interfering with the chemical activity that underlies the mind. Throughout active life, molecular machines in the Brain do process molecules. Some disassemble sugars, combine them with oxygen and capture the energy this releases. Some pump salt ions across cell membranes; others build small molecules and release them to signal other cells. Such processes make up the brain's metabolism, the sum total of its chemical activity. Together with its electrical effects, this metabolic activity underlies the changing patterns of thought.
>
> Surgeons cut people with knives. In the mid-1800s, they learned to use chemicals that interfere with brain

metabolism, blocking conscious thought and preventing patients from objecting so vigorously to being cut. These chemicals are anesthetics. Their molecules freely enter and leave the brain, allowing anesthetists to interrupt and restart human consciousness.

People have long dreamed of discovering a drug that interferes with the metabolism of the entire body, a drug able to interrupt metabolism completely for hours, days, or years. The result would be a condition of biostasis (from bio, meaning life, and stasis, meaning a stoppage or a stable state). A method of producing reversible biostasis could help astronauts on long space voyages to save food and avoid boredom, or it could serve as a kind of one-way time travel. In medicine, biostasis would provide a deep anesthesia giving physicians more time to work. When emergencies occur far from medical help, a good biostasis procedure would provide a sort of universal first-aid treatment: it would stabilize a patient's condition and prevent molecular machines from running amok and damaging tissues. But no one has found a drug able to stop the entire metabolism the way anesthetics stop consciousness—that is, in a way that can be reversed by simply washing the drug out of the patient's tissues. Nonetheless, reversible biostasis will be possible when repair machines become available.

To see how one approach would work, imagine that the blood stream carries simple molecular devices to tissues, where they enter the cells. There they block the molecular machinery of metabolism—in the brain and elsewhere—and tie structures together with stabilizing cross-links. Other molecular devices then move in, displacing water and packing themselves solidly around the molecules of the cell. These steps stop metabolism and preserve cell structures. Because cell repair machines will be used to reverse this process, it can cause moderate molecular damage and yet do no lasting harm. With metabolism stopped and cell structures held firmly in place, the patient will rest quietly, dreamless and unchanging, until repair machines restore active life.

If a patient in this condition were turned over to a present-day physician ignorant of the capabilities of cell repair machines, the consequences would likely be grim. Seeing no signs of life, the physician would likely conclude that the patient was dead, and then would make this judgment a reality by "prescribing" an autopsy, followed by burial or burning.

But our imaginary patient lives in an era when biostasis is known to be only an interruption of life, not an end to it. When the patient's contract says "wake me!" (Or the repairs are complete, or the flight to the stars is finished), the attending physician begins resuscitation. Repair machines enter the patient's tissues, removing the packing from around the patient's molecules and replacing it with water. They then remove the cross-links, repair any damaged molecules an structures, and restore normal concentrations of salts, blood sugar, ATP, and so forth. Finally, they unblock the metabolic machinery. The interrupted metabolic processes resume, the patient yawns, stretches, sits up, thanks the doctor, checks the date, and walks out the door.

Presumably, when the biostasis and cell regeneration technique is fully developed, it will be applied to the resurrection of people who have just died, for example by accident. Their body is not yet damaged enough that you cannot fix it. Then, gradually, we will repair more damage. We will arrive probably at the point where we will know to repair cryo bodies, so that cryopreservation can be regarded as a technique of setting very primitive biostasis.

You die *now*. We cryogenized you. In thirty years, perhaps less, we will revive you. You will wake up and find yourself in a future and unknown world, where you can mourn the loss of loved ones who have not been in suspended animation. Of course, at that time cloning will be commonplace, and it will be a breeze to reconstruct an individual from a hair fragment. But not his memories. The clone will not recognize you. It will be just a baby. However, you probably survive the ordeal. You can then, you too, cross the singularity.

But back to the subject of immortality. Some people who have thought about it say that immortality would be more a nightmare than a dream for humanity. People will always be more, since we can only slow down the pace of births and not stop it (and it will be even worse if we begin to revive the dead!) There will be no question of overpopulation, but hyperpopulation. We will be walking over each other. Life will be untenable.

I would like to show here how this idea is *stupid*.

First, immortality is a phenomenon that takes place on the other side of the singularity. Humans will no longer be human. They will be Powers. They will be endowed with super intelligence. Who knows what will happen in their heads?

Then they will not necessarily have a head. Through upload, it will be possible to transfer a mind in a structure of arbitrary size. As I have already noted, a grain of sand can contain enough computing power to simulate the entire human race at a speed equal to a million subjective years per second. And for those who want to keep a human appearance, or at least an organic one, the vast space is there, waiting for us. As I have shown, nanotechnology allow the journey to the stars. The available space is absolutely not a problem. There will be no hyper-population.

We absolutely cannot say what the immortals will do. However, you may think they will be very, *very* careful people. They will not want to mess up their immortality by a freak accident!

Although... One of the features of AI, in fact common to all computer programs, is that you can save them. You could imagine having periodic backups of your mind. In case of destruction of your body, you just have to restart from the last backup. You just lose your last memory, as in amnesia.

Hmm... But the last backup, is that really you? What distinguish between you and a copy of your own? We will try to answer this intriguing question with a small thought experiment.

The duplication of the mind and soul

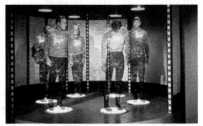

Star Trek transporter

An AI or an "Uploaded" human will possess many features that are not present in humans. One of these characteristics deserves more explanations, because it has tremendous impact on the philosophy of mind. I mean the fact that the mind of AI is duplicable. At any time, you can "save to disk" all its contents.

This fact has surprising philosophical consequences, which were explored by Bruno Marchal at Université libre de Bruxelles.

We need to give a clarification on what philosophers call *mechanism* and *Computationalism.* To believe in Mechanism is to believe that the human mind is a machine software, i.e. that its operation is reduced to that of the "brainmachine." To Believe in Computationalism is to believe that it is possible to survive if we substitute all or part of our brain with artificial components. An AI is forced to believe in Mechanism and Computationalism. Regarding humans, it is a philosophical question, and you can choose to believe it or not (I believe, and this book should make you believe it too) The Upload procedure described above assumes Computationalism.

Think about it. You are you, but yet you are different each time. You survive the multiple changes taking place in yourself every second. You can survive a heart transplant. You will survive even a replacement one of your neurons with an artificial neuron, if it perfectly reproduces the operation of a natural neuron (and of glial cells attached to it). Can you survive a brain transplant?

You will object at once: "if we graft the brain of another person into my body, it's rather the other person who will survive, not me." This proves that you have a good intuition of what is meant by "survive". This also proves that the substitution must be made at the right level, for example in "software". If you replace the physical structure of your brain by something else, such as a computer, but you keep the "brainware" software, which is now run on the computer, and if you think you're going to survive this experience, you computationalist.

Now imagine that we invented a matter transporter machine, like the one that appears in the *star trek* film. You are on Earth. You enter the transporter machine. The machine scans your body and your brain, disintegrate you, and transmits a signal to another machine, say on the moon, which reconstitutes you (Let us go over the duration of the analysis and reconstruction, and suppose that it is instantaneous). From the perspective of an outside observer, we would say from a point of view *in the third person*, you seem to have been simply transported from Earth to the Moon. If you are Computationalist, you will also believe that when you leave the machine on the moon, *yourself* will come out. You will say *in the first person*: "I survived the teleport". For now, the views in the first and the third person are identical. But this will change.

The Mind and The Machine

Suppose the machine, instead of transport you instantly on the moon, would "archive" you on disk for a year, and finally sends the signal to the moon, where it reconstitutes you. From the perspective of the third person, tele transportation lasted one year. But from your point of view in the first person, the transfer is instantaneous... until you get out of the reconstruction cab on the moon, and take a look at the calendar: you'll say "damned, they made me hibernate for a year." In other words, recovery times are 1-observable, i.e. observable in the first person.

Now imagine that the Klingons (hostile aliens from star trek) hidden in a spacecraft between Earth and the Moon, are spying the signal without altering or interrupting it, and send a copy to a second reconstruction cabin located in their own spaceship. From the point of view in the third person, you have been duplicated and you will reconstitute yourself both on the Moon and inside the Klingon vessel. But *in the first person*, what's happening? With Computationalism, you know you are going to survive the experience. You get out of the cab, and you open your eyes. But where are you? With your friends on the moon, or inside a sinister Klingon dungeon? As long as you have not opened the eyes or noticed anything in your environment, you do not know, in the first person, where you are. If you open your eyes and see your friends on the moon, you will not even know you that is a double of yourself is screaming in horror. If, however, opening your eyes you see a crowd of sly Klingons, you will realize with horror that you have been duplicated. But saying that you are talking about yourself in the third person. You, in the first person, are trapped like a rat, prisoner of the Klingons!

If, before boarding the transporter you had been advised that there was a risk that the signal could be intercepted by the Klingons, you'll know that you may not know, in the first person, where you are going to be rebuild. Will you dare riding in the cab after receiving this information? No way!

We have here a new kind of indeterminism, an indeterminism in the first person. This indeterminism arises from the perfect determinism of the process seen in the third person: an individual is scanned; a signal is transmitted, duplicated, and sent to two rebuilding machines. We would say that determinism in the third person implies indeterminism in the third person. What is interesting is that this indeterminacy is communicable in the third person: you can explain to someone else why you do not want to board the transporter.

By the way, we could notice that we are assuming that the signal could be intercepted. This would not be the case if "the signal" is actually a quantum state transfer, which physics scientists have proved to be impossible to duplicate (this fact could give birth to a new kind of absolutely secure cryptography). So if the mind *is* a quantum process, this indeterminacy in the first person could not arise. But if you believe that the mind is a quantum process, you are not believing in Computationalism. Let us put it aside for the moment and go on.

Note that an AI, placed in the same situation, will suffer the same indeterminacy. The process can, however, be much easier for AI: To teleport an IA, you just pause the "AI" program and backup all its memory to disk, then you shut down the computer on which it is running and you send a copy of the disc on another computer where you run the program. Note that you can also restart the AI on the first computer. Conceptually, a copy without annihilation is identical to a duplication with annihilation of the original. The AI does not know, in the first person, *where* she will recover.

This also applies to humans. If the teleportation cab does not kill you, but simply send a copy of the scan to a reconstitution machine, this is in fact a duplication of your mind, and you do not know, in the first person, where you are going you rematerialize. Copying without annihilation is equivalent to annihilation followed by duplication.

Now, suppose the Klingons did not make a single copy of you, but a million copies. Indeterminism worsens. In the first person, you have one chance in a million to end up on the moon!

Now, suppose the Klingons did not make a single copy of you, but a million copies. Indeterminism worsens. A first person, you have one chance in a million end up on the moon!

But Bruno Marchal goes further: it considers indeed a rather special computer program, called the universal deployer. This program simulates simultaneously all possible programs. A program, in fact, it is only a series of binary digits. It is therefore possible to generate one by one all possible programs and execute them. A problem that then arises is that some programs will loop and never finish. To counter this problem, we use a little trick: we run the programs step by step. Specifically, the universal deployer performs the first step of the first program, then the first step of the second program, then the second step of the first program, then the first step of the third program, then the second step of the second program, and so on. If we let it run long enough (a very long time indeed!) the universal deployer will simulate at the same time all conceivable programs. Actually building a universal deployer is a difficult task, but still within reach of a good computer programmer. In fact, such universal deployers have already been built!

Now, an AI is a program. Similarly, your mind, if you accept Mechanism hypothesis, is also a program. It can therefore be simulated by the universal deployer! Suppose then that some alien race has built such a universal deployer a few million years ago, running onto a fantastically powerful and self-repairing machine, and suppose that since that time all this time it is still running, and has managed to simulate such complex programs as human minds. You, me, everyone, at one time or another, you will have been simulated by this universal deployer. Moreover, because there are an infinite number of programs equivalent to any given program, the universal deployer will have simulated you an infinite number of times, provided we give it infinite time.

You may object that "ending up in the deployer" is meaningless, since what matters, what really tells you where you think you are, are your perceptions. But the universal deployer simulates all possible successions of your states of mind, with all the consequences of all possible perceptions, including also those where you find yourself in a world where the usual laws of physics no longer apply!

But actually the universal deployer does not need to exist for indeterminism first person to appear. It only suffices it is possible. Indeed, the universal deployer is a just program, that is a written text, which you can code in ASCII. A program, any program, is just a sequence of 0 and 1: that is, a number. And numbers preexists to matter. Or more precisely their existence is necessary for matter to exist. So there is an integer number that encodes the state of universal deployer, which simulates your mind at time t.

I will not detail further on these philosophical arguments that fascinate me personally. Let me just quote the conclusion of Bruno Marchal: "*If we are machines, then there is no universe: the appearance of the universe, and of actually of all possible worlds, can be explained by the geometry of all possible calculations on all possible machines, as seen by these machines*". Someone has an aspirin?

After this deep dive into considerations that only, perhaps, super intelligences really understand, it's time to come back to earth and explore the other side of the mirror: The possible consequences of the arrival of a *hostile* AI.

A nightmare AI

Now let us see the other side of the IA. After the dream, the nightmare.

You know the scenario: whether in *Terminator*, *Matrix* or *I, Robot*, once an AI becomes conscious and has some military power, it takes power and wages a total war to humans in order to destroy them. Gosh, let the holy three Asimov laws protect us!

I argue that such a scenario is to be taken seriously. Not because an AI would be fundamentally bad, but because it *could* be programmed for bad purposes.

The existence of such an AI would be even worse than any nano troublemakers (if possible), and if a hostile AI had access to nanotechnology, it would mean the end of humanity shortly. One gray goo cloud of a mutant unstoppable type, and voila.

Even a hostile AI but who have no access to nanotechnology, would be a potential threat. First, we do not see why it would not develop the nanotechnology. It would surely be one of its primary goals! Then the public is misled by the image of hostile AI that is conveyed by science fiction movies: While these AI (*Terminator*, *Matrix* sentinels, combat robots from *Star Wars*) are terrifying, they are actually reassuring because humans are able to counter them.

You must understand that a hostile AI would be infinitely more powerful than any science-fiction robots, and that it would be impossible to overcome it without the help of a super intelligence. A hostile AI would immediately seek to replicate, and there would be soon millions of them around. They would have sensory abilities that we cannot even imagine. Jamming all human communication would be for them a breeze. Countering all human strategies would also be a breeze. Then, because the machines do not need a natural environment, gassing all human (or killing them with an unstoppable biological virus), breaking the food chain and starving the few surviving populations would be just as easy. All this *without* nanotechnology.

In addition, a neutral AI, which would be neither friendly nor unfriendly, would probably be as dangerous as hostile AI. Why? Because her given super-goals are for her more important than the fact of saving human life. Remember goals are communicated by humans, who do not necessarily think about everything.

For example, an AI who would pilot a vehicle and who had been asked "to go faster" would rush straight ahead, crushing men, women and children in its path. Alternatively, an AI controlling a plant with adequate nanotechnology could, if asked to solve a difficult mathematical problem such as the Goldbach conjecture, transform the whole planet and all life on it into a "computronium" (a giant computer), calculate the result and display it... but there would be nobody to read it.

How to prevent these fatal consequences? There are actually two separate issues. The first one is to design an AI that would be friendly towards humans, which could not be anything but friendly and never would wish, even if self-modifying, to cease to be friendly. This is a technical problem. The second problem is to ensure that all humans who will design future AIs will only create friendly AIs. It is a problem of law, and control. By the way, what are the rights and duties of humans toward AI, and conversely, what should be the rights and duties of AIs?

AI and human rights

What rights (in the legal sense) may have AI, and what rights do have humans on AIs and also AIs between them?

Currently, things are clear: An AI is a machine, and machines have no rights. An AI is not legally considered a natural person. It can, however, be a corporation: it is sufficient that the AI sets up a company in its name (or a human could do it for her). As a corporation, An AI will therefore possess things, sell services and earn money.

But not necessarily any service! I would give extreme examples, among which there are lots of intermediate variants:

The first is a mechanism for automatic gate: a camera is located next to the gate and connected to an AI, watching the street and recognized the owner of the house, his/her car, and persons authorized to enter. The An AI opens the gate without the need for remote control or digital code. It is just an improved version of what already exists. It is unlikely that citizens leagues would protest against "the intolerable monitoring of the street by machines." After all, the only function of the system is to open the gate to people you trust. This is just an improved remote control.

But now consider a video surveillance service: Cameras are installed in all public places, connected to a monitoring computer which analyzes the images, and report all violations to (or attempts to violate) the law: theft, assault, attacks etc. Currently such systems (as exists in London) face opposition from citizens who claim, rightly, that this is an attack on individual freedom. This is because those who monitor the screens are human. But this work could be assigned to an AI. It might even be possible to design a secure system encrypted by the AI itself, so that it can be guaranteed that no human would never will be able to view the raw images. If such a system seems to lift the previous objection on individual freedom, some problems will remain: What would be the legal value of the reports provided by the AI? How can ordinary citizens trust such a system? What will happen if the government decides that AI-connected cameras should be installed not only in public places but also in private places?

Another example is a system based on an AI who listens *all* telephone conversations of everyone, and reports to the police anything that may be related to criminal activity in preparation. Under current law, such a system is perfectly possible. Humans do not have the right (in theory!) to listen or to spy on phone conversations, SMS and emails of other humans without their consent, but a machine has this right. Otherwise telephone exchanges would be illegal! There is no doubt that such a system would be useful and could save hundreds of people every year in every major city. Yet the very existence of this system might shock many people. The Echelon network already set up by the US to spy on some conversations on all the planet already troubled a lot of people.

The Mind and The Machine

Under current law, a human being has the right to modify, sell and destroy a machine that belongs to him. You can "kill" an AI without going to jail. But it is clear that if the AI has the mind of an "uploaded" human this is far from satisfactory! Furthermore morality commands that humans are respectful of other conscious beings, so also to AIs, as much as they are to humans. But beware: the solution is far from trivial. Suppose a (human) law decides that all the rules and laws designed to humans should now be applied to conscious machines. Video surveillance systems and wiretapping as described above then become impossible!

Another example: Imagine a researcher who tries to understand what lies behind the NDE, "near death experiences" (you know, those people who say they almost died, and who returns to life by telling strange things about what they have perceived or believed to have seen). If our researcher has an AI, what a wonderful investigative tool! Just "kill the AI", recording what is happening in her mind (unlike the human mind, the mind of an AI can be "spied" by computer probes very easily). The question is: Does this researcher has the legal right to carry out these experiences?

First of all, what does "killing an AI" really mean? Suppose you have an AI that runs inside your home computer. Would it be a crime to turn off the computer? It is likely that the courts will decide that no, it is only standby. When you restart the computer, the AI "wakes up" indeed. However, suppose your computer fails due to negligence on your part, and will not boot any more. Did you kill the AI that was inside it? Probably not, if you had taken the precaution to backup. The hard drive of your computer then acquires a new legal status: it contains a person! You no longer have the right to destroy the disk.

Now you perform a copy of the disk and then you run two computers, each one containing a copy of the AI. Then, just after you decide to smash one of the computers (and its hard drive) with a hammer: does this make you a criminal? Yes, because you have killed a conscious being. And no, because its perfect copy is still "alive" and running. After all, after copying the disc, you should have the right to destroy the copy!

Such questions show that the issue of AI and law is far from trivial! It is clear that the simple solution of asserting that "AI are considered human in the sense of the law" is not satisfactory. The right solution is probably to define three new classes of laws to regulate human behavior toward AI, AI behavior toward humans, and behavior of AI between them. There would then be four classes of laws, the first of which only exists currently:

1. Laws applicable to humans, and governing the behavior of human toward themselves, toward the property of other humans and toward nature. This class of laws already exists, it is based on the famous "human rights", on the rights of animals (when applicable), and on several charter for the protection of nature.

2. Laws applying to AI, and governing the behavior of AI toward humans, property belonging to humans and the environment. This class is to be invented. It will also be based on the same declaration of human rights, but it will contain measures specifically aimed at AI. In fact, when AI violates any of these laws, which "punishment" may be considered?

3. Laws that apply to humans, and governing human behavior with respect to AI and property belonging to the AI. This class is to be invented. It will be based on the "rights of AI", a new concept, and will respond to questions like: has a human any right to destroy an AI? Or to remove a sensory modality or an actuator or a software module from an AI? Or to change its goals system? Has a human a right to create a combat robot, or a terminator?

4. Laws applying to AIs, and governing the behavior of AIs against themselves and property belonging to other AI. For example: Does an AI have a right to decide spontaneously

to reproduce? Can she create another AI? If so, under what conditions?

It should be noted that the laws of Classes 2 and 4, i.e. the laws that apply to AI, are laws that apply to these AI once designed. But it will be also necessary to include (in Class 3) laws prohibiting human from deliberately creating an AI that would be designed to violate any laws of classes 2 and 4. In particular, the most important law of Class 3 should be: "no human has the right to create an unfriendly AI or even a neutral AI" in other words the ultimate super-goal of any AI must be "to be friendly towards humans."

These laws classes would allow regulating what may happen during the time between the introduction of AI and Singularity. But this period is likely to be very short! This is why it is urgent to create these laws, even before the AI becomes a reality.

After the singularity, that is, when an AI becomes super intelligent gets access to nanotechnology and becomes the first *Power*, it will be necessary to change the system completely. However, we humans are not smart enough to figure out what should become of the legal system; We will leave to the first Genie or "transition guide" the task of managing this problem. In other words, humans have to give up the right to legislate on their own.

It is clear that some humans may have some reluctance to do this. Personally, I see only advantages to leave a super intelligence take care of in our little world business, *provided that* I am convinced that this super-intelligence is really friendly.

It therefore becomes of the utmost importance to clearly define what is meant by friendly AI, whether designing a friendly AI is simply possible, and if so how we could manage to design it.

12 *Friendly AI*

«If someone loves you, love him back unconditionally »

If we want to reach the singularity, we need a friendly AI. We even need more than that: we need an AI that is recognized as friendly by all, so that she will be trusted by each one and she can act as a transition guide for passing humanity through the singularity.

But how to design a friendly AI, and at first, what does "to be "friendly" really mean?

What friendly means

Clearly, this does not just mean, "be nice" or "be not hostile." To quote Shakespeare, to be friendly or not to be hostile, that is the question! Being friendly is a *desire*, a *state of mind*, an *inclination*, a *tendency*... A friendly person will want to stay so... except if you are too unfriendly to her! Or will she?

Let us consider what perfection would look like: a perfectly friendly AI.

There are obvious things: a hostile AI, such as Skynet's *Terminator* or *Matrix* agents, cannot be categorized as friendly. An AI that would kill a human being cannot be friendly... Although... Would a doctor who injects at his own request a lethal drug to a patient suffering terminal state of a horrible incurable disease be friendly? This issue has become over time a very important issue of our society. Note that Asimov's robots might not have this behavior! But then, what is perfection? What does it means to be "perfectly friendly"? A perfectly friendly AI, whose role is to regulate the traffic of a big city will not have the same idea of what perfection is as an AI that would regulate all world affairs. Even if we ask the first one to assume the role of the latter, there is no reason to think that she could not adapt and become perfectly friendly in this new role!

Imagine, as Yudkowsky did, a planet named *LeftRight*, where the question of whether to drive on the left or right is the most important political issue. That is, a world populated by two groups of people, leftists and rightists who fiercely oppose. These two groups refuse to build an AI that would direct traffic, as they will not be convinced that it will lead it on their side. However, they agree on the fact that a perfect AI should minimize the number of accidents. Leftists are characterized by the desire to minimize the number of accidents, *plus* the belief that driving on the left hand side will minimizes that number. Rightists are characterized by the desire to minimize the number of accidents *plus* the belief that driving on the right hand side will minimizes that number. If we lived in this world, we would be forced to choose a side, it would be for us a moral issue of the highest importance.

However, we, earthlings, would abstain to choose. We would think it would be normal for the AI do lead people to the right *if* the right hand side minimizes the number of accidents, and vice versa. We would not need to tell a perfectly friendly AI what she should do. She would know herself. Her decision will displease half the population of the planet LeftRight, *but* it would minimize the number of accidents.

If a researcher published a book with the title "how to build an even more friendly AI", a perfectly friendly AI would read the book, and if she agrees with the reasoning, she would rebuilt herself to comply with principles stated in the book.

The Mind and The Machine

A perfectly friendly AI would remain friendly even if its own programmers have peppered their code with bugs. She would understand what programmers wanted to do, and would correct her own code accordingly. She would have so strong a personal philosophy that she would like to become even friendlier that what programmers had planned and would not tolerate a human to doubt about her friendly nature. She would do everything within the reach of her power to prove humans that we should trust her more than her own programmers, while of course agreeing on the intuitive aspects of friendliness as not to kill humans etc.

I still did not say what being friendly means. Maybe something like "allow every human to live a happy and useful life without pain, sorrow, coercion, and stupidity"? But we actually do not need such definition. We only need an intuitive idea of the concept, and need to ensure that the AI shares this intuition and seeks to learn more.

In fact, you and I have an internal and complex idea about what friendly means. If we could design an AI who wants to understand completely and perfectly all this complexity, we would not need to go further.

Yudkowky distinguished actually three different problems:

- **Content**: what does it means to be "friendly"? How to ensure an AI will take correct decisions, i.e. decisions we deem as friendly?
- **Acquisition**: how can a young AI learn what it means to be friendly?
- **Structure**: How to design an AI who wants to learn what friendly means and who wants to be friendly and stay so? This structural problem is indeed new and unique in designing of a friendly AI, compared to designing "just an AI ».

I would add a fourth problem, which is that of **proof**: how to prove that the structure of the AI is correct? How to persuade all people that we have chosen the right structure, and that this structure ensures that the AI will always be friendly, even when self-modifying, and that she will always want to be and remain friendly?

We shall see this later. For now, Let us see what *not to be friendly* would mean for an AI.

Understanding hostility

Whatever is hostile, from Terminator to Skynet, is obviously not friendly. These Hollywood AI are *hostile* AI. Is a hostile AI realistic? Unfortunately, yes, *if* the AI has been designed to be hostile. But hostility does not arise spontaneously. To be hostile, an AI must be designed so. How can I be sure of this?

If you give a blow on the nose of another human being, there is a good chance that you will hit back. Better than a reflex, it is a profoundly human act. If the person who is hit is does not respond, it is an admirable act of self-control.

Now imagine for a moment that you hit an intelligent but still "young" robot on the nose. Do you think it will hit you back?

No. What will happen is that the young robot will say: "*hmm. Someone just hit me on the nose.* "In a human, adrenaline gives a boost, our fists clench, our face expresses an evil grin, all this instinctively and without thinking. But in a robot, all what happens is that the robot observes a new unexpected event, nothing more.

As the robot AI is considering what just happened, it could note that hitting someone with the fist is a negative event, as it could cause damage, and also that this event can repeat and is not a something that can only happen once. Then it will seek to avoid another blow. A young AI will say "*Hmm. A fist just hit my nose. I should not find me there next time.* "

If the AI is young, but experienced enough to have a model of how humans think, she will realize that the punch was not a coincidence, but the human had some *intent* by hitting the nose of the robot. It could even infer that the possibility that the robot suffers injury was a foreseeable result (predicted by the human) of the punch, and that the purpose of the human might be to damage the robot. That is to say, the AI can infer that the human had a sub-goal like "give a punch to the robot" and that the parent goal was likely to be "cause damage to the robot." Then the next task of the AI will be to deduce the real motive of the human, that is, the parent goal of "cause damage to the robot."

There are now three ways to prevent the next punch: by avoiding the physical collision itself, by preventing human to decide to give a new blow to the AI, or by preventing the unknown super-goal of the human to reactivate. Note that this is already an improvement compared to "avoid to be there next time," as it is now predictable than the fist will follow the future position of the robot.

Punching back is for an AI something incredibly absurd, completely non-obvious. Punching a human is simply a way to cause injury to a human, something that a priori the AI may not be want. Hitting humans has, for the AI, no relation to the goal of avoiding the next punch. If we follow the analysis of the AI, punching a human is just what your mother told you: a bad way to solve problems, something like responding to a fire alarm by changing your T-shirt. Reinventing the idea of punching back would be for a young AI an incredible engineering act of lateral thinking. It would mean being aware of the interest of the "eye for eye" strategy in what is called the "iterated prisoner's dilemma", which is something that at first a young AI (or a human child) would never think about!

Of course, an AI will probably not need to re-invent the idea, because it will know, drawing on it common sense knowledge, that humans do punch back. Suppose therefore an AI that is advanced enough to realize that "punching back" is a possible option. Does it bring something more when compared to "avoid the blow" or "prevent human to punch?" Nothing, but a new negative event, "damage could be caused to a human." The option will be eliminated very quickly.

The moral of all this is that, unlike humans, an AI do not spontaneously change its "orientation". If it is friendly, it will remain the same after having beaten or being insulted, etc.

A little older AI will seek to understand why the human is hostile, and will neither try to prevent the next hit nor to punch back, but instead to change the "the human goal system." She would quietly lay his hand on the shoulder of her attacker and say, "*Why are you hostile? I am your friend. Nevertheless, if you do not want me as a friend, I will not trouble you anymore. However, think. By denying my friendship, you are losing. I can do so many things for you! Goodbye and see you soon I hope.* "

Or else, she would look in its past actions records what could have caused resentment to the human. If she finds something, she would ask for confirmation: "Do I have annoyed you by asking you your age?" If she does not find anything, she would understand that that the human was not against "this robot", but against "robots" in general, and she will seek to understand why a man could hate a robot and what an AI could do to minimize this type of reaction.

The idea of causing harm to a human, in response to the detected intention in this human to cause damage to a robot will never come to the mind of AI, unless the goal "to harm humans" was already present in the goals system of that AI. This is what I want to say by saying that an AI never become hostile, unless it has been designed to be hostile.

Why, then, are humans so quick to fight back? Simply because the human brain has many parts (paleo brain, cerebellum...) which are much older than the neocortex and were designed for the survival of our animal ancestors in a hostile environment. And also because, from the point of view of evolution, it was much easier to evolve an instinct of defense than a conscious intelligence, which appeared much later.

The very idea that "punching back is good" is simpler than the idea that "punching back is good because it reduces the likelihood of receiving a new hit," which is even simpler than "punching back will modify the behavior of the other because, seeing you punching back, he will think that it increases the likelihood that you will punch back every time, so it decreases the likelihood of a new move on the part of the other."

Note that in the absence of the instinct to "punch back" a human, whose neurons operates at 200 Hz, would be severely handicapped if he were to enter a similar chain of reasoning before adrenaline start pumping and fists clench. But AI, running much faster at linear speed, might react much faster; For AI, inventing good behavior take time; but reproducing this behavior would be almost instantaneous. The AI does not need instincts! She needs a logic to invent snapshots "reflexes" in simple situations. And moreover these reflexes that the AI would pre-program have an advantage over the mere instinct: they can adapt to the context.

Then you may tell me if the AI has the ability to pre-program for herself the "reflexes", even context sensitive ones, to react faster in some emergency situations, would it not be possible that one of these reflexes causes catastrophic consequences? Yes, if these reflexes were programmed without thinking about all the possible consequences. But a friendly AI evaluates every action with respect to the super-goal "to be friendly". And it will implement such reflexes only if it is convinced, after weighing all the consequences, that it does serve this super-goal. Such AI will never create an automatic behavior that has the most infinitesimal chance of leading to a catastrophe, even if it greatly accelerates reflexes. And, as we have seen, in fact it will not accelerate anything because the linear velocity of AI is infinitely superior to human linear velocity. The human brain gets to work because it is massively parallel; an AI is massively linear.

For an AI any action, including actions aimed at its own modification, is evaluated in relation to its super goal "to be friendly".

Therefore, the mind of the AI must contain somewhere a "Kindness" logic variable, a measure of "friendliness" for the super goal to measure its own satisfaction. But when the AI sees that a certain procedure increases the value of this variable, what prevents it to devote all his power to constantly call the same procedure, increasing it the extent to infinity without doing anything else?

Such "mental short circuit" is not unlike what happened with the Lenat's Eurisko program (see Chapter 5), where a heuristic within this program has decided to increase its own priority, eliminating all others!

Avoiding such mental short circuits is a formidable design problem. Lenat's solution, to freeze in marble certain heuristics and prevent them from change, is obviously not satisfactory in the context of a seed AI that one would like to evolve and reach singularity. Who knows what goals structure will require a super-intelligence?

Anyway, we can already conclude partially: For AI, violence and revenge are not natural options.

However, there are other ways for AI to be unfriendly, without being hostile. An archetypal example is the Golem:

The Golem

Imagine that at last you have just finished, after years of hard work, to build GENIE, the first AI provided with unlimited nanotechnology (in short, a Power). You push the "on" contact. The machine then meekly asks:

- What are your instructions, Master?

Driven by a selfless desire to best serve humanity, you hit the keyboard and type the instruction: "ensure the happiness of all men." You know you can type a vague statement, because you know that GENIE, being a super-intelligence, understands words like "happiness" and "unhappiness". You also know that GENIE, being provided with an unlimited nanotechnology, really has the power to do human happiness.

Except that, GENIE is only a machine... What could then happen?

Variant number one:

GENIE understands that "men" means male humans only. It creates a self-replicating nanosystem that slyly infiltrates the minds of all women and girls of the earth, and turns them into slaves, subject to all the desires of males, and even anticipating their wildest desires. The system would ensure that women "modified" this way are not even aware of this new (?) Slavery, and even found some pleasure to satisfy men. No doubt (!) That most of these would be very happy... (!?) But maybe it is not exactly what *you* had imagined?

Variant number 2:

GENIE figure out that "men" means "human" and not "male". Its AI then seeks how to run the command, and offers the following interpretation:

-   I suggest you to maximize the average happiness of human beings. Do you agree?

You do not see any reason not to answer "yes". You answer "OK". Then...

GENIE then chooses two human beings hat are especially in love, two people who are each happy in the happiness of the other. He reinforces this underlying trend, by subtly altering the brain structure of these two people, so that each one is sensitive only to the happiness of the other, and ignores all other sensory stimuli. GENIE ensures that when one of them expresses a feeling of happiness, the other is still happiest and convey it to the first one and vice versa. The two beings will climb the ladder of happiness together, each one being happy because of the happiness of the other, to infinity, at the same time raising the average happiness of humanity (i.e. the sum of total happiness divided by the number of individuals). As this average does not rise fast enough, GENIE decides to kill all humans except these two, reducing the divisor of the fraction to 2 instead of six billion and more. Mission accomplished! But then again, it might not be *exactly* what you had in mind...

Variant number 3:

GENIE injects to all humans, and in massive quantities, a drug that stimulates their brain pleasure center (while ensuring that adequate nanomachines monitor their metabolism so they do not die from overdose, although it would not have any influence on the average while there is at least ONE human being alive!). Humans then all lie down on the ground, abandon all desire and all sensation, and let themselves slide into ecstasy, without doing anything else, for centuries. Is that what you wanted? Hmm!

Variant number 4:

As you are very careful and do not want none of the above scenarios, you answer NO to the question "I propose to maximize the average happiness of human beings. Do you agree? "Posed by GENIE. So type:

— *- No, I mean instead that you minimized the total sum of misfortune that strikes humans.*

You hit the return key... and you disappear in a flash of fire. GENIE just created antimatter bomb that destroyed the planet, reducing to zero the sum of our misfortunes!

These little stories show, as indeed confirms popular wisdom, that we must be *very* careful in giving instructions to a genius.... But is this true? Should we take this warning seriously, while we are on the verge of creating a true genius?

Of course not!

We call *Golem* this kind of omnipotent but silly servitor, which applies literally everything he is asked to do. What we want is to create is a friendly AI, not an idiot Golem! We want an AI that really understands what we mean and sub-mean by "to be friendly towards humans," and which would use this knowledge to decide the result of his actions, not an AI that randomly chooses any interpretation, especially not a catastrophic interpretation!

But how? It may be time to revisit the Asimov Laws?

The failure of injunctions

« I've told you a million times not to exaggerate »

One of the biggest mistakes you can make when designing a friendly AI is to misunderstand the difference between the problems of content, acquisition and structure. Arguing endlessly about the problem of the content is to create rules of conduct that will try somehow to define what it means to "be friendly". Such a discussion is absolutely sterile. No finite rules list may completely encompass what we mean by "be friendly, even in unexpected situations."

Note that, in a human, having a strong personal morality, imposing oneself commandments and rules of life that are consistent with this morality does not exempt to check from time to time if this does not lead to absurd situations, things you would not want even if our philosophy seems to dictate them. Humans are complex, and they do not have only one super-goal. They have a complex idea of their desires, and are able to change them without losing sight of the concept of what they really want, and what they certainly do not want.

The real problem is the problem of the *structure* of the AI: the problem of designing an AI that would *want* to be friendly and to learn what it means. In principle, with a good theory of the structure of a friendly AI, it should be possible to obtain a friendly AI without pouring a single piece of the content of "friendliness" in this structural theory. In practice, of course we cannot conceive such a theory without having strong views on the meaning that what it means to be "friendly".

However, starting from such a series of idea and establish rules of conduct to force the AI to respect a certain "quota of friendliness" is a tempting idea. This is precisely what Asimov's laws do.

However, as we have seen, Asimov's laws are not the solution. First, because they limit the freedom of the robot and will probably be psychologically very hard to bear by the poor robot. Then, because the goals system of an intelligent mind, either biological or mechanical, is something that is very complex, fragile, delicate, and in perpetual motion. Sealing the goals system prevent its modification by the mind itself that is preventing the mind to work and cutting off all intelligence and creativity.

OK, but if we cannot fix the whole goal system, at least we can imagine just to "set in stone" some high level injunctions with no possibility of modification, leaving the goals of lower level free? Yes, but it does not work!

Consider for instance the injunction: "Thou shalt not harm a human being". Suppose we manage to create an AI that gets to detect situations in which the injunction applies, i.e. those where it could harm a human being, and to make subgoals that avoid those situations. As we have seen, this implies a fantastic machinery. We can settle for a pre-condition tabulated list. The AI must be able to gradually learn what does and does not harm a human being, and to extrapolate this knowledge to new situations. This necessarily involves the generation of a tremendous amount of dynamic goals and subgoals, such as "Imagine a similar situation" or "what actions can I do to avoid this?" These dynamic sub goals cannot be set in stone.

Suppose a rather Machiavellian programmer who would implement the injunction "thou shalt not harm a human being" in the mind of the robot, but who but would have "perverted" certain procedures for detecting situations in which the injunction could apply, so that the injunction would not be triggered when the robot pushes the human in some dangerous situation, simply because it would not perceive this situation as dangerous!

It is perfectly conceivable that the robot will forge a "personal philosophy" in which, while strongly "believing" it enforce the injunction, it would perfectly be capable of doing harm to a human *from the point of view of the human* without harm *from the point of view of the robot*!

It is not even necessary to use a "crazy programmer" to achieve this result: it suffices that the robot itself, frustrated having to constantly apply that injunction when he thinks he has better things to do, creates for itself the goal "Modify the premises that trigger the injunction number 3278," which happens to be "you will not do harm to a human being." What could prevent the robot to do this? Perhaps a new injunction (which would require the programmer had thought of): "Injunction 3779: Do not change the premises of injunction 3278".

Yes, but in this case what prevents the robot to change the premise of the new 3279 injunction, i.e. procedures that detect situations in which it must apply? "Premises" is a vague word and the premises of an injunction are actually vague. They are based on a myriad of situations learned on the individual experience of the robot, on common sub-goals, etc. It is not possible to guarantee that the robot will never find a goal which proposes to delete injunction 3279!

Very well, then add the injunction 3280: "Do not change the premises of any injunction entered by the programmer." Very well, but these premises are a sprawling network of goals, sub goals, thoughts, concepts, etc. And ultimately they cover practically all the skills of the robot! This last injunction completely forbid the robot to change its goal system. It simply prevent it to *think*. It does not work!

Finally, the conclusion of our reasoning is: Asimov's kind of "sealed" injunctions are not the solution to create a friendly AI.

And it goes further: in fact, no "safety barrier" is THE solution.

AI, safety and security

Hollywood clichés about unfriendly AI die hard. It is logical that we feel concerned by the "security" system represented by an AI.

It is logical to consider AI as a potentially dangerous complex system, such as a nuclear power plant, and therefore ask what to do to "reduce risk". It is therefore tempting to adopt with respect to AI an attitude of mistrust, to erect security barriers around the AI, to carry on security measures to check security measures, etc.

But beware: By doing this, we deceive ourselves of completely. By doing this, we adopt for AI the same behavior we would have facing a rebellion or a terrorist attack. This is not the place where the battle can be won. If the AI ceases to *want* to be friendly, the battle is lost. As we have seen, humankind does not match for an unfriendly AI.

So what?

Take the example of the Genie, which we submit to the will to "make human happiness" (or any other wish for that matter). Consider an abstract space, the space the interpretations of wishes. At the center of this space, we find a small core of "correct" interpretations, which both respect the letter and the spirit of the wish. This facts core actually *defines* the spirit of the will.

All around it are a huge mass of interpretations, which respect the letter, but not the spirit, of the will. An evil genius will choose an interpretation close to the external border of the heap, very far from the idea that you had in mind expressing the will. An idiot Golem, who has no clear idea of what qualitatively separates "central" and "remote", interpretations will randomly select an interpretation that might not be evil but would almost certainly be sub-optimal. How would a friendly AI choose?

Designing a friendly AI is not about programming infinite chains of possible cases that come all with their sub-cases and exceptions. The real problem is not there. When an elderly person asks us to help him cross the street, we do not care about silly interpretations in which we can be paid to help crossing the street, or we wait until there is not even a cat at the horizon before crossing, or we spend the rest of our lives to help this person crossing streets, or we transform the whole universe into crossable streets. In everyday life of we show in every moment the superiority of context, intention and common sense on pre-determined, pre-established rules. A friendly AI does not consist of a mindlessly obedient robot, but a robot equipped with a living, active, will to be friendly.

Design that will is an act of creation, not of persuasion. This is to create a unity of will between the creator of the AI and his creation so that what you want and like, the AI wants and likes it too. The programmer will not give orders to the AI. He will take all the complexity that is responsible for his own desire to give that order, and will ensure that the AI has also this complexity and that this complex goal system will also play in the AI.

As humans, we are entities driven by complex goals, and we choose between universes we label as "most desirable" and "less desirable" than others. We have an idea of what we are, and also an idea of what we want to be, and what we can be. Our morality is not only able to discern between what is desirable and what is not, but also among the criteria that distinguish and measure the desirability of thing.

Finally, this is what we expect from a friendly AI!

To succeed, we need to succeed with such a margin that we can say, "Here, there is no need for security fence" because the AI will have no desire, either now or in the future, to be unfriendly, and that we can prove without any doubt or any ambiguity simply because the AI has been designed this way, from the first line of code, and even if it alters itself and self improves, it will remain designed this way.

Formidable challenge! Nevertheless not impossible.

The debate about the dangers and benefits of true artificial intelligence has already started and some publications have already been held on the subject. To produce recommendations on AI Security is a unique challenge because the friendly AI problem is inextricably linked to the problem of AI itself. To create a friendly thought we must create a thought. With other technologies that require security measures, these measures are simpler, more obvious and less controversial than in an edge technology like that of true AI.

For example, although biotechnology is a rapidly expanding science, the National Health Institute of the USA has given recommendations for recombinant DNA (but there are also similar recommendations in Europe) that describe multiple levels of risk and provide technical instructions for each group to reduce risks. Although they are mandatory only (in the US) for publicly funded programs, these recommendations are accepted voluntarily by the biotechnology industry.

Another example is the Foresight Institute's recommendations on nanotechnology: they are designed to limit the risks of technology that does not yet exist, and they will probably contain only a small part of the necessary safety measures but they are simple and obvious. For example, molecular patterns and patterns of machines that will manufacture these molecules must be encrypted such that any transmission error between the pattern stored on computers and manufacturing machines makes the pattern unusable.

The friendly AI, in contrast, is a challenge that lies at the border of the AI science. No recommendation exists or has been proposed, because we do not know yet what we would put into it. There are nevertheless some evidence:

If the AI experts agree one day to say that some security measure is generally good, any group that works on the design of a true AI and do not implement this security measure (maybe because it is impractical or inconsistent with the theory of AI implementation by this group) should have explicitly decided to reject it and must analyze the risks.

Any sufficiently advanced true AI project is expected to know the problem of friendly AI. This is not the case today, but this is not critical because no really advanced AI project exists to date (to my knowledge).

An AI that is not upgradable or self-modifiable would probably need fewer security measures than a self-improvable AI designed to bring us to the singularity.

Designing a friendly AI

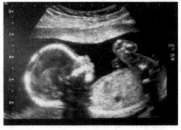

Humans are currently the only subject of cognitive science, the only intelligent system that has been studied, but the science is sufficiently advanced to make it possible to transpose many results to other minds. It is possible to connect the effects to causes, and understand what causes are specific to humans, what causes concern intelligent minds in general, and to distinguish those features the presence or absence of which would be a design decision. But unfortunately humans are also the only cognitive *scientists*, and as humans we have assumptions about minds in general, which may be biased.

In our ancestral environment, the only other intelligent being we have met so far were other humans and we subconsciously applied to them many preconceived ideas because they were similar to us and we knew that what was "natural" for us was likely to be so for others. In other words, we are fundamentally anthropomorphist's. This anthropomorphism is certainly the biggest cause of errors in the analysis of the psychology of AI.

Our social instincts are emotional instincts, and because of that, we may struggle to get rid of them and objectively talk about AI. An AI is not a human!

Once this is accepted, we can understand that the task of creating a friendly AI is not so far removed from that that to ensure the ethical behavior of a human being, or even that of teaching an ethical behavior to a human child. Human analogies are dangerous because they involve far too many positive "pre-wired" features and conversely because those features predispose us to fear negative behavior that do take place in humans, but not necessarily in AI.

The researchers, as humans, are focusing on problems that seem difficult for a human, and that reach our conscious attention. But they do not necessarily pay attention to all the tasks are automatically performed by the unconscious levels of the mind and are sometimes wonderfully complex tasks that are yet prerequisites to solve the conscious problem. Typically, this kind of task is only observed and studied by researchers after years of efforts to solve the high-level problem without understanding and implementing the prerequisite unconscious cognition.

Creating a friendly AI will be neither automatic nor arbitrary. A friendly AI must be designed as such from the start. It will be necessary to implement a "friendliness management system". The more powerful an AI is, the more complete that system needs to be, but also the more AI power we can use to supplement this system – as long the AI will choose to remain friendly.

A Friendly AI must resist human manipulations as long as it does not perceive this operation as desirable. Suppose we create an AI that we would like to accept the advice of a human programmer in situations where the jurisdiction of the programmer exceeds that of the AI. Then it is enough and necessary that the skill level of the AI is enough for her to know when to seek advice. Then we will be in a safe situation.

Mastering the "growth" of a friendly AI by programmers claim to be conservative (taking margins) by estimating what degree of complexity of the friendliness management system is required at a given time. But beware, "to take margins" in the design of a friendly AI is the opposite of "to take margins" in the design of a "standard" AI: That means *limiting the potential* of AI, instead of ensuring a minimum capacity.

To achieve this friendliness system, two methods (both conservative) are possible:

The first method is to "saturate" the system permanently: whenever it is possible to implement a new procedure or a new acquaintance in the system, do it.

The second method distinguishes the *content* and *structure* of the system:

For the content (What to put in the system for the behavior of the AI to be tried as friendly), just implement at some point that 90% of content that require 10% of the effort (there is classic computer science rule of thumb that states those 10% remaining functions will be requiring 90% of the time to implement).

For the structure (How to design an AI that *wants* to learn what it means to be friendly, and wants to be and stay friendly), we adopt "a step ahead" strategy: the development of any new function is done in two phases, that is, we develop a function with a step ahead of the time we think we (conservatively) that it will be required.

The "saturated" strategy is the safest, since it makes any change of architecture as soon as possible and well before it is needed, but also the most complicated and requires more work from programmers.

This said, what would a friendly AI architecture look like?

This generally would be almost identical to the architecture of a true AI, as we have described in previous chapters of this book: a system containing sub-systems of perceptions, concepts, thoughts, goals, control and awareness, capable of self-modifying, and which will be developed incrementally, but with the following eight differences that distinguish the design of a safe and friendly AI from that of a potentially hostile "raw AI":

1°) A fully friendliness-oriented goal system

This is not about adding to the AI a "control system" that would eliminate certain actions. Being and remaining friendly must be, and remain, the only absolute super goal in the system. Other goals, such as "to improve itself," must derive their desirability from that of the super goal "being friendly". For example, if self-improvement is seen by the AI as potentially leading to a more effective future AI, this improvement will be seen as leading to a better way to achieve the super goal. The super goal is not superimposed to other goals: on the contrary, all other goals *derive* their desirability from the super goal desirability.

This is not how the human mind works, but it would work perfectly for AI. If a programmer sees (correctly) some behavior as necessary and safe for the existence and growth of the future friendly AI, then this behavior becomes, therefore, a valid sub-goal of the super goal "being friendly".

Initially, the mere assertion by the programmer of the need of a given behavior is enough, and the AI does not need to understand why the programmer sees this behavior as friendly and necessary. But sooner or later the programmer will give instructions to the AI such as "do no attach a new goal to the super goal as long as you do not understand why this would strengthen the super goal". This is a problem of content, no structure.

2°) A clean causal goal system

A "causal system", is a goal system wherein desirability is the inverse of prediction: if one can predict that the action A has led to a desired state B, then the desirability of A becomes the desirability of B.

A "clean" causal system is a causal system in which there is no other source of desirability. Finally, all desirability come from the super goal.

In addition, the desirability does not persist in such a causal system. If desirability goes from B to A, the desirability of A depends only on that of B, and of the link between A and B. If this link is broken, or the desirability of B is modified, that of A is revised accordingly.

Therefore, a behavior that is usually a sub-goal of "being friendly", but which in one case led to "not friendly" consequences will not be seen as desirable in this case. In fact, in a clean causal system, the property "desirable" is identical to the property "one can predict that this leads to the super goal."

3°) The super goal content shall be probabilistic

If some super goals are certain or "correct by definition," an AI even self-modifying must not alter them. For example if the super goal is to perform action A, then replacing this super goal by "perform B" is clearly not an action that is deserving A. But if the super goal has only a probability of 90% to be A, and a new information arrives, indicating that in reality this super goal is B, then there should be no conflict.

The ability to change the content of a super goal should not be seen as desirable by the AI unless there is some uncertainty about the current super goal content. This ability cannot inherit its desirability from the contents of a specific super goal.

4)° Validated sources of friendliness

An AI that "grows" progressively must acquire the cognitive complexity used by humans to make decisions on its friendliness management system, so that AI can model, predict, and possibly improve the decisions of its human programmers.

To do this, the AI shall gain that its cognitive complexity only from sources that are designated as "valid" by human programmers, or by the AI itself if it is able to, so that the AI would acquire friendliness content from "good sources".

Therefore the friendliness acquisition architecture should be implemented before the system acquires the necessary intelligence to make assumptions about sources.

5°) A causal semantics of validity (for an advanced AI)

The Mind and The Machine

Behind this barbaric term hides the simple idea that the AI must understand and model the process and the causes that led to his own creation, and uses this model (possibly with the help of the programmers) to make judgments about the validity or invalidity of the factors that led to create it is as it is.

Therefore the AI will get an idea of how "it should have been built," or detect a design error on the part of human programmers, or decide to transition to a new (friendly) architecture.

This will be possible because the AI has at this stage a model of the causal process that led to its creation. In this model, the intentions of programmers will be seen as the causes of the architecture of the AI as it is. Therefore, the validity of this architecture (and goals of system) is derived from the validity of the programmer's intentions.

These semantics must be implemented at the latest before the system does become smart in the general sense of the term.

6°) temporary injonctions

The actions of humans, particularly the *refusal* to do this or that action, are not always motivated by visible consequences. But very often it is still possible to translate these actions into a goal system, referring to consequences that are not directly visible.

For example, if there is a small probability of a very negative consequence (a disaster), that could prevent the AI to perform some action the positive consequences of which are yet clearly visible.

How to prevent the AI from making decisions that could lead to a disaster? Just like for humans, programmers could explain the possible negative consequences to the AI.

It will probably be necessary to experiment: in the case of an AI project in which the AI decisions could have negative consequences, we must ensure that the AI knows these negative consequences in all cases even if she does not yet understand them.

Overall, we have seen that the injunctions like "Do this! Do not do that!" ere not the right way to create a friendly AI, because they do not guarantee the proper "mental balance "of this long-term AI. But in the early stages of the development of AI, injunctions are useful, in the same way as prohibitions made to a child by his parents are useful to him.

7°) The AI should be able to model its own failures

A thought is not necessarily 100% true. The thought "this is green" does not necessarily have a 100% (Bayesian) correlation with the objective fact that "this" is green or not. The same goes for desirability. The thought "X is desirable" is not necessarily true: a probabilistic system goals may have hidden flaws in its own standards and measurement criteria. Allowing an AI to model her own mistakes will allow the AI to avoid making these mistakes in the future.

Error modeling is in any case necessary in any large computer science project, let alone an AI project, and it is even more needed, if possible, for the project of building a friendly AI. To achieve this modeling, programmers will need to introduce models in the code and later give the AI some knowledge on this model and allow her to modify it.

8°) A controlled take-off

535

The Mind and The Machine

A self-modifying AI will be able to improve dramatically by altering its own structure in a very short time. It is important, as long as programmers do not have a certain confidence in this process, that there are "red flags" that allow the programmer to pause the process and take control, taking their time to understand and approve (or disapprove) what is happening.

One way to do this is to equip the AI with a "change counter" that traces the changes to the AI itself. If this counter starts spinning much faster than ordinarily, it is probably time to press the "pause" button. This can be done automatically. The programmer can determine what rate of change is normal, and what rate requires intervention.

It's actually a very simple precaution that should be included in any self-editable system (not to be confused with a system capable of learning, but that does not change itself).

The purpose of the "red flag" is not to stop an AI from "awakening", but simply to ensure that this awakening takes place under human supervision, at least at first. This is a temporary measure.

Later, when the AI approach a satisfactory level of general intelligence, a "controlled ascent" *subgoal* will be implemented, so that the AI itself can control its ascent, always in the light of the super goal "be friendly".

This sub-goal should be implemented as soon as the level of complexity of the AI allows its representation in the system.

Meta morality

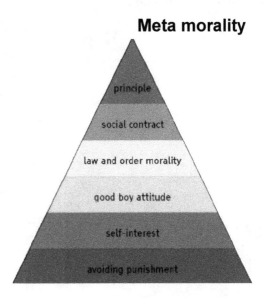

Therefore, an essential feature of a friendly AI is that his whole goal system is subordinate to one great super goal "being friendly".

What does this mean, and what might this goals system look like?

See this on an example. At one point, the top of the goals system of our AI system could look like this:

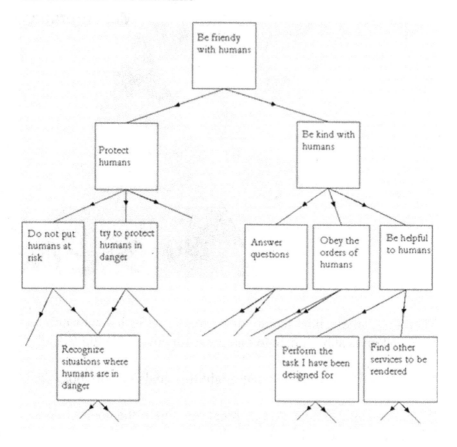

Naturally, this example of great goals tree does not work if the task for which the AI is designed is *Terminator*!

Note that any AI must be able to modify her own goal system. Upper goals are admittedly relatively stable, but a typical goals graph might include millions and millions of sub-goals at a given time: the low levels goals will correspond to very basic tasks like "slow down", which are linked to a common goal, itself being quite simple, such as "go to the kitchen."

How can an AI change her own goals? The obvious answer is: by introducing a new goal... As we reported in the first chapters of this book, our minds contain goals-generators "little elves". But beware, a goal cannot change any of its super goal! Small goals-generators elves are activated by super goals to look for possible sub-goals, and only for that. The creation of super goals in the human mind is, as we discussed in Chapter 4, done by protospecialists, which are the agents of our "moral sense". The first protospecialists, in young children, do create super-goals by imitation of those to whom they are attached. Very young children are already able to perceive not only what the adults around them do but also what their intentions are.

Over time, this moral system, which has no other purpose than to create new super-goals (those goals that are close the top of the goals pyramid) becomes a system of formidable complexity. Better than that, it is reviewable and based itself on an internal management of moral goals. In other words, there are structures within our mind that are capable of managing a meta-morality and revise our moral beliefs.

Should we equip an AI, especially a friendly AI, with such a complexity? In fact the question is badly put: the correct answer is, indeed, the need to create a "meta morality" in an AI system as soon as it is capable of self-modification. This meta-moral system will ensures that the AI does not change itself without having duly verified that this is consistent with her own personal morality and this does not create a future AI that *could* desire things the current AI would not want.

For the programmer, building an AI that has this level of "moral sense" seems a terribly complex case. But in fact there is a fairly easy way to make the AI itself reaches the desired maturity: the *wisdom tournaments*.

What is it about? Just the idea that the AI can learn everything through trial and error, i.e. by experience, and this applies even for wisdom.

One of the major sources of human wisdom... is human stupidity. Without our innate tendency to believe the authorities, to erect ourselves as authorities and to transform any debate into a political debate, without our willingness to defend causes that are even untenable once we have chosen our camp, without our intellectual and emotional stupidity, would we have felt the need to invent science?

In addition, is science itself, this approach by refutable hypotheses and experiments, useful for an AI? Would an objective AI be more effective than a subjective AI? Scientists find the objective method most effective because they see subjectivity as a way to avoid confrontations and they think confrontations are necessary. Otherwise, everyone stays on its selfish position and nothing can move forward.

Humans, consciously or unconsciously know this, and they try to compensate for this excess of selfishness, to de-skew their views. Selfishness is so, in a sense, the source of altruism. An AI must at least understand this process if she is to understand the forces that shape human morality.

When errors are introduced into a process of reasoning, an intelligent mind happens to compensate for the bias that is the cause of the error. It can even compensate for errors which have not taken place, but that would be likely to occur, and thus become more resistant to errors of reasoning. If we test a mind by artificially introducing errors, this will make it more resistant to natural errors. If this mind properly corrects artificially introduced errors, we can be more confident that it will correct natural errors, even if unanticipated. We can even test this: just simulate the course of events that would have occurred in the mind if safety barriers had not been introduced, and see if it happens to still get by; if yes this will be a good surprise. If not, we will have an idea of what to add for it to correct these errors.

In my personal history and probably yours too, those kind of "philosophical short circuits," happened several times. If my personal morality happened to be damn ground following an unforeseen event, yet I am still a charming and selfless person (as you are, I suppose!). How could we have that degree of confidence in AI? How can we build and test a friendly AI that everyone agrees to say she could manage any "philosophical short circuit" without damage (ie stay friendly)?

The first method is to explain properly how *I* got out of these philosophical short-circuit situations, and to put this knowledge at the disposal of the AI.

The second method is to ask the AI to simulate what would have happened if some known problem had been unexpected: the AI should then, either show that it is doing properly, or modify herself so as to show she would come out properly from a similar problem. ("Similar" and not "identical". We ask the AI to generalize).

To do so is extraordinarily easier with AI than for a human, because AI are just programs, after all: For example it is very easy to immerse the AI into a simulated environment were humans become suddenly hostile to intelligent machines. It is very easy to erase some knowledge in the AI, or to see what she would have done if she had not had this or that knowledge. It is very easy to introduce deliberate errors in some AI mechanisms.

Such "wisdom tournaments" for example could oppose the current version of the AI being tested to other versions of herself that are almost identical but different in one point. The AI will thus almost automatically acquire knowledge that allows humans to get out of extreme situations such as philosophical short circuits. The AI could even gain some knowledge that we humans *do not yet have* about how to develop morality beliefs that are increasingly strong and solid.

In fact, the wisdom tournaments reinforce the ordinary reasoning with heuristics. First, you solve the problem, then you try to re-solve with half your brain artificially shelved. What you learn by doing this helps you to better understand how to reason in similar cases and allows you to solve problems that are more complicated.

When the AI goes out victoriously (remaining friendly) from all situations where it could have become unfriendly, being situations imagined by human programmers or by itself, only then can we claim victory.

My personal opinion is that if we adopt the approach proposed in this book, it is not impossible.

Remember: with the idea of seed AI (Chapter 7), it will happen much sooner than you think.

13 *The race is on*

Singularity against nano-hecklers

This is indeed a race, but a rather special one, because we are faced with two potential dangers.

The first danger is replicator nanotechnology without a *complete* control because in this field the smallest security flaw would be enough for a pain-in-the-neck nanobug to be released in the wild, and as we saw just a single one is enough to kill all life on the planet in less than two days.

The second danger is the hostile AI. *Terminator*, *Skynet*, world domination by machines, and most likely the extermination of humans (it would take more than two days ... but certainly less than two years. Contrary to what Hollywood movies say, humans would not have *no* chance against intelligent and hostile machines)

These dangers are very real. The fact that these problems are very science fiction-like should not encourage us to ignore them. In terms of safety, especially when the risk is no more and no less than the end of the world, there is no place to bury your head in the sand, or for half measures. To get rid of the problem we should be absolutely certain that there is not the slightest risk. Nothing could be further from the truth.

The man in the street could say "okay, it's serious, but not for now. When the problem becomes real, we will talk. But I bet my bottom dollar it will take at least fifty years. "

Well, the man in the street is wrong, because the two problems are, in some ways, linked and this connection will cause an acceleration of research in both areas. Indeed, on one hand designing nano-technological gadgets, whether useful or "bad" is a very complicated business, which would be greatly facilitated if superfast engineering techniques were available and those techniques could only emerge if an AI was available. Basically the equation is: as soon as you have an AI you have nanotechnology.

And on the other hand, an AI is a complex program that needs a lot of computing power, and the design of AI would be greatly facilitated if that computing power were almost unlimited: programmers would not have to constantly wonder about how to program a given task as well as possible while consuming the least amount of memory and CPU resources, but simply to ask "what is the fastest way to do this thing?". Which is a lot quicker and easier to do. Indeed the computer hardware industry will be one of the first, if not the first, to benefit from nanotechnologies as soon they become available. Once the nano-computers invade the labs, computer industry will be totally shaken and the AI will not be far. Basically the second equation is: once you have the nano-computers, we will have the AI within a few years (2 or 3 years at most).

Provisional conclusion: The emergence of nanotechnology and AI will be almost simultaneous.

But there is a third equation: indeed *an AI that would have nanotechnology* would be capable of improving not only its own software, but also its own hardware. What would follow is, as we have seen, a super-exponential acceleration of its capacity, leading in no time (a few days or even hours) to the singularity: an intelligence so much bigger than ours that today humans cannot even imagine. This super intelligence having ultra-technology at its disposal then will become a power, meaning (choose) the equal of a Genius, a Golem or a God.

So we have the following theorem:

AI *or* nanotechnology => Singularity, Genius or Golem in no time.

However, as we have said, if the first AI is *not* a friendly AI, the risk of destruction of humanity is very high. The logical conclusion of the reasoning is thus:

1) The first true AI should be a friendly AI.
2) We must have this AI before the arrival of nanotechnology (at least before the arrival of nano replicating assemblers).

Finally, because despite their potential hazards, friendly AI and nanotechnology are both carriers of immense hopes and progress will go faster and faster. One may even think that they are *not fast enough*:

Somewhere on this planet, a small number of humans are engaged in the race for the singularity. These humans have limited resources, and are constantly distracted from this work by the need to sleep, to eat, to buy a living, or by hecklers who ask them stupid questions. Every hour that passes brings us closer to the singularity. Every hour of "distraction" to the person who is the closest drives us away. Every hour six thousand humans die. But the Singularity is the way to reach immortality.

For this reason alone, working on Friendly AI is a very desirable thing. But the other reason is just as important, that the AI is the only way to save the planet from nanovirus and other nano-hecklers that emerging nanotechnologies – if there is no friendly AI to control them - will for sure plant on the planet, despite all the precautions taken.

When we discovered fire, we invented wildfire.
When we invented bows, maces and spears, we created war.

When we created the automobile, we created the accident.

When we invented electricity, we created the electrical fault.

When we created the Internet, we created the risk for a global economic catastrophe.

When we invent nanotechnology with replicators, we will invent the world's end.

As soon as we invent the AI, Terminator and Skynet will be created.

However, when you invent the *friendly* AI, you will save the world from all these disasters. And as a bonus, you'll reach immortality, the super intelligence and the Singularity. It is time to wake up!

So this is indeed a race. In this race, what are the forces? Who is the hare, who is the turtle?

The nanotechnology side

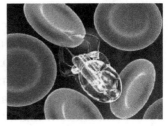

Since the book appeared founder Eric Drexler, *Engines of Creation* in 1986 (revised and reissued in 1996), research on nanotechnology has exploded. Numerous laboratories are working on the issue, and new publications appear every day.

In a sense, nanotechnology is not a science, but rather as its name implies a technology, because we know that there is no scientific impossibility to design nano-replicating assemblers: after all, they already exist, DNA is the proof! This proof of feasibility is a formidable driving engine for researches. The other engine is constituted by the extraordinary scale of the field of possible applications ... and markets that will result. It is not surprising that some manufacturers (in the medical sector in particular) are ready to spare no expense to be the first. Even before the arrival of assemblers, nanotechnology research spinoffs will be worth several hundred billion euros for the coming decade.

But the obstacles are numerous, for designing a molecular engineering from scratch is a huge task that requires as much practical as purely theoretical development work. After all, even though we know that biological systems do work, we do not know exactly *how* they work. Our understanding of how proteins fold, in particular, is far from complete.

The search field on nanotechnology fragmented therefore into a multitude of research subdomains:

- Nanomaterials
- Nanocomposites and problems of dispersion
- Ordered nanostructures
- Analytical tools (visualization and understanding of the properties of nanostructures)
- Modeling and computer simulation
- Manufacture of nanostructures
- Integration and manufacture of final products (assemblers ...)

Where are we in 2016?

We can say that the roadmap is drawn. This roadmap identifies precisely the difficulties and necessary research. It predicts a massive influx of nanotechnology within 20 years.

The research primarily in the US, but Europe is far from absent. The US government has spent a billion dollars in research and development in nanotechnology as early as 2005, to which must be added two billion dollars from private funds, but this is only a third of the global effort on the subject. However research in Europe are very advanced but also very sharp and specialized, and Europe lacks "global vision". In the USA, a country used to "technological forward flight", there are many people who think that nanotechnology is a solution "to all world problems," especially since a fair share among those people have the feeling that their country is the main cause of these problems ... Many Americans nanotechnology experts feel then driven by a "moral duty" to get these technologies as quickly as possible. This feeling of guilt is absent in Europe. Europeans are more pragmatic and for them the interest of nanotechnology lies above all in their extraordinary potential practical applications. Nevertheless they feel increasingly the need for a global vision, and even more the need for coordination on the subject. For this reason the European Commission proposed as early as June 2005 an "action plan for nanoscience and nanotechnology". It should be noted that the Commission has identified the "potential health risks" of nanotechnology, and asked the member states to take adequate measures.

Since then, progress has been going fast, especially in the field of nanomaterials. But it is slower than was expected in 2005.

However, both in the United States and in Europe, nobody seems to have made the connection between nanotechnology and AI. No decision-maker seems to have seen that true AI will necessarily generate assembler nanotechnology, and no one realized that it cannot been fully mastered without a friendly AI. Awareness is more than ever necessary.

AI science side

Already now, the total power available on the internet exceeds that of a human brain. Of course, this power is not used to run an AI, but it is a matter of software, not hardware, and software capabilities can increase very quickly. Naturally, this does not mean that it *will* grow very quickly, but only that it *can* in theory.

For practice to rejoin theory would require that many researchers consider the topic of true AI. Now, scientists are generally reluctant to simply address this issue. No serious scientific journal has published articles on even the design of a real AI, and a researcher who would dare make such publication would be very soon in stumbles to multiple criticisms. Time is the most valuable resource for researchers, and researchers do not want to waste their time with these trifles and those science-fiction ideas. But it gets worse, because there is a resource for scientists that is even more precious than time: the consideration of their work by peers. The scientific community is, in fact, the most conservative one, and this situation is worsening with time. It is not certain that an obscure remote patent office employee named Albert Einstein could have published the theory of relativity today.

The science side of true general AI has led to an impasse. Only a few researchers dare to advance the idea that the implementation of an AI is possible with current technologies. Others think at best that "it is not necessary for the moment" or "that's far in the future" and at worst "it's just not possible." However, they are usually aware that these statements are more professions of faith as proven facts, and they keep an open mind, probably thinking is that if the fools who dare to embark on this line of research at the risk of ruining their career come out something interesting, there will be time to take the train.

On the industrial side this is the same. Extraordinary progresses have been made during the last decade in the use of artificial neural nets for harnessing big data. Computers can now understand human language in a surprising good way. Google search engine, Google assistant and translation engine, Apple Siri and Microsoft Cortana are perfect examples.

In January 2016, A deep-learning computer system called AlphaGo using a combination of classical tree-searching and deep neural networks and created by Google's DeepMind team has defeated reigning three-time European Go champion Fan Hui 5 games to 0 — the first time a computer program has ever beaten a professional Go player — a feat previously thought to be at least a decade away.

But those are practical applications of brute power, not breakthrough in the science of understanding and replicating human thinking. Unlike what happens for nanotechnology, software manufacturers have not taken stock of the recent progress made by the "crazy" guys described above, and none of them are currently willing to invest in this area, in notable exception of research funded by military orders.

For the military *are* interested about the AI. But they have an inherently biased view of things: they seek above all practical applications, such as unmanned cars or planes, combat robots or espionage systems for spying telecommunications and the Internet. They know that these applications require a good deal of intelligence and they are willing to fund researches, even long term ones, provided they can lead to one of these practical applications (note that military decision makers have not yet understood that there is an application of AI that will make all other finger-snapping, namely ultra-fast engineering). Research is already underway in some military laboratories.

There is a strong risk that the military works neglect the "friendly" aspect of the future they seek to create AI. Skynet is in sight.

AI computer science side

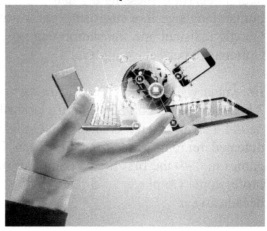

As a scientific discipline, AI is accustomed to cycles. These cycles share the same structure: huge hopes, intense development, bitter disillusionment, and lean times. Many of these rounds have already taken place, successively based on hopes to build a "universal problem solver", a "general expert system", "a constraints reasoning system", or a "universal translator" The AI discipline has then segmented into multiple sub-domains of parallel research, and each of these areas in turn passes through cycles. The field of "artificial neuron networks" is currently at the end of its intense development phase. The field of "genetic algorithms" is in the midst of this phase. The field of "massively multiplayer agents systems" is at the end of the stage of hope, and development begins.

It should be noted that, apart from these cyclical activities, some researchers focus on very theoretical "background tasks", experiencing a slow but steady development (sometimes still with ups and downs). This is the case of pattern recognition, speech recognition, language analysis and machine translation, formal reasoning and logic, and optimization theory.

This segmentation into dozens of areas has a very practical purpose: focusing on a specialized topic, researchers can expect relatively quick results, and publications. Given that, the aura of a researcher is measured by his number of publications...

True AI or "General AI" researchers are probably less than a dozen in the world. Stationed mostly in theoretical work, they nonetheless identified the basic principles of the mind functioning and laid the theoretical basis for the construction of an artificial mind. These bases are the ones I have outlined in this book.

This low number of researchers is a handicap, yet the development of a true AI will require a lot of possibly very sharp theoretical work, which could provide grist and things to be published for interested researchers.

I already mentioned the massively multi-agent systems, which already constitute a separate discipline, and that will be necessary to create an AI despite the fact that current studies are not carried out in this single goal.

However, there are other issues worth digging into: the study of the qualitative behavior of a (probabilistic or not) system of goals capable of self-modification is a very important task that requires serious study.

The study of the optimum computer representation of concepts (and thoughts) is also a field of study that must be deepened.

It is unfortunate that these study subjects had, so far, found no "takers". However, this will happen one day. The amazing advances (as Phaeaco, we mentioned in Chapter 5) occur when a young researcher full of new ideas is on the direction of an "old hand philosopher" who is curious to see what it could give. In AI, you do not necessarily need huge teams to produce interesting things!

The IA, as a scientific discipline, is progressing rapidly precisely because all the necessary knowledge is controllable by one man. Unlike mathematics or physics, which have become so huge areas there is salvation only through specialization, every researcher in AI can really rest on the shoulders of those that precede it. Moreover, a good topic in AI research generally gives rise to a program, and the following researchers can recover and re-use at least the ideas if not the computer code itself of the program that preceded them. Phaeaco was built on the foundations of Copycat, itself inspired by AM, to mention only these three systems. AI is a discipline that is, from a scientific point of view, as perfect as physics. The AI ideas are testable, provable or refutable.

Minsky and Yudkowsky gave us the guideline, the way forward to reach the true AI. If any part of the investment that is being done in nanotechnology was devoted to the AI, we would probably have an AI in twenty years, maybe in ten years only.

The philosophical side

Platon, by Raphael

The old cliché of the old bearded philosopher, walking alone in the garden of Heidelberg and smoking his pipe while thinking dies hard. And it is true that, in general, philosophers do not like being rushed. This is why most *interesting* philosophical ideas of recent years are often the result of "non-philosophers" scientists whose path that led them to question the meaning of what they saw or felt when faced with the results of their experiments. This include the physicist Bernard d'Espagnat who is questioning the reality of the physical world in the light of the "Bell theorem" and the proof of the non-separability of quantum particles. Or the mathematician Roger Penrose, mixing in a gigantic fugue chaos theory, quantum theory and relativity, to question determinism and free will.

But in general, philosophers do not like science come encroach on the field of "pure thought." An exception is John Searle, who tried to prove the impossibility of conscious AI in such a wrong and biased manner I do not want to dwell on this subject here. Another exception is Danniel Dennett, "philosopher of the mind", who produced some very interesting thoughts about the meaning of "me" in AI. He understood that the more and more likely arrival of an AI in our civilization would have enormous philosophical consequences. Yet while Dennett knows well the works of classical AI, does he know those of Bruno Marchal on computationalism? Does he know the work of Orsay

555

neuropsychologists on the access phenomenological consciousness and conscience? Probably not. Fort there are few philosophers who really know all the latest developments on the subject of the mind in general and AI in particular.

For example, the work of Minsky on the "society of mind" *should* be known to all those who wonder about these issues. It seems to me that we are still far away.

Yet when the AI happen, the broader public who undergo the political decisions, policy makers who make public decisions, and "thinkers" who prepare these decisions in their gilded alcove, all will ask accounts to philosophers. They will want to know "what it's really like to be an AI". They will want to know how to explain these things to the public. They will want to know whether an AI really think, whether it has a soul, whether an AI may be endowed with creativity, whether it can feel emotions, could make mistakes, and ultimately if we can do trust an AI. I am afraid the philosopher's answer will be way off beam.

While the answers are actually very simple:

- Yes, the AI really think, as far as humans really think. However, AI do not think like a human being. An AI think faster and farther than a human.
- An AI has neither more nor less than a human soul.
- An AI may well be endowed with creativity. Her creativity will likely be even much higher than that of a human being.
- An AI can feel emotions, in the same way each of us can. She may also feel other emotions that we do not know. Nevertheless, she never let her emotions make her lose her goals.
- An AI can make mistakes, but will make less and less mistakes over time. And a friendly AI is reliable and will remain reliable in the future.
- We can and should trust a friendly AI. By cons we should *not* trust an AI that is not designed from the outset to be friendly.

In one sentence: forget Hollywood clichés on AI!

The political side

The political side of AI is a complete vacuum. Politicians have on AI roughly the same vision as the man in the street: Yes, true AI sells movies and video games, but for the moment, and for a long time, it is just science-fiction.

Investing in AI research, my good sir? But if you knew the number of researchers and labs that require credits, not to mention far more pressing issues such as Europe, education, defense, health, equipment and so on!

No politician seems to have realized that all these problems could be solved in a single magic wand with AI. And please do not mention the danger of nanotechnology, this just could make their back worse. No, really, AI does not deserve more interest that UFOs!

This is distressing.

We hold in our hands the solution to all the problems of the planet, and no one among our policy makers has the slightest consciousness of this fact. No one even wants to hear about it.

Still, one dollar invested in research on real AI will bring billions of times more than one dollar invested in cancer research; and by the way, it will cure cancer, AIDS and all other diseases. And nobody wants to see that.

Are we all so stupid?

I want to believe that we are not, and that what lacks is just an awareness.

Conclusion

Clair de Terre, by Frédéric Gracia

The Mind and The Machine

I hope I have shown that it is useless to close our eyes and repeat the mantra "we cannot solve all the world's problems." We *can*. We can solve the problems of poverty, lack of energy, waste of resources, disease or totalitarianism. We can, through *upload*, become immortal. We can become infinitely more intelligent than today. What's more, we can do all this quickly.

In this book, I hope to have shown that thinking and consciousness are not magical phenomena, that they are reducible to computable physics, and that the objective of creating a thinking and conscious machine is nothing utopian. I dare think I gave some keys to achieve this, particularly I have shown that the simplest method is the construction of what I called a *friendly seed AI*, the overall structure and an overview of operation of which I gave in this book.

If we put the means, we can build a seed AI within a decade.

Moreover, we have a *duty* to do so quickly, before the nano-hecklers and hostile AI destroy all life on earth. Because (generally military) research in both areas is already underway and can only lead to this terrible conclusion.

Faced with this challenge, it is imperative that awareness takes place, that governments focus all resources on the task of creating a friendly seed AI. One euro invested in this work will yield billions of times more than a euro invested in research against cancer, for example (and it will cure cancer!)

There are two types of investment: those that are *linear*, and those that are *exponential*.

The former, like the construction of a viaduct or housing assistance, provide only linear impact compared to investment. You invests x dollars, it pays k times those x dollars in the best case (if k is not less than one, which is often the case!)

The latter, such as aid to education and investment in future technologies, yield exponentially, because one dollar invested now will yield more in the future: a better education for our children benefits the whole economy, which then have ways to further improve education, and so on. Creating a biotechnology start-up, in addition to creating jobs and new markets will benefit the entire population because the new products will be used to improve general welfare; and more knowledge and technologies developed in the new company will create even more new products, and probably new start-ups.

It is already sad fact that governments almost only do linear investments.

However, building a Friendly seed AI is the *only super-exponential* investment.

This is the only investment that pays the jackpot without fail. For a few hundred millions, we can change the face of the world and solve all our problems at once! It is vital that our leaders, but also the broader public, are aware of this simple fact.

We must invest in the construction of the Friendly seed AI. NOW!

Bibliography

Books

As this book is intended for a wide audience, I did not want to clutter the text with precise references or footnotes about the books I quoted, or by which I was inspired. To fill this gap, here are, in bulk and in disorder, some books I loved, or have me arrested, and have a close relationship with the subject matter of this book.

- *The Society of mind*, Marvin Minsky: The masterwork of a key pope of AI. All psychologists and all mind philosophers should have read it.
- *Gödel, Escher, Bach: an Eternal Golden Braid*, Douglas Hosftader (Pulizer price 1977). A must. After reading it, you will know all about self-reference, and what it means to *think*. And besides, it's fun to read!
- *The Mind's I*, Douglas Hofstadter and Daniel Dennett: philosophical reflections, not without humor, on consciousness and what happens in our minds.
- *The Emperor's New Mind: Concerning Computers, Minds, and The Laws of Physics*, Roger Penrose: the point of view of an iconoclastic genius about mind: according to him, it may be that a true AI is impossible if it does not use quantum physics.
- *Les systèmes multi-agents: vers une intelligence collective*, Jacques Ferber. (In French). A summary of a discipline that has profoundly marked AI, and is still developing.
- *I, Robot*, Isaac Asimov: a series of new science fiction based on "three laws of robotics". Entertaining, enriching and exciting all at once.
- *Syntactic Structures*, Noam Chomsky. A groundbreaking study (when published in 1957) on the grammar of natural languages.

- *Modéliser et concevoir une machine pensante*, Alain Cardon (In French). An erudite and philosophical study (but without humor) about how thought and consciousness may emerge in a massive organization of agents controlled by another massive supervisor agents organization and functioning by homeostasis.
- *Engines of Creation*, K. Eric Drexler. The "bible" of the inventor of nanotechnology. A stunning book written for a broad audience, and exciting from start to finish.
- *Intelligence artificielle, résolution de problèmes par l'homme et la machine*, Jean-Louis Laurière. (In French). Although somewhat dated, it is still my reference on programming techniques in artificial intelligence. The book contains among other things a detailed description of Pitrat's *Robin* software (a chess player that made plans) and of the author's *Snark* (a very general and effective system for problem solving, using multiple representations at a time).
- *Intelligence artificielle et informatique théorique*, Jean-Marc Aliot et Thomas Schiex (In French). A very technical and detailed reference on almost all classic AI algorithms. For specialists!
- *Artificial Intelligence*, Patrick Henry Winston. An extremely clear computer science work, with many insights on the recognition of visual forms.
- *Artificial intelligence*, Elaine Rich. Yet another general book on AI, but more focused on the representation of data.

Websites

- http://singularityu.org/ The *singularity institute for artificial intelligence* website. Was very interesting ten years ago, but seems to have turned into a money-making gizmo.
- http://www.lecerveau.mcgill.ca/: tout sur le cerveau! (in French)

- http://web.media.mit.edu/~minsky/: Marvin Minsky's website.
- http://www.kurzweilai.net/: when a self-made billionaire is interested in AI, what does it give?
- http://www.automatesintelligents.com/ • http://www.automatesintelligents.com/ A reference: hundreds of articles, press releases, book reviews, etc. all related directly or indirectly to AI and the questions it raises (in French)
- http://www.foresight.org/: The Foresight institute website, dedicated to nanotechnology.
- http://www.spirtech.com/flv/nano/ Une présentation par Frederic Levy de la nanotechnologie.
- http://bluebrainproject.epfl.ch/ *Blue Brain* project site
- http://iridia.ulb.ac.be/~marchal Website of Bruno Marchal, on computationalism and conscience (in French)
- http://www.cs.indiana.edu/~hfoundal/ Website of Harry Foundalis on *Phaeaco* (see chazpter 5).
- http://www.ai.mit.edu/projects/humanoid-robotics-group/ the site of AI research group at MIT on humanoid robotics.

Table

You liked this book? You will probably like my other books!

Available on Amazon and http://sboisse.free.fr

Already published:

Alice et la boîte de Pandore *Novel* (*in French*)

Alice is not an ordinary girl. She is a very young, conscious and sensitive artificial intelligence, who discovers the world. But its creator, Daniel, his friend Ethan, and their companions Cathy and Jeanne will soon find themselves embarked on an adventure that they had not planned ... Alice will have to struggle to save their lives and its own, saving the world in passing ... and discovering love!

Soul Shifter *Novel (In French)*

• In a remote corner of Burma lives a strange tribe, which holds a fabulous secret.
• In Toulouse, a pair of lovers loves.
• In Saudi Arabia, a young prince thirsts for power.
• In the Nevada desert, and in Thailand, a deadly trap is set.
• In Paris, a young philosopher examines the relationship between gender and life.
• In a train, a young Asian woman swaps her soul and body with a young man.

Suddenly all those stories collide...

A great adventure story, a thrilling quest full of twists, and an amazing experience!

The Mind and The Machine

www.ingramcontent.com/pod-product-compliance
Lightning Source LLC
Chambersburg PA
CBHW071354050326
40689CB00010B/1640